Is LIVING WELL STILL THE BEST REVENGE?

VIGNETTES OF OLD GEORGIA:
The Presence of the Past
in Athens, Atlanta, and Augusta

By
BOWDRE PHINIZY MAYS JR.

Cover Image: The Charles H Phinizy house at 519 Greene Street August GA.
Copyright © 2013 Bowdre Phinizy Mays Jr.
All rights reserved.
ISBN: 1477583335
ISBN-13: 9781477583333

DEDICATION

To my grandmother Frank Crowell Clark (later Mrs. John Walter Inman and thereafter Mrs. Llewellyn Goode Doughty) and to my great aunt Mary Lou Phinizy, both of whom kindled in me a sense of family and interest in history. And also to my wife, Lynn Alexander Mays, and daughters, Tracy Mays Olmsted and Katherine Mays Bunker, who all have made my life. And finally to the grandchildren and whoever may come after.

PREFACE

Webster defines "vignette" as, in general, a picture, illustration, or depiction in words; this is what I have attempted to do herein as, in most cases, I have personal knowledge of or I have obtained corroboration from other sources of the events discussed. My family has urged me for some time to commit to paper these vignettes, and in so doing I follow in a way the ancient Japanese custom of an old codger writing a sort of chronicle of his life and memories.

I am told Teto Barrett once said to an Augusta newcomer that the three most interesting families here are the Barretts, the Cummings, and the Phinizys. Teto may have a point, but in these vignettes, I focus not only on my Phinizy and other ancestors as well as some close family friends, believing that, indeed, there is some fertile ground to uncover in some other less well-known ménages. Barretts and Cummings were always good friends with many Phinizy generations and with all the other families depicted; also, Ferdinand Phinizy II of Athens married as his second wife Anne S. Barrett of Augusta, so their direct descendants are related on both sides.

This work is not intended to be a study in genealogy; it is only a general outline of the lives of those closest to me in memory and history supplemented by family lore, recent research, and stories told to me during my early life and following my retirement and return to Augusta in 1992. While I am not exactly ancestor obsessed, I always have enjoyed the reminiscences one hears, and even today I much regret having not listened more and asked more questions; but the fact is that one's interests change, so that in late maturity I do wish I knew much more regarding my family and their closest friends on both sides.

Since my retirement in 1992, I have wanted to write these family memories and mini-biographies because, to a large extent, this combination of fact and memory defines who I am now and who I became. I trust those persons and relatives in these vignettes also will become "friends" of my immediate family, thereby permitting them, like me, to live across several generations. To me, many of these ancestors and friends still live on, and I think about many of them every day.

PREFACE

For the readers I should like to state that the book certainly can be read from start to finish or front to back; however, it also can be digested and chapters read in whatever order suits the reader's fancy. There are places in the book where facts or stories are repeated to remind the reader or to relate to the general context of a particular chapter or topic. This does ensure that any reader will stay in the picture and not be lost particularly should one peruse at random.

I should be remiss if I did not sincerely thank all who have aided in providing oral memories and tales and written input, and I give credit to certain published accounts as listed in the bibliography. The initial persons included Teto Barrett, Mary Lou Bussey, Frank Inman Mays, Genie Selden Lehmann, Craig and Marie Cranston, Inman Mays, Ashby Taylor, Calhoun Witham, Pat Walsh, and my great niece, Mary Hull Palmer, who found Frankie Clark Inman Doughty's scrapbook deep in the recesses of her great-grandmother Dandy's (Frank Inman Mays) secretary.

As I grew up in Augusta, my aunt Louise Mays Bussey also amused and filled me with family lore and stories of various Augusta personages. She was a fascinating talker who always gave me time. Part of the charm was that she treated me as an adult. She saved newspaper clippings that with her scrapbook and pre-marital diaries greatly assisted me. Her late youngest daughter, Mary Lou Bussey, proved to be an excellent authentic source, particularly on the Mayses and Phinizys at 519 Greene Street (Chapter III) and relative to our great-aunt's life and residence on Milledge Road (Chapter IV). After my retirement in 1992, Mary Lou and my immediate family became much closer than the usual first cousins. She died in 2005, and I miss her dearly.

Many others gave input and support; these include my original mentor Bryan Haltermann, Dawson Teague, Starkey Flythe, Jane Chandler, the late Phil Harison, Sr., Cassius Clay, Frances Stevenson, Mary Mell Battey, Marie (Frenchie) Battey Bush, the Del'aigle family (Katie, Jerry, and Kevin), their Del'aigle cousin from Birmingham, Alabama, Virginia (Ginger) Elizabeth Sandon-Mylius, Betty Butt Slaton Wallace of Atlanta, Harry Vaiden, Al Williams, Cobbs Nixon, Florence Blanton, Tom Robertson, Mary Barrett Robertson, Frank Mays Pride, Stedman Clark Mays, Sr., Harriet Bowdre Mays McAllister, Marquin Barrett, and Hale Barrett on the divorce tribulations of Jacob Phinizy II. Nancy Cumming Connolly was helpful with the later life of Pat Walsh as were Al Cheatham and Peter Stager on the Drury Family. Isabelle Robertson Maxwell provided certain details relative to family connections..

Many thanks to Virginia Banerjee of Redding, Connecticut, for opening the door to the "Bowdre Saga"; thanks also to Ann Carter Burdell Boardman for her consistent interest and help through the years and to Erick Montgomery for his continuing long-term advice on the Mays family forbears and those issues relative to publication chores.

The "Ridgely Story" data in large part derives from the assistance given by Elizabeth Lehmann Jones of Baltimore,

PREFACE

goddaughter of the late Elizabeth Ridgely Dohm, her Dohm children (Mary and Bill) living in Dallas, and the military historian Russell Brown of Augusta.

Patty Gray of Sandy Springs was very helpful in discussing the Richard Gray Gallogly saga, particularly Gallogly's later years. Dolly Fortson Adams was kind and sensitive in assisting with the Milledge Road shooting details and providing pictures of her parents. Charles Rivers furnished aid with the Alexander "cotton problem."

Gratitude and acknowledgement are due in addition to the author's kinsfolk including Nina and George Inman, Andrew Inman, the late Laura Ann Phinizy Segrest, John Phinizy Spalding, Anne Segrest Freeze, Anne Fortson Freeman, the late Bert Gary, Laura Gary Van Geffen, and Osborne P Mackie.

The late Bradley Hale and Alex Hitz of Atlanta and Dr. Randolph Smith of Augusta gave me very pertinent facts that lend color to these writings. This is true also of the recollections of Wyck Knox; Robert Knox was helpful with facts concerning Thomson, Georgia.

Frank Martien, Frank Barrett's great-grandson and Anne Barrett Derry's grandson, supplied much interest and support including pictures from his grandmother's scrapbook. The late Anne Felton of Macon, Georgia, (and her daughter Polly) provided interesting recollections of Tracy Duncan Cohen and North Winship together with photographs.

I convey thanks to the Atlanta History Center, The Georgia Trust, Historic Augusta, and the Washington

Library in Macon for providing useful data and dates. And finally a huge debt of gratitude and a cup full of kudos to Debra Lanham for her assistance and computer skills over many years. I would also like to thank my editor Bessie Gantt for her many suggestions and ideas relative to the final draft. If there are any omissions above, such was purely unintentional.

This publication of this book was greatly aided by a generous grant from The Porter Fleming Foundation.

B.P.M. February 2013

PREFACE

TABLE OF CONTENTS

Chapter I   Clarks (including profile of Frank Crowell Clark, later Inman and then Doughty), Doughtys (including the Burdell, Butt, Calhoun, Derry, and Jackson links), De l'aigles, Inmans, Ridgelys: FAMILY ARCHIVES AND ROOTS   1

Chapter II   Bowdres, Crawfords, Hamiltons, Mayses, Phinizys, Yanceys: MORE GEORGIA FAMILY ARCHIVES AND ROOTS   139

Chapter III   519 Greene Street Ménage: To the Manner Born   205

Chapter IV   The Private World of Mary Lou Phinizy at 814 Milledge Road   275

Chapter V   Potpourri of Milledge Road Minutiae: Who Was Who on Milledge?   321

Chapter VI   Miss Tracy and Mr. Roddey: A Window into 2150 Battle Row   395

Chapter VII Frank and Bowdre: The Way They Were	455
Chapter VIII The King Family in Augusta and Europe: A Cursory Sketch	507
Chapter IX John Walton and Pat Walsh: The Best of Friends	565
Chapter X The Alexanders of 1027 Telfair Street: The Real "Lucinderella"	619
Chapter XI Bowdre Phinizy Mays, Jr.: A Life Spent Largely Abroad	633
Chapter XII B.P.M., Jr.: Coming Back to Augusta: with Epilogue and L'envoi	761

CHAPTER I

Clarks (including profile of Frank Crowell Clark, later Inman and then Doughty), Doughtys (including the Burdell, Butt, Calhoun, Derry, and Jackson links), De l'aigles, Inmans, Ridgelys: Family Archives and Roots

As I explained in the preface, this is not intended to be a genealogical treatise except in the sense that I am writing in part about relatives. But all of these people were participants in the Augusta scene for many years; while many were private in their lifestyles, some of the others occupied high-profile positions in the business and professional fields. The names of a number are no longer well known (except to the few who might frequent on occasion Magnolia or Summerville Cemeteries); nevertheless, it is my hope the following word portraits in Chapters I and II will be found to be of at least mild interest to all curious with regard to past Augusta history and the town's mores. In all respects I am not searching for any highly sanitized history but will set out the facts as I found them. All of the persons discussed in Chapter I, and in Chapter II for that matter, are related by direct descent or from marriages producing descendants. There is even one case of two first cousins marrying, both for the second time, following the early death of spouses.

CHAPTER ONE

CLARKS:

The Augusta Directory for 1841 lists "our Clarks" as follows: Clark, Rackett & Co., wholesale and retail jewelry store, corner Broad and McIntosh (7th Street); J. S. Clark residence Ellis between Washington (6th) and Centre (5th Street); Horace Clark, Jeweler at Clark, Rackett, & Co. I am not certain if any of the other Clarks recorded also are related; although, one, Francis B. Clark, Bookkeeper at Haviland, Risley & Co., could be a relative of Joseph Stedman Clark (1808-1875) and his wife Caroline Mealing Clark (1818-1899) from whom I am directly descended on the maternal side—this because their son, Francis William Clark, was my great-grandfather. His dates were 1843-1891. In the book *The Silversmiths of Georgia*, the author relates that between 1816 and 1860 there were several Clarks in the silver, jewelry, and watch business working in various firms or partnerships. First F. Clark & Co., then F. & H. Clark, (when Francis and Horace were partners), followed by Clark, Rackett & Co. in 1840 when George Rackett became a partner.

After Rackett died in 1851, the firm name later appears to have reverted to just Clark & Co. It is very likely the older Francis, Horace, and Joseph Stedman Clark were brothers. When Horace died in 1854, he bequeathed his property to his brothers and sisters; then he appointed his brother Joseph Stedman Clark an executor with William J. Mealing. While the estate is reported to have been "considerable," Horace was ill the last years of his life and lived with his brother.

Final expenses and claims on the estate are said to have exhausted the capital. Whether or not Joseph Stedman Clark was a partner or employee of one of the Clark silver/jewelry stores is uncertain. Nevertheless, when Rackett died the February 1851 newspaper notice stated the partnership was dissolved and all claims against the concern were to be sent to "Horace Clark and J. S. Clark, surviving partners."

It is definite, however, that the Clark firm must have been the leading jewelry/silver/daguerreotype sellers in Augusta during the middle years of the nineteenth century. This is confirmed from continuous advertisements in local, daily, and state newspapers. Silver plate and sterling were sold and silversmithing/manufacturing of items done in-house as well as imported. My sister has old Clark & Co. flat coin silver utensils she received from her great-aunt Mary Stedman Clark Ridgely as a wedding present in 1947. Judge Scott Allen in recent years donated Clark & Co. flat silver to the Augusta Museum of History, while the museum itself purchased for its collection at auction a Clark-made silver pitcher for $6,000 several years back.

The *Augusta Chronicle* edition of May 4, 1899, reported on the death of Mrs. Joseph Stedman Clark (née Caroline Mealing) in New York City where she lived with her son Horace of the Seaboard Airline Railroad. Mrs. Clark was eighty; her body was brought to Augusta and interred here. The *Chronicle* further wrote that her late husband's jewelry business had been at the then William Schweigert Jewelry Store location between 8th

CHAPTER ONE

and 9th on Broad Street. The curbstone in front still bore the name Clark, according to that report.

My great-grandfather Francis William Clark (but always called Frank) married Ruth Eve Doughty at St. Paul's Church November 25, 1868. Aunt Mary Lou Phinizy probably would observe it thus: "He married up!" This due only to the fact that the Clarks were in commerce (i.e., merchants or tradespeople), while the Doughtys were more in the professions! Following the wedding, the couple lived first in Macon and later in Raleigh and Norfolk. Frank Clark appears to have been employed as the general freight and passenger agent of various railroads: Raleigh and Augusta, Raleigh and Gaston, and the Carolina Central system of railroads. Later he was the general passenger agent of the Seaboard Air Line which then had established a rail connection between Augusta and Norfolk. Frank Clark had an older brother, Horace P. Clark, who lived in New York City until he died in 1914. Horace too was a railroad agent. On occasion the Horace Clarks made visits to Augusta, stopping at the Bon Air Hotel in April 1906 and at the lower Broad Street home of his niece Frank Clark Inman and her husband, John Walter Inman, in March 1900.

Frank Clark and Ruth Doughty had four children: Frank (sometimes called Frankie) Crowell Clark who married first John Walter Inman and then Llewellyn Goode Doughty; Ruth Doughty Clark, who died an infant; Mary Stedman Clark (later Ridgely); and the youngest, Horace Doughty Clark, who probably was named for his uncle Horace.

Horace Clark died young at only thirty-nine in Opelika, Alabama, where he worked as the representative of the Augusta cotton factor Garrett and Calhoun. Horace was married to Florida (called Dolly) Echols of Opelika and sired two children, a boy and girl named Horace Doughty Clark, Jr. and Jean Clark. After the death of Horace in 1920, Dolly remarried to a traveling salesman whose given name was Luther. The latter often would visit my father on Broad Street during his periodic trips to Augusta.

After Frank Clark's death in Norfolk on December 1, 1891, Ruth Doughty Clark returned home to Augusta with her three children. Then following their marriages, she made her last home with her younger daughter, Mrs. Marion Ridgely, on Kings Way. According to the death certificate, she died at 2307 Kings Way at over seventy years of age. Her complete dates are given as May 24, 1846–November 3, 1916. My mother, then twelve years old, remembered her as a stern and somewhat irascible old lady!

Profile of Frank Crowell Clark, later Inman and then Doughty:

The first adult I really remember and vividly recall was my beloved grandmother on my mother's side. She was known as Frank (but often called Frankie) Clark Doughty. She frequently would sign her notes as F.C.D. My nurse Mamie Byrd and my sister's nurse called Nursie Coleman are not in truth as firmly implanted in my memory or affection as is F.C.D.

CHAPTER ONE

Grandmother was the only "Grannie" I ever knew, and I was her first grandchild. From the very beginning she showered me with endearments, hugs, and love, always having time to spend with me. Early recollections are our afternoon car rides, Willie Washington at the wheel of her late-1920s dark green Buick (black trim with huge yellow wooden wheels). I must have been three or four when almost every day Grandmother drove by to collect me for a spin. She was usually accompanied by her sister, my great-aunt "Ted" Ridgely whom I called Auntie T.

As I grew up into the years of the early to mid-1930s, we became even closer because for some of those years my family all lived with Grandmother in the Lake Forest Drive house she had built circa 1930. In those days Lake Forest was not in the city; the Sand Hills Cottage-type house is now known as 2914 Lake Forest Drive. Grandmother continued her devotion and concern for my welfare, was interested in my school life, and encouraged my reading habits starting with *The Rover Boys* series of tales. I certainly spent more quality time with her than with my parents who were busy with three or four other children and my father's daily work downtown. She treated me almost as an adult as she talked about our family, her own life, and her travels through the years. To summarize, Grandmother, in point of fact, was the first person I ever actually loved. As I learned more about her personality and life, I came to genuinely admire and respect her contributions and behavior over her lifespan. What follows is her story.

Frank Crowell Clark was born October 27, 1873. She apparently was named for her father whose name was Francis but who always was known as Frank. The middle name Crowell was her Grandmother Doughty's maiden surname. Eliza Margaret Crowell was born in New Jersey and must have had a relative named N. Savage Crowell, M.D. who died at age thirty-eight in 1867. This doctor is buried in Magnolia Cemetery on the large Doughty plot. Crowell's marker states he had been Assistant Surgeon Confederate States of America.

Little Frank was pleased to receive a sister January 8, 1875, when she was just over one year of age. The new arrival was named Mary Stedman Clark (always called Ted) after her father's sister who, following her marriage in 1858 to Louis De l'aigle, usually was called Aunt Mary Clark De l'aigle. The Clark girls, so close in age, remained inseparable and intimate all their lives. They were wonderfully devoted and caring of each other, even after marriage, perhaps in the way that only nineteenth-century sisters could be! This notwithstanding their quite different personalities and outlook.

Frank was the prettiest and liveliest of the two, more vivacious and animated than Ted who nevertheless was sweetness itself and even tempered in all matters. Frank had beautiful auburn hair with a natural curl and a pretty and rather seductive face, all of which added to her pep, high spirits, and enthusiasm.

We know little concerning Frank's education which, whatever it was, must have taken place at home or in public schools in the places the family lived: Augusta,

CHAPTER ONE

Macon, Raleigh, and Norfolk. There apparently was no "finishing school" for her, possibly due to lack of funds as her father died when she was in her late teens. She did possess an interest in reading. I have a leather-bound copy of *Under the Lilacs* by L. M. Alcott signed "Frank Crowell Clark, Xmas 1887" in a fancy but beautiful script. Travel too is a fine educator, and I was often told of the trips the family made by rail to New York City and other eastern points. As Frank Clark's father was a railroad agent, they always garnered free passes. Wilmington, North Carolina, and the adjoining Wrightsville Beach was often a destination to visit their Clark-De l'aigle-Munds cousins.

Grandmother frequently alluded to trips to New York City; on one such occasion the little Clark girls aged about six and seven were in the F.A.O. Schwartz toy store where they appear to have acquired a small wooden tricycle. They had their picture taken with this three-wheeled vehicle and were so charming and beautifully attired that one gentleman (who turned out to be a high-profile New Yorker, i.e., an Astor, Gould, or Vanderbilt) was much taken with this encounter and spent time with the little girls and their adult chaperone! I have a picture of the sisters with the three-wheeler.

On trips south to Augusta in warm weather, all rail car windows were wide open and cinders and dust flew all about. Then the Clark sisters over and over would sing, "Black and dusty going to Augusty!" Frank as a girl was very musical and probably took various music lessons as a child. She eventually played the piano "by ear" as they say and until almost her death always had a piano in her living room. This was a baby grand if my recollection is not faulty.

Growing to young adulthood, Frank was a pretty, popular, and much sought-after Augusta belle following the Clarks' permanent return to Augusta circa 1891. Her close friends included her Doughty first cousins, Daisy Berry, Nina Cohen, Henry North, Miller Robertson, Anita Phinizy, Willie Mickel, William Butt, and the William Martins to mention a few names. She must have met John Walter Inman of Atlanta shortly following his arrival in 1896 to open a cotton factoring office. They were married in 1897 at St. Paul's Church. Frank was twenty-four at the time, and Walter (as he was called) was twenty-nine. Their first child came rapidly but died at birth May 4, 1898. His stone is located in the Clark-Doughty section of Magnolia Cemetery and marked J.W.I. Jr. In 1899, Cordelia Dick Inman arrived followed by a son, Walker Patterson, in 1900 and Ruth Doughty in 1902. The Inmans lived on lower Broad, then numbered 445, but also had a summer home called Golden Camp outside of Augusta, a distance of around eight miles and situated at a higher elevation. I believe Golden Camp was located in the "Bath" area.

The happy Inman life became a tragedy in August 1904 when Walter was caught in a severe downpour of rain in his open car and suffered an extreme chill leading to death at the young age of thirty-four. Frank was pregnant and gave birth to their twins November 27, 1904. My mother was one of the twins, also named

CHAPTER ONE

Frank Clark Inman, but her twin brother, named John Walter Inman, lived but a month. With his death, Grandmother at age thirty-one had already lost two babies and a husband.

As a relatively young matron of a non-retiring but very happy personality, Frank, following the mourning period (or in those days probably still in it) found herself pursued by her first cousin Llewellyn Goode Doughty, a widower since 1901 with one daughter, Jean, who'd been born in 1896. L.G. (as my Mother always called him) was forty-two when Frank married him in St. Paul's Church at 1:30 p.m. April 16, 1906. Frank's mother, Ruth Doughty Clark, gave the bride away. There was a small reception at the bride's home to drink to the health of the newlyweds before their departure on the bridal trip to New York and other points north. Their engagement had been announced at a chafing dish supper given by Mr. and Mrs. Porter Fleming at their home. The details of that function appeared in the local newspapers around St. Valentine's Day 1906.

Frankie told the story that while in New York City on their honeymoon, Llewellyn for some reason pinched her good and hard; she said she really made him suffer that night!

Soon after their return the Doughty couple were "at home" in a large columned house numbered 1012 Greene Street. I recall this house from my youth, which was then occupied by The Knights of Columbus organization. Painted yellow (either brick or wood), there were white columns across the front to the second-story roof. The Doughty family and their Inman children and cousins remained at this address until building 2321 Kings Way circa 1916-1917, a Wendell-designed residence.

Before her second union to her first cousin, Frank took the train to Atlanta to tell Father Inman (her father-in-law) of the wedding plans. He apparently asked her to desist and not to marry just then. Perhaps he thought it rather soon after his son's death. Aunt Mary Lou Phinizy later would say that "Frankie married again before her first husband was cold in the casket." That was nonsense of course, but in that era I guess a mourning period of twenty months was deemed inadequate! Father Inman said he would leave her $50,000 (at that time around at least $250,000 or more in spending power) if she delayed her second marriage plans. Hence, she missed this legacy when Walker Patterson Inman died in Atlanta November 23, 1907, about nineteen months subsequent to the nuptials. Nevertheless, there were continuing cordial relations between Frankie Doughty and the Walker P. Inman family of Atlanta with whom she and the first Inman children visited from time to time. This was particularly true with respects to Mary Inman Gray, the late Walter's sister.

Frank and Llewellyn had a child, an unnamed boy, who died at birth in 1907. There followed a beautiful girl, named Mary De l'aigle for her great-aunt Mary Clark De l'aigle, born February 24, 1910. The infant Mary De l'aigle Doughty died at sixteen months after an illness of one month on June 21, 1911. Thus two

CHAPTER ONE

more infant deaths in Frank's life, now totaling four! However, the worst tragedy yet came just a month later at Sullivan's Island (where the entire family had gone for the summer) when the eldest Inman child, the lovely Cordelia Dick Inman, named for her paternal grandmother, contracted typhoid fever about July 20, 1911.

It was not known at first that the fever was typhoid. On the advice of the local attending physician, the twelve-year-old patient was brought home to the Pine Heights Sanitarium in North Augusta. Initially it appeared to be a light case, but she did not rally sufficiently and finally died following a "crisis" on Augusta 17, 1911. This loss was understandably a disaster for Frank. Adding to Frank's obvious grief over losing her fifth child, was the fact that Cordelia was a beautiful girl of twelve and considered one of the loveliest in Augusta. With a wonderful sweetness of nature and beauty of character, Cordelia herself spoke very eloquently of her womanhood soon to come. She had been voted "Queen of the Carnival" for the benefit of the Children's Hospital. And to lose two children to God within two months was almost too much of a burden for Frank to carry! What a sorrow for the entire family! At her funeral conducted from 1012 Green Street all sang the hymn "Onward Christian Soldiers," a favorite Cordelia loved to hear during her illness.

Frankie clearly was sustained by her faith and her religion. This combined with her innate focus on the positive probably allowed her to go forward with her head held high and a smile on her face. In her part diary-part scrapbook, however, Frank pasted hair from and flowers held by her two daughters; she evidently was utterly distraught as attested by the following diary entry:

> The world seems dark indeed, and it is long before we can see that God still loves us and that he loved those born to us better than we did ourselves. He sees down the way, He takes them out of the trouble here to Himself there to keep safely for us.
> My dear little baby will know no other home [this must refer to Mary De l'aigle];
> My Cordelia with a life so full of promise and everything to make her happy, as much as I loved her, God loved her more.
> There is comfort for me—it is a glorious thing to be the Mother of two little angels; a part of my being looking into the Father's face and receiving the love and happiness that we can form no idea of; and then I think it makes Heaven more like home for me. I know that next to the Savior they will be the first to welcome me. They have gone from the troubles of earth to the joys of Paradise.

No one really knows what life will bring. While the loss of five children, and particularly the death of one child of twelve, must have been traumatic and heartbreaking, still Frankie had her other three children: Walker, Ruth, and little Frankie, who now were the recipients of her devotion and love. I have a wonderful picture of the four of them all gathered around a table where Frankie is seated with book in hand. The time must have

CHAPTER ONE

been around 1912-1913. Understandably, Frank tended to spoil her only son and two remaining daughters. As always the girls continued to be dressed in lacy dresses so that when my daughter Tracy first saw a picture of Frankie and her brood, she said they all looked just like the Romanov grand duchesses of the 1900-1914 era! And many in Augusta have in recent days remembered seeing this family as so described in the Greene Street area. See the photograph in this book.

And, as a lawyer or the Oracle of Delphi might say, Frankie still had her health, a devoted second spouse who was well off and provided fine furnishings, and many servants combined with both carriage and motor car transportation. Frankie had a Victoria carriage for her own personal use, and there were stables/garages behind the 1012 Greene Street and 2321 Kings Way homes. Besides her husband Llewellyn's success as a cotton exporter and as president of Riverside Compress Company, Inc., plus other business interests, Frankie's Inman children all had trust funds from their paternal grandfather after 1907. She also had inherited about $250,000 in assets from Walter Inman. Hence, life was not all total bleakness and despair on the material side.

The leading local architect of the World War I era, Henry Wendell, had designed the Doughtys' large, handsome house circa 1916-1917 at 2321 Kings Way. Here Ruth, Walker, and Frank spent their early to late teenage years. As their mother still was comparatively youthful (forty-three or forty-four years old at the time), she was active in social affairs at night, leaving Llewellyn at home on occasion. This might involve parties at the country club with her friends (i.e., the Billy Butts, Bryan Cummings, Miller Robertsons, Porter Flemings, and Will Whites, all of whom now lived on "The Hill") or participating in entertainments offered to the US military stationed at Camp Hancock. On some nights when she was out, my mother remembered playing casino or another card game with her stepfather whom she called L.G. Teto Barrett said a small crowd including her brother Gene Baker, C. B. Law, and others would gather when L.G. had retired upstairs and play sardines—squeezing into a small closet or drawers! Tracy Duncan Cohen once told me that my grandmother's crowd during World War I and the early 1920s was "silly and frivolous!" She had seen them dancing at the club and made the decision not to comport herself on that model when she aged!

Ruth was sent to finishing school at Briarcliff Manor, New York, and Walker to Culver Military Academy in Culver, Indiana. Ruth did well at school in sports and academics. Like her mother, Ruth was musical and studied violin; she had her own instrument and learned to perform accompanied by her mother on the baby grand.

Frankie's younger daughter, known as "Little Frank" or "Frankie," was growing up rapidly as a very popular girl with both boys and girls. Little Frank first had a pony cart and later her own auto. She had been born with a natural white-streak birthmark across her dark brown hair. Many ladies later would pay their hairdresser to dye such a white streak onto their hair. As with all

CHAPTER ONE

mothers and daughters, there was the usual friction on occasion: Little Frankie would remark how stupid this or that was, and Frankie's standard reply was, "Isn't it amazing how such a stupid mother could have such a brilliant child!"

Frankie Doughty must have wondered many times what she had done to deserve such fate when one early Saturday morning, June 12, 1920, she was notified that her precious eldest daughter, Ruth Doughty Inman, named for her maternal grandmother, had been killed in an automobile accident about twelve miles from Augusta. Ruth, born in 1902, was in her eighteenth year having just returned home the Friday evening before from attending her brother's graduation exercises at Culver Academy in Indiana. She also had herself just completed a third year at Briar Cliff School in New York and had returned home for the summer. According to the press reports, Ruth was charming, vivacious, and recognized as one of the most beautiful of Augusta girls.

Teto Barrett recalled seeing Ruth about this time at a country club dance as a pretty girl with dark hair and dressed in red. This may have been the Friday night prior to the accident for Ruth was due to depart for a house party on Tybee Island, Savannah, at 7:00 a.m. Saturday, June 12. The house party was to be hosted by Miss Edna Maxwell whose sister and brother-in-law, Mr. and Mrs. George Blanchard, were the chaperones. The family story is that Frankie Doughty had begged Ruth not to go by car to Savannah because of her recent absences from home. Ruth naturally wanted to be with her Augusta friends and won the day!

The accident happened at 7:35 a.m. just outside of Augusta on a curve at the intersection of the old and new Savannah roads. The car, a Templar, was said to be rolling at seventy miles per hour and at that speed could not make the forty-five-degree-angle turn. As a matter of fact, the location was often referred to as Dead Man's Curve. There was a bridge at the spot over Big Spirit Creek, but the large red automobile speeding before the curve at sixty to seventy miles per hour never made the bridge. The vehicle skidded and turned over, rolling over three times and stopping upside down in the creek. Ruth in the front passenger seat was thrown from the car to the ground as were the two rear occupants; the driver, Mr. Antonio W. Davison, stayed at the wheel and was not pinned beneath the car. In the rear were William Cozart of 436 Greene Street and Joe Mathewson of 616 Greene. All three men, while shaken up, were otherwise uninjured.

Ruth was not instantly killed. Her right temple was gashed in a wound of about 1¼ inches. She rose from the ground and with the assistance of the young men walked to a store a few yards distant where she collapsed and died before a doctor arrived ten to fifteen minutes later. It was thought that in falling from the hurtling car, her head might have struck a rock so violently as to cause concussion of the brain. One news report says Ruth uttered, "Oh, Lord," as she first staggered to her feet before wavering.

CHAPTER ONE

The latest blow to Frankie Doughty must have been just staggering. She had lived now to have six children predecease her, something all mothers dreaded and that few, even in the 1920s, ever experienced. Again, her inherent and deep-rooted faith combined with the support of family and myriad good friends must have brought her through this tragic situation.

Ruth Inman was paid several written tributes the day of her funeral at St. Paul's Church and in an *Augusta Chronicle* piece. The funeral took place at the church at 6:00 p.m. Sunday, June 13, with young friends as pallbearers: Charles Mell, Jr., Montgomery Harison, Joe Lee, Jr., Levings Brown, Ernest Sherman, and Richard Stearnes. The church was filled with people and hundreds of floral designs and cut flowers so that the chancel was almost completely covered. Her special girlfriends followed the pure white casket covered with a large pall of pink roses and white lilies. The services were concluded at Magnolia Cemetery at the Doughty-Inman plot.

The press and church encomia or citations found Ruth Inman one of the fortunate ones of earth who from babyhood had been beautiful and lovely in every way. Through life to a young adult, "her roses held no thorns, the road of life held no rough places." Death came so swiftly that she quickly opened her eyes in Heaven. All were asked to think of her as always young, always beautiful, always happy as her radiant young beauty would never be dimmed by age nor dulled with tears or disillusion. Future heartaches and sorrow would be spared her. Sympathy for her sorrow-stricken mother knew no expression or bounds;

yet, Frankie remained with Christian resignation in her heart as she must have grappled with why a merciful God would permit such a tragedy.

Judge Henry C. Hammond wrote the editor of the *Chronicle* a letter recounting the facts known surrounding the accident as a lawyer would. His conclusion was simple: the driver of the seventy-horsepower Templar should be condemned for his reckless driving manner which put at risk both the car occupants and all who passed on the road that early Saturday morning. The judge termed the driver, Antonio Davison, "a demon man at the wheel."

Frankie had written the following in her diary when Cordelia died, which at this new very bleak time must have given her a modicum of comfort and solace:

> Not now, but in the coming years, we'll read the meaning of our tears, and then perhaps we'll understand.

Frankie Doughty then lost her second husband and first cousin, Llewellyn Doughty, who died October 21, 1921, at age fifty-seven. The cause of death was listed by Dr. M. S. Levy as uremia with hemiplegia/arteriosclerosis secondary and contributory. Aside from his wife and stepchildren/cousins, he was survived by one daughter, Jean Councill, née Doughty, brothers, and sisters. L.G.D. had been ill and confined to his 2321 Kings Way home for several months. There seems to have been at least a partial stroke, so in essence he had retired from his successful cotton business. He was

CHAPTER ONE

senior partner in the firm L. G. Doughty & Co. The surviving member of the cotton factoring business, B. T. Low, paid Frankie Doughty $100 monthly for several years after L.G.D.'s death in return for continuing to employ the original name of the firm. Thus her spouse's demise was a further sadness for Frankie and another reason to continue the deep black mourning still worn for Ruth.

St. Paul's Church reported in its August 1918 publication *Church Bells* on a new memorial. This was the installation of a new altar of white Vermont marble, massive but simple in design, ornamented on the front with a carved border and in the center a mosaic cross surrounded by a wreath. The re-table has the thrice "holy" in gold mosaic. The altar was the production of W. W. Leland Co. of New York and was consecrated in the new church (the fourth on the site) subsequent to the 1916 fire. The church announced it was the gift of Mrs. Llewellyn G. Doughty (Frankie Clark Doughty) in memory of her two little daughters, Mary De l'aigle Doughty and Cordelia Dick Inman, and her mother, Mrs. Ruth Doughty Clark. Why Llewellyn Doughty himself is unmentioned remains unclear!

Then on Sunday, October 12, 1924, there was a special benediction service at St. Paul's Church for the memorial pulpit, a second gift from Frankie Doughty, in memory of her daughter Ruth Doughty Inman. The pulpit was used for the first time the same Sunday when the Rev. Julius A. Schaad preached a sermon titled "Saved by the Foolishness of Preaching." The new pulpit was made by the Gorham Company of New York City from an original design. It was made of mahogany with carved borders and the emblems of Alpha and Omega and featured a cross and symbolic palms in the center panel. The pulpit still bears a small brass plate on one side with the very touching inscription:

To The Glory of God and in memory of another precious daughter, now with Him in Paradise,

>Ruth Doughty Inman
>1902 - 1920

Without doubt memorials such as the two described are rather perfect and solid expressions of a mother's love should one know the facts leading to their erection.

In the Winter/Spring of 1922, Frankie must have decided to take daughter Frank (who had followed her late sister Ruth to Briar Cliff Manor School by then) and join the Will Whites for a three-month tour of Europe. Frank was then seventeen or eighteen years old. Cornelia White would accompany her parents with a friend and neighbor Elizabeth ("Baby") Burdell, the sixth member of the group. They sailed from New York on the White Star Line's *S. S. Majestic* on June 17, 1922, and returned again on the White Star Line sailing September 13 from South Hampton to New York on board the *Olympic*, the sister ship of the *Titanic*. This was the first visit to Europe for the two "Franks" who were still dressed in mourning garb. The itinerary included France, Italy,

CHAPTER ONE

Switzerland, Germany (Munich, Dresden, Berlin, Potsdam, Cologne, and Frankfurt), Holland, Brussels, back to Paris, then London.

Their first stop after landing at Cherbourg was Paris and the Westminster Hotel on the Rue de la Paix. I think it still exists. Then to the South of France starting at Marseilles, Italy from top to bottom (Naples really) and back up to Venice, Milan, and the Italian lakes. Frank found Lake Como and Bellagio "the most beautiful spot I have ever seen." They stayed at The Grand Hotel (still there amid beautiful gardens to the water's edge, I think, as we also stayed there in years past). Then touring Lake Como by boat and by car to Stresa where Will and Nina White said in all their travels they had found the Hotel Grand and Iles Borronmées unequal in its setting and elegance on Lake Maggiore. These hotels probably were considered the Villa D'este of that 1920s era. Stresa today is rather commercial and not fashionable.

Frankie's son Walker also was in Europe that same summer with a group from Georgia Tech where he was enrolled. His friend and first cousin Marion Ridgely, Jr. was along as Walker's guest. Frankie worried constantly, as her diary reveals, about their safety (as a mother naturally would) and arranged to rendezvous with Walker's group in Rome on July 12. She minuted that she hated to leave them for Naples at 1:30 p.m. I wonder about their own feelings as jolly youths full of life on their first trip abroad! While back in Paris later on August 24, the diary notes it was Walker's twenty-second birthday, so he still was much on her mind. And rightly so after losing six of her children! During the course of their separate itineraries, she had met the "boys" several times, including July 12 in Rome for the first time and then again in Rome July 16 when Walker and his three companions took her in their car on a drive around the "Eternal City" before the Doughty-White party entrained for Venice. There was another brief meeting in Venice July 19 and in Munich on August 3, which is where she last saw Walker on the trip.

A sad event occurred in Venice when Frankie met Mrs. Hartman with a group of girls from Briar Cliff School at the Royal Daniele Hotel. Several girls had been friends of Ruth Inman, and seeing this group made her sad and tearful. The diary makes it clear she wanted Walker with her. She wrote, "God bless my boy."

The Doughty-White group returned to Paris for a long visit of about ten days on August 24, coming from Brussels. On arriving at the Continental Hotel on the Rue Rivoli, just down from the Place Vendome, Frankie found a note from Harry-dele Hallmark. Harry-dele also was a great friend to Louise De l'aigle Reese, Frankie's first cousin. Both ladies were staying nearby at the Hotel France et Choiseul. No mention appears in the diary about the death of Aunt Mary Clark De l'aigle July 3, 1922, in Wilmington, North Carolina. This was Louise Reese's mother. In those far-off days there was no question of returning by air for the funeral which took place in Augusta on July 6. However, the family must have cabled both of them.

CHAPTER ONE

Harry-dele Hallmark appears to have been sort of a "Martha Stewart" of her day but probably with more aristocratic connections, i.e. not the Hamptons trash! She was born in Pensacola, Florida, in 1867, the daughter of Harry and Adele Hallmark who obviously combined their given names for their child. Harry–dele grew up in Augusta, her parents having died when she was very young. Her career began in journalism as society editor of the *Augusta Chronicle*. Later in Philadelphia she was editor of the woman's page of the *Philadelphia Public Ledger* and The Philadelphia Press; subsequently, she served as fashion editor of the *New York Times*. Her frequent columns on fashion and the "art of living" were a daily feature article of the McClure Newspaper Syndicate and published by more than a hundred newspapers in the United States and abroad. Harry-dele wrote under the nom de plume Anne Rittenhouse.

"Anne Rittenhouse" continued to visit friends in Augusta, notwithstanding her career in the North and also made at least two trips to Paris each year to view the fashion collections. Mrs. John Harper Davison of Augusta was a close Harry-dele connection, and I recall her daughter, Alice Davison Smith, talking to me about Harry-dele when I first went to New York City in 1948-1949. During the 1922 trip Harry-dele took the ladies to visit all the important "dressmakers" (so Frankie termed them) of that day: Worth, Jenny, Paquin, etc., according to Frankie's diary. She wrote the following: "Crazy once in my life, but all of Paris is wild and crazy, and I may never come again!" Thus she explained ordering two gowns for her daughter plus one gown and a silk coat for herself! And further she wrote, "Shopping all afternoon, Frank and I alone in Paris." Then, "Met Elizabeth Allen Burwell and Mrs. Herbert on street." They were well-known Augusta residents.

Frankie always seemed to deplore needless extravagance (which is why I reviewed the Harry-dele shopping expedition) and constantly stressed to never invade capital. She is said to have inherited $250,000 in assets when her first husband, Walter Inman, died in 1904. What she received from the second spouse, Llewellyn Doughty, I do not know except that it is likely his estate had to be shared with his only child, Jean Doughty Councill. The house at 2321 Kings Way was sold in 1924 for $35,000 rather fully furnished; although, Frankie took out family silver and furniture important to her. The buyer was a Northern winter resident who insisted on his new accommodation being on a "move-in" basis. The price seems low to us today for a large furnished Wendell house, but in purchasing power it probably would be more than twenty times that amount in today's money.

After returning from Europe in September 1922, Walker at some point in the next year seems to have quit Georgia Tech and gone to Florida to take part in the general boom period there. He bought a boat (I guess we should call it a small yacht) and was living in Miami. Frankie and her sister, Ted Ridgely, took the train and made their first visit to Florida to be with Walker and, undoubtedly, also to check on his pursuits! There is a

CHAPTER ONE

photo of the two sisters in white yachting caps on the stern of Walker's boat. Frankie was enchanted with the Addison Mizner-type Spanish colonial architecture, and after returning to Augusta engaged Willis Irvin to draw plans for a classic Spanish colonial-style house at 2204 Kings Way. These plans date from June 1924 with the architect even responsible for including Spanish-type wall lights, sconces, and chandeliers of the period. Aunt Mary Lou Phinizy always referred to the home "as that ridiculous house your grandmother built."

The 2204 Kings Way house was finished at the end of 1924. Meantime, Frankie's only living daughter was married September 3, 1924, and Frankie made one trip to New York City to buy Spanish-style furniture for the new residence. Her former house at 2321 Kings Way had been sold mainly fully furnished as mentioned. Sloan and Company sold her many of the furniture items, a few of which can be seen in the picture included of the 2204 living room. These included a sofa, a marble-top wrought iron console and mirror, Spanish armchairs, Chinese-red-painted twin beds for her guest room, and a large desk/secretary with a carved drop-down front for writing purposes ala Mizner.

In that era, sleeping porches were the rage, so very soon after occupying her new residence, she added to the left-side rear a screened-in porch on the ground floor with an enclosed windowed sleeping porch above. With this addition, she had three bedrooms plus the sleeping porch for warm weather on the second floor. A one-car garage was a separate structure at the end of a rear lane running behind the house. To supplement the Spanish-Florida ambiance, Frankie also installed a parrot of gorgeous colors on the open side porch. This bird soon learned to duplicate the voice Frankie used in summoning her chauffeur, Willie Washington, from the garage; Willie rapidly tired of the unnecessary trips at the sound of his name!

At the end of her first full year in the house, Frankie was asked by her Doughty cousin, Elbert Jackson, to host his New York City mentor James Montgomery Flagg for the 1925 Christmas visit to Augusta Elbert had planned. Elbert was the son of Crowella Doughty Jackson, Frankie's first cousin, and a special favorite who later was to marry Constance Wright of Augusta. Flagg of course was still in the public eye as the painter of the World War I famous US military recruitment poster featuring the slogan "Uncle Sam Wants You!" While in Augusta, Flagg was given a guest card to the country club by Frankie and from all reports had a fine time enjoying much bootleg liquor and the end-of-the-year festivities. Flagg also did drawings of Frank and Bowdre Mays and Donald Bussey, the latter a close friend of Elbert Jackson. As a gift to his hostess, Flagg painted a watercolor of the old Greene Street Court House, one of Augusta's oldest and finest structures but tragically torn down in the early 1950s. A copy is included in this book of the local building the artist chose to paint as a fine example of old architecture in Augusta.

While discussing the Flagg visit to 2204 Kings Way in later years with my mother, I told her how the Lotus

CHAPTER ONE

Club in New York City (where Flagg had been a member) contained in their grill room and the men's bath downstairs a number of his paintings. My mother Frank called Flagg a "liquor-head" who was much older than "their crowd" and who obviously indulged a great deal more compared to their "twenty-somethings" group! Flagg apparently liked the South and also made visits to the Charleston, South Carolina, area where he did local watercolors of Folly Beach and some of the noted Charleston townhouses. I saw several for sale at a well-known South Carolina dealer's shop a few years back. The prices asked were about $8,000 each.

Around 1930, Frankie Doughty sold the Spanish Kings Way house to a Mrs. Hardwick for $14,000 and built her final house, a Sand Hills Cottage, at what is now 2914 Lake Forest Drive but was then out of the city with no number. One important catalyst for this decision was the move of the Ridgely family to Lake Forest following the sale of their house next door on the Kings Way side. The new development known as "Forrest Hills" was a mid "Roaring Twenties" creation anchored by the luxurious Forrest-Ricker Hotel built at its highest point, surrounded by brick streets and with lots and curving roads well laid out on the adjacent acres. The Forrest-Ricker Hotel and its golf course would provide Augusta with a new location for tourists and perhaps help to staunch the Florida stampede.

Mr. William E. Bush sold Frankie a lot on the high or east side of Lake Forrest (sometimes called Lake Forrest after Forrest Adair, an early investor in the new development) for either $250 or $500. There are two stories relating to the price for about a ½-acre property. At this stage, 1930, lots were not selling well, and the developers, including Blanchard and Calhoun, were naturally anxious to encourage new building. The lot was almost directly across the street from the Ridgely house with narrow empty lots on each side. On the left side was the house built for William Wright Phinizy (called Billy) and later occupied by William S. Morris, Jr. and his family.

As Frankie always admired 914 Milledge Road and its Sand Hills Cottage, such was to be her theme; three dormer windows were on the roof opening into two bedrooms and one bath between them. The master bedroom and bath were on the ground floor that also contained living room, dining room, pantry, and kitchen. There was a basement with servant's toilet, coal-fired furnace, storage area, and small back porch. She clearly intended this to be her final abode ensuring that one bedroom upstairs had its own sink for a servant or nurse.

The yard was planted and planned by herself with James Robinson who furnished the items she wanted including two magnolia trees on either side. From pictures she obviously transplanted cedar and other items from Kings Way; also constructed was a brick walkway from the street to the front steps edged by a low boxwood hedge and camellias behind on either side. The entire house and yard, including a separate garage in the rear, probably cost about $6,000-$7,000.

CHAPTER ONE

Another possible reason for the sale of 2204 Kings Way could be that Frankie suspected she was not as well off as she surmised following Llewellyn Doughty's death in 1921. This certainly became apparent after the October 1929 crash when her two surviving children began to experience their own financial difficulties. Will White often gave his advice as a successful businessman, but we don't really know how effective his input was. My mother said it was not very. The truth is that Frank Clark Doughty lived a life of total devotion and almost unselfish love; when her children had needs, she responded with alacrity—i.e., with loans or cash—even perhaps dipping into principal if necessary. Aside from the loan to my father and gifts to my mother, she also loaned her son, Walker, $5,000 in the early 1930s. At one stage I know she sold a diamond ring to William Bush and also a diamond brooch, perhaps to the same buyer. There is a mystery relative to the assets of $250,000 she is said to have inherited from her first spouse.

Frankie's amusing comments on our "Great Depression" will preface her report on the 1935 trip to San Francisco to the Garden Club of America annual meeting. This is as follows with no corrections to the original typing. She probably wrote the report for her local club, Sand Hills. The "Mary" mentioned is Mrs. Isaac W. Read, president of Sand Hills 1934-1936.

No doubt you have all heard the word <u>depression</u>, but believe it or not, when the Japan trip was being discussed I decided if it were humanly possible I would go.

Lying dormant for fifteen years in the back of my Safe Deposit box in the Bank, was some stock, and like Jack of the Beanstalk fame I took it out and sold it for a pot of Beans. Being the happy possessor of a 2 x 4 garden, I hastened to plant my Beans. The next morning looking from my window I saw the Beanstalk had begun to grow, and with it a request to our President to join the Garden Club tour.

It took all the combined efforts of our doctors to keep Mary from dropping dead with "heart failure" when I 'phoned her. After two days of nervous waiting a reply came from headquarters that I could go.

Now as to how cheap the trip could be taken, was the next question: First deciding to go up on the day coach to Atlanta — my plans changed when an invitation came to ride in a Cadillac. Instead of staying at the Ansley Hotel I went to the Biltmore; instead of occupying an upper berth we had a drawing room to Chicago.

Stopping over in Atlanta Thursday night we left Friday afternoon at six for Chicago where we joined the Garden Club Special the next day (Latin day) at 9:35 P.M. The Garden Club Special that left New York on Friday the 19th was composed of fourteen cars, two observations, two diners, baggage and the rest compartments and drawing room cars. Getting on the train we found our berths were all made up and we were more than ready to tumble in. I being

CHAPTER ONE

Jack of the Beanstalk fame, and having short legs and a good climber, the upper berth fell to my lot. Soon the lights were turned out and we were sound asleep. My "buddie" for this trip being our Garden Club treasurer and acting for the President, thoroughly felt her position and beautifully dressed in a blue "robe de nuit" lay back in luxury in the lower berth like Madame Recamier, still full of her importance, she too was soon asleep.

Feeling the call of nature, I had to descend my ladder which reached from the upper berth to the floor. Madame Recamier having read her Bible before retiring, began to dream dreams and like Jacob she saw angels ascending and descending the ladder, when in reality it was just poor little me trying to climb back on my perch quietly.

Easter Sunday morning, services were held in one of the observation cars. It was very crowded, women were sitting on the floor eager to take part in the service.

On the train were Mr. Brown and Mr. Beel, who had the trip in charge, they gave us the little green book which told the names and addresses of those on the trip. The observation cars were filled with large baskets of all kinds of beautiful flowers, radios, writing desks with souvenirs, and post cards. It was a merry party; everyone meeting old friends, and I, many, many new ones.

Sunday afternoon we suddenly saw what appeared to be a mist rising, and after discovered it was a dust storm. Soon we began to protect ourselves in every way, some tied scarfs around their heads, which Nina White wished she had done, for the mirror told that the white hair which we glories in, was an indescribable color..

Waking up next morning and looking from the windows, we saw the rugged Rocky Mountains. This scenery cannot be imagined, it has to be seen to believe.

The next point of interest was the great Salt Lake and Salt desert — and on through Utah and Nevada and California to Berkley, where we took the Ferry to San Francisco, then registration at the beautiful Fairmont Hotel where we were given a book containing a program of gardens to be visited later. Given a few minutes only, to refresh ourselves and by ten o'clock we were on our way to visit gardens. We started with a police motorcycle escort fore and aft, dipping down one long hill and up another, out California Street. Another thrill came when we were winding through Golden Gate Park and drive along the beach with the Pacific rollers breaking below us.

I must speak of the beautiful scenic "sky Line Boulevard" ride: First through the truck gardens and then through the wild flower fields, all gold and blue, and then the Crystal Spring Lake country.

The Woodside-Alberton gardens were <u>beautiful</u> and then we enjoyed luncheon Followed by more gardens and afternoon tea.

CHAPTER ONE

I suppose the July bulletin has given you full account of the annual meeting held Wednesday, April 24th at the Fairmont Hotel. I need not speak of this, but needless to say, we were bursting with pride when Mrs. Alonzo Boardman's name was read out as having received a much coveted medal.

Thursday, April 25th, conservation and __ side committee meetings, then followed same program of visiting gardens.

Friday, the horticultural meeting; program same as preceding days.

All of our evenings were free, and the consensus of opinion was, that it was very well arranged, because after our eyes had feasted on beauty of gardens and arrangement of flowers, at luncheons and teas, we were glad to be free to relax and meditate. No elaborate dinner was given, as we had at the Bon Air, but the Garden Clubs of Hillsborough, Woodside-Atherton, and Piedmont concentrated all their efforts into one wonderful luncheon given on Wednesday in the Banquet Hall of the Fairmont Hotel. Preceding the luncheon for a half hour, we enjoyed cocktails. Words are indeed inadequate to express the beauty that burst upon our view when the glass doors were opened and we were invited in for luncheon. In anticipation of our trip to trees would have bloomed, the room was profusely decorated with natural flowering fruit trees.

Hanging at the far end, was a deep blue curtain, on either side, full size trees of Cut leaf maples, in front of them stood great branches of pink Judas trees. Along The sides of the room, high above the tables, were full sized fruit trees, double Flowering crab in full bloom. The Officers table on a slightly higher level and Placed against the blue curtain, had a cloth of soft blue covering it. The center- Piece being four Chinese containers filled with the most gorgeous flowers of Every kind and description. These were linked together with a rope of flowers Of every color.

The small tables, with different colors organdie cloths, varied in their central decorations. Some had huge coral fans with "bird of paradise" flowers, some Easter lilies and forget-me-nots in containers of white shell, on a Hawaiian surf board rider with hibiscus, another with that glorious rose "Golden Emblem" and pink gladiolus, another a horn of plenty filled with yellow azaleas and lilacs. another decoration was a Japanese container holding purple and pink iris and lanterns. I could not possibly tell you of the dazzling beauty of these tables, most artistic in every respect. It was a triumphant thing, a real achievement I have never seen anything in my life to equal the picture.

Immediately after this elegant luncheon, we started for a tour of the City and ended in the afternoon for tea with Mrs. Silas Palmer, where the San Francisco Garden Club had been invited to meet us.

On Thursday we crossed the Bay into Piedmont. All of these gardens are on hillsides, very artistic and

CHAPTER ONE

never-to-be-forgotten perfection of bloom. The crowd was divided for luncheons and teas, and so ended a delightful day.

On Friday we visited the Hillsborough Gardens, another day of sunshine, after seeing so many flowers and so much color in Piedmont the day before, we were glad to see gorgeous old trees. Mrs. Edward White said she owned the finest liveoak in captivity. Of course, these gardens were filled with glorious color too. We enjoyed lunch and afternoon tea in the gardens, and so ended four perfect days. There was not a hitch in the entire San Francisco proceedings. We were joyously welcomed, royally entertained and sent on our way to Honolulu and Japan surfeited with beauty.

After stopping in Honolulu the group went on to Japan for several weeks being magnificently entertained in Tokyo, Yokohama, Kyoto, Nara, Nikko, etc. before taking side trips to what is now South/North Korea and China. The tour concluded in Shanghai, which Frankie's diary praises as a real "New York." The GCA group transited the Pacific Ocean on the *Tatsuta Maru* and *Chichibu Maru*, large liners of the NYK Line. Frankie kept a diary that I have given to the GCA archives as they were searching for such items to augment their scanty records. One New Jersey lady on the trip Mrs. Henry Jens is the grandmother of Marshall Jeanes whom I met on a GCA trip to New Orleans in 2004. Frankie noted her name as a companion in her diary. Unfortunately, part of the diary was missing, but there were pictures including one group of the entire party sitting on the deck.

Predictably for the era, Frankie described Japan and its people as charming in every way. The group was entertained by Japanese royalty (Prince Chichibu, Hirohito's younger brother, Prince Konoye, and Prince Tokogama) and the nobility (i.e., Baron Mitsui, etc.) and saw fabulous private gardens normally not seen by the public. No mention of the Japanese incursion into Manchuria; although, fighting then in China was at a rather low ebb as both sides were maneuvering for a better position. These were the "warlord" days in most of China.

The group taking the side trip to China crossed by train ferry to Pusan and traversed the then Japanese territory of Korea into China. A stop was made at Keijo (Japanese name for Seoul), Korea, where Frankie bought some of the beautiful brasses. China she found dirty and backward (compared to what she had observed in Japan). Stops were made in Mukden, Manchuria, Peping (as she termed it), Nanking, and Shanghai, which she considered a very cosmopolitan center and where after a long visit the group boarded the Japanese NYK liner *Tatsuta Maru* for the return voyage to Kobe through the Inland Sea of Japan. She thought the Inland Sea reminiscent of the Italian lakes. On to Yokohama again, Honolulu, San Francisco, and Los Angeles where the party disembarked and toured the city and Beverly Hills. By train to the Grand Canyon and finally back to

CHAPTER ONE

Atlanta where her son, Walker Inman, waited to drive her home to Augusta.

It is interesting that the GCA tour lodged in the Grand Hotel de Pekin in the present Chinese capital and at the famous Cathay Hotel in Shanghai, the latter a real art deco creation and both still operating. On the outward voyage from Honolulu to Japan via the *Chichibu Maru*, a young Japanese girl (who I believe was working on the vessel) committed suicide from the liner by throwing herself overboard. The ship turned back in an attempt to search but to no avail. At one point Frankie opened a raw oyster and found a small pearl that she had set in a ring at Kobe for her only granddaughter, Frank Inman Mays whom she called "Baby Sis" in the diary.

Both Frankie and Nina White were interviewed by the local press on arriving home as such a long trip then was big news! Hence, I am quoting one of the newspaper accounts conveying Frankie's general report on her once in a lifetime journey to the Orient:

> Whatever Mussolini may think of Japan and however badly Japan may treat China Mrs. L. G. Doughty says the Japanese are just the finest people in the world. Mrs. Doughty has recently returned from a trip to Japan and China where she was one of 125 American women representing various Garden Clubs of this country. It was her first trip to the Kingdom of Flowers and she kept a diary from day to day. A peep into the pages of this diary reveals a flood of such words as "thrilling", "gorgeous", "exquisite" and a

dozen more like them. If "the adjective is the enemy of the noun", as they taught at school, then the nouns in Mrs. Doughty's note book have a lot of enemies.

While Japan was the chief destination of the group, Mrs. Doughty got one of her finest thrills in Honolulu. In fact, if she is good, she expects to go to Honolulu when she dies. Here it was that she saw the three-mile drive lined with night blooming cereus which so enthralled her. Every day is "Lei Day" in Honolulu, but the group had the additional pleasure of striking the islands in May, the time of the national celebration of "Lei Week:, and the gorgeous flowers, perfume, music and confetti made a combination long to be remembered. But it was the sunny atmosphere, the languorous, carefree life, so different from the buzz and bustle of America that attracted her most, she says.

After Honolulu there was a long ocean voyage. But she declares she didn't mind it, the ship was a miniature world and her fellow passengers were most agreeable. She made many friends, as anyone would guess who knows Mrs. Doughty and her capacity in that direction. They arrived in Yokohama on May 13 and went straight on to Tokyo where they met many charming Japanese and saw beautiful gardens of every tree type and size. She says that through the extreme courtesy of the Japanese they saw many private homes and palaces. Here she saw a Japanese play that

CHAPTER ONE

she found most unusual and interesting. The names of the Japanese towns which she visited trip lightly from Mrs. Doughty's lips. It was in Nikko that her first mishap occurred. Here she sprained her ankle and back on a Saturday afternoon excursion. It didn't seem bad at first, but the next morning she was so stiff she could hardly move.

"My mind became possessed with the idea of what would become of me if I couldn't go on with the rest of the party," she said. "So finally I decided to spend the whole day in a tub of hot water. I did this and let me tell you something, I prayed as I never prayed before in my life. I just told the Lord plainly that I was doing my part, and for Him to do His. Believe in prayer? Well I should say I do. And the next day I went on with the party."

Another exciting moment was when she lost her purse. At least she left it behind her. The group had been entertained at a lunch in a very lovely garden. Lunch was served under a big striped tent, red, white and blue in honor of the American guests. After lunch they were to be carried across a charming lake in a boat. When they were almost at the lake Mrs. Doughty discovered that she had left her purse. For a moment her heart sank. That purse contained all of her traveler's checks as well as her passport. No one offered to go back with her so she went alone. But she wasn't alone long. She soon found a man in the garden. Now the friends of

Mrs. Doughty know that a man in the garden where she was wandering was as inevitable as the serpent in the Garden of Eden, only the man was much pleasanter. He was a "Gentleman from Japan", but he spoke English in true Gilbert and Sullivan style and together they found the purse and started for the lake only to find that the boat and the crowd had departed. Nothing daunted, Mrs. Doughty consulted her new friend who put her in a workman's cart and sent her around the lake to meet the rest of the party.

From Japan the party, or that part of it to which Mrs. Doughty belonged, went to China. They visited Korea and Manchuria, so much in the newspapers lately. Words fail her when she tries to describe China. She says that they saw soldiers all around, but no fighting or disorder of any kind. She also says that the Great Wall of China really is GREAT and as for the shops, well, it was fortunate that she found that purse because she saw some fascinating things to buy for her family, especially the numerous children who adore her and looked forward to her homecoming with mixed feelings of affection and anticipation.

On the way back she stopped in California and other points in the West. The Grand Canyon she describes as "God's Paint Pot" and says nothing she saw impressed her more.

CHAPTER ONE

It has been said that the trip was arranged in order that Japanese men and women might see how independent American women are. Well, whatever the reason they could hardly have found a better specimen than Mrs. Doughty. She says that it will taker her weeks to collect her ideas in any sort of form, but with her little notebook she has collected memories enough to last for many years to come, pictures of pleasant days and mysterious, alluring nights that when she "is too old to dream" will be hers "to remember."

During the remainder of her life the only travels I know of were to Sullivan's Island with her grandchildren, to Hendersonville, North Carolina, each summer to escape the hot summers in Augusta, and to Edisto Beach after she bought a cottage on the beach circa 1936. Several times she took friends to Edisto as a house party including her sister Ted Ridgely, Annie Robertson, Mamie Martin, May Cutts, and perhaps others. As the ladies always dressed in white summer attire, a neighbor subsequently wondered who all those older nurses were staying in the cottage! In North Carolina, Frankie always was a guest (probably a paying one) of Mrs. John J. Cohen (Nina White's mother) at her summer home on Hebron Street near the Farmer's Market in Hendersonville, North Carolina. One summer in the early 1930s, she rented the Lake Forest Drive house to the Gene Howerdds before they built their own first residence on Bransford Road.

IS LIVING WELL STILL THE BEST REVENGE?

Following the birth of her fifth Mays grandchild, Sam Warren Mays, February 8, 1937, Frankie decided to turn the Lake Forest Drive house over to her daughter and move to a small re-done cottage in the rear of what had been the Kellogg house situated on the property now known as Montrose Court just off Cumming Road. While the Kellogg property is now destroyed, at that time Dr. Colden Battey had converted the main dwelling into several apartments. The Ridgelys, having sold their Lake Forest Drive house, took one, and Frankie rented the rear cottage facing the Ridgely front steps to their unit. Her friend Colden Battey gave Frankie carte blanche to do what she wanted with the interior and its surroundings. She soon had James Robinson make a new garden, planting hedges, shrubs, trees, and flowers. There was a new walkway to the front of the cottage that contained a living room, dining room, bedroom, bath, and kitchen. Here she resided until late 1938 or very early 1939 when she sublet her cottage all furnished and boarded with her sister Ted Ridgely at their Milledge Road house. The Ridgelys had left their apartment sometime before when "Pap" Ridgely had become full-time manager of the Augusta Country Club and was offered the house at 671 Milledge owned by the club. This was to be F.C.D.'s final move.

Frankie knew she suffered from high blood pressure. Unknown perhaps to some, however, were the symptoms of angina pectoris. Her physician, Dr. Lansing Lee, was advising and wanted her to come to University Hospital for a day or two for complete tests. This she agreed to do

CHAPTER ONE

in early 1939. Meantime, she attended a cocktail party hosted by Frank and Bowdre on Lake Forest Drive in early December 1938 and carved the Smithfield ham into paper-thin slices as she was a beautiful carver. I remember seeing her in a long black lace evening costume, joking with the many guests who included her own generation too, i.e., Harry Goodrich, the Eugene Murpheys, Annie Burdell, etc. She left early with Willie driving her back to Milledge Road. I walked with her to the car and requested more Rover Boy books for Christmas.

Then a few weeks later I accompanied my mother to drive Frankie for her tests at University Hospital. As it was to be at least an overnight stay, I carried her small black case to the car. Frankie climbed into the front seat, looked at her daughter, and said, "Darling, you look so pretty!" Mother sort of disavowed this compliment but must have been pleased nevertheless. Arriving at the old University Hospital (the Barrett Wing, I think), Frankie was put in a wheelchair, which I pushed to her room following registration. This was the last time I saw her.

As I recall now, my parents received an urgent telephone call early the next morning (February 1, 1939) advising Frankie had passed away suddenly from an attack of angina. She was only sixty-five and would have turned sixty-six in October 1939. Today with more modern medicine and methods she would not have died most likely. The car returning from the hospital appears to have awakened me, but as it was still dark I must have slept again. But very early thereafter Mary "D" Goodrich came into my room to tell of Grandmother's sudden and unexpected death. She said no school today and sent me over to spend the day with Helen Wright on Bransford while my sister went to see Betty Phinizy at her home. I recall bursting into tears while Mary "D" hugged me.

The funeral service was at St. Paul's at 11:30 a.m. with John Hines officiating and burial following at Magnolia Cemetery. The family first gathered at 671 Milledge where the casket had spent the night. Nina White brought large baskets of wonderful camellias to insert all around Grandmother who they all said looked beautiful, if such a term is appropriate in these circumstances. Aunt May Inman Gray, her sister-in-law, came from Atlanta with her son, and old friends from New York City, Harold V. Smith and Boykin Wright, Jr., sent beautiful floral arrangements. Mother allowed me to attend being the oldest grandchild, but my sister was unhappy she could not go. The Fielding Wallaces sent their town car and chauffeur to drive Frank, Bowdre, Walker, and Alice Inman and me to the service. Bowdre, Sr. and Bowdre, Jr. sat on the rear jump seats. The Wallace chauffeur was well known to Frank as he had driven her also to her 1924 wedding at St. Paul's.

St. Paul's was packed as Frankie's popularity had continued, and at the internment on the Doughty-Inman plot, all of mother's intimate lady friends were in a line at the rear of the plot, including Mary "D" Goodrich, Julia Fargo, Anna Wilkins, Helen Wright, "Sis" Mell, Louise Mays Bussey, and several others. To help substantiate what I have written about my beloved grandmother, I am including the obituary printed by the local

CHAPTER ONE

press, the article written by Louisa K. Smith (L-K-S), also a close friend, and the resolution of the Widows' Home. Finally, the tribute from The Sand Hills Garden Club, read at their meeting and written by Tracy Duncan Cohen:

MRS. DOUGHTY DIES AT THE HOSPITAL; FUNERAL THURSDAY

Services Will Be Conducted From St. Paul's Church for Prominent Augusta Woman

---

Mrs. Frank Clark Doughty, widow of Llewellyn G. Doughty, died at five o'clock Wednesday morning at the University Hospital, after a short illness. While Mrs. Doughty had not been well her condition was not considered serious by her family and her death came as a great shock to them and to her many friends.

Funeral services will be held at St. Paul's Church on Thursday morning at half past eleven. Rev. John E. Hines will officiate and interment will be in Magnolia Cemetery.

Honorary pall bearers will be Bryan Cumming, William B. White, William M. Butts, B. T. Lowe, Dr. W. H. Goodrich, Dr. F. Lansing Lee, Andrew Perkins, J. P. Doughty, Frank Calhoun, Rodney Cohen, Sr., and Charles Phinizy. Active pall bearers will be Robert Martin, Emile Barinowski, Charles Houston, Charles

Whitney, Charles I. Mell, Montgomery Ridgely, Jack Wilkins, Gould Barrett, Barney Dunbar and Henry Gardner.

Mrs. Doughty was the daughter of the late Frank W. Clark and his wife Ruth Doughty Clark. She was born in Augusta and most of her life was spent here. Her first husband was the late J. Walter Inman, of Augusta and Atlanta. After the death of Mr. Inman she married the late Llewellyn Doughty a prominent Augusta cotton man.

Mrs. Doughty was a woman of unusual charm. A great beauty in her girlhood she never lost the sparkle and gayety that won her friends and admirers wherever she went. She loved people and they loved her and she won a place in the social life of Augusta that will be hard to fill.

She was a member of St. Paul's Church and was an energetic worker on all committees. She belonged to the Sand Hills Garden Club and was a delegate to the International Convention of Garden Clubs when it met in Japan some years ago.

But it was in her home life that she found her greatest happiness. She loved children and young people and her grandchildren found her a delightful and sympathetic companion. During the last year she had made her home with her sister, Mrs. Marion Ridgely, on Milledge Road.

CHAPTER ONE

Mrs. Doughty is survived by a daughter, Mrs. Bowdre Mays, a son Walker P. Inman, a sister, Mrs. Marion Ridgely, stepdaughter, Mrs. Jean Doughty Council, a niece, Miss Elizabeth Ridgely, a nephew Marion Ridgely, Jr., and nine grandchildren, all of Augusta and a niece and nephew in Atlanta.

L-K-S
- The Value of a Smile- (1939)

I sometimes wonder just what part of us, of our personality and of our experiences, we will be allowed to carry with us to another world. Perhaps it will be those things that will add most to the happiness of that "Beautiful Isle of Somewhere." If so there are more smiles in that land today because of two women who lived their lives among us and who, within a few short hours of one another left to go into the sunset.

These two women, Harriet Hanson and Frank Doughty, were different in many ways and yet they shared certain thing in common. Both had met with more than their share of the rough places in life. Each had lost a favorite child in a terrible accident when those children were just reaching maturity. Both women met their troubles with heads up and, centering their lives and affections on the children who were left, gave themselves to those children and to the friends among whom they lived.

But there was something else which these two shared, something rare and valuable, something which cannot be bought. That something was a sense of humor, a tolerance of the human weaknesses of others and the ability to smile under conditions which would have broken the spirit of most of us.

I shall always remember both of them as laughing and can any of us ask more than that we shall leave with our friends the money of a smile? Only a day or two ago I met Frank Doughty on her way into the hospital. She was laughing with a small grandson and called out to me not to let all the parties be over before she got well enough to go to them.

The last time I saw Hattie Hanson she was in great pain, but she was laughing it off and making fun of herself in spite of it. Is it any wonder that I shall remember them both with a smile?

Both women had the gift of making others laugh as well as of laughing themselves. They could be the life of a party. But they both shared that understanding of the troubles of others, perhaps because of the wounds in their own hearts, that made them real friends in times of sorrow.

Both had known the pleasures of wealth and both had seen wealth melt away, like the fairy gold of the old tales.

CHAPTER ONE

Hattie Hanson had that rare gift of being able to give herself when she had nothing else to give. Many a young man or woman in this town read of her death with tear wet eyes and grateful hearts. When money failed she gave "herself, her soul and her body" to those in need.

She had a gift for friendship and during her long illness she was surrounded and tenderly cared for by the friends of her school days. Her devotion to her old mother was a tender and beautiful thing.

Frank Doughty had the happiest nature I have ever known. Her laugh was so contagious that she could set a whole room laughing. She was a devoted mother and grandmother and to see her at Christmas, surrounded by a group of grandchildren, pushing and pulling them through the crowded shops, laughing and chattering while she did so was a sight that I shall never forget. The tie between her and her only sister was something that only sisters can understand. The town is the richer for the happiness that these women brought into the hearts and lives of those who knew them.

They have passes into a country where there is no pain, "neither shall there be any tears." And when they stand before the great judge of all and offer Him their lives, I think that he will choose as their greatest gift a sheaf of smiles, for surely, even in heaven, they are happier for a smile.

WIDOWS HOME BOARD ADOPTS RESOLUTIION ON MRS. F. C. DOUGHTY (1939)

At a recent meeting of the board of managers of the Widow's Home the Following resolutions were adopted in memory of Mrs. Frank Clark Doughty, Member of the board who died February 1:

"First: That in the passing of Frankie Doughty, we bow in faith and trust to Him who knoweth best what is good for His children.

"Second: That we shall sorely miss her and her willing helping hand and inspiring courage and love.

"Third: That we shall ever remember her in loving affection and strive to emulate her shining example.

"Fourth: That we extend to her bereaved ones tenderest sympathy and understanding.

"Fifth: That a copy of these resolutions be sent to her family, a copy be spread on the minutes and a copy be sent to each of the daily papers.

(Signed):
>"Mary F. Martin,
>"Annabel C. Coe,
>"Florence M. Lester."

CHAPTER ONE

The Sand Hills Garden Club
Augusta, Georgia
(1939)

Mrs. Doughty

All Augusta, and particularly we of the Sand Hills Garden Club, were shocked and saddened by the death of Frankie Doughty. It's hard to associate death with one so vitally alive.

Mrs. Doughty was a member of the Sand Hills Garden Club for many years. She was with us in the early days when the very close union was formed. Once upon a time she journeyed as our representative across the seas to far-away Japan, and brought back wondrous tales of the things she'd seen and done.

She had a rare talent for creating a charm about her, and with her impulsive restlessness built for herself many houses upon this earth. Over each she waved a magic wand.

Her gaiety was infectious — she loved life and laughter — little children — her own little children. She loved the world and was much beloved.

But it was not written that she should ever grow old — hers was not the temperament to watch for the lengthening shadows of late afternoon; so, with the sun still high in the heavens and a smile upon her lips, she slipped away to yet another home — this time, one not built with human hands.

She will be missed where-e'er she walked. We extend our deepest sympathy to her immediate family, and to all who knew her well.

t.d.c.

CHAPTER ONE

__ DOUGHTYS:

From the early years of the nineteenth and twentieth centuries, the Doughtys were fairly numerous and indeed even prominent in the business and social life of Augusta. In the Augusta Directory for 1841, E. W. Doughty is listed with his residence on the "Corner of Ellis and Cumming" (10th Street). Doughty also was said to be connected in business with "Geo. R. Jessup and Co." who were wholesale and retail grocers. Another Doughty listed in 1841 was Charles W. who according to the advertisement (in the directory) operated a family grocery and provision store at 215 Broad Street. There was a bar (in the store's rear) supplying wines, liquors, and cigars. The ad also featured two tea chests marked with Chinese ideographs. The Doughty clan appears to be mostly English in origin, and I have read that our line here originated with a John Doughty of Rye, Westchester, New York. We do know that the first generation in Georgia purchased 1,000 acres of land in Hancock County, Georgia, in 1795. Their names were Ebenezer Wesley and Rachael French Doughty; Rachael Ann is said to have been brought up in Bristol, England. This couple hosted the "Methodist Society" in their Augusta home on Reynolds Street 1798-1800 before the Methodists built their first church on Greene Street. This became St. John's with the present sanctuary built in 1844.

So we know Ebenezer's middle name, Wesley, must have been an homage to the Wesley brothers Charles and John or Methodism itself. Ebenezer is Hebrew for "Stone of Help," and its diminutive "Eben" is used often. My interest in Ebenezer Wesley Doughty of the second generation derives from the fact that on my mother's side he was her great-grandfather, my great, great. He was the son of Ebenezer and Rachael with dates of 1809-1887 and married Eliza Margaret Crowell from New Jersey. Ebenezer became a very successful cotton merchant, the couple raising ten children. In this recollection we will focus on several of their children and their descendants, some of whom married into well-known Augusta families. These include Burdell, Butt, Calhoun, Derry, plus Jackson and will be all mentioned with relevant facts as this narrative proceeds. At some point it appears Ebenezer deserted Methodism for he was buried in 1887 from St. Paul's Church.

Ebenezer and Rachael's eldest son, William Henry Doughty (1836-1905), was a well-known physician, as was his own son, William Henry Doughty, Jr. (1856-1923), with both father and son faculty members at the Medical College of Georgia. Doughty Senior was practicing medicine in 1858 at Center (5th Street) and Broad, he served in the Civil War as a surgeon in the C.S.A., and established in 1863 the second military hospital at Augusta on Broad Street between Washington (6th Street) and Center (5th Street). Following the close of hostilities, Doughty resumed his medical profession May 17, 1865. From 1868 to 1877 he also filled the department chair at MCG. as professor of material medica and therapeutics. At about the same time he also took part in the revival of the *Southern Medical and Surgical*

CHAPTER ONE

Journal, becoming one of the editors. He was a frequent contributor to this and other medical periodicals both before and after the Civil War. He was a sometime member of the Georgia and American Medical Associations in addition to many other civic and charitable organizations. His work was key to establishing a new Board of Health in Augusta and reforming sanitation after the yellow fever epidemic in 1876.

In the early antebellum years, another faculty member of the Medical College of Georgia was Dr. Louis Dugas (anatomy and physiology). With his numerous connections in France, Dugas purchased books and paraphernalia in Paris and returned to Augusta in 1834 with the makings of a medical library. Dugas, Paul Eve, and George Newton, all MCG physicians, had deepened their medical abilities by working in France where advanced research was then being accomplished. This kind of medical background was a great boon during the embryonic era of MCG. Dugas and Paul Eve were studying in France at the time of the 1830 Revolution; Dugas the year before had dined with LaFayette on July 4 in celebration of the holiday. Dr. Louis Dugas was MCG dean 1861-1896.

Doughty senior in 1855 married Miss Julia Sarah Felder from Sumter, South Carolina, a daughter of Dr. and Mrs. William L. Felder. She was an older relative of Annie Robertson and Mamie Martin who both resided in Augusta. The senior Doughtys were blessed with ten children of whom those mainly pertaining to this narrative are Mrs. William Elbert Jackson, Mrs. Lewis F. Butt,

Mrs. William M. Butt, Mrs. James Dargan, Dr. William Henry Doughty, Jr., and Mr. Llewellyn G. Doughty. The Doughty residence was 903 Greene Street situated on the northwest corner of Greene and 9th Street; while now destroyed, several of the adjacent structures behind still exist as good examples of the Second Empire style. One interesting fact relating to the 903 Greene Street Doughty house is the still-existing commercial townhouse behind what is now known as 307-309 9th Street and discussed earlier. This was treated by Doughty Senior as an investment property, and by 1891 Sang Sing and Sing Lee had moved their Chinese laundry to the first floor. The upstairs was residential and occupied by various people including at one point Sang Sing. Dr. Doughty's heirs sold this property for $8,000 in 1917.

An interesting cutting from the *Augusta Chronicle* of February 6, 1901, reports on the large (300 guests) masquerade ball the doctor, Julia, and the Misses Doughty gave at "Walker's" in honor of a Miss Dargan from Atlanta, indicating their activities on the social scene.

Two of the Doughty girls married Butts: Elizabeth (but always called Betty) wed William M. Butt in 1898 and Clara, Lewis F. Butt, in 1904. Lewis was the brother of Archibald Willingham Butt of *Titanic* fame. William M. Butt was their first cousin with his family providing an Augusta home for Mrs. Pamela Butt, née Pamela Robertson Boggs, and her sons following the early death of their father, Joshua Willingham Butt. Pamela and sons were rather impecunious after the loss of Joshua, so Archie and Lewis grew up in Augusta in Billy Butt's

CHAPTER ONE

home and were close always with the Doughty clan and their circle. Archie lost his father at age fourteen and later attended Sewanee (University of the South) where his mother was a librarian occupying an apartment in the library itself.

Archie Butt and his April 1912 heroism in loading women and children into lifeboats from the deck of the *Titanic* is recalled today and remembered by the Butt Memorial Bridge in Augusta, dedicated by President Taft in 1914, and a fountain in Washington, DC placed on the Ellipse close to the White House in 1913. Archie was aide to both President Theodore Roosevelt and President William H. Taft during their White House years.

As Archie never married, his personal effects came to his brother and sister-in-law, Lewis and Clara Butt, as Pamela Butt had died in 1908. Of these items, two appear of particular interest today: the "How Box" of Chinese manufacture containing silver cups/goblets and a cocktail shaker all heavily chased and embossed with Chinese motifs and an Imperial Chinese manuscript issued by one of the emperors. Today all the Butt memorabilia, which he likely acquired during his service in the Philippines circa the Spanish-American War, is now the property of John Wallace, a Butt/Doughty descendant on his mother's side, in Atlanta. Archie ended his military career with the rank of major having also served in Mexico and Cuba.

Billy and Betty Butt were great friends with Frankie Doughty and her second husband, Llewellyn. Betty

Doughty Butt always said Frank was her best friend, first cousin, and also sister-in-law after her second marriage to Llewellyn Goode Doughty, her brother. This second Llewellyn had been named for his uncle, major C.S.A., who was killed at age twenty-four at Petersburg, Virginia, June 23, 1864. His name is remembered on a tablet at St. James Church on Greene Street. Apparently at one period both the William Butt and Lewis Butt families lived on Hickman Road at what they termed "Butt Huddle"! The William Butt home still stands at 1001 Hickman Road. They had one daughter, Julia, who married John Slaton, Jr. of Atlanta, and the Slatons were the proud parents of Elizabeth Butt Slaton who now as Betty Slaton Wallace is my Doughty-side cousin in Atlanta. Betty Slaton Wallace's father, John Slaton, was the nephew of Georgia governor John M. Slaton, who in 1915 commuted the death sentence of Leo Frank in that famous murder of a female pencil factory worker. Frank then was taken by a mob from the jail and hanged in Marietta, Georgia, near where Mary Phagan was murdered. This was a horrible example of "lynch law" in the South.

    I shared with Betty Wallace a great picture of the two friends Betty Butt and Frankie Doughty dressed as gypsy fortune tellers (and pretending to smoke cigarettes) at the Richardson fancy-dress ball held at the Bon Air Hotel December 31, 1925. As I write this, I am again reminded of the joke (then considered a trifle risqué I suspect) told of a crowd of Butts all arriving en masse at the theatre where all the "butts" found seats! But today that word is considered just a natural term and used openly even on television.

As inferred, the four surviving daughters of "old Dr. Doughty" (as some even today recall him) were as close as sisters could be. These were Crowella Doughty Jackson, Clara Doughty Butt, Elizabeth Doughty Butt, and Lucy Doughty Dargan. While Clara and Betty were discussed previously, we should mention that Crowella was the mother of Elbert Jackson who married Connie Wright of Augusta. His artistic mentor was James Montgomery Flagg with his career largely spent in New York City and Long Island. Elbert and Connie had issue and were buried in the Wright section of Summerville Cemetery. An interesting note is that on the Jackson side Elbert has also a descendancy from Ferdinand Phinizy I. The Jacksons at one point lived at Montauk, Long Island, New York, and were the parents of twin daughters, Crowell and Connie.

Lucy Doughty seems to have married at age thirty-eight James T. Dargan who owned a well-known insurance adjusting business in New York City. The Dargans lived for many years in Scarsdale, New York, where they often received both Butt families and Jacksons on visits.

As Dr. Russell Moores confirmed in conversation, Dr. William H. Doughty, Jr. probably was more well known and a more important factor in Augusta medical circles than his father. This because Doughty Junior (1856-1923) first made his greatest mark in bringing the Medical College of Georgia into the twentieth century by ensuring the full and prompt implementation of the

Flexner Report in 1910. Flexner surveyed medical schools as a result of the AMA Council on Medical Schools and Hospitals and Carnegie Foundation pressure. The emphasis was to be on more quality education at all levels and to clean up the dirty physical facilities previously prevalent at many schools, including Augusta's MCG.

Doughty, Jr. (on MCG staff for operative surgery and surgical pathology) was elected dean in May 1910; immediately it was obvious this new regime was going to make over in every way the old M.C.G. from plant, curriculum, and procedures to professors and their assistants. Local political and financial support was secured with the assistance of the then Augusta mayor, Thomas Barrett, and a fundraising committee chaired by Joseph Rucker Lamar and lawyer William H. Barrett. With the complete backing of the Augusta City Council, the new University Hospital was finished in 1915 and financed by a bond issue. During this period MCG also became the Medical Department of the University of Georgia, replacing what Phinizy Spalding called "a somewhat tenuous" relationship in his history of MCG.

Doughty, Jr. had graduated from UGA and then taken his doctorate of medicine from MCG in 1878. Following postgraduate work in New York, he began his own practice in Augusta. By 1886, both Doughtys, Jr. and Sr., were medical supervisors for an Augusta mutual life insurance company. Later Doughty Jr. was chief surgeon for several railroads; all these positions were of course in addition to his ongoing work at MCG and as consulting surgeon for University Hospital. He

CHAPTER ONE

also was president of the Georgia State Board of Health and a member of the AMA as well as the Georgia and Richmond County Medical Associations. A most illustrious career by any measure.

When Doughty Jr. died in June 1923 of an infection following extraction of a tooth, he was succeeded as MCG dean by Dr. William H. Goodrich, a close colleague who was the author of a history of MCG. Harry Goodrich, a close family friend and neighbor, stayed as dean until 1931 and subsequently as superintendent of University Hospital from 1938 to 1945.

And now brief comments on three more well-known Augusta families whose present descendants have Doughty blood relationships.

BURDELLS:

Current family members interestingly have a double descendance/relationship from both Ferdinand Phinizy I (the immigrant) and from James P. Doughty, Sr., son of Ebenezer Wesley and Eliza Margaret Crowell Doughty. James Doughty, Sr. (1849-1929) married Laura Bignon, a descendant of French Huguenots from Santo Domingo, in 1873. At some point they must have converted to the Roman Church as his funeral in March 1929 took place at St. Patrick's (now Holy Trinity) on Telfair Street. However, James P. Doughty, Sr. was confirmed at St. Paul's Church April 5, 1868. The Bignons always were connected to others from Santo Domingo, i.e. the LeGardes, Roulets, and Del'aigles.

The Burdell connection arises from the marriage of James P. Doughty, Jr. with Julia Melville Burdell (sister of Carter) in 1903. Their issue comprised one son, William Wesley (but always called Billy), and two daughters, Julia Melville and Sarah Burdell. In 1919, the wife Julia Melville died, and J.P.D., Jr. later married Almeda Petit. J.P.D., Jr. lived from 1879-1952. Both father and son were familiar figures along Cotton Row and the Cotton Exchange.

The four Burdells who came to Augusta from Waynesboro as orphans in the last part of the nineteenth century following the death of both parents were Thomas Ferdinand, Carter, Sarah, and Julia Melville. For a time, they lived in one of the 7th Street houses owned by Mary Lou Yancey Phinizy. This house today is

CHAPTER ONE

numbered 415 7th Street and usually known as the Lamar house.

The only son of J.P.D. Jr., Billy Doughty (1908-1981), married Mary Elizabeth Erbelding in 1931, and there was issue.

CALHOUNS:

Aside from the Doughty connections, my mother's side of the family also were close to the Cozarts as they all lived barely a block apart on Kings Way; my mother Frank Inman even called Mrs. Cozart "Aunt Bessie." Bill and Isabelle Cozart both were in my mother's 1924 wedding (Isabelle as matron of honor), and later Bill's brother, Martin Cozart, became a staunch friend in the 1920s-1930s.

Back to Ebenezer and Eliza Crowell Doughty again—they had a daughter, Mary Beach (called "Beachy"), who married St. John Moore. The St. John Moores marriage in 1858 was cut very, very short by St. John's untimely death in July 1861. We do not know if such was war related; although, St. John had previously served in the Oglethorpe Infantry. This union was blessed with two children, Fanny Ermine Moore and St. John Moore, Jr. In the 1870 and 1880 Augusta census the mother and two children were living with her Doughty parents.

Fanny Moore wed Francis Augustus Calhoun, and they had issue consisting of Ermine, another Francis Augustus, Jr., and Beachy Doughty. Ermine never married, Frank married Elizabeth Cozart, and Beachy was betrothed to Reginald McGran Dales, yet another Burdell-Phinizy relative!

Fanny's brother, St. John Moore, Jr., was in the cotton business with Doughty relatives and in 1899 was one of the incorporators of the Augusta Country Club having formerly been connected with the Bon Air Golf enterprise, the club predecessor. St. John Moore, Jr.

CHAPTER ONE

married Julia Flournoy Carter whose only child, a son, died quite young. While Julia lived on until 1926, the circumstances of St. John's death are most unsettling: he was found dead at 2:30 a.m. October 26, 1902, in room sixty at the Planters Hotel! He was lying atop a rug dead when Dr. Joseph Greene arrived a few minutes after. The paper reported he had been at the hotel a few days "and was drinking some." The paper also reported St. John thought he had pneumonia and told a bellboy to summon his physician, Dr. C. A. Blanchard, who had been treating him.

St. John Moore, Jr. appears to have been a popular Augustan with his sudden death a shock. His picture hangs today with other founders at the country club. Within the context of the present Calhoun generations descending from William Cozart Calhoun and his wife, Anne Carter (Bootsie), St. John Moore, Jr. was Billy's great-uncle. Bootsie says her late father-in-law, Francis Augustus Calhoun, had his name legally changed from St. Augustine!

The present Calhoun relationship with my family branch is because Fanny Moore was Frank Clark Doughty's first cousin and, therefore, Frank Calhoun's first, but once removed. Some now would term it second cousin.

DERRYS:

Still another Ebenezer and Eliza son was Joshua Jones Doughty (1841-1914). He served in the Confederate army as a second and first lieutenant in the Oglethorpe Infantry and later in the Georgia Light Artillery. He was wounded and captured near Washington, DC. Even though in Augusta there was a long tradition of free black men and women, Joshua was one of three defendants charged with killing one Captain Heasley of US Colored Troops attached to the Freedmen's Bureau. Defense attorneys included H. H. and J. B. Cumming, and after trial Joshua Doughty and one other accused were found not guilty. The third defendant was sentenced to hang with the presiding military judge changing the death sentence to fifteen years in a New York penitentiary.

He was well known in Augusta as Uncle Josh and had a house called Lumpkin several miles from Augusta but still in Richmond County. On June 17, 1866, he was confirmed at St. Paul's after a baptism there June 8 of the same year. Joshua had three marriages with children from the first and last unions. When his last child was born, he was fifty-six years old, and in total he fathered seven. Joshua was the head of J. J. Doughty & Co., a large cotton brokerage concern following in the path of his father and other family members.

Josh's three wives were Alice Lumpkin Allen, Terrence L. Anderson, and Mary Rosine Nixon, daughter of J. W. Nixon. However, this account is mainly concerned with the issue from wife number one: primarily Mary Lumpkin who married William R. Derry. Their

CHAPTER ONE

children were Josh Derry and William R. Derry, Jr. The last named married Anne Barrett (daughter of Frank and Sadie) in Athens, Georgia, October 29, 1933. Billy and Anne Derry's grandson Frank Martien is avidly interested in his ancestors and has been very helpful in my research principally on the Barrett side. He was named for his great-grandfather Frank H. Barrett. All of this data shows that indeed there is kinship through the Doughty side of our families.

Mary Lumpkin Doughty Derry had a sister, well known in Augusta, named Lillie May who was born without complete hands but who lived on to age eighty-three. She never married. Then there was a half sister (born of the third Nixon wife), Gwinnett Doughty, born in 1894, who became a nurse at the United States Marine Hospital in Baltimore. She married a Baltimore banker, William J. Casey, at age forty-two. While I will not dwell on the Doughty brothers of these sisters, I will further comment on the Derry brothers.

Billy (1909-1980) and Anne Barrett Derry (1910-1985) had a happy marriage. Both are buried in Summerville Cemetery Augusta with Anne's parents. Joshua Doughty Derry (1910-1983) married a Chicago belle, Dorothy Bard, of Highland Park, in 1936. Josh then was manager of the Chicago office of Fenner and Beane. A terrible tragedy ensued when Dorothy Derry was a crime victim in their home and died. I believe the police never caught the killer. Josh later lived in Naples, Florida, where Frank Martien visited his great uncle prior to his death.

There were two suicides in the Doughty family in the twentieth century:
1. Ebenezer Wesley Doughty (1874-1930), son of Charles and grandson of the Ebenezer from whom our account begins. He killed himself March 3, 1930, with a gunshot wound to the head near Washington, Georgia. He was a noted cotton buyer, aged fifty-eight at the time, and a passing motorist found the body and reported two notes addressed to his wife and son were found in his car. The car was headed toward Augusta and parked on the roadside.

    This E.W.D. was considered quite an authority on cotton and built the interesting Japanese/Chinese style house still existing on Lake Forest Drive. His two sons were known as Eben W. Doughty, Jr. and Llewellyn Doughty. Eben Jr. was given the name of his infant brother who had died at age two following the kick of a horse.

    I do not know if this suicide was due to the onset of the "Great Depression" involving cotton or the 1929 stock market collapse.
2. The second Doughty to take his own life was LeGarde Setze Doughty (1897-1957), a son of James P. Doughty, Sr. The French name derives from J.P.D., Sr.'s French wife, Laura Bignon, who was connected to the LeGardes, Roulets, Barbots, etc. even including the De l'aigles and Gardelles.

    He died in an Atlanta hospital at age sixty of a gunshot wound to the head apparently

CHAPTER ONE

self-inflicted. Doughty had been found in his home with a revolver nearby. At this period he was employed by the *Atlanta Journal-Constitution* having been with the *Augusta Chronicle* in the past. He was a writer and had poems and stories published through the years in the *New Yorker*, *New Republic*, *American Mercury*, and other periodicals.

In one *Augusta Chronicle* column in 1945 "L.K.S." (Louisa K. Smith) reviewed his new novel *The Music Is Gone* with praise and interest. This book was dedicated to his son, LeGarde Setze Doughty, Jr., who was killed in action February 29, 1944, while flying as a pilot over Italy during World War II. *The Music Is Gone* deals with a Southern theme and features a country doctor and his crony, a judge. Both the sweet magnolia and seamy sides are revealed through their eyes always in a most human way. There were other favorable book reviews for *The Music Is Gone* when it was published in May 1945, particularly from *Time Magazine*.

DE L'AIGLES:

The Mays family connection with the De l'aigle clan begins with the marriage of my great-great aunt Mary Stedman Clark to Louis De l'aigle March 17, 1858. Mary Stedman was my great-grandfather Clark's sister on my mother's side, while Louis De l'aigle was the grandson of Nicolas (French spelling) De l'aigle, founder of the Augusta De l'aigle family. Nicolas was a French émigré, an early member of Augusta's French community, and his story is an interesting one involving some important bits of history.

Nicolas was born in 1766 as a son of one Charles Frederic Louis De l'aigle in Attancourt, Haute Marne, France. Nicolas was christened the same day of his birth as per the baptism record and then legitimized according to the leading De l'aigle genealogist Virginia Mylius, who advised they have the relevant document. Nicolas appears to have spent some time studying holy orders, as he served in a Paris church in 1791. Considering his birth facts this would make sense for a younger son with no inheritance or immediate prospects. And this period of early 1791 was a heady time in the first part of the 1789 French Revolution.

The royal family left Paris from the Tuileries Palace the early morning of June 21, 1791, undetected, on what is known as The Flight to Varennes. The royal family and their entire entourage were detained and returned posthaste to Paris from Varennes, near the Luxembourg border, the event serving as a real catalyst finally leading to the elimination of the monarchy and the creation of

CHAPTER ONE

the first French Republic on September 21, 1792. There also was the continuing saga of the nonjuring priests who all had refused to take the oath of allegiance to the National Assembly. In short, this was the prelude to the Reign of Terror and a good time to leave Paris. This Nicolas did on May 18, 1792, when he departed his native land for the French colony of Saint Domingue in the West Indies. This is the large island today consisting of both Haiti and the Dominican Republic.

In that era the island was divided between the French Saint Domingue and the Spanish Santo Domingo. However, after the French Revolution, the French did succeed in obtaining cession of the entire territory. The immediate problem facing Nicolas De l'aigle when he left France was the truth that "The Black Napoleon" (Toussaint Louverture) was in the process of wresting control of the colony from the French following the August 22, 1791, slave revolt called The Night of Fire. Two thousand whites were killed and 180 sugar and 900 coffee plantations destroyed. Then in the counter-terror 15,000-20,000 blacks and mulattoes were murdered from a pre-revolt population of about 500,000 with whites then at around 30,000 only.

So on his arrival in Saint Domingue, Nicolas must have encountered a chaotic situation arising from the slave revolt encouraged by a "modern Spartacus," Toussaint Louverture, and mainly attributed to the French Revolutionary proclamation of equality between blacks and whites. In 1801, Napoleon I had to send his General Leclerc (married to Pauline Bonaparte and a great favorite of her brother, now the emperor) to the island to again reassert France's central control. Meantime, the British invaded the French portion of the island, as did the Spanish from the west, to add to the unstable situation. Maps show that the British army took the parish of St. Marc where Nicolas is said to have lodged in 1793-1794.

It is said by the modern American De l'aigle genealogists that the family was closely allied to the famous Dukes of Guise and fought for the French king during the Crusades. The De l'aigles were given privileges of nobility and allowed to buy property. There exists a De l'aigle coat of arms, a twin-headed eagle, which probably accounts for the family name today. The Guise family was popular with Catholics and wanted one of their dukes crowned king at Reims; there was the heated cry of "A Reims," and the Guises wanted to establish the Inquisition in France as well as the confiscation of all property owned by Protestants—this all in the sixteenth century when the last Valois king, Henry III, had the then Duke de Guise murdered in 1588.

Nicolas De l'aigle was the first of the family to leave French soil (Saint Domingue) for the United States in 1794. There are two accounts of the subsequent events, so I shall set out both. The De l'aigle family says Nicolas escaped in a "feather bed," was put on a ship to Charleston, South Carolina, and then went on to Savannah. He was a merchant in Savannah where he ran a store on Moore's Wharf. Here he sold French imports, flower bulbs, and also slaves. Considering that in Saint

CHAPTER ONE

Domingue there was one of the best slave markets in the world, this last endeavor probably was organized prior to his departure.

Terence Battey (aunt of Frenchie Battey Bush) as a descendant of Mme. Nicolas De l'aigle by her first husband, M. LeGarde, wrote an interesting article in the *Augusta Chronicle-Herald* some years ago when the handsome De l'aigle house on Greene Street was destroyed to make a path for a super highway; the property stood between 4th and 5th and initially extended back to Telfair Street. Miss Battey recounted how Mlle. Mary Margaret Blinn found love and marriage on Saint Domingue where she became Mme. LeGarde. Two girls were born, and all were finally forced to flee the island due to an insurrection. Some persons were concealed in sugar barrels. The LeGarde family was lucky to be on the same ship with Nicolas De l'aigle and bound for the United States. Mme LeGarde insisted on taking a nurse, and when the captain of the vessel objected, this French mother, thinking quickly, said, "If you leave the nurse, you take away my baby's food!" The captain gave in!

Pirates boarded the ship. Nicolas De l'aigle gave the Masonic sign, and he and his LeGarde friends remained unharmed. The vessel was looted, some passengers murdered, and others made to walk the plank! Miss Battey wrote that the LeGardes debarked at Savannah with De l'aigle proceeding to Augusta. If he then did go to Augusta, he had to return to Savannah as noted before and because we know Nicolas became a naturalized US citizen in Savannah December 16, 1803. Records state that he had been a US resident for seven years and in Savannah as a resident for five years.

The Battey recollection tells how Nicolas had cloth buttons on his clothes covering gold pieces that even the pirates did not discover! Land then in Augusta was selling for about .25 cents an acre; De l'aigle soon, we are told, owned 14,000 acres of both town and plantation lands. He also founded the De l'aigle brick manufacturing works, participated in many Augusta civic endeavors (i.e., the plan to construct the Augusta Canal in 1845), and had become a leading citizen by his old-age death in 1853. His monetary inventory at his death was valued at $193,260 and included slaves, cattle, land, houses, lots in Augusta, plus stock.

The imposing De l'aigle house at 426 Greene with its three-story brick edifice was built in 1818. It had been sort of a center for the French-American community. On July 14, Bastille Day, there was a gala celebration featuring a formal dinner with tablecloths piled one above the other depending upon the number of courses to be changed following each course. When the Marquis de LaFayette visited Augusta March 23-25, 1825, Nicolas De l'aigle made an address of welcome at the Planter's Hotel in French on behalf of the local French citizens. The Battey account also states LaFayette was entertained in the De l'aigle home at 426 Greene Street as a part of all Augusta en fête to honor the last surviving major general of the American Revolution.

After M. Legarde died in Savannah, Nicolas brought Mme. LeGarde and daughters Cleo and Emma to

CHAPTER ONE

Augusta. The widow LeGarde and De l'aigle wed with the girls raised as his own. The couple had one son, Charles, who by his many progeny is responsible for the spread of the De l'aigle surname to this day. Another interesting fact is that the Battey article states Mme. LeGarde was born in France whereas the De l'aigle genealogist records her place of birth in 1766 as Saint Domingue, West Indies. She died in 1849 in Augusta and is buried at Magnolia Cemetery.

Charles De l'aigle and his wife, Martha Watkins, had fifteen children together. Their first was Louis Nicholas De l'aigle (1830-1868); he married Mary Stedman Clark as reported in the first paragraph, and aside from several children who died as infants, there were two surviving daughters who had interesting but very different lives.

The oldest and least known in Augusta was Martha Stedman De l'aigle (1859-1913), also called "Minnie." She married James Dickson Munds, son of a Methodist minister, from South Carolina. The Reverend James Theus Munds became a clergyman at age eighteen and was a descendant of a family with English roots who were Tories during the American Revolution. They returned to Jamaica, from where they had originally traveled to South Carolina, due to their loyalist sentiments, but came back to this country about 1785.

The Munds family by the early 1850s were in Wilmington, North Carolina, where the Reverend was posted and had married. There were four children, all boys, with three of them having the first name James!

Hence, all four were called by their middle names. One family history has the young minister as a "circuit rider," but poor health intervened, and the family moved to Columbia, South Carolina, were he died aged but thirty-four. The widow and four boys then returned to her family home at Wilmington sometime after May 1863.

Minnie De l'aigle and James Dickson Munds also had four children; however, this recollection intends to largely focus on the first and fourth born, James Theus and Louis De l'aigle Munds, for these two were the Munds descendants most closely associated with Augusta relatives and our family friends. The brothers apparently were reared in comfortable circumstances as their father and his three brothers were druggists and operated two shops. Although there was a difference of eight years between Theus and De l'aigle, as they were known, they prospered mightily. By the 1920s they were operating Munds and Winslow in New York City with seats on both the New York Stock and Cotton Exchanges. In addition, the firm was a member of the Chicago Board of Trade.

Both brothers were living the good life in the 1920s with Park Avenue apartments, trips to Europe, summers on Long Island at Southampton, visits to Augusta and Florida (Palm Beach) in winter, staying in Newport and at The Greenbrier in White Sulphur Springs, West Virginia. This was the Roaring Twenties, featuring a booming economy and stock market. At one point Munds and Winslow had a total of eight offices (six in

CHAPTER ONE

New York City itself) with branches in Pinehurst, North Carolina, and Augusta. H. A. Richardson was manager of the Augusta, Georgia, branch, and one of the New York City offices was located at the Vanderbilt Hotel, 34th Street and Park Avenue. Mr. Richardson was also associated with the Bon Air Vanderbilt Hotel in Augusta and apparently one of the leaders in attracting winter visitors to Augusta.

James Theus Munds V (1882-1938) married Elsie Welsh Saltus, daughter of novelist Edgar Saltus, in 1917 with a St. Thomas Church Wedding on 5th Avenue. They were divorced in 1930, but their daughter, Josephine Munds, continued to live with her father in New York until his death. Then she moved to Paris to reside with her mother who remarried several times. In 1945, Josephine married a Swede, Sven Malmberg, and moved to Sweden where there is issue. Josephine told a Munds family chronicler her father and uncle built a great fortune, lost it in the 1929 crash, rebuilt it once more, only to lose it the second time.

In October 1939, the executors of the J. Theus Munds estate sold at a Parke-Bernet sale his very handsome furniture, silver, porcelains, and other household effects. The total brought $26,507 for 417 lots. Today the collection of mainly Georgian and other eighteenth-century items surely would bring forty or fifty times that total!

When Theus Munds died April 18, 1938, in New York City, he was only fity-six and then living at No. 4 East 72nd Street, just off 5th Avenue, an excellent address to this date. The stock brokerage firm then called Munds, Winslow & Potter with a main office at 40 Wall Street, New York City, was a partnership terminated October 29, 1938, and some persons joined Laird, Bissell and Meeds as partners. However, Louis De l'aigle Munds then seems to have been housed with the new firm but not as a partner.

Louis De l'aigle Munds, the younger brother to Theus, had much charm and personality by all accounts. Born in Wilmington, North Carolina, in 1890, he had a youthful nickname of "Soupsadle" or more likely "Soupladle," perhaps due to his childhood girth! Married three times, De l'aigle, as he always was called, lived mostly in Manhattan at various addresses including 399 Park, 740 Park, 941 Park, and finally in 1945 residing at 245 East 72nd Street. In the 1920s and early 1930s there also was a rented house called Hedgerose on First Neck Lane at Southampton, Long Island. It appears quite clear De l'aigle and his first two wives lived in a rich and great style!

Anna Foley was the first wife, married in 1918 and divorced in 1927 with no issue; the second marriage was with the beautiful Dorothy Frowert on July 11, 1928, in New York City at her father's house, 45 East 85th Street. Dorothy had been recently divorced herself from Sheward Hagerty, Jr. in a Reno action. The Munds couple had one son, Louis De l'aigle Munds, Jr., who was born April 30, 1929. This second marriage continued until November 1939 when Dorothy and De l'aigle divorced, apparently in Nevada—three days following that

CHAPTER ONE

divorce, she married Raoul Fleischmann in Carson City, Nevada. He was publisher of *The New Yorker* magazine.

While married, De l'aigle and Dorothy seemingly liked Augusta and returned every winter stopping at the Bon Air Vanderbilt. Besides Augusta friends, they knew many of the winter residents also staying locally. The *Augusta Chronicle* wrote of a dinner party the Munds hosted in January 1933 at Fruitland Tea Room on Walton Way. This piece is quoted below particularly to show the guest list, including what one might call the "movers and shakers" in Augusta society of the era! Our mayor then was Tom Barrett, Jr.; also note the presence of Clifford Roberts who was the moving force in the formation of the Augusta National Golf Club. Roberts at one time was connected with Reynolds & Company, New York stockbrokers, and obviously knew the Munds in New York City. The Augusta National formally opened in January 1933.

> Mr. & Mrs. Munds of New York Entertain With A Beautiful Dinner
>
> One of the loveliest social affairs of this week was the dinner party given Tuesday evening by Mr. and Mrs. De l'aigle Munds, who are spending some time at the Bon Air Vanderbilt, At Fruitland Tea Room on Walton Way.
>
> The guests were seated at a beautiful table where an artistic arrangement of pink roses and sweet peas in

the pastel shades were used in effective combination with the silver and crystal table appointments and pink candles in silver holders.

Mr. and Mrs. Munds' guests were Mr. and Mrs. Frank Calhoun, Mr. and Mrs. Henry Garrett, Mr. and Mrs. Eugene Hoke, Dr. and Mrs. Hugh Page, Mr. and Mrs. William T. Gary, Jr., Mr. and Mrs. Julian Barrett, Mr. and Mrs. Frank Carpenter, Mr. and Mrs. William Kitchen Barrett, Mr. and Mrs. Arthur Card, Mr. and Mrs. Dawson Teague, Mr. and Mrs. Bowdre Mays, Mr. and Mrs. William H. Wallace, Jr., Mrs. Winslow, Mrs. Carter Burdell, Mr. Clifford Roberts, of New York, Mr. Geddings Jowitt, Mr. Jacob Lowrey, Mr. Martin Cozart, Mr. Thomas Barrett, Jr., Mr. Charles H. Phinizy, Jr., Dr. W. H. Goodrich, and Dr. Everard Wilcox.

Genie Lehmann, one bright local lady and a centenarian, recalls Fruitland Tea Room as located on the Old Berckman property, perhaps in a section of the old manor house that is now the Augusta National Clubhouse. Maybe the tea room had moved to Walton Way by the time of this function as the club did open that January. Frank Capers also remembers that his Aunt Marion Pope, Mary "D" Phinizy, and probably Frank Mays had been involved in running this party establishment.

There exists at the Museum of The City of New York, 1220 5th Avenue, a collection of photographs showing contents of the De l'aigle Munds apartment at 740 Park

CHAPTER ONE

Avenue in 1934 that included very elegant furnishings and a large diamond brooch with some colored stones in a flower motif. Their heavy social schedule continued, and business to an extent must have prospered with but a few wrinkles such as Princess Dolgorouky bringing a lawsuit for $2,900 in damages. This former lady-in-waiting to the Russian czarina, wife of Alexander II, alleged an unauthorized purchase of stock in a "short-sale" transaction!

New Years Eve 1937 found the De l'aigle Munds couple hosting a "Dutch treat" dinner at one of the large East Side hotels where the tab was $15 per person compared to $6 at the Broadway hotels, but not including drinks. Those charges must have included music, cabaret, and dinner! From the New York press reports, there were many gala groups marking the passage to 1938.

Unfortunately, 1938 and 1939 brought a run of bad luck to De l'aigle. Firstly, the senior partner of Munds, Winslow & Potter, his brother Theus Munds, died in April. The remaining partnership was terminated October 29, 1938. Dorothy left him with the divorce effective in 1939, and the New York Cotton Exchange suspended him in trading for one month. Also Mr. Winslow died in his eighties about this time. We know little about De l'aigle's business following this period.

Circa 1941-1942, De l'aigle married for the third time Miss Lilly Hoskins who I believe had trained as a nurse. One son was born February 14, 1943 in New York City; he was named Theus Scott Munds and has issue. De l'aigle and Lilly continued to visit Augusta in the winter, sometimes en route to Florida. I recall one visit when they came to our house for a mint julep session probably in early spring. My mother Frank fixed her tall silver iced teas with crushed ice and put them in the fridge to develop a mist on the outside before adding the bourbon and mint. I was sent down the front walk to welcome the visitors who parked their large foreign or perhaps Lincoln car at the Lake Forest Drive curb. I still remember the leather-covered seats that I had never seen before. Later De l'aigle drove the group to the then out-of-town Colonial Club to dine and probably gamble as I know there was a craps table and probably blackjack in this Wrightsboro Road place.

In March 1952, at only age sixty-two, De l'aigle died in St. Augustine, Florida. He was buried in Wilmington, North Carolina, where he had been born. Survivors listed in the news report were Lilly Hoskins Munds, wife, and two sons, Louis De l'aigle Munds, Jr. and Theus Scott Munds.

A close relative to Theus and De l'aigle lived in Manhattan during their zenith and also not so stellar years. This was an aunt, their mother's younger sister, Louise De l'aigle Reese, whose dates were 1864-1945. She was christened at St. Paul's Church July 12, 1864, but she hardly knew her father, Louis De l'aigle, who after his Civil War service died at only thirty-eight years of age from a bowel infection. He ended his war service as a captain in 1864 having been assaulted by a party of cavalrymen and wounded in the face and head. Prior

CHAPTER ONE

to the war, he was a lawyer. So Louise and her sister (who became Mrs. Munds) were raised mainly by their mother, the widowed Mary Stedman Clark De l'aigle (1840-1922).

Although the De l'aigle family genealogist gives her birth years as 1841, the silver baby cup she later gave to her namesake, Mary De l'aigle Doughty, has January 4, 1840. engraved as her date of birth. The cup, which now belongs to my brother Stedman Clark Mays, also is marked Clark & Co. on the bottom as the maker. This was the Clark family business at the time. Being left a widow at but twenty-eight years of age with several children to bring up and considering the very difficult Civil War aftermath, the future may have appeared a bit bleak. However, she still had both the Clark and De l'aigle families for support and perhaps financial aid. In any event, a house was constructed for Mary Clark De l'aigle in 1873 at the corner of Greene and Monument Streets. The number is now 551 Greene with the residence saved from destruction a few years back as an excellent example of Second Empire style by Augusta's premier nineteenth-century architect and builder William H. Goodrich.

By 1875, Mary Clark De l'aigle, still a young widow of thirty-five, was accepting "paying guests," to supplement her income. One of these boarders, as many now term them, was a young Irishman of thirty-one named Charles Dawson Tilly. On his gravestone is the following inscription: "Glorious in youth and beauty, gallant and brave Charles Dawson Tilly, a young Irishman was tragically killed in the last duel fought at Sand Bar Ferry." The question: Why is this foreigner buried on the beautiful Magnolia Cemetery plot occupied by the Louis De l'aigles and their immediate descendants?

Tilly came from Carlow, Ireland, attended Dublin University, and also studied in Paris. Coming to the United States circa 1865, he arrived in Augusta in 1869 as an employee of Branch, Scott & Co. and later in 1873 entered upon the business for his own account. It is likely the work involved cotton factoring and shipping. Tilly obviously was close to the widow De l'aigle and her immediate family, and in due course there were rumors apparently of a romantic relationship between Tilly and Mary De l'aigle. Tilly accused George E. Ratcliffe of spreading these rumors and wrote demanding to know who had initiated these slanders that Ratcliffe was repeating. Ratcliffe replied refusing to name his source and stating the innuendoes had been common knowledge for years! Hence, it was simply impossible to designate a specific authority!

Tilly was something of a hothead it appears as he then said the Ratcliffe response "added insult to injury" and demanded full satisfaction per the code duello. So following this peremptory challenge both named seconds to arrange the duel: Tilly selected J. W. Harris, and Ratcliffe, W. H. Chew. The latter is related to Dr. William Chew of Augusta as he happens to be his great-great nephew. Then friends of the two duelists urged them both to cancel; Tilly and Ratcliffe only agreed to a twenty-four-hour stay and decided to meet and shoot

CHAPTER ONE

it out at 3:00 p.m. December 16, 1875, at the Sand Bar Ferry dueling fields.

The rest of the story, as they often say, is history; but for those who don't know, Tilly won the coin toss to decide word and position. Tilly then elected word—i.e., his second, Harris, would shout, "Fire, one, two, three, stop." So Ratcliffe won position or choice of where to stand. As Ratcliffe had accepted the challenge, he had chosen six-inch Colt navy pistols, which on the "word" were aimed and fired at each other from ten paces. A bullet hit Tilly's right side above the hip and finally rested under the skin on the left side. A report stated Tilly wanted a second shot, but he was seriously wounded and unable to continue. En route back to the De l'aigle house, Tilly was joined by Dr. DeSausure Ford who began his ministrations at once. The bullet was removed, but the patient's condition showed no improvement during the night. He died at 8:05 p.m. the following day.

Tilly saw the minister of St. Paul's Episcopal Church before he passed away and also freely forgave Ratcliffe according to the account in the *New York Times*. Tilly hoped God would forgive him as he had done relative to his opponent. All knelt around the bed as the clergyman recited the Lord's Prayer.

Mary Clark De l'aigle never remarried. She lived between Augusta and Wilmington, North Carolina, and New York City when older, as her two surviving daughters resided in those two cities. However, she never completely severed her family ties to Augusta; for example, in November 1916, Mary De l'aigle presented St. Paul's Church with a beautiful and valuable private silver communion service made to order by Gorham of New York. This service of solid silver plated with gold consists of chalice, pyx (bread box), cruets, and spoon. The service was to be employed by clergy administering communion to the ill or at very small church services. The gift was given in loving memory of her two De l'aigle daughters who died as infants. This splendid memorial was blessed by St. Paul's rector on All Saints Day, November 1916.

The other Augusta connection Mary De l'aigle cherished was through her Clark nieces, Frankie Clark Inman Doughty and Mary Stedman Clark Ridgely, her namesake. The Clark sisters themselves always were close companions of similar age and had often visited Aunt Mary De l'aigle in Wilmington and probably also in New York City.

In her eighty-third year, Mark Clark De l'aigle, having been in poor health for some time, died in Wilmington at the home of her granddaughter, Miss Anne Munds. Her surviving daughter, Louise De l'aigle Reese, was then in Europe for the summer; hence, Anne Munds and the two grandsons, Theus and De l'aigle Munds of New York City, brought the body to Augusta for burial in Magnolia Cemetery on July 6, 1922. Rev. G. Sherwood Whitney of St. Paul's officiated at the graveside service soon after the arrival of the train from Wilmington. While her Augusta niece, Ted Ridgely was present, Frankie Doughty also was in Europe and unable to attend the simple funeral service.

CHAPTER ONE

We will end our account of the former Augusta De l'aigles by relating salient details from the life of Louise De l'aigle Reese who today appears known principally for building the gatehouse/sexton's lodge at the entrance to Magnolia Cemetery on 3rd Street.

As recorded previously, during the last full year of the Civil War, Louise entered the world. Christened at St. Paul's Episcopal Church in July 1864, she barely knew her father, Louis De l'aigle, who died at the early age of thirty-eight in January 1868. We know nothing of her early schooling; we always thought maybe she had attended The Berry School (now called Berry College) in Rome, Georgia, as her will bequeathed a legacy to that institution in return for a bronze plaque in her name. However, Kevin De l'aigle advises that Berry only began to admit girls in 1909, and Louise would have been forty-five at that time!

Louise most likely attended some finishing school in the Virginia or Philadelphia area. She met and married her first husband, H. B. Seyd, called "Otto" and of German ancestry. Otto was born in Philadelphia but died in 1906 in Augusta where he was buried at Magnolia on the "Louise De l'aigle plot." Her second husband was Dr. Robert Grigg Reese who was born September 23, 1866, near Petersburg, Virginia.

Dr. Reese became a most eminent eye surgeon who maintained his office and consulting room at 50 West 52nd Street in New York City. By the time of his demise on October 8, 1926, he had built a very successful and profitable practice. The Reeses also had a Manhattan townhouse at 160 East 63rd Street.

IS LIVING WELL STILL THE BEST REVENGE?

The Reese marriage must have been a quite mature liaison, as being free from Otto Seyd after 1906, Louise was in her mid-forties and the doctor was just two years younger. Louise was of an intellectual bent, a definite Francophile, and most likely very proficient in French. Above all, the Reese couple had their aristocratic Southern backgrounds to build upon. Dr. Reese mentioned in one of his wills, for example, his family cemetery plot in Staunton, Virginia, which is where Woodrow Wilson was born. Love of travel abroad also seems to have been an interest: in 1923 they traveled together for a tour of the Mediterranean and the Near East on the liner *Homeric* of the White Star Line. The *Homeric* was a smaller sister to the larger White Star liners *Majestic* and *Olympic*, famous in the 1920s for their Atlantic crossings. These last two named also were the great sister ships to the ill-fated *Titanic* which sank in 1912.

One early trip Louise made to France was in the early years of the 1900s when she traveled with her father's sister, Virginia De l'aigle Hopkins. According to the De l'aigle archives, Louise was close to her Aunt Virginia. However, by the 1920s it appears Louise was making almost yearly visits to Europe, always with long stays in France, unaccompanied by her spouse. In July of 1922, she was in Paris stopping at the Hotel France et Choiseul where her friend Harry-dele Hallmark also was staying. At that period Harry-dele was the well-known women's writer on clothes and domestic areas for newspapers and magazines including the *New York Times* and Philadelphia

CHAPTER ONE

papers. It was reported that Harry-dele went to Paris, Northern France, and Belgium soon after the Armistice in November 1918.

Writing under the nom de plume of "Anne Rittenhouse," Harry-dele wrote features that were published daily in more than one hundred newspapers in the United States and abroad. Born in Pensacola, Florida, but growing up in Augusta where she became the society editor of the *Augusta Chronicle*, she lived at 20 East 76th Street in New York City in her last years. She died in a Philadelphia hospital in August 1932 at age sixty-five and was buried in Magnolia Cemetery, Augusta. The news report of her death states she had retired from newspaper work and had just completed a biography of Georgia's English founder, Oglethorpe.

Kevin De l'aigle lives in New York City and has found much data on the Reese couple and their lives in the 1920s. Louise and the doctor were living separately when he died in October 1926. He was living in an apartment above his office at 50 West 52nd Street; Louise had sailed for Europe on June 19, 1926, so she had been abroad for several months when Dr. Reese died. She was still living in her townhouse on East 63rd, and her husband owned the house on West 52nd Street, now a part of Rockefeller Center. The question is, were they living separate lives when both in Manhattan? There were no children. Dr. Reese's estate was reported at $600,000 gross; I do not know if that sum includes the 52nd Street house. For that time this was a handsome till; the entire income from the estate was to go to the widow Louise for her life with the specific legacies paid only following her death. One exception was an immediate legacy of $20,000 to his nephew and medical partner, plus the entire practice provided Dr. Algernon Reese (his nephew) paid 20 percent of the medical proceeds to Louise each year until her death. Algernon also was to have use of the 52nd Street premises for five years provided he paid "taxes, interest on mortgage, and upkeep." Algernon Reese, licensed to practice medicine in New York State, in addition was left a further legacy of $50,000 to be paid after the death of the decedent's widow.

Theus and De l'aigle Munds, nephews of Louise, were willed $20,000 apiece to be paid when the estate and all items were finally settled on Louise's demise. Any residue remaining following all payments was to go to New York Eye & Ear Infirmary for the erection of a glaucoma pavilion to be known as the "Reese Pavilion."

Dr. Reese's instructions relative to his wife and her continuing income for life does infer at a minimum a deep fondness and affection of long standing.

In 1928, a news item stated Louise Reese listed her townhouse (160 East 63rd Street), between Lexington and Third Avenues, for sale at $100,000. The William B. May Co. "held" the property. However, I wonder if the sale ever materialized as she was living at this address when she died in the house in 1945! She also (circa 1930-1931) must have leased the house to her niece, Elsie Saltus Munds (former wife to her nephew

CHAPTER ONE

Theus Munds), when she was in a divorce situation. The press about then reported also on a sub-lease (which often happened in New York City) arranged by the original tenant. Kevin De l'aigle said the East 63rd Street house would now be worth around $4.5 million; and this estimate was a few years back! I believe Louise never sold the townhouse; if she did, the news reports are wrong, even if she leased it back from the new owners.

During the late 1920s Louise Reese began to spend the winter months in Augusta; at first she rented on Milledge Road and then in April 1929 purchased land on Meigs Street, extending to Hickman Road on the opposite side from two "Doughty sisters," i.e., Lucy Doughty Dargan and Clara Doughty Butt (Archie's sister-in-law). On the Ansley Street side was the house of Elizabeth Doughty Butt, third Doughty sister and married to William M. Butt, Archie's first cousin. All these Butt properties were known in the past as "Butt Huddle"! I believe there were two dwellings on the adjoining sites dating back to the early 1900s with the total land described as about two acres when she sold the property to Ira Stone through Camilla Von Kamp in 1942. Louise paid Clara Butt $17,500 and Lucy Dargan $5,000 for the properties. A small portion of 50'×50' was at once hived off to a friend, and then she either tore down or remodeled the existing buildings into a rather French-inspired cottage with a separate garage and rooms above and surrounded by a wall on the Meigs Street side.

Her new winter residence was named Le Manoir Fleuri, which was engraved on a stone near the entrance gate. Then the gardens were planted making this an Augusta showplace. Louise was given credit for employing workers to make her extensive gardens once the Great Depression arrived.

I have not yet been able to determine who designed the gardens, which included Italian cypresses, boxwood, fine camellias, and flowering shrubs. There was a marble fountain from Italy in the entrance court and several other bronze and marble ornaments situated in the three different gardens. I have read that these gardens are on a tract of land given to George Walton, a Georgia signer, by the state in 1802.

Louise Reese would occupy Le Manoir Fleuri during her annual winter visits south. She often had house guests and usually an unattached man from the North or Europe; some today might tend to designate these men as "walkers" or more vulgarly "gigolos"! Her close Augusta friends included Louise Broyles Barrett, Augusta Smith, Jake Lowrey, and John Walton, among many others. She was a non-resident member of the Sand Hills Garden Club and often showed her gardens to the public and privately as she did during the 1932 Augusta meeting of the Garden Club of America.

During her winter sojourns in Augusta, Louise often entertained with evening dinner parties. Frank and Bowdre, my parents, were asked on many occasions and apparently went, especially in the 1930s. However, I do recall Frank rather complaining about these invitations

CHAPTER ONE

and wanting to invent an excuse to avoid going! Until Frank's mother died in February 1939, they most likely attended when asked and probably tended to avoid the invitations after Louise's first cousin, Frankie Doughty, passed away. At one of these early 1930s parties, Frank and Bowdre began to develop a lasting friendship with John Walton who was just back after living in France.

Today Louise De l'aigle Reese is mainly remembered for the donations to Augusta of the cemetery portrait gallery located in the sexton's lodge at the entrance to the city cemetery called Magnolia. The charming lodge was of course also donated and constructed in 1940 following approval from Mayor James W. Wooddall and the city council. The style appears rather Virginian/Jeffersonian or Palladian with its clean lines and its crowned dome. In the late 1950s a staff writer at the *Augusta Chronicle*, Mary Carter Winter, called the family portrait gallery hanging in the lodge rotunda "probably the world's most unique gallery of family portraits."

Louise De l'aigle Reese was interested in the history of Magnolia Cemetery as her great-grandfather, Nicholas De l'aigle, donated land to the city circa 1818 to develop what is today a total of sixty acres. The city purchased land for $800 from the academy trustees with Nicholas giving part of his old plantation and brickyard. Hence, Augusta then had a public burial site and no longer used St. Paul's churchyard.

Engraved in stone over the front door is "A Daughter's Tribute to the past, a tender and heroic Mother and an Old Plantation." In the front rotunda room are hung portraits of the immigrant Nicholas De l'aigle, his grand-daughter-in-law, Mary Clark De l'aigle (wife of Louis), and charcoal drawings of Louise De l'aigle Reese and her two husbands, Otto Seyd and Dr. Robert Grigg Reese. In addition, there is large drawing of the young Irishman, Charles Dawson Tilly, who was killed in the last duel fought at Sand Bar Ferry. Recently, the Jerry De l'aigle family has placed a portrait of Virginia De l'aigle Hopkins, the aunt of Louise and to whom she was close, as an appropriate supplement to the "picture gallery."

There are two principal De l'aigle plots at Magnolia: one is the "old site" where the American family founder and his immediate family are buried, and the second is the "De l'aigle-Reese plot" facing De l'aigle Avenue around 7th Street. The latter is probably the most elegant family section in the cemetery and was apparently fully developed by Louise Reese in the late 1920s. The focal point in the middle of the lot is a handsome Celtic cross of marble finely carved and surrounded by a semi-circular-type seat in marble. All the individual markers are elaborately and elegantly carved with complete details relative to dates, sometimes poetry, and distinctive inscriptions. It is likely some graves were moved from older plots, i.e. Louise's Clark grandparents and her infant sisters and their nurse. Tilly's stone is particularly finely inscribed as is that of Otto Seyd, her German first spouse. Louis and Mary Clark De l'aigle are buried together as are Louise herself and Robert G. Reese under huge flat marble markers.

CHAPTER ONE

Louise Reese died aged eighty-one on June 29, 1945, at her New York City townhouse on East 63rd Street. She died of pneumonia, apparently without any lingering illness, as she had as made her usual summer down payment on a rental at Sands Point, Long Island. She also had engaged the summer cottage for 1946! The will was detailed with many bequests and the final monetary residue left to the Berry School. The Augusta house on Meigs Street already had been sold in 1942 to Ira Stone of Augusta, so except for the New York residence there was no other real estate.

The will was written in 1944 and, in part, stipulated the following:

- Japanese cultured pearls to Louise B. Barrett;
- All silver marked M. S. Clark to her first cousin, Mary Stedman Clark Ridgely, (her friend John Walton is said to have recommended this bequest); some of this flat silver was given to my sister, Frank, on her marriage in 1947, by her great aunt;
- Books: works of Mme. De Sevigne to a friend and letters between Horace Walpole and Madame du Deffand to Jacob Lowrey, Augusta; remaining books in her library to The Berry School;
- $1,000 to Miss Augusta Smith, Augusta;
- Mrs. J. Ashby Taylor, personal effects and $1,000;

--- Town Hall, New York, $1,000 to endow a chair in her name;
--- To her grandnephew, Louis De l'aigle Munds, Jr., the two life insurance policies totaling $25,000 on the life of his father as she owned these assets.

Her closest relative, nephew De l'aigle Munds, was left nothing. We have the definite impression that there was an estrangement between these two at this period.

One of her executors was a New York attorney named Egbert W. Doughty. I wonder about his connection, if any, with the Georgia Doughty's? Louise from all reports gave very detailed instructions to her executors relative to her cremation and burial on the handsome marble-filled cemetery section she owned. The bronze urn with ashes came from New York and was placed under the oil painting of her mother in the rotunda of the entrance lodge she had ordered built. The service was held at the gravesite where hymns were sung by a tenor voice who was paid ten dollars, as she had instructed. The City of Augusta sent a large wreath of flowers, and her local friends visited and left flowers the day of her interment.

My own personal interaction with cousin Louise Reese probably first occurred one Sunday at St. Paul's Church where I often accompanied my grandmother, Frankie Clark Doughty. I was introduced by Grandmother, who explained the relationship to her first cousin, Louise Reese, and to her mother she called Aunt Mary Clark De l'aigle. Louise wore bright paint on her face and always

CHAPTER ONE

tied brightly colored scarves around her neck ending in a large bow. The only other occasion I recall is when Louise came by our Lake Forest Drive house about 1940 and brought us children a large box of candy. There was a Lincoln Zephyr sedan in black driven by a white chauffeur in full uniform. The car drove up the side driveway to the backyard where Cousin Louise alighted. Louise again looked just as I have described before. She was not pretty but did make an impression hard to ever forget! Teto Barrett once told me she looked like a monkey, which may have been true but was not a very charitable remark!

There are currently Munds descendants of both Theus and De l'aigle living abroad and in various parts of the United States.

__INMANS:

This recollection begins with the arrival in the American colonies of three English brothers: Shadrach, Meshach, and Abednego Inman. Abednego followed his two older brothers and is the direct ancestor of those we today know as the Atlanta and Augusta Inmans.

The name "Inman" appears to be occupational in origin: coming from the term "innman" usually applied to a inn-keeper in the Middle English period. However, some etymological authorities say "innman" applies to the keeper of a nobleman's town house rather than to a country landlord. The name "Inman" we read is still often found in UK's North Lancashire Province and was in Yorkshire poll tax records in the fourteenth century. The 1953 edition of *Burke's Peerage* lists a Philip Albert Inman who was created the Baron Inman in January 30, 1946, and sworn into the Privy Council of Great Britain in 1947. Baron Inman also was appointed Lord Privy Seal in April 1947.

During my first trip to London in December 1952, I discovered in Upper Bond Street a shop called Inman Brothers; this was sort of a small Brooks Brothers or J. Press establishment selling woolens, ties, caps, etc. Cousin George Inman also visited this store in later years. On another London visit I entered and found that "Old Mr. Inman had just retired," so I was informed by the clerk.

The two older brothers, Shadrach and Meshach, are supposed to have emigrated to the British colonies in 1767. They probably came first to Virginia

CHAPTER ONE

and later to North Carolina and Tennessee, the latter being still wild and "Indian Country" in these early days. Abednego followed his brother, circa 1777 or a bit earlier, as one report states he married Mary Ritchie at Limestone, Virginia, that same year. She was born in 1757 and died in 1836 having had eleven children. Another publication by the American Historical Society infers that Abednego and Mary Ritchie (who came from Wales) married in 1777 and soon came to America.

We are told the mother of these three Inman boys, with names obviously taken from the Holy Bible (Daniel chapter 3), was Henrietta Harden or Hardin (as spelled in this country). Henrietta must have been quite impressed by the wonderful story of Shadrach, Meshach, and Abednego with King Nebuchadnezzar when these names were chosen! After all, the king promoted the three men in the Babylon province when they strongly defended their belief in their own true God. Their father was Ezekiel Inman.

It is known that Shadrach and Abednego took the oath of allegiance to the American colonies, March 4, 1777. Shadrach's commission as a major was signed by John Hancock, then president of the Continental Congress. Shadrach Inman, Jr. is the "brave captain Inman" (so-called by many historians) who was killed at Musgrove's Mill in Burke County, North Carolina, August 18, 1780, while leading a company of Georgia militia against the British and Tories. Young Captain Inman left no descendants.

IS LIVING WELL STILL THE BEST REVENGE?

The three Inman brothers were all involved in the Indian and border warfare in Georgia and South and North Carolina. In one fight with Indians, Abednego Inman received a scar on his forehead made by an Indian tomahawk; he was left by his assailant thinking him dead. The story as told by Abednego's great-great-great-grandson, Arthur Crew Inman (1895-1963):

> That man first appeared on the records as living in the county of Georgia renowned for its poorness of soil even then, the 'Tobacco Road' country. At or before he reached his majority, he trekked across South Carolina and began taking up a series of homesteads in North Carolina. He was tried for treason, that is, loyalty to King George, and acquitted. He and his two brothers determined to join Daniel Boone, a neighbor of theirs in North Carolina, in his projects in the then wilderness of Kentuck. They set out, were ambushed in Cumberland Gap by the Indians and Meshach killed. Abednego and Shadrach lay in a hollow log for days, hiding. Then they retraced their steps and settled in what became the independent State of Franklin. Abednego became a justice of the peace. He was a major in the Battle of Kings Mountain. He moved to Dandridge where he took up the allotment of land due veterans. He enlarged his holdings. He was Justice Of the Peace. He bought slaves until he had twenty-five. He refused Andrew Jackson his daughter in marriage. When he was no longer a justice of the peace, at least on one occasion he "shot up the town." He led a wild, free, often

CHAPTER ONE

lawless life, and one gets a picture of an arrogant, shrewd, reckless-within bounds man "taking nothing from nobody."

The British were defeated at the Battle of Kings Mountain, South Carolina, October 7, 1780. Abednego Inman also was with soldiers from the Watauga and Holston settlements who went to Col. Clark's assistance when the state of Georgia was taken by the British. There also are documents dealing with preparations for an expedition against the Cherokees in 1788. One account states Abednego was a private in rank during the American Revolution; however, by the time he was living in Eastern Tennessee, Jefferson County, he had the rank of major—this in 1793 when he served as foreman of the first county grand jury.

After Tennessee became a state in May 1796, Abednego was appointed magistrate by Governor John Sevier at the first court held at Dandridge, where he resided. He was a member of Hopewell Presbyterian Church and is buried in the Revolutionary Cemetery in the center of the town of Dandridge on land originally owned by his son, the third Shadrach Inman. Abednego, the last of the three immigrant brothers, died at Dandridge, Jefferson County, Tennessee February 2, 1831.

We now turn to the second son of Abednego and Mary Ritchie Inman, as these are the direct forebears of the Atlanta and Augusta Inman descendants. John Ritchie Inman (1788-1836) married in 1806 or 1807 Jane Walker (1791-1831). They had sixteen children of whom three infants—a boy and twins (a boy and girl)—were burned to death in a fire December 24, 1811. John and Jane Walker Inman would be my great-great-grandparents, Abednego my great-great-great-grandfather, with John and Jane's son, Walker Patterson Inman, my mother's grandfather and my great-grandfather. This is also true relative to Walker, George, and Andrew Inman, all three born in Augusta and sons of my uncle Walker Patterson Inman II. Nevertheless, in the latter's family once the eldest son was born, the two Walkers always were known as Walker Sr. and Walker Jr. This designation continues to this day.

Although most of the written history relating to the Atlanta Inman clan seems to mention Samuel Martin Inman and his cotton factoring enterprise, S. M. Inman & Co., as the large and rich Inman Company best remembered, the facts indicate on study that his uncle, Walker Patterson Inman, was the first real money maker and the early major financial backer of S. W. Inman & Co. S. W. Inman & Co. was formed by Walker's brother, Shadrach Walker Inman, but his son, Samuel Martin Inman, ran the business later and changed the name to S. M. Inman & Co. By 1891, the *Atlanta Constitution* announced that the Inman firm was the largest cotton house in the world. There were over 500 employees handling 500,000 bales of cotton worth $20 million dollars annually.

The foregoing is mainly background to the Walker Patterson Inman story that will be the principal focus of the remainder of this recollection and also include

CHAPTER ONE

his various descendants. Walker Patterson Inman was born 1828 in Huntsville, Alabama, where his parents had moved after the fire at Dandridge, Tennessee. However, when Walker Patterson Inman was quite young, the entire family removed back to their former home in Dandridge, Eastern Tennessee. It was here that Walker Patterson Inman began his business career with a dry goods firm started by his older brother, Shadrach ("Shade") Walker Inman, who was responsible in part for rearing him, as their parents died while their children still were very young. By the time of the Civil War in 1861, Shade was a wealthy man and a plantation owner as well as a town merchant and public figure.

The Inman plantation was between two and three miles square and featured a large gristmill, a saw mill, and a row of slave cabins. By the Civil War it is said that Shade's estate was worth about $100,000. Federal troops destroyed most of this property, as the family had been Confederacy supporters while some of their neighbors were Unionists. After the war ended in 1865, Shadrach moved his family to Atlanta because of continued federal harassment on his plantation and in the store.

Actually, the first Inman to move to Atlanta was Shade's younger brother, Walker Patterson, who earlier had reached Atlanta in 1859 as agent for the Northwestern Bank of Ringgold, Georgia. Walker Patterson had married Harriett Cordelia Dick April 1, 1858 in Dandridge, Jefferson County, Tennessee, where their wedding license was issued. The document also was signed and attested to this marriage April 1, 1858, by the signature of one who appears to be a minister. Harriett's nickname was "Cord." She was born in 1840 being some twelve years younger than Walker Patterson Inman. The couple sired four children, two boys and two daughters, all of whom were born in Atlanta. These were Mary (May), William Henry, John Walter, and Harriet (Hattie Fannie) Inman in this order. One early indication of Walker Patterson Inman in Atlanta as a resident was November 1861 when Walker Patterson Inman and wife joined the First Presbyterian Church.

Early in the Civil War Walker served in the cavalry, but he was thrown from his horse and sustained a serious back injury thus shortening his military career. He continued his banking activities through the conflict and also was working in dry goods through a wholesale house called Inman, Cole and Company located in the Franklin Building on Alabama Street. Circa 1864, when Atlanta was under siege by the Union army, Walker Patterson Inman and family fled to Augusta where they continued to live even after the war's end as their Atlanta house had been burned along with the other businesses. Walker then established and ran a dry goods store in Augusta.

Rumor has it that Walker had at least a bale of cotton to be sold at war's end, thereby putting him immediately in funds! However, during the Civil War Walker's brother, William H. Inman, stayed up north and very likely could have provided capital to restart the family dry goods and cotton factoring trade. Perhaps Walker also had funds pre-war located in northern or English

CHAPTER ONE

banks and, therefore, was not left only with Confederate assets! In any case, it seems clear that the custom of storekeeper accepting cotton as payment for dry goods was prevalent so that Walker both before and following the Civil War was acting also as a cotton factor and selling cotton bales to an agency in his own name.

Probably around 1867-1868 Walker and his family returned to Atlanta where railroads destroyed in the war were running again and that city recovering. By this time the cotton business was flourishing in Augusta with Walker, his nephew Samuel Martin Inman, and Samuel K. Dick working together to trade cotton. Mr. Dick must have been related to Walker's wife, née Cordelia Dick, and was to become in the future Sam Martin's brother-in-law. As a close-knit family unit, the Inman clan was to become a strong force in Atlanta and indeed in the South in this new post-war era. They had access to northern capital and eventually expanded their business activities into railroads, cotton mills, cotton pressers, making cotton steel hoops, clothing factories, banking, insurance, etc.

It appears that one reason for this early success was the Inman ability to access northern capital with their own cotton agency in New York City as soon as the Civil War ended in 1865. Under various names the Inman New York agency always was in the picture for the life of their cotton trading. John Hamilton Inman, nephew of Walker Patterson Inman, went to New York City to join his uncle William and formed the cotton firm of Austell, Inman & Co., and later the Inman firm became Inman, Swann & Co.

As a member of the Inman, Swann firm, John H. Inman helped organize the New York Cotton Exchange in 1870-1871. The Inman company had representatives on the exchange board until the 1920s. The New York Inman outlets of course worked closely with the southern offices who supplied the raw cotton to be sold in the north or to Europe.

The Inmans took a leading role in making Atlanta a symbol of the "New South." The family was active in many civic pursuits through the years and served on various committees to implement new growth and rapid expansion. There were real estate interests with the development of Inman Park by the East Atlanta Land Co. and the creation of Ansley Park where one street is Inman Circle. Inmans were investors in the Terminal Hotel which burned in 1908; that fire cost the Walker Patterson Inman estate $35,000.

The Inman clan stayed away from Georgia politics generally by refusing to hold office; however, their influence was employed behind the scenes, and at one point Sam Martin Inman served on the Atlanta City Council while Walker Patterson Inman held office on the Fulton County Commission. The family support turned largely to local schools (Georgia Tech, Agnes Scott), hospitals (Grady), and their Presbyterian faith. Several Inmans were elders of the First Presbyterian Church of Atlanta where Walker was a ruling elder and senior officer when he died.

Walker P. Inman secured control of the *Atlanta Journal* in the late 1890s and even served as the president of

CHAPTER ONE

the paper which was established in 1883. Other Inman family members owned a sizeable holding in the *Atlanta Constitution*, which had been founded in 1868, and then was led by Henry W. Grady who was very pro-business and pro-industry. The Inmans endorsed the New South campaign through these news outlets.

Inmans also participated in the social and cultural life of their city; in 1910 the New York Metropolitan Opera Company with Enrico Caruso came to Atlanta to give five performances after leading citizens jointly pledged $40,000. Inman men always have been members of what we know today as the Piedmont Driving and Capital City Clubs; this is true over the many years back to the time when the Piedmont Driving Club was known as the "Gentlemen's Driving Club" and the founding of the Capital City in 1883.

Walker Patterson Inman's two sons predeceased him, while the two daughters lived on beyond his death at age seventy-nine on November 23, 1907. He was buried in Oakland Cemetery with his residence (I assume) listed as 478 Peachtree Street. His wife Cordelia had died on the same day in 1902, and he remarried a Miss Francis Jones in 1905 who survived him. We have no information relative to Miss Jones and wonder if she was sort of a "trophy wife," an old friend, or perhaps a housekeeper/secretary type? In the will her first name is spelled "Frances."

For the era, it appears that Walker's final estate was quite substantial in both liquid assets and real estate. A trust of $150,000 was devised to his four minor grandchildren in Augusta: $50,000 in cash and $100,000 in Atlanta real estate. The trustees named were son-in-law James R. Gray and James F. McGowan, the latter being his late son John Walter Inman's partner in the Augusta Cotton factoring business. Other money and real estate bequests totaled $240,000 to various family members and to charity, with the final residue of his estate to be divided equally between his two surviving children, May Inman Gray and Hattie Fannie Brandon.

In estimating the total value of the Walker Patterson Inman estate at his death, it would appear to be well over $1.5 million. This sum derives from tax rolls in 1914 on property Hattie Inman Brandon then owned assuming May Inman Gray owned the same ($257,700) and the fact that he wanted to leave legacies of $50,000 to each of his eight grandchildren in Atlanta. The aforementioned is what his granddaughter, Frank Inman Mays, always reported. Hence, Inman daughters May Gray and Hattie Brandon each must have inherited in cash and real estate $350,000 or more.

The eldest son of Walker Patterson Inman was William Henry Inman, born in 1864 but passing away at age thirty-eight in 1902. However, William Henry had married Nanaline Holt of Macon, Georgia, by whom there was one son also named Walker Patterson after his grandfather. Nanaline Inman later married the tobacco tycoon James Buchanan Duke, and there was a daughter, Doris Duke, being the half sister of another Walker Patterson Inman II. When she was thirteen, Doris Duke inherited $70 million from her father; her subsequent life story is

CHAPTER ONE

well known. I believe there still today is an Inman nephew to the late Doris Duke residing in Colorado.

An interesting sidelight is that Nanaline Holt Inman was devised $50,000 and his grandson by her $75,000, both bequests to be paid one-third in cash, one-third in real estate, and the final third in stock or personal securities. The grandson is named Walker Patterson Inman, Jr. in the will even though he was not a junior technically, but I believe the second person to carry this name. The second son of Walker Patterson Inman was John Walter Inman born January 16, 1870. Raised in Atlanta, he attended local public schools and graduated from Boy's High School. Following in the footsteps of his older first cousin, Samuel Martin Inman, who had been a student at Princeton when the Civil War started, he too attended Princeton University class of 1891. For subsequent Inman generations, Princeton also seems to have been a popular choice. John Walter always was called Walter, probably to differentiate him from another older first cousin, John Hamilton Inman, who died in 1896.

Following the death of John Hamilton Inman, who had been in New York City for some years as the representative of the Inman Cotton "dynasty," there were organizational changes with S. M. Inman & Co. divided into three main branches: Atlanta, Augusta, and Houston, Texas. Our Inman grandfather, John Walter, worked in Houston circa 1893-1894 as a southwestern Inman cotton representative and then about 1895-1896 moved to Augusta for work at the Inman & Co. cotton branch office. The Augusta office seemingly prospered for by 1904 the turnover reached $17 million according to press reports. Eventually, Inman and Company in Augusta had three partners: John Walter Inman, W. H. Inman, and James F. McGowan, with Walker P. Inman of Atlanta providing financial assistance as needed. W. H. Inman died in 1902 with Inman & Co. continuing with Walter Inman and James McGowan as co-partners. McGowan was the grandfather of my school friend, Henri McGowan, Jr.

John Walter married Frank Clark at St. Paul's in 1897 and immediately started a new Inman family with enthusiasm. A first son arrived in 1898, named John Walter Inman, Jr., but did not live; followed by Cordelia Dick, named after her Inman grandmother in Atlanta, in 1899; a second son in 1900, Walker Patterson Inman, named for his paternal grandfather; another daughter, Ruth Doughty Inman, came in 1902, named for her maternal grandmother; and finally and posthumously for John Walter, twins November 27, 1904, called John Walter Inman Jr. and Frank Clark Inman for their parents.

In Richmond County off the Milledgeville Road some "5-6 or 7-8 miles from Augusta" (as the press reported), Walter Inman and James McGowan built two country homes on property they named Golden Camp. The two houses were only completed the summer of 1904 on what was known as the highest hill in Richmond County. The Inmans were in their house (the McGowans not yet in theirs) in late August 1904 when Walter drove his

CHAPTER ONE

car into Augusta to his office on a Saturday. While the Atlanta and Augusta papers somewhat differ in their reports, the essence appears to be that "an accident [probably meaning a mechanical problem] disabled his machine." Walter, attempting to find the difficulty, was completely drenched by a heavy rain shower and then suffered a severe "congestive chill." The family carriage driving in from the city brought him back to Golden Camp where he went to bed.

His doctor, William H. Doughty, Jr., advised bed rest, and Walter seemed much better on Sunday after a night of repose. However, Sunday night around nine p.m. Walter died in his bed having been attacked with "apoplexy." Another verdict was death due to "congestion" or " a ruptured blood vessel" with "excessive fat about the heart" given as the reason or cause of sudden death. He died at once before any doctor could arrive at the rural retreat at only thirty-four and a half years of age.

The funeral was held at the 445 Broad Street residence with many prominent Augusta gentleman acting as honorary and active pallbearers, including names such as Barrett, Cumming, Alexander, Phinizy, Tobin, Walker, D'Antignac, Charbonnier, and Boykin Wright. The music and flowers (both from Atlanta and Augusta) were impressive, and the attendance both at the home and later at Magnolia Cemetery was large. Walter's father had taken a private car over the Georgia Railroad and arrived in Augusta with the immediate Inman family, Inman relatives, and close friends from Atlanta.

Walker Patterson Inman had lived to see his only two sons predecease him! What sadness!

In those days the *Chronicle* wrote about the wills of well-known persons following the local probate. The news article reported on the simple and clear language relative to an estate estimated at $250,000 with the corpus left to the wife and children "share and share alike." Mrs. J. Walter Inman was co-executor with brother-in-law James R. Gray. The estate comprised cash, bonds, stock, and the deceased's share of Inman & Co.

Father Walker P. Inman apparently continued providing funds as needed to the Augusta Inman & Co. until his own death in November 1907. Walker P. Inman obviously thought highly of James F. McGowan who continued to run the business until there was "an embarrassment" in 1908 due in large part to two terrible storms that destroyed a major portion of the 1908 cotton crop! Inman & Co. then ceased business and Mr. McGowan died in January 1909. He too died at a young age, being but forty-five years old.

The widow Inman bought a new plot at Magnolia Cemetery and had erected an imposing and handsome granite marker engraved "Inman" in large letters. She in later days turned this plot over to her surviving son, Walker P. Inman, who with his wife, Alice Perkins, is buried thereon with his father and my mother Frank's little twin brother, the second John Walter Inman, Jr. who lived but a month.

With his two sons having predeceased him, Walker P. Inman then was left with two surviving daughters and

CHAPTER ONE

his grandchildren in Atlanta and Augusta. The youngest daughter, Harriet, named for her mother and born in 1873, married Morris Brandon, a prominent Atlanta lawyer, a graduate of Yale University Law School and previously Vanderbilt. He died in February 1940 leaving his wife (known as "Hattie Fannie") and three sons, Morris Jr., Inman, and Nathan Brandon. The family residence then was 550 West Pace's Ferry Road. I do not recall my mother ever mentioning the Brandons, although Mr. and Mrs. Morris Brandon, Sr. are listed as guests at her 1924 wedding in Augusta.

Gene Ellis, now resident in Augusta, but formerly of Atlanta, tells me that one of the best public schools in the capital is named for Morris Brandon. Frampton E. Ellis, her late father-in-law, was one of the honorary escorts from the Atlanta Bar Association at the Brandon funeral in 1940.

Inman Brandon, their middle son, also was a well-known Atlanta lawyer having graduated from the University of Georgia and Yale Law. His legal practice in Atlanta began in October 1930.

The elder daughter, May Inman Gray, born March 6, 1862, married James Richard Gray November 16, 1881. This union produced three daughters and two sons: Cordelia Inman Gray (later Brumby), Frances Gray Gallogly (later Yankey), Jennie Dick Gray (later Pearce), James R. Gray Jr., and Walker Inman Gray.

The Gray family resided at "Graystone" 2882 Peachtree Road, N.E. for many years with Gray admitted to the bar in 1879 becoming a junior partner with

Judge W. D. Ellis in a firm called Ellis, Gray and Ellis when W. D. Ellis, Jr. also became a partner.

The Gray association with the *Atlanta Journal* dates from 1900 when he purchased the stock of Senator Hoke Smith. In the same year Gray became editor and general manager of the paper. In 1905, he secured a controlling interest in the *Journal* and was elected president and editor, which positions he held until his death June 25, 1917. The Gray family continued their ownership and management of the paper until circa late 1939 when ownership was sold to James M. Cox.

James R. Gray was most public spirited and supported Atlanta's Oglethorpe and Emory Universities as well as Agnes Scott College. He was instrumental in launching the movement for Atlanta's first spring music festival which developed into the annual week of grand operas.

Mrs. James R. Gray Sr., known to my mother and the Augusta family as Aunt May Inman, continued on at Graystone in Buckhead. In the late 1920s it appears some of her children and grandchildren still were residing there too or in adjoining houses. Aunt May was educated at Mary Baldwin in Staunton, Virginia, was a member of the Georgia Society of Colonial Dames, the Daughters of the American Revolution, and the North Avenue Presbyterian Church. She eventually became chairman of the *Atlanta Journal* Board with her son Inman Gray as president and other son James R. Gray, Jr. as vice president and editor.

CHAPTER ONE

It was written of May Inman Gray that "she was a worthy daughter of her family, with all the charming heritage of the Old South, its grace and its poise."

The football season of 1928 was in the usual autumn motion when on the night of October 16, Willard H. Smith, clerk in a drug store at Boulevard and 8th Street (McRoberts Pharmacy) was shot and murdered as he tried to resist a robbery at the store where he was employed. Two Oglethorpe University students, called "thrill slayers" were arrested and subsequently were the focus of a sensation throughout the South, and indeed the country, by their trials. The two students accused of murder were George Harsh, son of a wealthy Milwaukee family, and Richard (called Dick) Gray Gallogly from the well-known and greatly respected Atlanta family. Gallogly was the grandson of May Inman Gray.

Some nights before (October 6th), S. H. Meeks, a clerk in an A&P grocery store at 1064 Hemphill Avenue also was shot and killed in a gun duel between the store manager and a youthful robber, later identified as George Harsh.

Harsh received a leg wound in the second hold-up and was arrested once the police had a tip-off about a college boy getting private treatment for his wound. Harsh confessed to the murder of Smith but insisted that in the grocery store affair, Meeks had been killed by a bullet from the store manager's pistol.

The Harsh confession named Dick Gallogly as his accomplice in both holdups stating that he drove the car and acted as the lookout at both stores. Gallogly was in Athens for the Georgia-Tulane football game and was arrested there and brought to Atlanta.

Gallogly denied participation in the "crimes," claiming he went to the doors of the two stores only to prevent Harsh from robbing the businesses. He was first questioned for more than four hours and stuck to his story.

The trials of Harsh and Gallogly were separate, with the Harsh trial first in January 1929. Harsh pleaded not guilty but made no effort to deny the facts, saying he had been drinking and did not know what he did! The jury returned a prompt verdict of guilty, and Harsh was sentenced to the electric chair.

Gallogly was defended by a large group of well-known Atlanta lawyers headed by the Arnold brothers. There were two trials both resulting in hung juries. At the third trial, Gallogly pled guilty and accepted a life sentence stating that he did so only to save Harsh from the electric chair. Harsh too was then granted a life sentence. Both men were assigned to different Georgia prisons, Harsh to Bellwood Camp in Atlanta and Gallogly to Milledgeville.

The late Calhoun Witham (my cousin) and his friend Alex Hitz sent me some background material on the Gray family around this period. May Inman Gray's two sons were Inman Gray who ran the *Journal* and was rarely visible and James R. Gray, Jr., who was said to be a delightful partying chap who was the father of their school friend at E. Rivers but behind Calhoun and Alex. This school friend was Dick Gray III, handsome,

CHAPTER ONE

of an olive complexion, and good at football. Alex and Calhoun also were at E. Rivers School with Inman Gray Gallogly (called Jim), the younger brother of Richard Gray Gallogly (called Dick). Both brothers were the first cousins of Dick Gray III and all grandsons of May Inman Gray.

The Grays and Galloglys lived then side by side on Peachtree; Alex, Calhoun, and Jim Gallogly often played in the side yard/garden at the Gray House. Both houses have since been torn down. Jim was described as nice but a rather "strange bird, cross-eyed, thick glasses, and a nerdy expression."

Prior to his arrest, it was said Dick Gallogly had shot out the clock at Hermance Stadium at Oglethorpe University. I do not know if George Harsh was his companion in crime relative to this instance, although Gallogly maintained Harsh did the shooting!

The events resulting in "thrill murder" and the subsequent legal (and perhaps not so legal) maneuverings carried forward for another twelve years wrecked the Gray family financially and socially in the words of my Atlanta informants. After Aunt May Gray died in January 1940, the Peachtree house was sold and became Atlanta's first serious restaurant called Hart's Peachtree.

Led by Grandmother Gray, the family conducted for twelve years a battle to obtain the release of Dick Gallogly. Three clemency pleas were denied; the first time he was eligible in 1932, Georgia Governor Richard B. Russell denied the request as did Governor Gene Talmadge in 1938. Although the case was really a "criminal cause celebre" with the general public showing little sympathy for Gallogly and Harsh, both scions of well-to-do respectable families, the Grays still persisted while the Harsh family contributed $50,000 to the injured parties.

I first became fascinated with the Gallogly case circa 1937-1938 when my grandmother Frankie Doughty was requested by her sister-in-law, May Inman Gray, to write the governor of Georgia (then Gene Talmadge) and plead for the commutation of his life sentence. This must have been the occasion when Talmadge refused to intervene. However, the story was a good lesson for me reflecting that bad actions do have dire consequences.

Later Dick Gallogly, with medical problems, spent time in Atlanta's Crawford W. Long Hospital where in May 1939 he married Vera Hunt who as a college student had played piano at prison. She then was described as a piano teacher in her early twenties. The newspaper pictures indicate she was most attractive in appearance and well dressed.

In October 1939, while Gallogly was being transported by car from the Long Hospital in Atlanta to the state penitentiary at Reidsville, Georgia, he pulled a gun on the two prison officials both then sitting in the front seat and ordered the car to stop. Gallogly was in the rear seat with his wife Vera and mother, now Mrs. Worth Yankey. The two guards were left by the side of the road in open country as was his mother who refused to continue as a participant in this escape.

CHAPTER ONE

The Gallogly couple then returned to Atlanta, picked up her car, and abandoned the prison vehicle. Spending the night in Alabama and one or two more on the road, they reached their destination at Dallas, Texas, where Gallogly surrendered to the local authorities and declared he wanted "Texas Justice." Dick claimed he was innocent of two murders but under a life sentence; he also stated he was the victim of "political persecution" due to "bad blood" between Solicitor General Boykin who prosecuted his case and the family-owned paper, The *Atlanta Journal*. Another defense was that all involved were drinking.

The Dallas attorney, Harold H. Young, was hired by Gallogly after he had read that Young had kept a Texas oil operator from being extradited to Louisiana in the "Hot Oil" scandal. Georgia Governor Rivers immediately drew a formal request to the Texas Governor W. Lee O'Daniel to send Gallogly, then in the Dallas County Jail, to Atlanta.

Governor Rivers also sent Georgia Attorney General Ellis Arnall to Dallas in order to personally deliver the extradition documents. Gallogly had surrendered to Sheriff Schmid in Dallas October 10, 1939.

One minor ancillary legal problem was that Vera Hunt Gallogly was under a $2,500 bond in Dallas and the subject of a $500 fugitive bond in Atlanta from a shoplifting case!

In short, all the Dallas legal maneuverings finally turned out to be in vain (and probably very expensive) as the Gallogly couple were returned to Atlanta.

Dick was sent back to jail; the final disposition of Vera's shoplifting case is not known. Although there was some speculation a charge against Vera might be made that she aided a felon (and probably provided him with a gun), I do not think this was ultimately pursued by the Atlanta authorities.

In November 1940, George Harsh was let out of jail on parole. However, the terms required that he stay twelve months in Fulton County. He was to be employed in the laboratory of an Atlanta doctor in the city. It was said he had been "a model prisoner" and had tried to pay his great debt to society with twelve years in prison.

Full pardons then were granted by Governor Rivers in January 1941 to Dick Gallogly and to George Harsh, who, as explained, was already on parole. A large number of other pardons also were signed on Rivers' last night of office. There was subsequently much talk that Gallogly and Harsh had rich and powerful families who had over the years spent liberally in the effort to free them.

Harsh following his pardon moved to Canada and served in the Canadian army during World War II. Apparently Harsh was a decorated hero at war's end!

As for Dick Gallogly, we are unsure of his whereabouts after his pardon. At one point he may have returned to Dallas, but to date we have no firm information on his post-prison life. Patty Gray (widow of Dick Gray III) recalls that Gallogly was married twice: first to Vera Hunt (with whom there was a son) and later to a second wife who presented him with a daughter. Patty Gray met the

CHAPTER ONE

Gallogly daughter at a Gray family reunion and told me she was a lovely person. That meeting was many years ago, and she does not even remember her name. It is said Gallogly died in Dacula, Georgia, June 22, 2002, at almost ninety-three years old.

It is a pity Gallogly's loving grandmother, Mary Inman Gray, who died in January 1940, did not live to see the battle she waged finally end in victory. I met Great Aunt May Inman Gray only once in February 1939 when she came to Augusta to attend the funeral of her sister-in-law, Frank Clark Inman Doughty. She was then seventy-seven years old and accompanied by one son. She must have been a strong personality, very protective of her children and extended family. Perhaps this is rather grandly illustrated by her handsome funeral plot at historic Oakland Cemetery in Atlanta.

The beautiful Gray plot features a weeping Niobe from Greek mythology; Niobe was turned to stone because she loved her offspring more than the Gods who were jealous and killed all fourteen (seven sons and seven daughters). Niobe is an example of pride humbled but also continuing to shed tears forever for her progeny.

__RIDGELY:__

Although the Mays family has no original direct blood relationship with the Ridgely clan, I include a short piece on how we are now connected. This is because from my earliest recollection I was in touch with Ridgelys in Augusta due to the marriage of my great aunt, Mary Stedman Clark, with Marion Gardner Ridgely. She was the only sister of Frankie Clark, my beloved grandmother; the two sisters were life-long close companions, being familiar and intimate as only two sisters can be. They talked by phone and usually saw each other daily. The sisters were virtually twins being born approximately fourteen months apart with Mary Stedman the younger.

My mother and her brother called their Aunt "Auntie T" as she was known to her friends as "Ted." We followed suit with the "auntie" pronounced as "ontie." Auntie T was a sweet, placid person with an open disposition to believe the best about a person. She was not as vivacious as her slightly older sister and probably not as pretty, but nevertheless always a good friend and popular with most. The Clark sisters, Frank and Ted, were well known as eligible young ladies in the social life of the city by the early 1890s. Their names also must have been a talking point!

Ted Clark (whose mother was born Ruth Eve Doughty) married Marion Ridgely January 8, 1903, at St. Paul's Church; this was reported in the local newspaper, but the church marriage records apparently neglected to record this wedding! She was twenty-eight and the groom

CHAPTER ONE

twenty-seven. Her brother-in-law, John Walter Inman, gave them the wedding trip to a point up North, paying all expenses. The Atlanta newspaper reported that Marion Gardner Ridgely was with the National Bank at Augusta and a brother of Lieut. Randolph Ridgely who was with Admiral Dewey at Manila in 1898 during the Spanish-American War..

The Ridgelys are an old prominent Maryland family with Robert Ridgely emigrating here circa 1664. His descendants did well with his great-grandson Charles building what is still known as Hampton Mansion near Baltimore. Hampton was said to be one of the largest and most ornate Georgian houses ever built in the United States. Originally the center of an estate of 24,000 acres, the Georgian and Palladian-inspired house was constructed 1783-1790. The house is now owned by the National Park Service and designated a National Historic Site. It was said that Charles Ridgely could ride twenty-seven miles across his property; however, by 1872 the total acres were down to about 1,000 by division among various Ridgely heirs. The house over the years accommodated six generations of Ridgelys whose wealth originated from iron ore as one chief source. Their furnaces supplied the American Continental Army with armaments.

So beginning with the first English émigré barristers, Robert Ridgely, in the 1660s, the family prospered greatly with marriages to names like Dorsey and Carroll and also government service; Robert the barrister became in 1670 the deputy of Baltimore County Province, and a later Charles Carman Ridgely served three terms as a Maryland governor.

The Ridgely connection with the South began when West Pointer Lieutenant Randolph Ridgely was on garrison duty at Savannah in 1844 and met and married Catherine Elizabeth Desaboye (of French descent) who was the owner of much land in Burke County where the county seat is Waynesboro. There was a prenuptial agreement in which the groom gave up interest in her estate unless she predeceased him; in this instance, he would inherit half and her family the balance. In other respects, the whole estate would be given to their children. The couple did have one son, Randolph Jr., who was born at Fort McHenry, Maryland.

Ridgely saw action in the US-Mexican War of 1846-1848 when he served gallantly before falling from his horse and, following a coma, dying in 1846 at Monterrey, Mexico. He had given important support in successful battles for his country and had been given a brevet promotion to captain as a result.

The Augusta/Grovetown military historian Russell K. Brown has written an interesting paper called "By Land and by Sea: The Saga of the Fighting Ridgelys." This paper deals with the four generations of this Ridgely branch who were conspicuous in serving their country on land and by sea. The other three generations, all also named Randolph, took part in the Civil War, Spanish-American War, and World Wars I and II. These Randolph Ridgelys all served with distinction with the third being named admiral in the coast guard

CHAPTER ONE

and his son also a coast guard aviator and commander during World War II in both Atlantic and Pacific operations. The admiral and his son were honored with various service medals and awards.

Following Randolph, Jr.'s Civil War discharge, he came to Burke County to farm on his mother's land. In 1870, he married Eliza Gardner Rhind from a prominent Augusta family at the newly established Church of the Good Shepherd on The Hill. Eliza was a founding member of that church. The couple raised five sons: Randolph III, Charles Sterett, Marion Gardner, Montgomery Rhind, and Conrad. Circa 1879, the Ridgely family moved to Augusta from Burke County and lived on Pickens Road at number 2247. This house is now owned by Clay Boardman.

Marion, also known to close friends as "Pap," was a keen sportsman all his life. A tennis player, at one time city champion in his youth, he played golf well into his eighties. Marion and Ted had two children, Marion, Jr. in 1904 and Elizabeth Rhind born in 1909 and named for her paternal grandmother. The family always was active at The Good Shepherd Church where Marion, Sr. was the senior warden for thirty-four years, up to January 1949. The Episcopal Day School's old Ridgely Hall was named in his honor.

Dot Manice, long-time Augusta resident, called Marion Gardner Ridgely "a very gracious gentleman of the old school." He played very key roles at the Augusta Country Club as member, secretary, treasurer, assistant manager, manager, and board governor for more than fifty years! He was one of the founders of the Women's Titleholders Golf Championship and always an inspiration to the young on good sportsmanship and manners. Pap was honored by the country club in 1992 when one of the rooms was named Ridgely and his portrait hung therein.

In her 1999 Augusta Country Club Centennial book on the club's history, the late Eileen H. Stulb paid generous tribute to Pap Ridgely and his many contributions to the club through the years. He was a golfing mentor to that author and to many others growing up and learning to play golf. Included in the book is a picture of a foursome including Pap, baseball legend Ty Cobb, Scott Appleby, and Frank Robinson, Sr.

Marion was a partner in an Augusta printing business called Ridgely Tidwell Company. Ted Ridgely also had a shop catering to the Northern tourist trade during the winter months on the ground floor, Walton Way side, of the Partridge Inn. The shop sold Ted's needlepoint and petit point items in addition to her lacework and other gifts. Marion was friendly with many of the winter visitors, proposed them for membership privileges at the country club, and became their golfing companions, including Scott Appleby and Julius Setze.

The Marion Ridgelys lived in houses now numbered 2218 Kings Way, 2913 Lake Forest Drive, and 671 Milledge Road. This last house has been demolished but was located on the site where the Milledge Road tennis courts are now visible. Then to the George Walton Apartments, their final residence. I last saw Auntie T in

CHAPTER ONE

November 1953 when I was in Augusta just prior to my assignment to Hong Kong. She was sitting on a bench behind the building on the sunny day when I went to say goodbye. I left but circled around and drove back five minutes later to hug her again. She later told my mother Frank how sweet this gesture was but also said she got the feeling I thought I would not see her again for I was leaving for three years. She was right, as she died at the age of eighty-two before I returned in 1957. Pap lived on a few more years until February 5, 1960, when he was in his eighty-fourth year. When I was in Augusta during the autumn of 1957, he treated me to lunch in the men's grill at the old clubhouse, and he was still managing to play the first and eighteenth holes which in those days still were parallel.

While Marion Gardner Ridgely, Jr. was married to Julia Wilcox of Augusta in 1928, there was no issue. He died in 1948 at the early age of forty-four and is buried with his parents and grandparents on the Ridgely plot in Summerville Cemetery.

Elizabeth Rhind Ridgely (1909-1987) was pretty, charming, and popular. Her best friend was Genie Selden Lehmann, and they both were Augusta debutantes in 1928. She was usually called Lib and attended Tubman High School in Augusta and Stewart Hall in Staunton, Virginia. Lib was very fond of her Aunt Frank (my grannie) who she said gave her a diamond ring her debut year of 1928 while they were in Aunt Frank's car pulling the "Bon Air Hill," Willie Washington at the wheel.

Lib was in love, apparently, with Dr. Charles Mulherin, who in the late 1930s was an intern at a large Texas hospital—probably Dallas or Houston. Mulherin married someone else, leaving Lib quite hurt. However, Lib did bounce back and married Carl Willis Dohm January 6, 1940, in First Christian Church, Augusta, as Carl had been divorced, and The Good Shepherd then did not marry a divorcé. The wedding trip was to Miami for two weeks; afterward they lived at 2709 McDowell Street and subsequently in Charleston, West Virginia, Charlottesville, Virginia, and Dallas, Texas. Carl was the Ruberoid Company representative when he came to Augusta.

The Dohms had two children, Mary Ridgely born in 1944 and Charles William born in 1950. Mary married Joseph P. Wilbert in 1968, and the son, called Bill, married an Irish nurse, Sheila McCarthy, in 1971. Both marriages have issue, and the two families still live in Dallas. Carl and Lib Ridgely Dohm passed away within six months of each other in the late 1980s, Lib departing first. We were then living in Athens, Greece; Lynn, however, happened to be in Dallas visiting her mother and was able to attend Lib's funeral. We always called on Lib and Carl during my stays there to see the Alexander family, and Lynn's sister, Jan O'Reilly, is friendly with the Wilberts.

As a short corollary to the Ridgely story, it may be of interest to include what I learned relative to the Rhind family when I was engaged in Ridgely research. Some of this data comes from the Victor Moore book

CHAPTER ONE

on the Good Shepherd Church history. The reader may recall that Randolph Ridgely, Jr. married Eliza Gardner Rhind in 1870 at the newly established parish. Her parents were James Rhind and Mary McKinne Gardner, and her brother, killed in the War Between the States in 1862, was William Montgomery Rhind. So this family had many blood ties with a number of the church founders.

The Rhinds were of well-known Scottish family stock; the Rhind branch in Scotland may be now extinct. One perished on one of the Crusades under the lead of a Scottish prince. "Rhind" likely is the modern spelling for the Charles Rhind who came to the United States from Aberdeen in 1796. He was born February 11, 1779. President Jackson appointed Charles as commissioner plenipotentiary to the Ottoman port to negotiate a trade treaty; he went to Constantinople and successfully completed his task. The US Senate ratified this treaty, but Charles declined the offer of resident minister in Constantinople.

Charles Rhind married well in 1809; the bride was Susan Fell, daughter of Colonel Peter Fell and Margaret Colden as well as granddaughter of Governor Cadwallader Colden of the then New York Province, 1761-1776. The granddaughter of Charles and Susan Rhind, Eliza Gardner Rhind, is the lady who pledged her troth to Randolph Ridgely, Jr. in Augusta. Her sister, Susan, married W. H. Barrett, and they became the great-grandparents of my friends and contemporaries Mary Barrett Robertson and William Hale Barrett.

IS LIVING WELL STILL THE BEST REVENGE?

Ruth Doughty Clark *Francis William Clark*

CHAPTER ONE

Grandmother and Grandfather Inman (Harriet Cordelia Dick and Walker Patterson)

John Walter Inman   *Frank Crowell Clark Inman*

2204 Kings Way living room, 1924 at Frank Doughty's new Dower House

CHAPTER ONE

Mary Clark De l'aigle

IS LIVING WELL STILL THE BEST REVENGE?

Frank Clark Inman Doughty with children (LtoR): Ruth Inman, Cordelia Inman, Frank Inman, Jean Doughty step-daughter, and Walker Inman

CHAPTER ONE

*Marion G. Ridgely in golf foursome at Augusta Country Club.
Ty Cobb is second from left
(Photo from Pap's grandson Bill Dohm of Dallas)*

The old Augusta Court House as painted by James M. Flagg in 1925 during his Christmas visit. The original now owned by Sted Mays.

Frank Doughty and Betty Doughty Butt in 1925 at Bon Air Hotel Fancy dress affair dressed as gypsy fortune tellers

CHAPTER II

Bowdres, Crawfords, Hamiltons, Mayses, Phinizys, Yanceys: MORE GEORGIA FAMILY ARCHIVES AND ROOTS

<u>B</u><u>OWDRES</u>: Our family always thought "Bowdre" originally was a French name (possibly Anglicized a bit); the name also had been initially a surname, and this we know for certain as it was the last name of my great-great-great-grandfather Hays Bowdre on my father's side. Over the years someone told me Hays Bowdre was a medical man, i.e., a doctor. My own investigation and research discovered the real story which has some fascinating aspects, at least to my mind.

IS LIVING WELL STILL THE BEST REVENGE?

Hays Bowdre is listed in the 1841 City Directory of Augusta living at 238 Broad Street. His grandfather, Elisha Bowdre, emigrated from Goochland County, Virginia, and paid taxes on the 1779 North Carolina (Randolph County) tax list. He finally moved to Columbia County, Georgia, where he died. As son of Elisha, Robert Bowdre, was Hays Bowdre's father. The Bowdre family may have been of French Huguenot origin.

The colonial Georgia marriage records (1760-1810) shows that Robert Bowdre and Sarah Hays married April 24, 1792, in Columbia County; however, I cannot explain the "Colonial Title" as late as 1792 up to 1810!

Hays Bowdre's dates are February 1, 1793-October 26, 1856, as per his grave marker; although, one newspaper report puts the death date as October 27, 1856. Hays seems to have been a merchant; one enterprise was a dry goods establishment called Bowdre & Claggett. Another business partner in this business was Hays's brother, Thomas Bowdre.

Hays Bowdre apparently prospered with, for the period, a fine till of assets estimated at about $85,000 on his passing. He owned 700 acres along Butler's Creek, owned various real estate, and sat on the board of a bank. The real estate included items also in Summerville. At various times he owned fifteen to thirty-two slaves, livestock, etc.

Hays Bowdre waited until he was about thirty-four years of age before marrying Mrs. Harriet E. Young, December 13, 1827 (as per one report), although the

CHAPTER TWO

formal wedding certificate signed by the minister is dated April 13, 1828, with the Georgia license approval issued December 10, 1827, by Richmond County. In any case, one child was born to the couple January 20, 1829, in Augusta. This little baby girl was Harriet Hays Bowdre. Unfortunately, this child never really knew her mother, as Mrs. Hays Bowdre died August 14, 1829, not quite seven months following the birth of her daughter and at barely twenty-nine years of age. She died in Greenville, South Carolina, perhaps out of Augusta then to escape the summer heat.

It appears that Hays Bowdre also was the guardian to some people of color who were free; some worked as his house servants. One was called Lucy, a mulatta with whom Hays had a son in 1824 named George Bowdre. Between 1830-1837 Hays and Lucy sired five more children all taking the surname Bowdre. Lucy obviously was sort of a foster mother to little Harriet Hays as was Mrs. Sarah McKeene, her grannie on her mother's side who may have lived with the family after her husband's death circa 1835.

In 1848, Hays bought Lucy and her children eighty acres of land in Warren County, Ohio. The land parcel was near Cincinnati; later the Bowdre Ohio clan moved to Jefferson, in the northeast corner of the state. Lucy's eldest son, George, married a mulatta Ann Fox in 1851. Another mulatta Susan Fox also went to Ohio with the Bowdres.

The amount paid by Hays for the Ohio land approximated $4,700-$5,000. Hays continued to pay the

Ohio taxes on the property until his death; thereafter, his executor, and by that time his son-in-law, Ferdinand Phinizy II, paid the taxes due. The Ohio Bowdres were listed as "colored people" but eventually I understand "they passed over"!

When I first learned about the "Lucy and Hays Affair," I surmised that Hays Bowdre wanted to hive-off as it were his common-law wife and their children for by 1848 the legitimate daughter, Harriet, was nineteen and therefore of marriageable age. In any event, Harriet married Ferdinand Phinizy II February 22, 1849, with the bridegroom obviously fully aware of the Ohio Bowdres.

The Hays Bowdre will left everything to Harriet B. Phinizy with the exception of two legacies to his mother-in-law, Sarah McKeene, and to his brother, Thomas Bowdre, the entire principal to revert to Harriet after their deaths. Mr. and Mrs. Hays Bowdre both were originally buried in Magnolia Cemetery, Augusta, but later moved to the Ferdinand Phinizy II plot at Oconee Hill Cemetery, Athens, Georgia. Mrs. Sarah McKeene also is buried on the same lot.

There still are persons residing in Thomson, Georgia, about thirty miles from Augusta, using the surname Bowdre. Thomson is in McDuffie County. These persons I am told are people of color. I have seen the 1810 Bowdre-Reese-Knox house, now owned by the Knox family and a usual stop on the Belle-Meade Fox Hunt. McDuffie County was created in 1870 and embraces lands once located in the pre-revolutionary

CHAPTER TWO

war colonial era known as Wrightsborough Township. The latter dates back to 1768. Once rail travel began, Wrightsborough declined; however, I have read that prior to the Civil War in and around the vicinity of Wrightsborough there was wealth with family names noted as follows: Hamiltons, Phinizys, Whites, Bowdres, Alfords, Barnes, etc. Wrightsborough or, as it is sometimes spelled, Wrightsboro is today listed on the National Register. The old church and cemetery still remain.

It indeed would be very churlish not to acknowledge and thank Virginia Banerjee of Redding, Connecticut, for alerting the author to the "Lucy-Hays Bowdre Ohio story" and for providing most of the dates relating to their liaison in Augusta. Virginia has visited Augusta twice in her pursuit of Bowdre information as she knew the family well in Ohio and has compiled much research about their Georgia past and current situation.

Two interesting footnotes to the Bowdre story were furnished by my niece Bowdre Mays McAllister. One is that a Charlie Bowdre fought with Billy the Kid out West and is now buried with him (William H. Bonney "The Kid") at an old military cemetery in New Mexico called Fort Sumner. I have a picture of the grave marker. Charlie Bowdre's parents were Albert and Lucy Bowdre and lived in Wilkes County, Georgia, and subsequently in Mississippi (De Soto County) where they owned a farm or, as people often still like to state, a plantation! Here Charlie was raised. Virginia Banerjee believes he was probably a nephew of Hays Bowdre.

Another rather esoteric and useless bit of lore is a soil classification survey denoting a "Bowdre soil series." This is defined as "deep, somewhat poorly drained soils" formed in Mississippi River Alluvium. The states concerned are Missouri and Mississippi.

CRAWFORDS

I first became aware of my Crawford ancestry when reading one of the newspaper accounts of my parent's September 3, 1924, wedding. In those days there were very voluminous accounts written in both the Atlanta and Augusta papers; one account noted that my father, Bowdre P. Mays, was the great-grandson of former Georgia Governor George Walker Crawford. I later learned he was buried on a plot in Summerville Cemetery with his wife and other relatives including my own grandfather, Samuel Warren Mays, who was the governor's grandson.

George Walker Crawford (1798-1872) was a lawyer, legislator, congressman, governor of Georgia 1843-1847 when the state capital was located in Milledgeville, secretary of war under President Zachary Taylor, and president of the State Secession Convention in 1861. This data is found on the historical marker at the cemetery together with the names of other notables also buried therein. All of this piqued my interest to discover more about the Crawfords.

My late aunt Louise Mays Bussey became interested in our Crawford genealogy in 1959 and recorded that the Crawfords in America were noted for their longevity and extreme height. The common American ancestor was one John Crawford who emigrated from Ayrshire, Scotland, to Jamestown, Virginia, in 1643. The Crawfords were said to be supporters of the House of Stuart; the great rebellion or Civil War in what we now designate the United Kingdom began in 1642 and such might have provided one rationale for the John Crawford's departure. He was accompanied by his son, David Crawford, from whom the Georgia Crawfords descend. Our Augusta branch first moved from Virginia to North Carolina circa 1767 and then to Columbia County by 1772.

The name Crawford in Gaelic means "the pass of blood" from "cru" ("bloody") and "ford", ("a pass"). It was said the immigrant John Crawford was the youngest son of the Earl of Crawford whose pedigree was notoriously longer than his rent roll! The title dates back to 1127 when a Scottish king conferred the distinction.

The chart below outlines the relationship of the three Crawfords with which this piece will principally deal: Peter Crawford, his son Governor George Walker Crawford, and William Harris Crawford. Peter, father of George, married his first cousin, was a native Virginian, a Revolutionary War veteran, and a man who was the power in Columbia County according to Alfred Cumming, one of the lieutenants to "King Peter"! This as per the Joseph B. Cumming memoir which also reports Alfred Cumming was mayor of Augusta in 1839 and later governor of the Utah Territory. In the time of "King Peter" Crawford, the Cummings of Augusta owned property in Columbia County. Peter died in 1830 having served many years as a state senator. The following is a simplified chart of Crawfords in this account:

CHAPTER TWO

David Crawford m Ann Anderson

Joel Crawford	John Crawford	Charles Crawford
m	m	m
Fanny Harris	Sarah Smith	Jane Maxwell

William Harris Crawford	Peter Crawford	m	Mary Ann Crawford

George Walker Crawford

While one large Crawford estate was near Appling and was said to comprise 1,900 acres run as a cotton plantation, both Peter and his son George lived near Belair, from 1837 a railway stop about ten miles west of Augusta. The train depot at Belair closed in 1931 having been open since the construction of the Georgia Railroad. The Crawford house at Belair caught fire in the 1890s and was rebuilt, but it was finally razed with nothing now remaining.

The large Crawford homestead near Appling in Columbia County, built by Dr. Nathan Crawford, an uncle, was called Oak Hill or Oak Hall (both names were used in old documents and newspaper reports). The house was said to be the oldest in the county prior to burning in 1968. A picture reveals a tall wooden structure with six columns across the front reaching to the roof. There was an iron balcony, eight rooms, and some windows with imported stained glass. Dr. Nathan Crawford's father was Charles Crawford, a militia company captain from Virginia and later North Carolina. His wife was the former Jane Maxwell, and their fourth child, Mary Ann Crawford, is the lady who married her first cousin, Peter Crawford.

Thereafter Peter and Mary Ann Crawford Crawford were the parents of the only Columbia County-born Georgia chief executive: George Walker Crawford. He was schooled partly at home and at the Kiokee Academy and graduated from Princeton University. His early life was a bit impaired by the duel in 1828 when he killed Thomas Burnside, a congressman who had criticized George's father. He tried to make amends for the duel tragedy by sending money privately to the Burnside family.

It appears that George Crawford developed a large estate from various professional and commercial business interests. He was the law partner of Henry Harford Cumming at one point and had extensive property holdings in Columbia and Richmond counties. For example, the 1874 map of Summerville by W. C. Jones depicts a substantial swath of land extending from the street "Battle Row" through what is now Gardner Street and on down Milledge Road including land of today's Augusta Country Club and the property directly across Milledge Road. This land is labeled "Crawford-Mays" on the map and abuts land then owned by H. H. Cumming

CHAPTER TWO

and now the country club and the original two golf courses. Sam Mays was the governor's son-in-law from November 1860 and was related to the Milledge family from whom this land in Summerville was purchased.

George Crawford was a Whig and elected Governor under the Whig flag. When President Zachary Taylor died in 1850 (also a Whig), Crawford resigned as secretary of war in the Taylor cabinet and returned to Augusta. He then resumed what has been called in the local press "a highly profitable law practice."

On the personal family side, George W. Crawford probably "married up" as his bride was Mary Ann Macintosh, born in Savannah and the daughter of John Macintosh and Mary McKinne. Four children were bestowed on this couple with the second one, Sarah Macintosh Crawford, eventually becoming my great-grandmother on the paternal side.

Governor Crawford is well known in Georgia amongst history/political scholars; nevertheless, his cousin, William Harris Crawford, is much more familiar on a national basis—this due to his very high-profile United States political and diplomatic career in the first half of the nineteenth century.

William Harris Crawford had a good pedigree. His mother was a Harris, and in that family there was a US senator and Tennessee governor. He was born in Amherst County, Virginia, in 1771 with his family moving to the Edgefield District, South Carolina, near Augusta and then to Appling in Columbia County, Georgia. William Harris Crawford was schooled at

Carmel and Richmond Academies, and in 1798 was rector of Richmond Academy.

Crawford studied law, passed the bar, and opened law offices in 1799 in Lexington, Georgia. He was elected to the state legislature by the Democratic-Republican Party and then elected to the US Senate in 1807 by the legislature. Crawford seems to have been an influential US senator, becoming president pro tempore in 1811. After Vice President George Clinton died in 1812, he became acting vice president.

William Harris Crawford, from his picture, was a ruggedly handsome giant of a man for his era at 6'3" tall and weighing over 200 pounds. Possessed of very regular features, clear blue eyes, and being active physically, he had a fine, logical mind. He married Susanna Girardin and purchased property near Lexington, actually two and a half miles from the town center in 1804. His home was named Woodlawn. The new wife was called a "planter's daughter" in news reports.

His Washington career must have been spectacular with a rapid rise to prominence, for one very influential backer was Albert Gallatin, long-time treasury secretary for both Jefferson and Madison. Crawford helped Gallatin with the passage of legislation in the senate relative to the National Bank Charter by giving a lucid, well-regarded speech. President Madison then in April 1813 appointed Crawford minister to the Imperial Court at St. Cloud outside Paris, France. This was in the final stage of Napoleon Bonaparte's First Empire.

CHAPTER TWO

Crawford's interest in commerce was one reason for the appointment to Paris. This era was difficult due to the War of 1812 when British cruisers were blockading US ports. The United States also wanted an indemnity from France relative to our grievances of violence against American shipping interests and a favorable commercial treaty.

William Harris Crawford did not speak French; however, he had the friendship of General Lafayette who briefed him often on local French politics. Soon after his arrival in Paris, Lafayette came to dinner; Crawford recorded that he "looked younger than he was," was very cheerful, and spoke of the United States with warmth and affection. LaFayette of course spoke and wrote English; he had named a son George Washington Lafayette.

Mme. De Stael, daughter of former French Finance Minister Necker from the "ancient regime," is said to have liked Minister Crawford who very likely was present at Crawford's salon receptions. She also was fluent in English. Crawford appears to have been rather internationally admired in general during his embassy. And who has not heard the oft-told tale that he was the only foreign envoy to whom Emperor Napoleon I himself had felt compelled to bow? Napoleon too must have been impressed with the American's height and poise.

Crawford performed his tasks in France abundantly well, even expertly, and then resigned his post in 1815 shortly following the end of the War of 1812. While sailing for America, President Madison named the returning envoy minister of war in his cabinet. Crawford moved on to secretary of the treasury in October 1816 where he remained until resigning in March 1825 at the end of the Monroe presidency. His first job at Treasury was to deal with what then was the huge national debt of $12 million incurred by the 1812 war. It was reported that general business and industry revived under his leadership and policy proposals.

In the February 13, 1978, issue of *The New Yorker* magazine ran section II of a profile on Georgia entitled "From Rabun Gap to Tybee Light." The year 1978 was of course a Jimmy Carter period, so the profile aimed to convey a sense of Georgia from the mountains to the sea for the reader. The article also pointed out that Georgian William Harris Crawford at one time was a politician who expected to be elected president of the United States.

Crawford very likely could have succeeded Madison in 1817, but, says *The New Yorker*, at the president's suggestion he agreed to let James Monroe take the job first, for the Georgian contender was only forty-four and could surely wait his turn! However, the best laid plans can often go astray, and Crawford suffered a serious stroke in September of 1823. His health did improve, so by 1824 he apparently was well enough to run even though "many canards" had been spread about relative to his real health. Hence, Jackson, Adams, and Clay wanted to run in November, and in the election Crawford finished only third behind John Quincy Adams and Andrew Jackson even though former Presidents Madison and Thomas Jefferson supported him. Albert Gallatin also endorsed him and agreed to run as the vice-presidential candidate.

CHAPTER TWO

As none of the candidates received a majority in the Electoral College, the matter was thrown into the House of Representatives where Clay, the powerful speaker, threw his strength to Adams who won the victory.

The newly elected President Adams offered Crawford the Treasury cabinet post in the new administration, but the incumbent declined. He then made plans to return to Georgia where on his arrival it is said towns vied in receiving him with a returning hero's welcome home. He went back to Woodlawn where his health improved; he then accepted a State Superior Court judgeship from Governor Troup at an annual salary of $3,000. The appointment was to the bench of the Northern Georgia Circuit.

Crawford continued as an active judge until his death on September 15, 1834. He was buried in the Crawford family cemetery at Woodlawn.

Governor George W. Crawford is supposed to have said, "The American Crawfords never forgot the Scotchman's prayer that they might not have a good opinion of themselves."

Three footnotes to the above:

1. Tony Aeck, Atlanta architect and husband of Frank Mays Hull, Judge for the Federal Appeals Court 11th Circuit, had the contract to renovate the former State Capitol Building at Milledgeville where Governor Crawford served four years. Judge Hull is the great-great-great-granddaughter of the governor on her mother's side.
2. When LaFayette made his final trip to the United States 1824-1825, the general came to call on

William H. Crawford in Washington, DC. They visited for three hours. One report is that Crawford refused to remove his hat at one reception for Lafayette hosted by President Monroe; this was attributed to his recent illness.

To show the appreciation for the services of Lafayette during our war with the British Crown, Congress during his visit voted to award the general $200,000 plus a so-called township of 24,000 acres with 6 percent interest to be paid on the cash. The township was a section of Tallahassee, Florida, which was incorporated as a city in 1825. The US Congress apparently hoped Lafayette or his descendants would reside there at times. However, Lafayette sold the land for $100,000 in 1827 to speculators.

3. Lafayette journeyed to the United States on the *Cadmus*, an American frigate bound for New York. He landed in August 1824. Also on board was another Georgian, John P. King, and he became friendly with the Lafayette party consisting of the general, his son George Washington, and secretary M. Levasseur. A valet also was included.

The Lafayette party reached Augusta from Savannah on March 23, 1825. They found there their friend from the *Cadmus*, John P. King. King was helpful in sending back to France all the gifts collected as well as extra personal effects not needed for the rough journey through Georgia and Alabama to New Orleans.

CHAPTER TWO

__MAYSES:__

In the late 1950s/early 1960s my Aunt Louise Mays Bussey began to study her family origins; she already knew much regarding her Phinizy-born mother but far less relative to the Hamilton, Yancey, and Mays antecedents. One day she drove out to the Belair area of Richmond County where many of the Crawford/Mays families once lived; she was looking for the site of her Grandfather Mays's land and house. She approached an old gentleman as he sat resting on the verandah of his country house. Did he know the Mays family who once owned many acres of farmland in the area? "Of course," the elderly man replied. "I knew all of them and not one of them was worth a damn!"

While the old man's rejoinder was very amusing, it does bring up the age-old debate relative to a family's social and business status: whether such in the final analysis just depends on money or ancestors reaching back for countless generations? In the Mays case it appears the financial position in our branch was rather parlous by the twentieth century while the family tree in America of ancestors goes far back to the early seventeenth century. There is even a legitimate coat of arms from the line of Reverend William Mays (Mease) of Virginia, the first to arrive in the future United States in 1611.

The name "Mays" has been spelled different ways: Mayes, Mayse, Mease, etc. and is thought possibly to be Dutch/English in origin. One theory advanced is that "Mays" is the modern form of the Dutch name "Maas" or "Maes" pertaining to a family living near the River

Meuse, which in Dutch is called Maas. It is documented that a number of persons with one of these Dutch appellations settled around Belfast, Ireland, and came over with William of Orange and his wife Mary (both Stuart first cousins) in 1688 when The Glorious Revolution of that year placed William and Mary on the throne of England. As there was the Hanseatic League and trading relations between Holland and England long before 1688, as well as a number of persons living in England with the Mays/Mease surname, it is obvious additional emigration had occurred direct to England years before and perhaps from what is now The Netherlands.

As I am concerned in this recollection with my own Mays genealogy and its origin, the following is an effort to trace in an interesting manner the future United States story:

1. Our side is directly descended from the Reverend William Mease who came across as part of the Virginia Company in their last party of colonists. He was an Anglican minister aged thirty-seven. The date was 1611, some eight years before the arrival of the *Mayflower* at Plymouth.

    Mease (Mays) was born in 1574 in England and was minister at the established church at Keoughton, some thirty-seven miles below Jamestown but on the same side of the river. This place is now called Hampton. St. John's is now the parish name (from circa 1830), and this church has over the years established five new mission churches. In St. John's there are memorials to the

CHAPTER TWO

early rectors (including William Mease) sent over from England by The Society for the Propagation of the Gospel.

2. William Mease (Mays) had two sons, John and Henry. We believe our branch descends from son Henry through one of his subsequent offspring again named William Mays. This William, born in Virginia, died in Lunenburg County, Virginia, about 1751. He married Mary Mattox who died after 1748. This union produced five children of whom the first, called Mattox Mays, married Dorcas Abney.

It is Mattox Mays and his wife Dorcas with whom we are concerned. Mattox died in 1773 in Halifax County, Virginia; widow Dorcas remarried William Hill and with her children, she left for the Edgefield District of South Carolina where there already were Abney relatives. The group as indicated included the youngest Mays child, Samuel, born in 1762 in Halifax County, Virginia, and also our direct ancestor.

Abneys in America descend from Abneys of Derbyshire, England. Their founder was Nigel de Albini, a brother-in-law of William The Conqueror who brought them with him to England from France in 1066. The Anglicized surname "Abney" derives from the Norman-French. There is an Abney coat of arms.

Pertinent to this story is the truth that a number of other Mayses emigrated to Virginia after the Reverend William in 1611 with also a number moving from Virginia to the Edgefield, South Carolina, District in the eighteenth century. One was a Joseph Mays from Virginia who settled Maysville, Georgia. Some say he was a brother of Samuel, the fifth child of Mattox and Dorcas; others dispute this fact.

An interesting addition, however, to our story is that Joseph Mays provides us with our Cherokee Indian connection through the marriage of his son, another Samuel Mays, to Nannie Adair. She was the daughter of Chief Wat Adair. Several of their sons also were Cherokee chiefs in the latter portion of the nineteenth century. These included Samuel Houston Mays and Joel Bryan Mays, children of Samuel and Nannie.

3. Samuel Mays married Nancy Grigsby 1793 in Edgefield District, South Carolina. He was a man of wealth and property and fathered ten children, among whom was my direct ancestor Rhydon Grigsby Mays and twin boys, Thomas Sumter and another Samuel Warren, the latter dying without issue.

Samuel Mays became brigadier general of the South Carolina forces during the War of 1812. Following the American Revolution he lived in Newberry County, was a member of the South Carolina Legislature, and a founder of South Carolina College, now the University of South Carolina. He knew General George Washington and had been directly

CHAPTER TWO

thanked by the US Congress for an act of bravery during the Revolution.

His dates were 1762-1816; he was buried in a Mays family cemetery near Greenwood, South Carolina, where he owned a large plantation. His last will also devised some 2,373 acres in Newberry District to various sons, and it speaks of additional tracts of land near the Saluda River and Edgefield District in South Carolina. Edgefield District then was far larger than today and included the Greenwood area. Sixty-three negroes were listed to go to his surviving wife and children.

4. Dr. Rhydon Grigsby Mays, fourth child of General Sam and Nancy Grigsby and my great-great grandfather, was born in 1801 and married a second cousin, Sarah Butler Smith, in 1823. She was the daughter of Luke Smith and Elizabeth Lamar. Sarah's sister Ann Lamar Smith also married Rhydon's elder brother James Butler Mays. Through the Lamars these ladies also were closely related to the John Milledge family. Georgia Governor Milledge and his wife Ann Lamar both lived in Sand Hills and are buried in Summerville Cemetery.

Contrary to the normal pattern of the family men attending the University of South Carolina, Rhydon obtained a medical degree from the University of Maryland. However, although he seems to have used the title "Doctor," we have no record of a specific medical practice. He graduated in 1823, the year of his marriage. We do know Rhydon was a strong Baptist and served as clerk of his church at Sardis; other members of the active congregation there included Smiths, Lamars, plus the Mayses.

Dr. Rhydon must have been of a pioneering spirit as he moved to Northern Florida and settled on the St. Johns River near Jacksonville. There is a story that his wife set out during the Civil War the first orange plantation in Florida. I doubt this as the Spanish were in the orange market many years back, so it is surmised the Rhydon Mays family obtained a Spanish Land Grant property already established to work and expand. Their home and property was at Orange Mills and said to be a place of beauty along the river in Putnam County. It is thought likely that the first grapefruit farm (rather than oranges) was started by the Rhydon Mays family.

By the time the Rhydon Mays family moved to Florida it must have been after 1843 when most of the Seminole Indians had departed for the Indian Territory. Nevertheless, it does appear brothers of Dr. Rhydon were also pioneering in Florida years before and probably during the Seminole Indian Wars.

We do know that Rhydon sold his Edgefield village property in 1846 for $3,500; this was the land and house purchased from William Prothro for $5,500 in 1838. The buyer was Francis H.

Wardlaw, a lawyer who drafted the South Carolina Ordinance of Secession years later. The elegant antebellum mansion was named Holmeswood by the Rainsford family who by now have owned the property for more than one hundred years.

5. The fourth child of Dr. Rhydon Mays and Sarah Butler Smith was my great-grandfather. He was Samuel Warren Mays, born May 10, 1831, in Edgefield County, South Carolina. He made a good marriage to Sarah Macintosh Crawford November 1, 1860, at her father's house in Belair, Richmond County, Georgia. Edward E. Ford, then rector of St. Paul's Church, performed the wedding ceremony. Sarah was the daughter of Georgia Governor George Walker Crawford, and her maternal grandmother was Mary McKinne. I am told the McKinnes currently occupy a rather high rung in Georgia genealogical circles!

At their marriage the bride was twenty-six and the groom twenty-nine; they produced nine children including several who died as infants and one boy who survived to age twelve. Two of the infant boys' deaths were sort of memorialized in that there were two George Crawford Mays sons and two named Rhydon Grigsby with the later and second pair living long lives. All the progeny were born at Belair, Richmond County, Georgia, where both Sam and his father-in-law owned land.

Samuel Warren Mays, being of the correct age, served as a captain in the Confederate army and appears to have retained the title after 1865. As a land owner, he farmed, and at one stage was owner of a gristmill and cotton gin in rural Richmond County. One of the original settlers of Belair was a Haitian, Mathurien Maresehal Verdery, in the 1790s; another was George W. Crawford. We know that the Verdery mill site in the late nineteenth century was owned by Sam W. Mays.

The Crawford home once stood for years near the newly constructed Dyess Parkway. The Mays couple and their children continued to live in the Crawford house until a fire partially destroyed the second and third floors which were partially rebuilt. Notwithstanding the new rebuilding, Sarah Crawford Mays apparently was unhappy with their accommodation, and a transfer to rented property on Greene Street took place in the 1890s. At this home, located at 605 Greene, Sarah took in "paying guests" at some point, and the couple left Augusta to live with sons George Crawford in Albany and Rhydon Grigsby in Thomasville probably circa 1912. These sons then were prospering in an enterprise called the Georgia Cotton Company.

Captain Sam died May 3, 1914, in Albany, Georgia, while Sarah, now largely blind, died in Thomasville, Georgia, nine months later. She then was visiting her son Rhydon. The Mays couple are buried in the Mays family plot at the Oak View Cemetery in Albany, Georgia. We visited this gravesite en route to Augusta from a "Georgia Trust Ramble" in Thomasville some years back.

6. The third child of Samuel Warren and Sarah Crawford Mays, Samuel Warren Mays, Jr., was my grandfather. Born June 6, 1865, in Belair, just after the termination of the Civil War in April, he spent most of his life in the Augusta/Belair vicinity except for his later work in Thomasville, Georgia, as a cotton factor, around the date of his marriage to Harriet Bowdre Phinizy. The wedding took place February 12, 1896, at the Phinizy House, 519 Greene Street, in Augusta. The rector of St. Paul's Church did the honors followed by a supper party at a number of round tables at the residence.

Hattie's family did not want this marriage. For starters, Sam was eight years older and by age thirty-one had not achieved what could be called a business success. Although Hattie's mother was well off, the bride still had but little in her own name; this situation spoke loud and clear that her mother's lawsuit against her paternal grandfather was a colossal mistake in retrospect. The case is discussed in detail elsewhere in these recollections and must be considered a pyrrhic victory at best.

Sam certainly was a popular man about town, playing a guitar and singing tenor, presumably with a good voice as he was cited at the Stires/Hardwick wedding in 1894 at Good Shepherd Church. However, he must have had little business drive, for his Thomasville cotton venture did not prosper, and by the early 1900s the couple had returned to Augusta where they separated. Hattie Phinizy Mays with her two Mays children then lived at 519 Greene Street and Sam probably with his parents at 605 Greene. There was no divorce; Sam died at age forty-one on June 13, 1906, still separated, although it is thought Hattie and her mother were considering a divorce before they learned (from lawyer Hamilton Phinizy) that her husband was very seriously ill.

Samuel Warren Mays, Jr. was buried at the Summerville Cemetery on his grandfather George W. Crawford's plot.

When my late youngest brother was born February 8, 1937, ten years after my own birth, there was much discussion about his name, i.e. what should it be? My mother Frank wanted a second girl, whom she intended to name Mary Del'aigle for her late Doughty sister; hence, she more or less put the decision in Bowdre's hands.

One idea was Benjamin Yancey, my father's great-grandfather and the beloved father of Mary Lou Yancey Phinizy who essentially raised my father. He had always called Mary Lou "mother" and not "grandmother." He also knew and was fond of great uncle Hamilton Yancey, her only brother, and called him Uncle Ham. When consulted, "Auntie" (Mary Lou Phinizy) favored Benjamin Yancey (her grandfather) or perhaps Charles Phinizy Mays (after her father), but at the time there already were two other Charles Phinizys living in Augusta!

The final decision taken was to honor his own father, Samuel Warren Mays, Jr., even though Bowdre barely remembered him, being but five years old when he died. However, he had been a jovial sort, and my father's sense of family may have prevailed. Perhaps it also was time to name a child after the father's side of the family!

7. The two children of Sam and Hattie were 1. Louise Mays Bussey (1897-1966) and 2. Bowdre Phinizy Mays (1901-1975). Their stories have been well covered in Chapters III and VII of this work.

Our branch of the Mays family only has two younger male descendants, my nephews Samuel Warren Mays, Jr. and Stedman Clark Mays, Jr, both unmarried. Hence, the surname Mays may disappear in our branch; although, our daughter, Katherine Mays Bunker, did use it as a middle name for her young son, Alexander Mays Bunker. I trust this may continue for, as this account reveals, the Mays do have an interesting ancestry over the past four centuries in the "New World."

END

Special Note:
Much of the information relative to the Mays Family in America originated from Erick Montgomery who is the husband of my cousin, Laurie, his charming wife. She is the direct descendant of George Crawford Mays, younger brother of Samuel Warren Mays, my grandfather. Additional data was compiled from the 1929 book *Genealogy of the Mays and Related Families* by Samuel Edward Mays of Plant City, Florida.

B.P.M.

CHAPTER TWO

__ HAMILTONS/YANCEYS:

In this section discussing family roots and origins, I finally decided to combine this segment, as on the Phinizy side the Mayses are related to all the three families. This is because Sarah Paris Hamilton married Benjamin Cudworth Yancey in 1846 in Athens, Georgia. That couple became the parents of Mary Lou Yancey, who married two Phinizy cousins and was my great-grandmother. As Aunt Mary Lou Phinizy, the only child by her second Phinizy marriage, often used to say to various relatives: "We are related on both sides." In particular, this comment also pertains to the Garys, Irvine Phinizy, and Doris descendants. The following elaborates.

Our Hamilton branch descends from one Captain James Hamilton, born in Ireland, who married Anne Fox Napier of Albermarle County, Virginia. Their marriage date was March 15, 1782, in Fluvanna County, Virginia. The two sons of this union were Thomas Napier Hamilton and James Fox Hamilton; both were born, I assume, in Columbia County, Georgia, as the Hamilton and Napier families had left Virginia and then put roots down as planters in Columbia County.

James Hamilton died in 1817 in Columbia County with his last will "proved" on November 17, 1817. He had been judge of Land Court, Richmond County, Georgia, in 1785 and sheriff of Columbia County in 1793. His wife, née Anne Fox Napier, also died in the same county. Through her Napier relatives Anne Fox too was descended from the Claiborne family of Virginia as her grandfather Patrick Napier had married Martha Claiborne in Virginia.

When James Hamilton's will was proved he left land to his sons and negroes (not called slaves) and still owned 1,000 acres of Ohio land. Peter Crawford with the two sons were the executors.

The two Hamilton sons appear to have married well: Thomas Napier in 1814 to Sarah Sherwood Bugg and James Fox to Eliza Frances Harriss circa 1828. It is Thomas Napier and spouse Sarah Bugg from whom my side descends.

Thomas and wife Sarah had a home called Woodville Plantation, Columbia County, and another residence in Athens. Thomas was an early student at UGA, graduating in 1807; thereafter he attended a law school in Connecticut. He seems to have been a successful man of business affairs. A founder of the Georgia Railroad Bank in Augusta, a promoter of the Georgia Railroad, a Georgia state representative in the legislature, and a trustee of UGA. He and Sarah were the parents of six children. We are concerned here only with the third child, Sarah Paris, for she married my great-great-grandfather Benjamin C. Yancey. Hence, this recollection relative to the Yancey/Hamilton combination will follow.

One final amusing point is the truth that to be eligible for Colonial Dames membership, ladies in my paternal family appear to have employed their Hamilton/Napier ancestors, namely one Thomas Napier, born in 1745 Albemarle County, Virginia, and died in Columbia

CHAPTER TWO

County, Georgia in 1804. He had been a justice of the peace and was commissioned a colonel in Virginia being then considered an eligible ancestor for descendants! These appointments pertain to Albemarle and Fluvanna Counties.

Now to the Yancey particulars: Benjamin Cudworth Yancey, a lawyer and US minister to Argentina, was born in Charleston, South Carolina, on April 27, 1817. He was the son of Benjamin Cudworth and Caroline (née Bird) Yancey whose antecedents came to South Carolina from Massachusetts (the Cudworths and Birds) and Culpeper County, Virginia (Yanceys who had come over from Wales in 1642). B.C. Yancey was a relative of "Charles of Buckingham," a Virginia Yancey who owned a large landed property and was very active in public life.

Young Yancey attended school at Mt. Zion Academy in Hancock County, Georgia, a school at Troy, New York, and graduated with honor from the University of Georgia in 1836. He completed his education with a B. L. degree from Yale Law School in 1837. Then to Alabama where he became master in chancery in 1838 for seven counties. Together with his brother, William Lowndes Yancey, he was the co-editor of the *Wetumpha Gazette* circa 1840. Later he settled at Hamburg, South Carolina, practiced law, and served for several terms in the South Carolina legislature. During this period B. C. Yancey owned much of the present North Augusta land; it was here in the Yancey house on the highest point of the North Augusta hill where the first child to Benjamin and his wife, Sarah Paris Hamilton, arrived September

27, 1848. The little boy was named Hamilton Yancey; apparently there was no middle appellation.

In researching the life of Benjamin, I found that there had been a first marriage to a lady named Laura Hines at Sparta, Georgia; there was a daughter born named Caroline (but always known as Caro), and her mother died soon afterward. Caro was born July 2, 1844; she wed Dr. Hugh H. Harris, son of the Alabama congressman Samson W. Harris. Caro of course was named for her Yancey grandmother, Caroline. The Harris union produced two girls and two boys. The oldest, Cousin Sallie, I met as a kid when she came to stay with her cousin Mary Lou Phinizy. Cousin Sallie was then an old lady afflicted with a sort of somnolence; she would break off in the middle of a conversation and then sleep for a bit! This was rather disconcerting even though she always came back after a minute or so and continued on with the conversation!

The second and last child of Benjamin and Sarah Paris Hamilton Yancey was a girl christened Mary Lou and born at their Cherokee County, Alabama, farm called Walnut Bluff on March 27, 1851. Yancey had purchased this property near the Coosa River in 1850. In a log house, four rooms and a hall, the new baby arrived. During the following year, 1852, Sarah Paris's father, Thomas N. Hamilton, sent carpenters and brick layers from Columbia County who built a substantial two-story house for his daughter. This home was burned in 1864 by the federal army under Sherman. According to the last will of Benjamin Yancey, this farm property had

CHAPTER TWO

been purchased actually by his father-in-law, Thomas Napier Hamilton, and was devised to his wife, Sarah Paris, née Hamilton.

The Benjamin Yanceys next lived in Atlanta until September 1858 when Benjamin accepted President Buchanan's appointment as resident minister to Argentina. He resigned and returned home December 1859 "due to the unexpected death of his father-in-law" as recorded later by son Hamilton Yancey. The *Dictionary of Alabama Biography* states that Benjamin Yancey declined also an offer from the president "through Secretary Cass" of the appointment as resident minister to the Court of St. James's in London.

Joseph B. Cumming in his memoir *Reminiscences 1893-1983* comments somewhat incorrectly on the supposed appointment to the Court of St James's and confused Benjamin C. Yancey with his political and more notorious brother William Lowndes Yancey. The fact is that William L. Yancey did travel to London in early 1861 and was there just before the Fort Sumter battle that began the Civil War. He was sent as the Confederate government's envoy by the Davis government, formed in February 1861 at Montgomery, Alabama. I am told Yancey was received by Lord John Russell, the British statesman and then foreign secretary. There will be a bit more on William L Yancey and his career following for this Yancey indeed was an interesting character!

A March 5, 1972, article in the Birmingham, Alabama, newspaper captioned "Then and Now" compared William L Yancey, nineteenth-century orator to

George Corley Wallace, his twentieth-century equivalent as a political firebrand. In 1858-1860 during the run up to the national political convention of 1860, Yancey condemned "a mass of wrongs" with his belief that a rupture of the Union was preferable to obstructing the expansion of slavery westward. Stephan L Douglas, the Yancey oratorical opponent, insisted that new western states must decide the issue. Douglas was the "champion of popular sovereignty," hence, both slavery (i.e. race) and bussing to desegregate schools in 1972 arose from old issues in effect showing once more how history tends to repeat itself!

William L. Yancey still was in London as a Confederate commissioner with Messrs. Dudley Mann and Pierre Rostas, the quasi-ambassadors of the Confederacy to England and France, when the British mail steamer *Trent* was stopped by the federal U.S.S. *San Jacinto* November 8, 1861. New commissioners John Slidell (headed to Paris) and James Mason (assigned to London) were kidnapped on the high seas which, as is well known, Britannia ruled! Slidell and Mason were held as prisoners of war at Fort Warren in Boston.

Prime Minister Palmerston and Foreign Secretary Lord Russell wanted to send a tough ultimatum: release these men at once or we will withdraw our ambassador from Washington. This of course, in those days at least, could lead to war! Although Queen Victoria is said to have described the Federalists as "ruffians," Prince Albert redrafted the note to Washington and toned it down considerably by offering to negotiate.

CHAPTER TWO

Slidell and Mason were released and continued their journey to Europe. Meantime, Mrs. Slidell saved all the Confederate documents carried (letters of credence) by hiding them inside her crinoline!

Contrary to their public stance, both British and French governments met privately with the Confederate envoys. Following the early Confederate victories in the war, both England and France actively considered recognition; the English encouraged naval construction for the relatively non-existent Confederate navy, and John Slidell was received by Emperor Napoleon III after the *Trent* incident.

The Georgian Robert Toombs was the first Confederate secretary of state. He had first been a US congressman and senator (1844-1861), was a truculent orator, and had visited many European statesmen during a 1855 sojourn to England and the continent. Toombs was an ardent admirer of the British constitutional monarchy; in camera at Montgomery in early 1861, it is thought he made very positive statements relative to the favorable attitude of the European governments. Hence, the missions of Yancey, Slidell, and Mason, etc.

While William L. Yancey remained in London until the first part of 1862 (about one year of residence), his brother, Benjamin, enlisted in the Confederate army in 1861 as captain of the Fulton Dragoons and was later named major of Cobbs Legion. Benjamin participated in the Virginia campaign and subsequently was appointed colonel in Georgia of state troops.

Due to the Confederate War conditions in 1861, the Yancey Atlanta home was sold with the family moving to Athens where Hamilton relatives lived. The two children by Sarah Paris Hamilton entered Lucy Cobb School (Mary Lou) and the University of Georgia (Hamilton). The latter was member of Chi Phi Fraternity and in the well-known class of 1868.

Eventually Benjamin Yancey and family left Athens post-Civil War and moved to Floyd County where he established Cloverdale Farm, near Rome, Georgia. Sarah Paris Yancey, née Hamilton, outlived her husband who died in Rome October 24, 1891. The Yanceys must have left Athens for the Rome area circa the early 1870s as daughter Mary Lou, after schooling further in Staunton, Virginia, married the eldest son of Ferdinand Phinizy II in Athens on January 23, 1870.

The Benjamin Yancey career, aside from his real estate and planting interests, also involved public service as he served as trustee of the University of Georgia 1860-1886, president of the Georgia Agricultural Society 1867-1891, and served one term as representative of Clark County in the Georgia Legislature. His beloved second daughter, Mary Lou Yancey Phinizy, wrote that his golden motto was "Duty without fear." His widow Sarah Paris lived on another year; she passed away at her daughter's country home at Grovetown, Columbia County, October 4, 1892. It was written of Sarah: "Blessed are the pure in heart for they shall see God."

The Benjamin Yancey final will devised all to his wife and children. Assets included real estate in Atlanta,

CHAPTER TWO

Alabama, Rome, etc., with bonds and equity shares in various railroads and enterprises. The Cloverdale Farm near Rome was a legacy to Mary Lou and Hamilton, his children by Sarah.

Hamilton Yancey known in our family as Uncle Ham apparently spent most of his adult life in Athens and Rome. Hamilton married Florence Patterson with whom seven children were born, three boys and four girls. One daughter was Claire (or Clare) Yancey Clark married to Austin Clark. Aunt Mary Lou Phinizy and I lunched with them in the fall 1948 at the St. Regis Hotel in New York City after having met them earlier the same day by chance. My mother Frank remembered Uncle Ham as a "charming old gentleman with a large white mustache." By 1931 Uncle Ham was acting as an agent in Rome for the prominent English property, marine, and casualty insurance company Commercial Union Assurance Company, Ltd. The business was conducted by The Hamilton Yancey Insurance Agency, Inc. from 209 N. Broad Street. The Yancey family was also shareholders of the Rome Fire Insurance Company where at one time Hamilton was an officer (titled secretary) for this enterprise. Today, however, the Yanceys appear best known in Rome for their former residence located at 906 E. 2nd Avenue. The main house is called Claremont.

Claremont was one of the first houses built in East Rome; it has been an upscale bed and breakfast for many years but first was lovingly restored for Mr. and Mrs. Charles C. Shaw who acquired Claremont in

1967. The Rome Area Heritage Foundation gave the Shaws an award in 1979, and the Georgia Trust honored them as well in 1981 for their outstanding restoration accomplishments.

Claremont is an elegant example of Victorian Gothic or what one can call Second Empire. It is now listed on the National Historic Register. Construction began circa 1878 on the cottage behind the main home; here the Yancey family lived until completion of the mansion about 1882. While Hamilton Yancey certainly lived here a large part of his life and definitely was closely involved in the buildings construction, some reports state his father, Benjamin, too was one of the builders.

A silver urinal (hidden in the wall) was incorporated on the first floor; I have not yet determined if sterling or plated-silver! There is also a large safe built into one wall of the entrance hall. Presumably this was needed in the early days when the address was a distance from the town center and there did not exist a bridge across the Etowah River.

Hamilton appears to have been known also as Colonel Yancey; if this title dates to the Civil War it is doubtful as Hamilton was but seventeen when the conflict ended. Perhaps he was in some sort of National Guard? He and his wife are described as possessing very polished manners and to-the-manner-born poise, courtesy, and graciousness to one and all. They are said to have been famous hosts with Hamilton ever gallant. On July 28, 1885, the Hamilton Yanceys hosted the second wedding of his beloved widowed sister, Mary Lou Yancey

CHAPTER TWO

Phinizy, to her second Phinizy, Charles Henry, in the library of Claremont.

One remaining work in progress relative to the Hamilton family is the subject matter in the two Hamilton oil paintings Mary Lou Phinizy gave in her will to our cousin Bert Gary. He had them cleaned, repaired as needed, and hung in his Augusta house. On the backs of the old gold leaf frames, Bert pasted labels—James Fox Hamilton and Emily Bowdre Hamilton—to designate the subject matter. As Mary Lou's mother was a descendant of Thomas Napier Hamilton, why would the Phinizy branch have the James Fox portrait? We have learned, however, that James did have a first wife named Emily Bowdre. Hence, the James Fox Hamilton descendants could have passed them on considering the Bowdre descendancy of Mary Lou Yancey's first husband and his given name Ferdinand Bowdre. We have seen photographs of the portraits and compared these with another Hamilton picture of James in the possession of Osborne Phinizy Mackie. It is not certain if the portrait matches! Bert's daughter, Laura Van Geffen, now owns these two paintings which are hung in her Maryland home.

The Yancey Family archives and papers were given to the Southern Historical Collection at the University of North Carolina Library, Chapel Hill, North Carolina. That collection includes all details relative to Benjamin's appointment as US minister to Argentina and, I believe, the William L. Yancey papers too. I gave two framed steel engravings of B. C. Yancey to the library in 2006.

Note: From Rome, Georgia, Margaret Mackie Wimberly and Marian Shaw very kindly sent data relative to the former Yancey house Claremont.

B.P.M.

CHAPTER TWO

__PHINIZYS: As I wrote in the preface, these recollections are not intended to be any genealogical study. Hence, in this Phinizy section I will deal mainly with the life and times of the grandson of the Italian "immigrante," Ferdinand Phinizy I. My rationale in this regard is threefold: 1. Rather complete family genealogical data already has been printed in the 1925 book *The Phinizy Family in America* by Ferdinand Phinizy Calhoun (a great-great-grandson of the "immigrante") and by the former's son F. Phinizy Calhoun, Jr. M.D., who in 1991 gave us *Grandmother Was a Phinizy*. This last book is a complete registry of Phinizy descendants and their allied families up to early 1990. 2. The second reason to focus now on the Italian's namesake and grandson, Ferdinand Phinizy II, who was the first child of Jacob and first son of the immigrant, is due to the truth that through two wives and eleven children most of these numerous descendants, living around Athens, Atlanta, and Augusta, are known to the writer. 3. And finally, Ferdinand Phinizy II was my great-great-grandfather and quite a strong and interesting character; he definitely appears worthy of our attention.

Ferdinand Phinizy I and his first wife, Margaret Condon, had five children: Sarah Phinizy, Jacob Phinizy, Eliza Phinizy, John Phinizy, and Marco Phinizy. There was no issue from the second wife, and it was a very brief marriage; however, all of the five direct descendants listed produced offspring.

To place the known descendants of Ferdinand Phinizy I, his first son Jacob and namesake/grandson

179

Ferdinand Phinizy II, in full perspective, in 2007 the total descendants from all five branches totaled 1,152; of that sum 716 pertain to Jacob with many of these directly descended from the eleven children of Ferdinand Phinizy II.

In January 1949, Dr. Ferdinand Phinizy Calhoun, the eminent eye surgeon from Atlanta, established at the University of Georgia The Ferdinand Phinizy Lectureship with an endowment as a memorial to his maternal grandfather, Ferdinand Phinizy II. Our Calhoun kinsman was a UGA alumnus, class of 1900. Through 2009 there have been nineteen lectures featuring many notables such as Harold Medina (1956), Eugene Black (1961), J. K. Galbraith (1968), Erskine Caldwell (1995), Walker Percy (our Phinizy kinsman 1978), Dean Rusk (1983), Jon Meacham (2007), and Richard Ford in September 2009. The lecture series held every few years is also the occasion for a family reunion. At the 2007 gathering in Athens, sixty-seven of the ninety-one persons present descended from first son Jacob and his son, Ferdinand Phinizy II.

The gift Dr. F. Phinizy Calhoun made to the University of Georgia Foundation consisted of real property. This property, when sold, was the basis for the endowment. The current approximate lectureship balance is about $175,000. In recent years, the lectureship occasion also has become our ideal venue for a Phinizy family reunion and several social events.

Through the years the former younger generations have become, as usually the case, more interested in their Phinizy ancestors (even if their surnames differ) so that apart from the formal lectures held in Athens at the university every two or three years, there have been very enjoyable trips to the Mississippi Delta, Augusta, Atlanta, and to the first home of Ferdinand Phinizy I near Lexington, Georgia, and named China Grove.

The continuing "Phinizy Phamily" reunion activity provides a sort of glue to keep the family together in the years ahead. For this we all must give a vote of thanks to our kinsmen Dr. F. Phinizy Calhoun, Sr. and Jr. and one also to the late Phinizy Spalding, his nephew John Phinizy Spalding, and those who serve on the latter's active committee.

In the family there always has been discussion relative to the origin of the name Phinizy (obviously neither Italian nor French although the immigrant fought on the American side with Rochambeau in the Revolution); several kinfolk, including myself, have been to Parma, situated in Northern Italy, in an effort to locate persons bearing that name. We only could find locals with surnames like Finici, Finizzi, or Finisee. Obviously then "Phinizy" is the Anglicization of his original name. While Parma always was said to have been the birthplace of F.P.I., his trunk brought to America had a "made in Naples" label. We do know he spoke French also; this he probably learned in Italy and improved during a period in France prior to joining the regiment ordered to America under Lafayette's supreme command. One conjecture is that the first Ferdinand actually came from a suburb of Naples called Palma Campagna. This is a story still to be continued!

In 1991, F. Phinizy Calhoun, Jr. recorded in his registry of descendants that a biography of Ferdinand Phinizy I was in preparation. I do not think this ever was completed, but in it "Phin" wanted to discuss all these unanswered questions relating to names, place of birth, etc. Hence, this is a work in progress.

Turning now to the facts on Ferdinand Phinizy II. His dates are January 20, 1819, to October 20, 1889. He was born at Bowling Green (now called Stephens) near Crawford, Georgia, in Oglethorpe County. As his Uncle John Phinizy then owned China Grove (residence of his grandfather), he likely was born in a separate dwelling occupied by his father, Jacob. Attending a local county school initially, he moved with his family to Athens where he began as a student at Franklin College. This college became the University of Georgia. F. P. II studied here for three years, graduating with honor in the 1838 class. A picture of the Jacob Phinizy residence in Athens is found in the 1925 book *The Phinizy Family in America* between pages seventy and seventy-one.

Our hero then turned to business pursuits, managing his father's plantation at Bowling Green followed by a contract from the Georgia Railroad to grade the first eleven miles from Athens to Augusta. This work was reputed to have been his first business success.

A move to Augusta soon ensued. With relatives and a college friend he was to be busy trading cotton for many years; the first firm was Phinizy and Clayton and later a

CHAPTER TWO

cotton partnership with his cousins Charles H. Phinizy and Joseph Morse Burdell. The partnership was called F. Phinizy & Co. Even after retirement and moving back to Athens years later, he continued to back several other Phinizy cotton houses—i.e., F. B. Phinizy, C. H. Phinizy, and Phinizy & Co., all situated in Augusta.

Aside from cotton, F. P. II was active as a director and shareholder in various railroads, several banks including Georgia Railroad and Banking Co., the Augusta Factory, and Southern Mutual Insurance Company. He introduced Southern Mutual to Augusta and became its first resident agent. The successor company to that F. Phinizy & Co. agency is known today as Dawson, Taylor & Company and is owned/managed by a Phinizy-Burdell descendant.

F. P. II met his first wife, Harriet Hays Bowdre, in Augusta. They were married February 22, 1849, when the groom was thirty and his bride twenty in a Methodist ceremony officiated by the Rev. Dr. Means. The picture I have of the bridal pair depicts the couple in evening/wedding attire, the bride with a lace veil on her head and wearing what is called a jewelry suite of necklace, bracelet, and brooch probably of pearls and diamonds. The marriage from all accounts was harmonious and free of discord. There were seven sons and one daughter born to the couple, all of whom lived to maturity. In order of birth:

1. Ferdinand Bowdre (my great-grandfather), 1850

2. Stewart, 1851
3. Leonard, 1854
4. Mary Louise, the sole girl and a F. P. II favorite! 1855 (her nickname was Lula, and a town/railroad stop in North Georgia was named for her!)
5. Jacob II (named for his grandfather), 1857
6. Marion Daniel (known as a grown-up as Uncle Manny. Always had a supply of beaten biscuits in his pockets; looked after by his older brother Jacob as it seems Uncle Manny did not deal from a full deck!), 1859
7. Billups (obviously named for F. P. II's sister Sarah who married a Billups from Virginia and later Mississippi), 1861
8. Harry Hays, born February 4, 1863, with his mother dying three days later!

We do not know what suddenly caused the death of Harriet Bowdre Phinizy three days following the arrival of Harry Hays, the eighth child and undoubtedly named for his mother but in a masculine sense. She was but thirty-four years old; her own mother, another Harriet, also died very young, not quite twenty-nine in age. At some point after his father-in-law's death in 1856, F. P. II had the bodies of Hays and Harriet Bowdre moved from Magnolia Cemetery in Augusta to the Phinizy plot at Oconee Cemetery in Athens.

CHAPTER TWO

F. P. II, in addition to pleasing his wife, must have had sympathetic feelings for his in-laws for he continued to provide affidavits or funds to pay taxes in Ohio to the Hays Bowdre illegitimate descendants following Hays's own demise. These details are fully reported in the Bowdre section of this book.

While F. P. II did not bear arms in our Civil War, he served as "finance agent" of the Confederacy, sold many Confederate bonds to raise funds, and participated in running cotton to Europe through the Union blockade. When hostilities began in 1861, he was already forty-two years of age. F. P. Calhoun in the 1925 account states that F. P. II "lost heavily" by the failure of the Confederate armies. Nevertheless, it is likely this shrewd Southern ancestor who had accomplished so much in business by the time of the war must have hedged his bets, as it were, so that by the end in 1865, he still had access to gold and US currency among other assets. Then there was cotton, and I wager he had a stored supply ready to trade immediately through former business connections in Augusta, New York City, and abroad.

We do not know if F. P. II moved to Augusta to separate himself and children further from the fighting in North Georgia and the 1864 siege of Atlanta. I think it likely some time was spent in Augusta where he had family and business interests continuing during hostilities. Could it have been at this period when he met Anne Barrett or renewed her acquaintance, assuming, as is quite possible, they had been introduced in prior years? Anne was the daughter of Thomas and Savannah

Glascock Barrett, prominent Augustans who had family connections also in Athens. It is even quite conceivable F. P. II and Anne had met long before in Athens. Anne Barrett had been married to a Mr. Davis; that union was terminated, and there was no issue. In any event, Anne and F. P. II married August 11, 1865, the bride being thirty-one and the groom forty-six years old.

The new Phinizy couple were blessed with three children: first a little girl, Savannah Barrett Phinizy, in September 1872; then a boy, Barrett Phinizy, arrived in August 1874; followed by the last child, Charles Henry Phinizy, in December 1875. Charles was the eleventh of the F. P. II progeny. Unfortunately, the baby girl Savannah lived but nine months. In both marriages many of the children appear to have been born in Augusta, perhaps due either to the fact that both wives were from Augusta or that the better medical facilities were located there. One interesting point is that following the birth of Harriet's last child in 1863 and the second wedding with Anne Barrett in August 1865, there was a large gap of some seven years before the arrival of her first issue in 1872. During F. P. II's first marriage all eight children came at intervals of but one or two years!

Initially Anne Barrett must have been very occupied in the rearing of her step-children, for all of them in age ranged from fifteen and fourteen years down to just two years in respect to the youngest, Harry Hays. However, Harriet's grandmother, Sarah McKeene, still was living amid the family in Athens and could have been of some assistance to the numerous nurses and servants. It does

CHAPTER TWO

appear that the younger step-children, for example Jacob II, Billups and Harry, were always close to Anne who had replaced their birth mother when they were so very young.

F. P. II maintained a country house near Athens; this is pictured between pages seventy-six and seventy-seven of the 1925 Calhoun book. Otherwise the large family lived on Hill Street, then a sort of bucolic suburb of the town. The Hill Street house, now labeled No. 889, had sixty-eight acres of land then and was bordered by Hill, Cobb, and Billups Streets. Apparently the gates to the land and house once stood at Milledge Avenue. The F.P. II final will said he spent summers here.

The more spacious residence was situated on thirteen acres above Athens on the road leading to Jefferson. This he labeled as his "Home Place" and was called the "Country House" by F. P. Calhoun in his 1925 book. F. P. II also owned real estate throughout Athens, mainly commercial, some of which is described in his 1889 will. Prior to his death, however, it was reported he had sold off a quantity of real estate to achieve more liquidity through bonds, stocks, and cash at interest.

No one disputes that F. P. II indeed was a veritable "Napoleon of Finance." He had particularly large holdings in the stock of Georgia Railroad & Banking Company, to note just one name, so that by the time of his death in October 1889 he was considered one of the wealthiest gentlemen (if not the richest) in Georgia. His total estate then was estimated at about a million to $1,250,000. Much of his wealth of course originated in the cotton trade. At that period a share in Georgia

Railroad stock was valued at $200, and he owned a bundle!

While he owned a hundred slaves at war's end, he never, it seems, was burdened with the plantation problems in the new and changed environment. Business boomed, and F. P. II had ready assets to invest. He possessed great business acumen and was always considered a shrewd man of business affairs.

He never went into politics but spent his free time with his family whom he loved; also he was very proud of his ancestors, especially his mother, Matilda Stewart of Virginia, and his maternal grandmother, Mourning Floyd, who was related to the Breckenridges of Kentucky.

F. P. II gave all his children a classical education and a start in life's journey. As each child came of age, he invested in them, as it were, to give each a leg-up in life. These financial advances were as follows:

Ferdinand Bowdre	$27,000
Stewart	$68,653
Leonard	$68,507
Jacob II	$65,392
Mary Louise	$71,993
Billups	$64,693
Marion Daniel	$20,000
Harry Hays	$23,500

It was estimated that prior to his death he had distributed to his family in assets including real estate about $500,000 in values. These advances to the offspring of

CHAPTER TWO

the first wife as they came to their maturity were to be set off against the final estate tally that also included real estate individually designated. In short, the residue of the entire estate, following the specific bequests went to the <u>surviving</u> seven children of the first wife. The emphasis should be noted for I underlined "surviving" as this meant my great-grandfather's wife and two children were deliberately excluded. The reasoning for this slight is quite well known in the family and makes a rather fascinating story to be told hereinafter.

Ferdinand Bowdre, the first child, was born in 1850. He attended the University of Georgia, graduating in what is sometimes called the "famous class of 1868." The Chi Phi fraternity published in the 1906 Year Book memories of college friends by one Emory Speer relative to the 1868 class. Ferdinand Bowdre (always just called Bowdre) is described as "tall, sinewy form, clear olive complexion, high colour, penetrating eye, of Italian lineage." He wore a droopy mustache growing from the upper lip and had coal-black hair. His photo is between pages eighty-two and eighty-three of the 1925 Calhoun book.

Some other well-known personages from the class of 1868 included A. Pratt Adams of Savannah; Louis LeConte; Howell Cobb Jackson; Henry W. Grady; Hamilton Yancey who later lived in Rome, Georgia, and became Bowdre's brother-in-law; and the Honorable Peter W. Meldrin of Savannah, later state senator, Savannah mayor, judge, and always close to the Phinizy family.

Bowdre married Mary Lou Yancey in 1870; the Chi Phi piece describes her as the "toast of all the collegians, a young girl who would have been the belle of any country on earth." Bowdre died in his young manhood, aged but twenty-seven, leaving the young widow and two children, my great uncle Bowdre and grandmother Harriet.

The cause célèbre of which I wrote arose following Bowdre's early death in 1877 when his executor and father, F. P. II, refused to pay the widow Mary Lou the entire proceeds of the estate corpus which appears to have been $100,000. The investments yielded about $4,000 per annum but the executors apparently decided to withhold $2,000 as the balance was sufficient for her support. She finally brought suit to recover all the income while she remained a widow. The year was 1884, the trial in Clarke County Superior Court, Athens, Georgia, with Hon. Joseph B. Cumming and ex-Senator Pope Barrow prosecuting for Mrs. Phinizy and Messrs. Erwin and G. D. Thomas representing F. P. II. There was a jury trial of two days with the verdict to give the widow the entire net income of the estate beginning January 1, 1884.

This was probably the first and only occasion in the life of F. P. II that he had been so challenged and confronted and then lost the battle! He was furious with the press, reporting he would carry the case to a higher court! I do not think he did; however, his relationship with his daughter-in-law was broken and made doubly embarrassing when in 1885 the widow Mary Lou Yancey Phinizy married her father-in-law's first cousin! This was cousin Charles H. Phinizy, still a bachelor at age fifty and who, the story went, fell in love with her watching her deportment during the trial in Athens!

So the victor in the lawsuit in the end really earned but a pyrrhic victory as her children did not participate in the final division of the F. P. II estate. In his will he took pains to leave grandson Bowdre Phinizy only $1,000 in Georgia Railroad and Banking stock and granddaughter Harriet $2,000 of the same stock. He further stated they were children of the second degree as his grandchildren and would be well taken care of by his late eldest son's estate. Too bad she did not wait a few more years before undertaking the legal action against F. P. II for he died of Bright's disease complicated by diabetes in October 1889 following the 1884 court and jury trial.

The loss of the legal action brought by his first daughter-in-law must still have rankled when he signed his final will/testament on January 16, 1889. Due to the prominence of the parties involved, there were widespread newspaper accounts (unfavorable to F. P. II); even the venerable *New York Times* reported on the case May 24, 1884, under a banner line that read

"Georgia Social Sensation"

"Unsuccessful attempt to cheat a young and pretty widow"

Hence, five years later F. P. II still carried a deep grudge against his first daughter-in-law and certainly proved such by virtually disinheriting his first grandchildren.

Apparently he could not adopt the very Christian ethic of forgiveness notwithstanding his charity, generosity, and strong belief and interest in the Methodist Church during his later years.

Many years later it was generally agreed in our family (but probably not in the other branches who benefitted by the F. P. II meanness!) that the lawsuit was a tactical mistake. This was the opinion too of Aunt Mary Lou Phinizy (daughter of cousin Charles H. Phinizy). Another way daughter-in-law Mary Lou Yancey Phinizy exacted a non-financial reward on her own was to expunge the first name Ferdinand from her son's given name in the family Bible! Thereafter he was to be called Bowdre Phinizy only!

The F. P. II last will was handwritten and dated January 16, 1889. Sons Leonard (a lawyer) and Jacob II were named executors; Alexander Erwin of Athens was appointed counsel for the estate. The amount of $60,000 to each devised heir plus real estate to his minor sons, Barrett and Charles Henry; I presume the latter had been named for his first cousin and business partner in the cotton trade in Augusta, Charles Henry Phinizy (cousin Charlie).

There had been signed a postnuptial contract between F. P. II and his second wife, Anne Barrett Phinizy, so that by January 1889 she received $188,000 in securities from her husband. He had been given in trust $65,000 after their marriage in 1865 and had grown this principal three times approximately also paying out over the years interest as desired each year. William H.

CHAPTER TWO

Barrett, Augusta lawyer, had been the trustee for Anne relative to her estate but had resigned in favor of F. P. II on January 2, 1873. This postnup obviously had the aim of ensuring that Anne's funds not be mingled in any way with the claims of the children from the first marriage.

F. P. II was a fervent member of the Methodist Church. He preferred country parishes and in particular one near Athens called Boggs Chapel that he founded and endowed. While he was said to be friendly with the clergy of all denominations, his youngest son, Harry Hayes, wrote that "it was late in life when he gave himself publicly to the service of his Master." The last will gave legacies to several Methodist churches but only on the express condition that no music of organ or other instruments ever be played! However, he liked congregational singing, and his funeral instruction requested specific songs with the final two lines to be repeated and "lines given out in the old style, two lines at a time." It appears he wanted harmony but unassisted by organ or cornet!

The youngest son, Harry Hays Phinizy, was only twenty-six when his father died. He was living in Brunswick, Georgia, working as a journalist. Harry graduated from UGA in 1882 with an A.B.; he was a member of Kappa Alpha Fraternity and seemingly also was a lawyer and member of the Georgia Legislature in 1888. However, his father's last testament makes clear there was a problem, for his entire inheritance was passed to Harry's older brothers Leonard and Billups in trust for Harry's life term. The testator further elaborated on his decision:

"with great pain but on account of the unfortunate habits of my said son Harry." Was alcohol consumption one of these unfortunate habits?

Harry Hays Phinizy must have loved and admired his father as he wrote and published a memorial book to honor him. All the various newspaper cuttings relative to the death and subsequent funeral service and burial on the family plot at Oconee Cemetery also were included therein.

The will also makes clear that Mary Louise Phinizy Calhoun, the only daughter by the first wife, was a very particular favorite of her father. F. P. II in addition appears to have liked his son-in-law from Atlanta, Dr. Abner Wellborn Calhoun. Mary Louise's nickname in the family was Lula, and her marriage in 1877 probably was welcomed by both families. My cousin and contemporary—and Mary Louise's grandson—Calhoun Witham knew her well from his birth in 1921 and told me stories of her Atlanta life. She gave him his first car and lived on to the grand old age of ninety. Her father, in addition to the legacy of an equal share in the final residue of his estate, devised a cash sum of $10,000 not to be counted in the ultimate division—this to strongly show his devotion.

As provided in the will, the surviving seven children of the F. P. II union all received equal shares of the estate residue, personal and otherwise; such must have approximated $125,000-$150,000 to each. This added to the advances already mentioned made them all rich indeed by the standards of the late nineteenth century.

CHAPTER TWO

The F. P. II funeral on October 22, 1889, must have been massive as friends and many relatives attended the service first from the Hill Street house and then afterwards at Oconee Cemetery. Two Methodist ministers from La Grange and Atlanta officiated with thirteen more Methodist clergies seated around the casket as was the immediate family. There were orations and hymns sung just as he had instructed with a minister lining out the words of the song.

All his children had arrived before the death from Atlanta, Augusta, and Brunswick. Colonel Charles H. Phinizy (cousin Charlie), then president of the Georgia Railroad and Banking Co., left for Athens the night before the funeral in his private railroad car. Accompanying him were the close Augusta friends of F. P. II: Mr. Barney S. Dunbar, Hon. J. G. C. Black, Mr. H. H. Hickman, and Mr. James Tobin. A special engine met them at Union Point to take them on to Athens.

The funeral procession was reported as one of the largest ever seen in Athens; there were pallbearers (Reeves, Charbonnier, King, Erwin, Cobb, G. B. Thomas, to mention a few) and an honorary escort of persons from Athens, Atlanta, Augusta, etc.

One lifelong close friend, the lawyer and Confederate statesman Robert A. Toombs, was not present as he had died in 1885.

Anne Barrett Phinizy, the second widow, was about fifty-five years in age when F. P. II went to his reward. If not in that position already she rapidly became the "grande dame" of Athens society and lived many more years to age ninety in 1924. It seems that once her marital chores were finished, and being on her own to call the shots, and with plenty of money under her control, Anne kicked up her heels and did what she wanted! She bought a new house on Milledge Avenue (now occupied by the Phi Mu sorority) and liked to spend money! When in New York City with her grown son Barrett, probably in the late 1890s or early years of the twentieth century, she saw a large diamond sunburst pin in the window at the Tiffany store. They went in, and Anne decided to buy the brooch priced at $8,000. Barrett told her she did not have that sum in the bank and therefore could not afford such an expensive jewel. She bought it anyway (probably selling a bond), and Anne Barrett Segrest Freeze today has this beautiful ornament. It was worn at her Athens wedding.

Anne S. Freeze tells the story of her great-grandmother's butler/driver named Douglas who every afternoon would serve champagne to Miss Anne or the "Lady Anne" as some addressed her. This took place on her wide Milledge Avenue house porch and included those who came to call. I also read a charming account of a dinner party given by Anne Barrett Phinizy at her residence. The Georgia governor, then chairman of the University of Georgia Trustees, was the honored guest. The dinner was one of those Edwardian affairs with white wine with the fish, red wine with meats, followed by champagne taken with dessert, plus an orange rum punch at some point! Then coffee and cordials to the ladies in the parlor and to the gentlemen sitting on the long veranda. Lady Anne's nephew, Willie Barrett of Augusta, was present at this dinner as he was then a student at the university and had been asked to escort a young lady staying near by.

A poem was written to this grande dame of Athens, Georgia, as her social charms and general demeanor must have fascinated the town. With this I end my recollection of F. P. II and his life:

> **"Lady Anne"**
> When slumber first unclouds my brain
> And thought is free,
> And sense refreshed, renews her reign,
> Lady Anne, I think of thee,
> I think of thee.
> When next in prayer to God above,
> I bend my knee,
> Then when I pray for those I love,
> Lady Anne, I pray for thee,
> I pray for thee!

Notes:
1. The 1925 book by Ferdinand Phinizy Calhoun has been reprinted by Higginson Book Co., 148 Washington St., P.O. Box 778, Salem, Massachusetts, 01970, phone 978-745-7170, fax 978-745-8025.
2. Although both the 1925 and 1991 books on the Phinizy family in America refer to the F. P. II second

wife as "Anne Barrett" and her great-granddaughter, her namesake (Anne Barrett Segrest—now Freeze), was so named, the F. P. II last will and postnuptial agreement spelled the given name "Ann." I have chosen to use "Anne."

3.

George W. Crawford, Governor of Georgia 1843-1847

CHAPTER TWO

Ferdinand Phinizy II and his bride, Harriet Hays Bowdre

Ferdinand Bowdre Phinizy

Stewart Phinizy (1851-1918) second child of F.P. II and Harriet Bowdre

CHAPTER TWO

Fake Phinizy Coat of Arms featuring the monkeys of Phinizy fame. Prepared by Stewart Phinizy. Latin inscription means:
"Press on Regardless"

Phinizy descendants in a group picture at the 2009 Phinizy reunion in Athens, Georgia at UGA Chapel

CHAPTER TWO

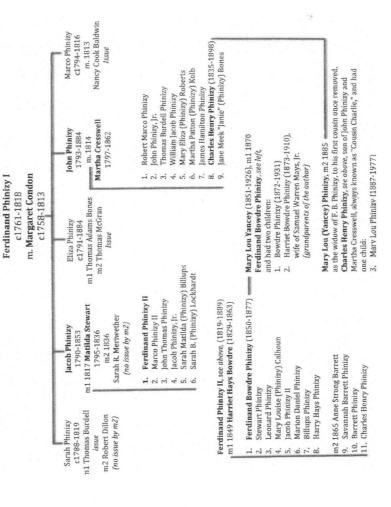

Abbreviated/Simplified Table for Immigrant Ferdinand Phinizy and Descendants

Ferdinand Phinizy I
c1761-1818
m. **Margaret Condon**
c1758-1813

Sarah Phinizy
c1788-1819
n1 Thomas Burdell
 issue
m2 Robert Dillon
(no issue by m2)

Jacob Phinizy
1790-1853
m1 1817 **Matilda Stewart**
1795-1836
m2 1836
Sarah R. Meriwether
(no issue by m2)

1. **Ferdinand Phinizy II**
2. Marco Phinizy II
3. John Thomas Phinizy
4. Jacob Phinizy, Jr.
5. Sarah Matilda (Phinizy) Billups
6. Sarah B. (Phinizy) Lockhardt

Eliza Phinizy
c1791-1884
m1 Thomas Adams Bones
m2 Thomas McGran
Issue

John Phinizy
1793-1884
m. 1814
Martha Cresswell
1797-1862

1. Robert Marco Phinizy
2. John Phinizy, Jr.
3. Thomas Burdell Phinizy
4. William Jacob Phinizy
5. Mary Eliza (Phinizy) Roberts
6. Martha Patton (Phinizy) Kolb
7. James Hamilton Phinizy
8. **Charles Henry Phinizy** (1835-1898)
9. Jane Meek "Janie" (Phinizy) Bones

Marco Phinizy
c1794-1816
m. 1813
Nancy Cook Baldwin
Issue

Ferdinand Phinizy II, *see above*, (1819-1889)
m1 1849 **Harriet Hays Bowdre** (1829-1863)

1. **Ferdinand Bowdre Phinizy** (1850-1877) ——— Mary Lou Yancey (1851-1926), m1 1870
2. Stewart Phinizy
3. Leonard Phinizy
4. Mary Louise (Phinizy) Calhoun
5. Jacob Phinizy II
6. Marion Daniel Phinizy
7. Billups Phinizy
8. Harry Hays Phinizy

m2 1865 Anne Strong Barrett
9. Savannah Barrett Phinizy
10. Barrett Phinizy
11. Charles Henry Phinizy

Ferdinand Bowdre Phinizy, *see left*,
and had two children:
1. Bowdre Phinizy (1872-1931)
2. Harriet Bowdre Phinizy (1873-1910),
   wife of Samuel Warren Mays, Jr.
   (grandparents of the author)

Mary Lou (Yancey) Phinizy, m2 1885
as the widow of F. B. Phinizy, to his first cousin once removed,
Charles Henry Phinizy, *see above*, son of John Phinizy and
Martha Cresswell, always known as "Cousin Charlie," and had
one child:
3. Mary Lou Phinizy (1887-1977)

203

CHAPTER III

519 Greene Street Menage: To the Manner Born

One fine old Phinizy House at 519 Greene Street in downtown Augusta still stands. This is the former residence of John Phinizy, and at his death passing to his son Charles Henry Phinizy. John Phinizy was the fourth child of the immigrant Ferdinand Phinizy I and lived to the advanced age of ninety-one, departing this world July 4, 1884. Charles Henry was his eighth child, born January 16, 1835. The house at 519 Greene has architectural merit and was built in the Regency or Federal style (the term most used in the United States) circa 1835-1840. The house has similar features to handsome buildings one can see still in Charleston and Savannah dating back to the early nineteenth century. Erick Montgomery of Historic Augusta believes it is very likely the design of Charles Blaney Cluskey, the architect of the Old Medical College (1835), as Cluskey, a naturalized Irishman, was then working in Augusta and, at one period, living also in Savannah.

The 1841 Augusta Directory lists John Phinizy on Greene "between Washington [now 6th Street] and Centre [5th]" so it is obvious that family was then firmly ensconced in their new home. What follows will be the story of the house and its occupants subsequent to the marriage of Charles Henry, still a bachelor and over fifty, to the widow of the groom's first cousin once removed, Ferdinand Bowdre Phinizy on July 28, 1885.

The "dramatis personae" or principals in this account are as follows:

1) Charles Henry Phinizy, known to the public and servants generally as "Colonel" due to his Confederate army military service but to all the rest of the immediate family, even including his wife and daughter, as "Cousin Charlie." His dates are 1835-1898.

2) Mary Louise Yancey Phinizy, born 1851 and married to two Phinizy gentlemen; she was widowed with two small children, a boy and a girl, at the early age of twenty-six. She was generally called "Mother" in the family and Mary Lou by her close friends and intimates, also sometimes Lou or Mamie Lou by the latter.

CHAPTER THREE

3) Bowdre Phinizy, born December 27, 1871, and therefore about fourteen when he acquired a stepfather; his own father, Ferdinand Bowdre, died suddenly of pneumonia in January 1877 at the early age of only twenty-seven.
4) Harriet Bowdre Phinizy, born December 24, 1873, and being about twelve when her mother married "Cousin Charlie."
5) Mary Louise Phinizy, born March 27, 1887, to Mr. and Mrs. Charles Henry Phinizy, always called Mary Lou.
6) Mary Louise Mays, born March 18, 1897, following Harriet's February 12, 1896, marriage to Samuel Warren Mays, Jr., who died in 1906; called Louise and sometimes listed as Louise Phinizy Mays.
7) Bowdre Phinizy Mays, born August 27, 1901, with his mother Harriet passing away in October 1910; hence, Bowdre and Louise became orphans early in life and were raised basically by their grandmother Mary Lou, always calling her "Mother", and their Aunt Mary Lou and Uncle Bowdre; Mary Lou was called Auntie.

It appears that about the time of the Mary Lou and Cousin Charlie's marriage in July 1885, contracts were let to upgrade all internal facilities and to redecorate the still handsome residence in the Second Empire or High Victorian style; some of the furniture probably then ordered was known as American Renaissance and similar to the French Second Empire. In those days, companies such as Tiffany offered redecorating and construction services for interiors, but we do not have hard facts at this time relative to what firm or contractor/architect accomplished the 519 Greene Street renovation.

The ballroom took up the entire right side of the main floor, contained twin fireplaces on the 5th Street side with over-mantels built to hold china vases and Old Paris urns. Two large gilt-framed mirrors were placed at each end of the room, which was forty feet in length and twenty-eight in width. Marble-topped gilt low consoles or pedestals were situated at the bottom of each mirror and held large bisque figures or statues of persons in eighteenth-century dress. All the foregoing can be seen from contemporary pictures.

The original house was three stories with a fourth story either added then or a bit later due to the new family situation. As was seen often in the 1880s, stained glass in lead surrounds with initials "C.H.P." was added above the front door and another stained glass window incorporated in an opening in the wall of the main staircase to the third floor. Spanish leather-embossed wallpaper was installed on the walls of the second-floor main entrance hall above the handsome parquet floor, while the ground floor and the wall wainscoting were finished with marble of a pinkish hue. We are not certain if the marble was original to the house or added during the late-1880s renovation; it probably was original.

The house indeed is a classic of its period, and all Augusta is fortunate in that William G. Hatcher, Sr. has rescued this splendid example of Regency/Federal

CHAPTER THREE

architecture; the house is now sometimes called Hatcher Center and has become a popular locale for receptions. 519 Greene Street is in excellent company if as we surmise it was a Cluskey project, considering Cluskey's work at the Old Medical College in Augusta and the elegant Governor's Mansion in Milledgeville, at one time capital of Georgia (1806-1868). Cluskey also is said to have designed the tombstone of Thomas Cumming in Summerville Cemetery, Cumming being an early mayor with title of "intendant" when first employed circa 1798.

Cousin Charlie had an interesting education and career. First educated at home and then in preparation for future collegiate courses at Richmond Academy of Augusta, he thereafter attended the State University, known in that era as Franklin College (in Athens), where he graduated in the class of 1853. Afterwards, he studied at West Point, not as a military cadet but as a civil engineering student under the tutelage of the esteemed Professor Mahan, teacher of science and engineering at the US Military Academy.

For several years subsequent to the end of tuition, he was employed as a civil engineer during the construction of various railroads in Georgia, North Carolina, and East Tennessee. This allowed him practical railroad experience and must have laid a good foundation for his most successful future work and railroad investments when he embarked upon commercial and mercantile pursuits very early in the post-engineering phase of his life. Cousin Charlie became a partner with his kinsmen, Ferdinand Phinizy II and Joseph M. Burdell, in a cotton house called F. Phinizy & Company. Later there were various cotton houses in Augusta called C. H. Phinizy & Company, F. B. Phinizy, and just Phinizy & Company, where he probably was also involved at one time before and following the Civil War.

He was so engaged when war began in 1861, and was among the first to volunteer. He was sent to Virginia as a first lieutenant in Company B of the Tenth Georgia Regiment, then under command of Colonel Alfred Cumming; later he was assigned to the adjutant general's department on duty with Brigadier-General Alfred Cumming and remained in service until General Johnston's final surrender at Greensboro, North Carolina, on April 26, 1865. Prior to the end of the war, he was made and commissioned a colonel of the 39th Georgia Regiment, which included the surviving veterans of General Cumming's brigade. Phinizy served in numerous engagements and large battles, including the siege of Vicksburg, Hood's campaign in Tennessee, Williamsburg, Sharpsburg, Missionary Ridge, Jonesboro, the second battle of Manassas, and all of the battles around Richmond, ending in that of Malvern Hill.

Following the termination of his military service in 1865, in the autumn of that same year, Charles H. Phinizy resumed his cotton house pursuits with his Phinizy relatives and continued the cotton factorage business in Augusta until around 1879 and apparently with much success. Then having been a director of the Georgia

CHAPTER THREE

Railroad and Banking Company since 1874, he was elected president in 1880 of the combined enterprise, remaining president of the railroad until it was leased in May of 1881. He continued until November of 1897 as the president of the banking company, a commissioner (one of six) in charge of the railroad, a director of various other southern railroads, and the president of the Augusta factory for five years from 1882. Charles H. Phinizy was said to possess a fine sense of business judgment and a superb administrative talent. In short, he was a resounding business success in the best sense of the word.

For the heated term in Augusta, i.e., June to October, some opine now, Charles H. Phinizy had a country home located in Grovetown. This house was situated among the pine groves with a fish pond of some size and an iron spring to supply (many said) water to restore one's youth more effectively than that era's "new sheep decoction" which was reported "to play hide and seek with death"! Grovetown was situated on the main line of the Georgia railway between Washington, Georgia, and Augusta and so was reached easily; being several hundred feet higher than Augusta, the Grovetown village had the reputation of being one very healthy region. A number of Augusta families (including the Stewart Phinizys, James Tobins, and Henry Cohens) had built summer cottages in the town, and there was an excellent hotel and even an Episcopal Church dedicated to the memory of the late poet Paul H. Hayne. The Stewart Phinizy home was called Villa Marion and the Cohen Home Cohencrest.

Apparently, those suffering from hay fever or asthma found great relief or even cures in the fragrant Grovetown ozone. Charles H. Phinizy was said to be so enamored of his country place as to be tempted away from the fall, winter, and spring sojourns at 519 Greene; his wife, Mary Lou Yancey Phinizy, and a most charming and lovely representative of her sex, was said to have made the Grovetown home "an idyl" with her beautiful children. The home was known as the Georgia "Sans Souci," with the master and mistress never happier than when friends and relatives shared it with them.

Aside from his undoubted and obvious business acumen, Charles H. Phinizy was credited with being genial and warm hearted, courtly in bearing, and most cordial in manner while a spirit of real delight to his friends. We have a picture probably taken in full maturity about the time he married for the first time aged fifty. The wedding to Mary Lou Yancey Phinizy, widow of his cousin since 1877, took place in Rome, Georgia, in the library at the home of the bride's brother, Hamilton Yancey, Esq. Staunch friends "attended Colonel Phinizy," and these included ex-Senator Pope Barrow, Honorable J. B. Cumming, Honorable John Davison, and Major Thomas P. Branch. An extended wedding trip to the "Northern Resorts" followed the ceremony. Our picture shows an elegantly dressed gentleman of the 1880s with brown-black hair and a full bushy mustache of the same color carrying a handsome walking stick of wood with a gold top engraved with his initials. The stick is in our possession.

CHAPTER THREE

The family story handed down is that Charles H. Phinizy fell in love with Mary Lou about 1884 at the trial when she brought a legal action against her father-in-law, Ferdinand Phinizy II, for the entire income and presumably control of her late husband's estate. Charles Henry Phinizy and Ferdinand Phinizy II were first cousins and, at one time, partners in the cotton factorage business. Hence, Mary Lou and her first Phinizy husband, Ferdinand Bowdre, and son of Ferdinand Phinizy II were close to Charles H. Phinizy from the time of their arrival in Augusta in the early 1870s, particularly since Ferdinand Bowdre also entered the Phinizy cotton firm, replacing his father in Athens.

Furthermore, Charles Henry's brother, Dr. Thomas Burdell Phinizy, was married to Frances Hamilton, who was the first cousin of Mary Lou's mother; the doctor's children were always close friends and relatives on both sides to Mary Lou, so it is more likely Mary Lou and Charles Henry were often thrown together in a social sense both before and after her husband's untimely and early death from pneumonia at age twenty-seven. I believe it more likely that Charles Henry advised Mary Lou on the legal action and obtained/briefed her attorneys, who it appears were also his good friends! Mary Lou prevailed and was awarded the entire income from January 1, 1884, with the balance of income added to principal retroactively. The capital was reported in the press as over $100,000, then a very important sum and quite "well invested" to yield about $5,000 per annum. The local paper reported that Mary Lou appeared both "dignified and retiring" on the witness stand and that to relieve her embarrassment, a large number of ladies of Athens accompanied her and were given seats within the bar!

So the year following the trial, Mary Lou and Charles Henry married on July 28, 1885, and once the renovations at 519 Greene were completed, they were "at home." Mary Lou retained her house at 415 7th Street (then known as 51 McIntosh Street) as rental property. This dwelling is now owned by Historic Augusta and called the Joseph Rucker Lamar House. The new establishment at 519 Greene must have been considered one of the most impressive residences in the then finest residential area. Mary Lou was most beloved by all family, relatives, and friends, including servants, help, and staff, and was a most handsome and very pretty, vivacious widow of only thirty-four.

The marriage appears to have worked on both sides. Charles Henry Phinizy was a man of much local position (then president of the Georgia Railroad Bank, plus other business interests) and ready for a family life of his own following the death of his father in July of 1884, his mother having passed on in 1862. Mary Lou with her boy and girl of fourteen and twelve probably wanted a "father figure" in their lives, particularly in view of the squabble with their grandfather and her father-in-law. Also, they both no doubt wanted companionship and love in their more mature years. Mary Lou must have been a celebrated hostess from all reports, with a large domestic staff and an acclaimed table in their elegant

CHAPTER THREE

Greene Street home. She obviously was quite sure of herself and had much confidence as her personal visiting card was engraved only "Mrs. Phinizy"! At some future date, she acquired a set of twelve French Limoges portrait plates hand-painted with the pictures of noted European ladies, mostly queens, all rimmed in cobalt blue and gold. One plate was painted in her own likeness as a young lady! We have these today in our dining room.

The marriage certainly provided her with a somewhat more prominent position and house besides bestowing on the young widow and two children a new family environment. Mary Lou did not have to change initials on her silver and linen and at the same time acquired a more impressive "screen on which to paint"! And after eight years of widowhood her background and parentage had given her perfect advantages. For example, in the mid to late 1880s she was a well-educated lady having schooled at both Lucy Cobb Academy in Athens and later at an Episcopal School in Staunton, Virginia. At the latter she even delivered the valedictory address circa 1869-1870.

Mary Lou Yancey Phinizy is often described as beautiful and radiant in both person and personality. Ever tactful and very considerate, she always was the central focus of a large circle of friends; and this circle was ever widening through the passage of years. She gave generous support, both time and money, to every institution working for the betterment of Augusta. Her specific civic endeavors included the following:

- Colonial Dames: when she died in 1926, she was the oldest living member in Augusta
- Daughters of the Confederacy: a faithful member
- Women's Club
- Committee to build Butt Memorial Bridge in 1914
- DAR: one of the original members of the Augusta Chapter founded in 1892; welcomed visitors to George Walton's house, Meadow Garden, at the 1901 opening ceremony
- YWCA: president from 1909, then serving many terms, finally becoming honorary president for life; the *Augusta Chronicle* editorial following her death in 1926 called her "Mother of the YWCA."

She appears to have endeared herself to all, white and black, young and old, fortunate and unfortunate, so that one resolution on her death read, "None knew her but to love her, none named her but to praise." Even her in-laws sang her praises and admired her innate sweetness of character. My mother Frank, her granddaughter in-law, spoke of her sincere kindness and charm saying how much she loved beautiful jewelry and handsome fancy clothes while Donald Bussey, grandson in-law, always felt much affection for the lady his wife Louise called "Mother." He often said she was the only Phinizy he ever really liked!

Joseph B. Cumming (1893-1983) in his *Reminiscences*, published by the Richmond County Historical Society in 1983, gives us a rather lovely and appealing portrait of Mrs. Charles H. Phinizy. He wrote that after the deepest

CHAPTER THREE

black and then gray mourning periods passed, she went into lavender which she never left. He wrote that this beautiful lady could be seen riding through the streets in her victoria "looking elegant, dignified and patrician, always wearing lavender." Joe Cumming wrote that such was not exhibitionism; "She just lived the life of a woman of gracious manners, refinement and position." However, his comment regarding her father is incorrect in that her father was Benjamin Cudworth Yancey, brother to the William Lowndes Yancey mentioned. Benjamin was minister to Argentina from 1858-1859, and he was appointed by President Buchanan but declined another appointment as minister to The Court of St. James's in London circa 1859.

Putting all facts upon the mahogany, I should probably state that the then Cumming legal firm represented Colonel and Mrs. Charles H. Phinizy and also The Georgia Railroad Bank as attorneys. Cummings and Phinizys also were social friends through the years up through the present generations.

As was the custom in the period of which we write (circa late 1880s through the late 1920s), help was quite abundant and relatively cheap. For example, 519 Greene was staffed in the early 1900s by Charles, Lewis, Lena, Mary, Janie, and on occasion by an Addie, Nancy or Martha, Julia, William, Elbert, Norvell or Alec for a time. The steady regulars were members of the Carter family who came from Grovetown. Lena Carter was the ladies' maid, her brother "Son" butler and chauffeur, and "Man" the yardman (Janie the cook was married to him). Another Carter brother and at a much later period Lena's nieces, Mattie and Carrie Belle, all were in domestic service. Still another Carter brother, Beesley, worked for my father at The Furniture Market. The Carters had a high percentage of white parentage having very light skin; one Carter had blue eyes and emigrated to the North where, as they say, "he passed"! Aunt Mary Lou Phinizy would say often that it was entirely possible the Carters were related to the Phinizy clan for both lived in Grovetown many long years!

Salaries and many partial advances were paid monthly, and the wages as recorded by the lady of the house appear to have been as follows: Lena $7.00, Charles/Lewis $15.00 to $18.00, Cook $10.00. There were some extras depending upon a six- or seven-day work week. A large party was given November 22, 1906, by Mary Lou Yancey and her daughter Mary Lou at 519 Greene; apparently a large evening reception with dancing (as the invitation notes) beginning at 9:00 p.m. The total expense is detailed at $958.00 including music $68.00, Land's Drug (probably for ice cream) $40.00, Tiffany $47.49, dance cards $4.00, Schneider's Department Store $224.96, and extra help $30.00. As Mary Lou was about nineteen and a half in age, this may have been her debut party. All of this just to reveal how our dollar currency has severely lost its former purchasing power. Even so, $958.00 appears too high for that era.

Mary Lou Yancey Phinizy wrote a number of aphorisms or epigrams in one of her journals; some were

CHAPTER THREE

rather obvious and commonplace, other perhaps on the cynical side. For example, to give a few:
- "Many waters cannot quench love."
- "Wine that maketh glad the heart of man."
- "There is a special providence in the fall of a sparrow."
- "What wound did ever heal, but by degrees."
- "Put money in thy purse."
- "On their own merits, modest men are dumb."
- "Take thine ease, eat, drink and be merry."
- "Apples of gold and pictures of silver."
- "Words are leaves, deeds are fruits."
- And she quoted Confucius: "Great souls have wills, Feeble ones have only wishes" and even Plato: "With necessity not even the Gods Contend!"
- "Assume a virtue if you have it not."
- Conundrum: "What is it one eats in the morning and drinks at night? — A toast!"
- "Prosperity is the very bond of love."
- "Human life is every where a state in which much is to be endured and little to be enjoyed."
- "Marriage is like putting your hand into a bag containing ninety-nine snakes and one eel. You may get the eel, but the chances are against you!"

She even quoted the Methodist preacher and hymn author John Wesley who gave a famous and simple summary of the duties of industry, economy, and liberality: "Make all you can; save all you can; give all you can." In the time of her first marriage to Ferdinand Bowdre Phinizy, Mary Lou attended the Methodist Church in

Augusta: I believe St. John's on Greene Street, near their 7th Street home, but then later switched her membership to St. Paul's Episcopal. The rationale handed down in the family was she wanted to serve wine at home parties, such not then permitted in the teetotalist Methodist religion. But she had attended an Episcopal school in Virginia, and many of her Augusta friends and relatives by the time of the second marriage in 1885 were Episcopalians. So at St. Paul's, Mother Church of Augusta, she became a devout and fervent member until her death in November 1926. Her children and grandchildren also were raised as communicants of St. Paul's. When the so-called "cocktail era" began in the early twenties or just prior, Mary Lou Yancey Phinizy served what she called a "Cherry Bounce" to her luncheon or dinner guests. Where necessary made with "aged corn liquor" and apparently with much in common with our present-day Manhattan cocktail. The Cherry Bounce was shaken with ice in a silver cocktail shaker then poured straight into about a four-inch-tall cocktail glass with a red cherry on the bottom.

Some twenty months almost to the day following their marriage, Cousin Charlie and Mary Lou Yancey (at ages fifty-two and thirty-six) had their first and as it turned out their only child. The little girl arrived March 27, 1887, and was christened Mary Louise after her mother but always called just Mary Lou. The book *Phinizy Family in America* by Ferdinand Phinizy Calhoun, published in the early 1920s, made Mary Lou a "printing-error bastard" by listing her birthdate correctly while giving the parents' wedding anniversary as July 28, 1895!

CHAPTER THREE

Little Mary Lou entered a household of largely older persons considering the ages of her parents and her half sister (fourteen) and half brother (sixteen) but also Phinizy cousins. There must have been a certain formality about life at 519 Greene considering the size of the establishment which at that time ran all the way through to Ellis Street with kitchens, garage, stables, and servant quarters either connected or semi-connected to the main residence facing Greene. Mary Lou grew rapidly and became very quickly "the apple of her father's eye"; however, it seems she also was very spoiled by all the attention as on a trip to New York City in the early 1890s Cousin Charlie returned with an English black and white steel engraving captioned "Spoilt Child" and showing a little girl of about five or six years beautifully dressed and deliberately pulling the tablecloth and all china and food set upon it from the table to the horror of several persons sitting or standing nearby!

This large engraving was framed and always cherished by Aunt Mary Lou who hung it in her dining room at 814 Milledge in years to come. I was living in Belgium when I inherited the engraving in 1977. As it was by that time badly foxed and moisture-stained under the glass, we employed an expert at picture restoration to remove the tan/yellowing marks. What a mistake, as the entire engraving started to disintegrate once the cleaning solution was applied. We should have left it as it was but did manage to extract from the restorer an antique French engraving (eighteenth-century) to replace the damaged

"Spoilt Child" which we had valued mainly for family sentimental reasons.

We have photographs of Mary Lou around ages four or five, eight or nine, and seventeen or eighteen; she is always well—even elaborately—dressed and looks like one of the Romanov grand duchesses from their late nineteenth or early twentieth-century pictures. She probably was a child given everything! Her brother Bowdre called her "Monk" as a pet name or sometimes "Daughter" imitating their mother, and Mary Lou appears to have really loved him. She told me her brother-in-law, Sam Mays (always called "Brother Sam") made the gift of her first bicycle when she was eight or nine.

We have no news of her initial education in Augusta whether at home or outside; there may have been some tutoring, perhaps in French, but we do know of "a dance party" for "little people" given by Mary Lou, maybe on her birthday, about 1900-1902 at 519 Greene. The local paper reported she received the guests accompanied by "Master John Pendleton King." The afternoon guests included "little people" girls and boys named D'Antignac, Hull, Phinizy, Verdery, Stovall, Barrett, Davison, Miller, Gary, Eve, Heard, Gardner, Coleman, Evans, Jeffries, Clark, Cohen, Alexander, Garrett, Davidson, Foster, and Walker (all well-known Augusta names). Mary Lou later attended Lucy Cobb Institute in Athens, Georgia, her mother being an alumna, and then off to her finishing school, Madame Lefebvre's at 122 West Franklin Street, Baltimore, Maryland.

CHAPTER THREE

Two early trips to Europe took place in 1905 and 1907 while she still was in the Baltimore finishing school. Later in her long life she told me a person could be well educated by strong reading habits and extensive travel provided one was keen and very observant. And follow that philosophy she certainly did most of her years. She was particularly fascinated by English and French history and read much concerning the seventeenth, eighteenth, and nineteenth centuries. The Bourbons and Bonapartes of France were favorites, including the Regency period following the death of King Louis XIV in 1715.

Mary Lou read the memoirs of Duc de Saint-Simon and many other autobiographical memoirs and biographical works of these periods. In England and Scotland, she visited almost every well-known locale, all probably already familiar from studies and perusal of the famous English authors and poets, i.e. Scott, Dickens, Trollope, Thackeray, and Tennyson. She was not exactly a "bluestocking" but nevertheless had literary interests even if not pedantic. I believe she sort of identified with the "Royals" of her day and those from the past, e.g. Marie Antionette, Marie de Medicis, Josephine and Napoleon I, the sisters of the emperor and Hortense de Beauharnais, daughter of Josephine and his sister-in-law at the same time. Hortense was of course the mother of Napoleon III, the final person on the French throne and the monarch who gave Paris much of the beauty we know today and which Mary Lou first inhaled on her initial visit to Europe in 1905 at age eighteen. She returned in 1907 with another group from Madame Lefebvre's school, including her friend Tracy Duncan from Macon.

While we have no record of the numerous trips to Europe made through the 1920s, there are diaries describing in detail the 1905, 1907, and 1911 journeys. In 1911, she visited Berlin for the first time and raved about this large city in its Kaiser Wilhelm II glory. The tour of 1911 was taken with her mother, Mrs. Leonard Phinizy and her daughter Marion Coles, then twenty-one, with her cousin our Mary Lou now twenty-four. Six others were included in this escorted tour which commenced at Naples where the ship first docked following a brief stop in Gibraltar.

Mary Lou's diary is amusing in describing the various people in the group and their leader. As for the beauties of Naples, she wrote, "Some imbecile says you should see and die, but I much prefer to get away alive!" She did not like the wet Netherlands, and on arriving at the Hague reported their hotel was "horrible" and that "nothing doing" as Josephine would say—Josephine being the French empress of course! Reaching Paris from Brussels, she minuted, "At last our ambition was realized and we were alive and in Paris!" But then after ten days in Paris and crossing the Channel to London, a letter arrived from Brother Bowdre that her dog "Tots, poor, fat, little Tots was dead." Mary Lou wrote in her diary, "The only object she adored on earth – God wots- was Tots." Tots was a Boston Bulldog with a screw tail.

CHAPTER THREE

Some friend, together with Miss Dina Taliaferro, sent Mary Lou on black-bordered mourning paper, a long memorial eulogy to Tots as follows:

In Memoriam
- Tots -
June 16, 1911

He is dead-
She has tears to shed:
Let her lie on the bed
Given up to unavailing
Weeping & Wailing.
Let her make noise,
Calling with choked voice,
"To age, turn to its mudder"
While we look on & shudder.

— · —

He is dead.
Our hope is fled.
And because he was over fed
So they said-
No kind by hand to pour castor oil
Fierce indigestion's ravages to foil.

2.   A screw tail Boston Bull
He was not beautiful-
Alas! Alack! Ah no
The more's the woe!
E'en though
Clad in a cap from Sorrento

And chic in all the latest Tots
From France-ring's, shoes & what-nots
He still were Tots.

— · —

Lives one so cruel who
Wouldn't mourn for Mary Lou
Far on the summer sea
With the trembling summer stars above
And never again to see
The Angel Child of all her love-
Twas all she knew of loves surpassing worth.

3. The only object she adored on earth
     God wots
     Was Tots
   Tots, poor old Tots has been claimed by his destiny
   Let's lay grisly away in the cedar wood chest any things of his-
   'tis bitter-Harness, cap & sweater-
   Wrap them in Lavender & rue
   The while we gently strew (Poor Mary Lou!)
   For-get-me nots on tots.

4. Alone, in the hot sand,
   By no cool breezes fanned
   He died-
   No friend beside
   To scratch his aching back
   Or his Sto-mach.
     — · —

CHAPTER THREE

A favorite has no friend
Hence at the bitter end
Tracy & Louise
No scolding tear can squeeze
Forth for Tots
Not
Knowing What's
What.
Only Dina & I
Sit sadly by
And cry
"Oh Tots, Tots, Tots
We sure did love you lots."

In late July 1911, the Phinizy party (without any guide—it seems the guide had left them before Paris) took a special steamer train for Liverpool where they boarded the *Mauretania*. The voyage was five days to New York, and Mary Lou wrote the ship "was exactly like an enormous floating hotel." She also told her diary their party spent one week on the road in England and Scotland without a "P.C." (I assume this means personal conductor), got along well, and behaved in a most respectable manner! By this time, Mary Lou had acquired a certain sophistication through experience. She was derisive in mocking the tour guide and the "sensitive plant" as she called his wife but at the same time wrote that he was quite intelligent. Mary Lou obviously felt the Phinizy party from Augusta would have been better served apart from this group!

In 1914, Mary Lou again was in Europe; she seems to have spent much time in Paris where her niece, Mary Louise Mays, then was to attend a finishing school with a group of girls chaperoned by Miss Leila Hill. Mary Lou stayed at the Hotel de la Tremoille in Paris (this hotel is still in existence behind the Plaza Athénée Hotel at 25 Avenue Montaigne). Also in Paris the summer of 1914 were other Augustans: Carolyn Cumming, the Traylors, and Marguerite Pressly whose father, Charles, was in the US diplomatic service at that time. Charles Pressly's wife was cousin or niece to Pleasant Stovall then US minister to Switzerland stationed at Berne. Marguerite Pressly eventually married Rudolph Joseph Kratina after World War I terminated and settled in Dresden; Charles Pressly served the United States as vice consul general in Paris during WWI and later lived with the Kratinas in Dresden. The entire family including their only child, Fredric, left Germany circa 1937-1938 and then resided in Augusta with Mr. Pressly and their German domestic, Elsa, who made wonderful meatballs. While in Paris, letters and diaries show that Mary Lou in 1914 did meet her then beau's Aunt Mina, Marchioness of Anglesey, who had lived in France for many long years. The beau was John Pendleton King who then was twenty-five and Mary Lou twenty-seven. Mary Lou too seemed to call her "Aunt Mina."

Finally, in late June 1914, Mary Lou left Paris on a trip to Austria and Germany. War was declared by several counties the first week of August, but apparently Mary Lou, the Traylors, and Carolyn Cumming were

CHAPTER THREE

able to leave Breslau for Dresden while one member of their party, Miss Louise Rowland, was turned back in Munich. Of course, the United States was not a party to hostilities until 1917, but I understand US Minister Pleasant Stovall and Vice-Consul Pressly were of great assistance in securing special passports or visas as needed to permit all the Augustans to book passage and return home at an early date without incident in the Atlantic crossing.

Aunt Mary Lou told me she chose not to marry; she certainly had opportunities through the years, and perhaps there was some added and normal pressure from her mother. We know that North Winship of Macon and John Pendleton King (grandson of the Augusta family founder) both were beaus and pursued her. There was talk she would become engaged to one of them inside the family and also outside. As late as the summer of 1914 Pendleton (as he was called) still was in the picture and kissing her farewell on the train as she departed for Europe. Some say William E. Bush was a later suitor, and they always remained close friends until their deaths.

There were other suitors, e.g. one called Dr. Herbert, and later her friend North Winship who became U.S. ambassador to South Africa in 1948. Previously his long diplomatic tenure provided him with consular posts beginning with Tahiti in 1910, Jerusalem 1913 (during the Turkish period), Petrograd through World War I to the 1917 Russian Revolution, Milan, Bombay (where the Winships imported their Italian butler Guiseppe), Cairo as chargé d'affaires, then a long spell at Copenhagen as consul general, (where he entertained in the early 1930s Logan Phinizy and her traveling companions), on to Warsaw as counselor in 1937 serving with Ambassador Anthony Biddle of Philadelphia, a personal friend of both Winships. In 1941, North was stationed in Toronto and in 1944 promoted to consul general at Montreal. He retired from the U.S. Foreign Service following a long and distinguished career of forty years in 1950. North had married Catherine Colfelt of Philadelphia in Paris in 1921.

The Winships maintained a Macon home, Breezy Hill, which they visited often between posts and when on leave; Breezy Hill was well known for its grounds and gardens with the rose garden of particular charm. Breezy Hill was situated on one of the highest points in Bibb County and formerly a retreat for the Jesuit Order. North was fluent in four tongues, including French, Italian, and Russian. He came from an interesting family being the grandson of the first white woman born in 1813 at Fort Hawkins as Macon was then known. North also was the nephew of General Blanton Winship, at one time governor general of Puerto Rico. North's dates are 1885–1968. What a life for M.L.P. had she chosen to accept his proposal! But as her great niece Mary Lou Bussey said, "Auntie always wanted to be a Phinizy!"

In her 1911 European trip diary, Mary Lou wrote down a poem called "Platonics." This appears written from a man's viewpoint but may well reflect her own sentiments which is why she thought to record the verses now repeated:

CHAPTER THREE

I knew it the first of the summer; I knew it the same at the end that you and your love were plighted — But couldn't you be my friend? Couldn't we sit in the moonlight, couldn't we stroll on the shore — with only a pleasant friendship to bind us and nothing more? There was never a word of nonsense spoken between us two — though he lingered oft in the garden when the roses were wet with dew. We touched on a thousand subjects — the moon and the stars above — But our talks were tinctured with silence and never a thought of love! A wholly platonic friendship you said I had proven to you could bind a man and a woman — the whole long summer through. With never a thought of folly — though both were in their youth — What would you have said — my lady? Had you but guessed the truth? Had I done what my mad heart prompted — gone down on my knees to you — and told you my passionate story — out there in the dark and dew? But I fought with myself and conquered; and I hid my love from sight; you were going away in the morning and I said a calm goodnight — But now when I sit in twilight or wander by the sea — that friendship "wholly platonic" comes surging over me, and a hopeless longing fills me for the roses, the dark and the dew, for that beautiful summer vanished, those moonlight talks and you!

Bowdre Phinizy was an important and obvious luminary, even a megastar (as one today might term it!), in the 519 Greene Street ménage—this because of his bright and brilliant mind, his career and accomplishments in the outside business world, and his prodigious scholastic achievements. He also seems to have been very affable, well liked, and charming to the ladies, with a genial and approachable attitude toward his fellow friends, colleagues, and workers as well as to all servants. My mother always said he liked to tease (when she knew him in his later years) and was apparently considered "good company" in his club life at the downtown Commercial Club and the Augusta Country Club on the hill.

After Cousin Charlie died at a too-early age in 1898, Bowdre Phinizy, then in his twenty-seventh year, took the place of his step-father/cousin as the senior and indeed only male family member in the household. Bowdre Phinizy was by then well prepared for this new role because of his spectacular academic and fledgling business résumés. Starting with Augusta public schools and the Webb School in Tennessee, his college education and various accomplishments follow:

- Graduate Princeton University A.B. degree 1892; A.M. in 1894;
- One of five who graduated Magna Cum Laude;
- Manager Princeton Glee Club of 25 voices; when touring they came to Augusta, Atlanta, Savannah, Columbia, Baltimore, Washington, Wilmington, Charleston, and Richmond one season with Augusta papers reporting the "Princeton Boys captured Augusta socially with their music, They were lionized and entertained on all sides." Much of their success was said to be due to the business

CHAPTER THREE

management of Bowdre Phinizy, a very popular and gifted young man; he also was business manager of the Banjo and Mandolin Clubs;
- Managing Editor *Princetonian*, a journal issued daily under his reign; this proved possible due to the handsome dividends paid to the student stockholders;
- President "Cleveland Club";
- Lacrosse Team member;
- Winner Whig Literary Society Essay Contest two years;
- Member Whig Debating Society, winning many prizes including the important "Lynde Debate" just before the commencement ceremony in 1892; he was called the "silver-tongued orator," and he was one of the final commencement orators and won cash prizes!
- Vice President Princeton class 1892;
- Awardee of one of three Nassau Literature Prizes, the highest academic honor from Princeton:
- Ivy Club Member, oldest at Princeton, where today his picture hangs in the club library;
- Greek memberships: Phi Beta Kappa and Alpha Delta Phi;
- School prophesy was that Bowdre would be US president!

Then after graduating from Princeton in 1894, Bowdre went on to Johns Hopkins (1893-1894); next to the University of Virginia for the 1894 summer law course; and finally to Harvard Law School in 1895. He was admitted to the Georgia bar in Augusta 1894 and soon opened his law office; although, in the interim, he had entered the newspaper business and undertook no actual law practice. From 1894-1896, he was a member of the Georgia House of Representatives, later in 1906-1907 and 1910-1912, member of the Democratic State Committee, trustee of the University of Georgia 1907-1923, and concurrently trustee of the Medical College of Georgia. He was later elected a director of the Southern Mutual Insurance Company at Athens.

The reason Bowdre Phinizy decided not to follow a legal career really came about through circumstances rather than by pure choice: apparently his mother or even Cousin Charlie, his stepfather, had loaned or invested funds in the *Augusta Herald* launched in late 1890 by former *Chronicle* employees. The *Herald* was fighting to stay alive, being still confronted by the mighty *Augusta Chronicle* when Bowdre Phinizy entered the scene in 1892. To preserve the family investment, Bowdre decided to become energetically involved in the newspaper's operation. Further investments were made in the form of *Herald* bonds, and T. J. Sheron became a partner with Phinizy. Sheron became business manager and Phinizy editor and publisher under an agreement that if one person died, the survivor would be the sole party who could acquire the stock of the deceased. Meantime, the partners began to seek out and purchase the minor *Herald* shareholdings dispersed previously. Sheron died in 1913 when Phinizy then assumed complete control continuing as editor and publisher.

CHAPTER THREE

As the editor and publisher of the *Herald*, Bowdre Phinizy revealed himself to be a man of some vision, bold and fearless in his approach to local and national events; initially somewhat flamboyant as editor and publisher, he seemed imbued with noblesse oblige toward his public and particularly all working classes. An example was his proposed bill while in the state legislature to require all railroads carry bicycles as baggage free of charge. This was a lifelong trait and was combined with an adventurous spirit and perspective. He appears to have adopted as his "*Herald* code" the need to promote public service, support the underdog, and arm to assist in always growing Augusta. He was very successful with his approach as the fledgling afternoon paper with its "Extras" gained consistently in its reach and, most essential of all, in increasing circulation. The new *Sunday Herald*, introduced in late 1898, also helped buttress circulation, which by the early 1920s had passed the morning *Chronicle*.

Large and loud headlines became a *Herald* feature even though Bowdre Phinizy himself was mostly a restrained and rather private person. For example, during the Spanish-American War in 1898, The *Herald* issued many afternoon "Extras" and planned to have news from Admiral Dewey relative to his attack on the Spanish navy at Manila Bay on one day. The expected news bulletin, however, failed to arrive, but the public still was clamoring for a press release. The *Herald* obliged with an "Extra" headline: "No News From Dewey." This "Extra" obviously caused some laughter but did attract the desired attention as intended! This approach and his innate patriotic mindset must have helped gain new circulation as did the rise of the middle class and its fresh significance to advertising.

The *Herald* also achieved much greater readership by reporting the triumphs of very normal ordinary men or women rather than focusing mainly on notables of the day. Another powerful *Herald* headline following Woodrow Wilson's capture of the Democratic Party's presidential nomination in Baltimore in 1911 was "We Win With Wilson!" Of course in those days the South was almost entirely backing the Democratic Party.

One interesting bit of trivia (but quite germane to the Bowdre Phinizy story to fully reflect his character) is the conversation Woodrow Wilson had with Bowdre's cousin, Ferdinand Phinizy, during the future president-elect's visit to Augusta in November 1911 prior to his inaugural March 4, 1913. Woodrow told Ferdinand that Bowdre had the second best scholastic record of any man who ever attended Princeton! Wilson said the B.P. record was second only to that of Aaron Burr, the third US vice president and son of the man who was president and founder of Princeton. Bowdre Phinizy, the story reported (but was this hyperbole?), was closer to Woodrow Wilson than any man in Augusta or perhaps Georgia.

President Wilson later offered him a diplomatic post in Europe, but Bowdre decided to continue with his newspaper career in Augusta. Wilson, of course, had been president of Princeton before he was elected

CHAPTER THREE

New Jersey governor. President-Elect Wilson also told Ferdinand Phinizy that it was not possible to get the Democratic Party nomination without the support of William Jennings Bryan who became Wilson's first secretary of state before resigning over the war policy.

In writing of the Bowdre Phinizy journalism career as his profession, I could not resist comparing him to the late William Randolph Hearst, Sr., relative only to the newspaper business. Phinizy was rather modest and retiring and certainly did not have the rootless extravagant lifestyle of Hearst; however, Bowdre seems to have agreed with Hearst that truth always is stranger than fiction and to be in accord with Hearst's central newspaper circulation philosophy as hereafter: Each reader had five basic interests—himself/herself, others, the world around them, where they came from, and where they were going. For a news publication to prosper, those wants and aspirations must be indulged.

During the first two decades of the twentieth century Bowdre Phinizy was involved in two interesting contretemps, both connected to the *Augusta Chronicle* and its then and future owners. The earliest affair was fisticuffs with a Mr. W. S. Brand, who as superintendent of the Georgia Railroad and a supporter of William S. Morris, Sr. (then treasurer of the Georgia Railroad), was asked to leave his office the day following an election for the Georgia Senate when Morris handily defeated candidate Phinizy in the primary. Apparently the entire campaign had been a most vicious one with the *Herald* constantly assaulting both Brand and Morris frequently. Brand had called Phinizy a liar in the *Chronicle*, so after the voters decided, Bowdre Phinizy acted to uphold his honor. Brand and Phinzy said nothing when they came together in the open on the sidewalk but commenced to trade punches. An onlooker reported Phinizy was routed and pushed down; the *Chronicle* account stated, "Phinizy was badly bruised while Brand had one of his fingers severely bitten." Phinizy is supposed to have declared as per *The Chronicle*: "I am satisfied. It had to come, and I did the best I could."

Although no one could have imagined it then, in 1908, the Morris family was destined to buy the *Augusta Herald* and then the *Athens Banner-Herald* (which Phinizy purchased in 1916) in years to come! Hence, the grandson (Billy Morris) and great-grandson (Will Morris) of Bowdre Phinizy's political opponent in 1908 were to be in the future firmly ensconced in managing and owning all three papers! Fortunately, I can report that we all now are good friends and very happy to be together in Augusta in the present era!

The second incident pertained to the then *Chronicle* principal shareowner and editor/publisher, Thomas W. Loyless. As a strong backer of Georgia Governor John M. Slaton's decision to commute Leo Frank's sentence of death following the rape and murder of a young teenager in 1913, Loyless and the *Chronicle* stood for the most part alone. Others, led by Tom Watson, a fervent populist, carried to new and extreme heights their calls for death to ex-Governor Slaton and to lynch Leo Frank. The matter reached a climax in August 1915

CHAPTER THREE

when masked men kidnapped Leo Frank, who then was in prison near Millegeville, and lynched him from a tree near Marietta, outside Atlanta. Loyless continued to defend Slaton and deplore the violence and flames Watson incited; Loyless obtained the backing of Slaton's successor, Governor Harris, to bring to justice those responsible for the lynching. Meantime, Tom Watson continued to agitate and appeal to those with rabid race and religious prejudices.

Our episode happened at the Commercial Club in Augusta on a chilly December evening in 1915. Loyless seemingly had been saluted by someone on the premises with the wisecrack "Hello Tom Watson"; Loyless believed the one liner came from Bowdre Phinizy (an antagonist on many issues), so he produced a pistol, thrust it up touching the Phinizy abdomen, and pressed the trigger. Fortunately, the bullet chamber was unfilled! Other club members quickly then parted the two men prior to any real damage or injury occurring. Neither the *Chronicle* nor *Herald* ever reported the fracas; although, a sheet called *Augusta Labor Reviews* did December 11. However, the *Augusta Chronicle* biography of 1960 notes that the *Labor Review* account wisely omitted another confrontation that December evening so long ago between Loyless and attorney Colonel Daniel Fogarty. Publisher Loyless was said to be "drinking" heavily on this occasion, and it is also obvious the others involved too had their passions excited by the fuel of alcohol!

On the personal side, Bowdre Phinizy was absolutely devoted to his mother and also to his two sisters;

such was even more apparent following the death of his step-father, Cousin Charlie, in 1898, making him the senior male at 519 Greene Street. This could also be one reason Bowdre finally decided to make his career in Augusta in journalism keeping in mind his brilliant record at Princeton where he first came into close association with Wilson. Perhaps the future President Wilson, acting as his academic mentor, encouraged him to study for his masters degree and to study law first at Johns Hopkins where Wilson himself took his PhD in 1886. Wilson matriculated at Princeton in 1875, graduating circa 1879. While an undergraduate, Wilson had preceded Bowdre in the Glee Club and as managing editor of the college newspaper, the *Princetonian*, so with Wilson's early boyhood spent in Augusta, naturally they had a good deal in common and many mutual acquaintances. As Woodrow's Aunt Marion married a Bones family connection and the Boneses also were a Phinizy relation, here again they found still another association. Wilson had joined the Princeton faculty in 1890 as professor of Jurisprudence; he acceded to the Princeton presidency 1902, serving until elected governor of New Jersey in 1910.

Whatever his rationale, Bowdre Phinizy, with prior academic training virtually unsurpassed and cum laude decorations from various universities, determined to give up any vision he may have at times harbored of a great career on Wall Street or another metropolis. He was said to have a mind quick to analyze, then reach a decision by reasoning, and thereafter able to favorably defend his decision. Bowdre also participated in social activities: at one time he was president of the "Merry Maker's Association" and the Commercial Club then located at 727 Broad. The Commercial Club was destroyed in the serious March 1916 fire and apparently never reopened. Bowdre organized the Augusta YMCA football team in 1894 and later played golf during the winter months at the Augusta Country Club links. He also was a member of the Elks and Biltmore Forest Clubs. One bucolic pursuit was to raise hogs and probably other farm produce at his mother's country home in Grovetown.

From all who knew him we hear of culture, extreme courtesy, charity, and reticence. One newspaper editorial after his too-early death said that in the social sphere he was a charming companion with a very keen sense of humor and a conversationalist eagerly sought by all who knew him. This report also stated "he was a polished gentleman to the manner born."

Beginning sometime after the death of James F. McGowan in 1909, Bowdre Phinizy grew to become very attentive to his widow, Margaret Charbonnier McGowan, who had been left with two young children, Henri and Margaret. By the late 1920s they had been "an item" (as some say now) for many years. The Phinizy side of the family said Bowdre would not marry as long as his mother, Mary Lou Yancey Phinizy, was alive, while the McGowans said Meta (as she was called) would never marry until after her only daughter, Margaret, had wed! My father Bowdre told me how he and Uncle Bowdre would take the streetcar from Greene Street to The Hill (circa 1916-1919); Uncle Bowdre would ride to the end of the line (Monte Sano Avenue) and then walk the one short block to Meta's house on Walton Way and Glenn Avenue while Bowdre first would drop off at the John's Road stop "to neck" with the Burum girls who lived on the corner! They both took the last Walton Way streetcar back to Greene Street.

The two "Bowdres" in the household appear to have been fairly close at this period; during the hot weather spell in Augusta "Big Bowdre" would move down to the ground marble floor from his private bedroom on the third floor left-side rear as would nephew "Little Bowdre" from his fourth-floor bedroom. Uncle Bowdre would have free passes from the railroads serving Augusta (probably in exchange for advertisements in the Phinizy-controlled papers), so the entire family had another good rationale to travel often; in addition, there was a connection with the old Vanderbilt Hotel on 34th Street in New York City, so the family always stopped there when in the city. My father also told me of the trip Uncle Bowdre took him on the summer of 1924 just prior to his marriage. The journey was to the then well-known resort hotel at French Lick, Indiana, noted for the waters and golf. According to Aunt Mary Lou, when her brother Bowdre entered the dining room one day, the head waiter greeted him with, "Are you with Mr. Mays's party?!" We have a wonderful picture of Little Bowdre at the French Lick resort in his white golf knickers. Mary Lou Bussey told me Big Uncle Bowdre slept late and often there was an empty liquor bottle in his trash basket in the morning! As children, they had to remain quiet when visiting 519 in the early mornings!

Bowdre continued to be his mother's host, as she entertained company often, and probably for business connections in the journalistic field as well. But rather suddenly in her seventy-fifth year Mary Lou Yancey Phinizy died November 16, 1926, at 519 Greene. She had gone on a trip to New York about six weeks before falling ill in Baltimore en route back to Augusta. Following her return she continued to fail and died of pneumonia. This was really the deathblow to the 519 Greene Street ménage; although, Bowdre Phinizy did not marry Meta Charbonnier McGowan until 1928. Meta's daughter Margaret married Julian Space of Savannah in 1927 and apparently then resided in Washington, DC where Bowdre and Meta married in 1928. The Spaces then accompanied the new bride and groom on their honeymoon before the Bowdre Phinizy couple returned to live in Meta's house on Walton Way following some remodeling.

Mary Lou Phinizy (with Lena Carter Glover her maid) boarded the train to Washington for the simple ceremony even though she had been quite hurt by one incident following their mother's death. The story is that one evening when Mary Lou was out, Bowdre escorted Meta to 519 Greene where they went through the house top to bottom, even opening closets, to determine what items of furniture, silver, personal effects, and household furnishings they wanted to take in the division provided under his mother's will. Mary Lou was hurt, and her good friend William E. Bush advised her to object for many of the furniture and jewelry items were acquired with her father's money! But it seems nothing could ever affect Mary Lou's deep affection and love for brother Bowdre, so in the final sharing, as one example, she actually paid Bowdre $750.00 so she might retain the entire large dining room table (it was in three sections) which originally had been the property of her grandfather John Phinizy. They also partitioned all the handsome jewelry, each taking one piece from the pair of large twin-diamond earrings; Bowdre chose the diamond bow pin and pearl and diamond "dog collar," while Mary Lou kept the diamond and onyx bracelet and perhaps other items. Bowdre asked about the Tiffany diamond Patek Philippe wristwatch, but Mary Lou said their mother wanted her young namesake, great-granddaughter Mary Lou Bussey, to inherit this. Mary Lou Bussey gave the watch to my wife Lynn with the request that in due course at her death the watch would be conveyed to her godchild, Elizabeth Law Olmsted, our granddaughter.

Mary Lou retained 519 Greene Street, Bowdre received the Grovetown property, and the two grandchildren, Mary Louise Bussey and Bowdre Mays, were given houses on 7th Street, Nos. 409 (now torn down) and 415, which is currently called the Lamar house and owned by Historic Augusta. Mary Lou Yancey Phinizy's personal fortune was divided into three equal parts: two parts for Mary Lou and Bowdre with the remaining third to the

CHAPTER THREE

grandchildren, whose mother Hattie will be examined shortly. Mary Lou now continued on alone at 519 and would do so until 1933-1934 when an illness led her to sell the property and move to The Hill. This latter phase of her long life will be covered in Chapter IV "Mary Lou Phinizy at 814 Milledge Road."

As Bowdre Phinizy decided to continue his basic "noblesse oblige" behavior in his final will, and because his bequests greatly enriched both the Medical College of Georgia and University Hospital, I have decided to report in some detail on his death and legacies. To an important degree Bowdre Phinizy is still an unacknowledged and really forgotten benefactor to Augusta and its population, and I am hopeful these comments will remedy the omission.

Bowdre died at his home, 2624 Walton Way, after an illness of ten days. His final malady was influenza resulting in pneumonia affecting both lungs; in due course his heart began to fail, and he expired early Sunday morning February 8, 1931, at only fifty-nine years of age. The funeral was the following Monday afternoon February 9 at 4:00 p.m. at the residence with interment in a new large plot in Westover. Sister Mary Lou Phinizy had her chauffeur, Son, deliver the key to the Phinizy Mausoleum in Magnolia Cemetery to the widow Meta who sent it back with word that other arrangements had been made.

The honorary pallbearers were headed by Dr. Eugene E. Murphey (his principal physician), Dr. R. H. Land, Judge William H. Barrett, James C. Harrison, D. G.

Fogarty, Hamilton Phinizy, L. H. Charbonnier, Charles Pressley, Henry M. North, John Phinizy, Thomas S. Gray, Andrew C. Erwin, Judge Thomas F. Green, and Jacob B. Joel of Athens while the active pallbearers were Lansing Lee, Ferdinand Phinizy, Coles Phinizy, Marion Ridgely, James Harper, Earl B. Braswell of Athens, Fielding Wallace, and Millwee Owens. When Meta Charbonnier Phinizy died in 1961, she was buried beside Bowdre and not with her McGowan first husband and progeny in Magnolia Cemetery. Her birthdate is listed as 1870, so it seems she was somewhat older than her second husband who was born December 27, 1871. No others are buried on the Bowdre Phinizy plot which is spacious and contains a beautiful white marble balustrade and urn as a backdrop for the two grave markers.

In the end, it transpired that the *Augusta Herald* endured for almost 103 years prior to being absorbed by the *Augusta Chronicle* and therefore ceasing daily publication after the final issue of Friday, April 30, 1993, the first issue having come out November 24, 1890. The *Athens Banner-Herald* is still active and occupies a new spacious and handsome building in the town. The *Augusta Herald* building at 731 Broad Street was destroyed in the large March 22, 1916, fire as was the Commercial Club building adjacent at 727 Broad. Bowdre Phinizy rebuilt the Herald Building at 725-727 Broad and occupied these new premises the fall of 1918. The new four-story building was on the site of the old Commercial Club. In 1949, the *Chronicle* and *Herald* partially merged operations,

CHAPTER THREE

and when in 1955 the *Chronicle* purchased the *Herald* and its office, the building became the "News Building."

The Bowdre Phinizy final will and testament was signed July 12, 1929. Aside from several specific monetary bequests only to be paid when the entire estate income might exceed the $20,000 requisite annual sum to be paid semi-annually to his widow, all assets (excepting real property such as the Grovetown estate and personal effects, silver, etc.) were conveyed into a trust. Upon the deaths of the donor and his wife, the entire corpus was to be divided into two equal halves: one moiety to be paid to the Medical College of Georgia as a memorial to the late Professor Leon Henri Charbonnier (father of Meta C. Phinizy) and the other to University Hospital as a memorial to Mrs. Mary Lou Yancey Phinizy, mother of the donor. Under the terms of the will, the University Hospital portion was to be used for treatment of the poor free of charge or would provide they be treated for a nominal sum. Based on recent research, the Medical College finally received $1,550,000 and University Hospital $1,755,563 for a grand total of $3,305,563.

The Medical College designated the memorial as the "Leon Henri Charbonnier Professorship," naming Dr. Robert G. Ellison as the first recipient with nine following. The medical historian in residence, Dr. Lois Ellison, advises that the bequest was the largest private donation in its history and entered the college endowment fund. The University Hospital had no endowment fund when these payments were made (1962-1965), and I understand the monies received were transferred to its construction fund in 1969 and employed to assist with the new building we see today. The trustees of the Phinizy estate had five years, as per the will, in which to dispose of all assets and terminate the trust agreement following Meta's death in May 1961; the Herald Publishing Co. had been sold in 1955 to Southeastern Newspapers, Inc. for $1.517 million but leaving the *Athens Banner-Herald* still in the estate. This important asset was sold in the summer of 1965 to William S. Morris III and his brother Charles who then were vice-presidents of Southeastern Newspapers Corp. Troy Breitmann of University's Foundation tells me that until very recent years the Bowdre Phinizy legacy was certainly the single largest bequest in its history. Thus the Bowdre Phinizy bestowal to Augusta and its citizens conformed rather closely with his wishes and in my view ought to be recognized in a more tangible manner, i.e., by a plaque from MCG and University Hospital. A former MCG president, Dr. Lombard Kelly, made this suggestion in the local press some years ago, but it does not appear to have been acted upon to date. However, in 2011, at my suggestion, Laurie Ott, president of University Health Care Foundation, had the Bowdre Phinizy name added to the hospital donor board in a very prominent location.

A grandson-in-law of Meta C. Phinizy told me before his death that her family at one point considered trying to break the Bowdre Phinizy final testament and trust estate but were unsuccessful, if in fact they did consult an attorney; reading the will again makes it clear that Bowdre, being a lawyer himself, had drafted

CHAPTER THREE

a document so concise and detailed in spelling out his intentions that it must appear the final trustees would be unable to revise the principal provisions—unless of course Meta herself was in dire need, which was never the case as per her grandson Henri McGowan Jr. who told me she had developed her own estate being very frugal! While the tax consequences of the time may have played a role in the Bowdre Phinizy estate planning and trust, in any event his memorials to Augusta indeed are worthy of three big cheers!

The three 519 Greene residents yet to be discussed are Harriet Bowdre Phinizy (born Christmas Eve 1873) and her two offspring, Mary Louise and Bowdre Phinizy, born 1897 and 1901 respectively. The progeny were the product of her marriage to Samuel Warren Mays, Jr. on February 12, 1896. Harriet (but always called Hattie by family and close friends) was about twelve years old when her mother, having been a widow for eight years, remarried their Phinizy cousin August 1885 in Rome, Georgia, as noted previously. Then the small Phinizy family moved from what is now known as the Lamar House on 7th Street to 519 Greene, Cousin Charlie's home, newly redone to receive them. We know Hattie attended some local schools (and probably had private lessons too—i.e., French, music, etc.) and then was sent to Lucy Cobb Academy in Athens following in the trail of her mother's education. A finishing school up north in the Philadelphia-New York City area completed the formal schooling. One Richmond County public school report gave Hattie a 96.6 average while the class average was just 87.7. Hattie then was aged eleven. Hattie was of a most attractive appearance with large beautiful brown eyes. These eyes must have been one fabulous feature for William Hamilton Hayne (always called Willie), son of the poet many called the "Poet Laureate of the South," dedicated the poem below to Hattie:

> "Beaux Yeux"
> (dedicated to Miss Hattie B. Phinizy)
> In that old legend of love and bliss
> The princess waked at her lover's kiss
> Though the maid had slept for a hundred years
> In the moss-grown court by the palace stairs
> No princess ever had eyes like these —
> (By the prince unclosed on his bended knees)
> Eyes of brown as a stream where the shadows lie
> Yet bright as the rays of the morning sky.

<u>Note:</u> Teto Barrett sent the original to Hattie's only daughter, Louise Mays Bussey, in 1961. Teto and her family are related to the Hayne family on the Michel side for Willie's mother was a Michel from Charleston. Willie's father was of course the noted poet Paul Hamilton Hayne.

As the Phinizy family moved to their Grovetown house for the summer months, and the Hayne family lived year-round at their Grovetown place called Copse Hill, it is obvious Hattie saw Willie often even if he was much older (seventeen years). I also wonder if there

CHAPTER THREE

was some kinship bearing in mind the Hamilton blood relationship with the Phinizys?

Hattie's closest girlfriend in Augusta was Katie Black, herself also a Greene Street resident and member of a prominent local family; we have a charming photograph of these two in a small carriage with one horse stopped on the then dirt Greene Street with Hattie at the reins. The 519 Greene Street house is in the background, and the picture probably dates to the early 1890s. Miss Katie Black lived to a ripe old age and often talked of Hattie and their friendship; when Frank Mays, Hattie's granddaughter, married Jim Hull, Jr. in 1947, Miss Katie sent them a silver candelabrum which she said Hattie had given her.

In 1923, the *Atlanta Journal* reprinted an old article about a cotillion given by the Young Ladies Dancing Club at Kimball House; there is a large picture of Hattie who led the cotillion with John W. Grant of Atlanta. I assume this was the "Grand March," and it was reported this event was the largest and most elaborate "german" of that season. The year must have been about the period when Hattie was making her debut. The *Augusta Chronicle* reported after Hattie's marriage that "she has been one of the most strikingly handsome and brilliant young society women in the state since her debut. A tall, queenly brunette with just that touch of indifference so tantalizing, yet with all so captivating, she has easily been a reigning belle wherever she made her appearance. Unusually intellectual, she is a woman of broad culture and rare conversational powers." We know nothing of her beaux; however, her picture album does contain studio pictures of two young boys, David Adams Calhoun and James E. Calhoun who may have been suitors when older.

Hattie finally determined to marry Samuel Warren Mays, Jr. even though her family apparently opposed the match. The Phinizy family said they felt Sam Mays was too old for her (he was some eight years senior), but I think the real reason is that they believed Sam was too much of a "playboy" and still had not proved he could support a wife and family. Sam came from good county stock going back to colonial times; he was christened at St. Paul's Church September 13, 1867, after his birth on June 6, 1865. On the Mays side they had lived in Edgefield, South Carolina, Florida, and at Belair in Richmond County, Georgia; his mother (whom everyone considered to be a great lady) had descended from the well-known McKinne/Macintosh lines. She was Sarah Macintosh Crawford, daughter of Georgia Governor George Walker Crawford and cousin to the well-known US ambassador and secretary of the US Treasury, William Harris Crawford.

The Sam Mays, Sr. house had partially burned at Belair, so the Mays family at some point rented a house on Greene Street where they took in several boarders. Sam Jr., now thirty-one, was a popular "young man about town" being always noted in the press of the era as one of the movers and shakers! He seems to have had a charming manner and was a social leader. For two years, he had worked in Thomasville, Georgia, as a

CHAPTER THREE

cotton factor, and to Thomasville Hattie and Sam went following their wedding (February 13, 1896) and honeymoon, which was said to be an extended bridal trip!

The wedding was quite a quiet affair held at the home of her parents, 519 Greene Street, at 8:30 p.m. Mr. and Mrs. Charles H. Phinizy were listed on the invitations as hosts, and Chauncy C. Williams, rector of St. Paul's Church, officiated. Intimate friends were present; the only attendants were a Miss Spenser of New York and Crawford Mays, brother of the groom. The *Augusta Chronicle* reported February 13, 1896, that an elegant wedding supper followed with all close friends of the bride, including Miss Katie Black, sitting at the bride's table with bride, groom, and bride's mother and brother (Bowdre Phinizy). The *Chronicle* further enthused that while the Mays-Phinizy wedding was quiet and understated, still none was of greater interest this season—this due to the fact that aside from the contracting parties belonging to two of the most prominent and influential families in Georgia, they both were exceedingly popular, each having a large circle of friends and admirers throughout the South. Julia Walton Houston, mother of John Walton and known to us as "Miss Julia," told us of Sam's jolly personality and general vivacity and how well he played the guitar; Julia then was married to Maurice Walton, Sam's close friend.

As would be normal in that time, Hattie came home to Augusta to have her child, Mary Louise Phinizy Mays, born March 18, 1897. Louise was but three and a half to four when the family seems to have left Thomasville for good, as she recalled very little of her short life in that town; at one stage they lived on Remington Avenue in a rented house but purchased another home at 606 N. Dawson Street in 1900. The Dawson Street property was listed as belonging to Hattie but was sold when the family returned to Augusta in 1901. There was some marital dissension (most likely due to lack of ready funds), and Hattie began to pawn or sell her silver. When her mother heard of this, she went by the next train to Thomasville and bought back all she could then returned to Augusta with Hattie and Louise. We are not now certain if Hattie and Sam separated for good then or after their son's birth in Augusta August 22, 1901. The second child, a boy, was named by Hattie after her beloved older brother, Bowdre Phinizy Mays. His uncle Bowdre was also his godfather at the baptism held at St. Paul's Church April 11, 1902, and presented this new family member a beautiful large embossed pap bowl and tray in silver, all properly hand-engraved. (When growing up in the Mays household, this item always appeared full of homemade mayonnaise for the table; now my wife Lynn more often uses it for flowers placed on a low table!)

The Augusta Social Register of 1906 listed the Sam W. Mays, Jr. couple as residing at 605 Greene Street with the Senior Mayses; I doubt this is entirely correct, believing that by 1906 the marriage rupture was total because long before Sam's death on June 13, 1906, Hattie's mother, Mary Lou Yancey Phinizy, discussed a possible divorce action with Cousin Hamilton Phinizy

CHAPTER THREE

(the noted local lawyer) who informed her Sam was very ill and even dying! He was ill for several months before passing away at only forty-one years of age. His obituary characterized him as "a young man of boundless energy, quick to think and act but of sound and conservative judgment, and with hundreds of friends in Augusta and Thomasville. He was a fine man and the loss is a loss indeed." Among the six pallbearers were Messrs. W. H. Barrett and Maurice Walton. Burial was in Summerville Cemetery on his grandfather Crawford's plot; there was no special marker until his daughter, Louise Mays Bussey, installed one in the early 1960s.

It appears Hattie at first continued with the usual social round after the suitable period of mourning dictated by that generation. She was present in late 1908 for a reception and dance at the Augusta Country Club where President-Elect William H. Taft and Mrs. Taft were guests as were Sophie Meldrim of Savannah and Tracy Duncan from Macon. Probably Sophie and Tracy were visiting Mary Lou Phinizy, Hattie's younger sister, as they became lifelong friends with Mary Lou as other chapters in this narrative do affirm. We have a certificate reflecting Hattie's entry into the D.A.R. in June 1893; we have not yet learned if she followed her mother into the exalted ranks of the Colonial Dames. Perhaps she then was considered still on the "young side" for that organization. Hattie also traveled to Macon in December 1909 for the Tracy Duncan-Rodney Cohen grand and large wedding where her sister was maid of honor.

What transpired next we only can guess, but some form of depression obviously occurred even though Hattie had the complete support of her mother and adored brother, notwithstanding her marriage fiasco. The story is she began to take laudanum (defined as tincture of opium) and paregoric (camphorated tincture of opium) to soothe and mitigate her pain. Genie Lehmann advises that the well-known Augusta physician, a Dr. Foster, was one instigator of this type of treatment to assist the ladies with their monthly curse! My grandmother's younger sister, Mary Lou Phinizy, refused to discuss this subject when I raised it late in her life. In any event, Hattie passed away October 16, 1910, only aged thirty-seven at 519 Greene Street, where she and her two children had been occupying the fourth floor. Her funeral was also at 519 Greene on October 17, 1910, in the afternoon at 4:30 p.m. The *Augusta Chronicle* reported on "her painful illness" of four months while the death certificate signed by Dr. W. R. Houston gave the cause of death as a case of pellagra. The *Chronicle* further stated that "Mrs. Mays was one of the leading young matrons of the city. Socially she was very prominent and was highly regarded for her brilliant mental qualities and was noted for her grace of manner and charming disposition." While her late husband was not mentioned at all, the listed survivors included her two children, mother, brother Bowdre Phinizy, half sister Mary Lou Phinizy, and her uncles Leonard, Stewart, and Jacob Phinizy then residing in Augusta. Her aunt Mary Louise Phinizy Calhoun of Atlanta and the other

CHAPTER THREE

Phinizy uncles—Marion Daniel, Billups, Barrett, and Charles Henry—were not mentioned.

Louise and Bowdre Mays were now orphans, at ages thirteen and nine respectively. I like to imagine that their grandmother, Mary Lou Yancey Phinizy, known to all and sundry as the essence of love and kindness, hugged them both in a long embrace and told them she now was their "mother" and should look to her always in such capacity. In future they only called her "Mother" as did their Uncle Bowdre and Aunt Mary Lou and indeed already had lived with them for some years before losing their parents—winters and spring on Greene Street and summers plus early fall at the Grovetown country house where we have pictures of both children with their older relatives.

The life pattern at 519 Greene was rather formal with a good deal of "company" for dinner (in those days served around 1:30 to 2:00 p.m.) and also "supper" in the evening when the hosts and guests often wore evening dress. Neither Louise nor Bowdre ever had a Christmas tree until they married, although there were wreaths and floral decorations. While the exact date and timing is unclear, Louise was sent to Baltimore to a convent (called College of Notre Dame of Maryland), sited on Charles Street. This was a boarding school run by nuns; Louise always said she learned to knit, crochet, and sew at this pious institution. Her younger brother, Bowdre, at age nine or ten was enrolled at the Stuyvesant School in Warrenton, Virginia, just outside Washington, DC. I do not believe sending the orphans away was due to any lack of love but more likely to the truth that their grandmother, now fifty-nine, was growing older while at the same time she still hoped and worked for the marriage of her son Bowdre (thirty-eight) and remaining daughter, Mary Lou, now twenty-three. Grandmother Phinizy liked to travel at this period—to Europe and the Northeastern United States. For example, in 1911 there was a long sojourn in Europe of three and a half months when the two Mary Lous traveled with Mrs. Leonard Phinizy and her daughter Marion as outlined previously.

Bowdre appears to have enjoyed his boarding school experience somewhat more than Louise hers; this is likely due to the King family, proprietors of the prep school Stuyvesant who befriended and always treated him as one of their own family. When his grandmother was away traveling during school vacations, for example, he was welcome to stay with the Kings who became very fond of him on a lifetime basis. Before departing Augusta, Bowdre knew and played with the local crowd his age (Billups Dunbar, the Mathewson twins—Joe and Tracy—mainly, plus others), and once when she was ill as a little girl he came to visit at their Greene Street house with a small bouquet of ivy he had pulled from a wall as Elizabeth (Lib) Fleming Boardman told me!

In reading the Louise Mays diary commencing January 1914, we find that she was then at a finishing school called Springside located in Chestnut Hill, a suburb of Philadelphia. Bowdre was still in Warrenton at Stuyvesant School and the two were in contact by the occasional letter; they also met in Washington, DC en

CHAPTER THREE

route to Augusta if their schedules meshed. Bowdre performed well at his prep school, winning silver cups and prizes and making his grandmother very proud. But reading between lines of Louise's diary, it appears there were some (perhaps natural under the circumstances) tensions on her part at home even though she wanted to be in Augusta with her friends; she clearly wasn't a favorite of her aunt and uncle as a now semi-rebellious teenager of seventeen. She did seem fond of her brother, Bowdre, calling him a "cute kid" now and destined to be a good-looking man; she wished he were older than she and opined that he probably did too! In April 1914, Louise was allowed to visit home (Bowdre then was not given permission by his family) and was told Auntie was going to marry Pendleton King.

It is clear that even at this young age of seventeen Louise thought she was madly in love with Donnie Bussey even though she enjoyed the company of many other boys at parties, etc. Her family always was partial to Boykin Wright, Jr. from the time he and Louise were king and queen in the grand march at the Kermess. As it turned out, Louise's family had other firm plans for her education having determined she would leave for Europe, Miss Leila Hill as the chaperone, with several other girls to attend a finishing school in Belgium, France, or Switzerland for at least a year and a half. Apparently the final decision on which school was to be made once their party reached Europe and had visited all the possibilities. Meantime, Louise returned to Philadelphia to finish at Springside after a round of

Augusta events with Donnie Bussey, Francis Calhoun, Bob Walton, a boy named Tracy Thorpe Jones, Jake Lowrey, Warren Bothwell, and a number of her girlfriends. One interesting bit is that while at Springside, Mr. Bush of Augusta was in town and asked Louise to take lunch one Sunday in Philadelphia, but the school principal (Mrs. Chapman) refused to give her permission! In April 1914 when in Augusta, the Louise diary reports the following: "Mr. Bush came down to supper tonight—I wish he would stop telling me how fat I am! He is certainly not one to talk!"

Because the future schooling and life of Bowdre is covered in great detail in Chapter VII, we now shall continue only with Louise until her marriage in 1917 and departure from 519 Greene Street. However, there is one final point which I trust is a fair assessment of the actual situation: I believe both Bowdre and Louise found it difficult to feel completely at home at 519. The environment was too stately, even a bit courtly, and in this very decorous home there probably were far fewer hugs and kisses than needed! The two teenagers very likely wanted to be on their own and left alone which in later life most find (as they equally did) impossible!

While at Springside in Chestnut Hill, Philadelphia, Louise did exchange letters with her father's sister Aunt Marion Mays Twiggs, who reported regularly on "Nannie" who I assume was grandmother Sarah Crawford Mays, then living in Albany, Georgia. Nannie was quite ill and finally died in Thomasville February 1915, her husband Sam, Sr. having passed away in May

CHAPTER THREE

the year before. Both are buried on the Mays section in the Albany Cemetery that we visited with Mary Lou Bussey and Erick Montgomery en route back to Augusta from a Georgia Trust Ramble a few years back. Louise appears to have been quite fond of Nannie and also her Aunt Marion who passed away suddenly following an appendectomy in January 1923. She too is buried on the Crawford section at Summerville Cemetery, her funeral having been conducted from the home of Judge and Mrs. William H. Barrett on The Hill in Summerville.

Accompanied by Auntie, Louise departed Augusta in early June 1914 by train for New York from where the party was to sail for Europe. William E. Bush joined the train in Baltimore; Louise's diary recorded that they gambled all the way to New York having much fun! They checked into the Collingwood Hotel where Miss Leila Hill joined them. Louise also reported that Auntie was nicer to travel with than she thought! The party sailed for Dover June 6 at 10:00 a.m., sitting at the captain's table on the *Kroon-Land* of the Red Star Line. Louise was seasick the first few days of an eight-day voyage and wrote that there wasn't a good-looking man on board when the captain gave dances at night! Louise did enjoy the deck sports, and after the stop at Dover the Augusta party continued on the ship to Antwerp, ending up in Brussels where they stopped at the Bellevue Hotel next door to the Royal Palace. Then on to Paris where they visited prospective finishing schools: in one were Louise Broyles and Isobel Robinson, but Louise Mays apparently thought little of the school.

It was decided Louise would proceed to Switzerland with the other girls to Rossinieres where they would lodge and study French at the Hotel Grand Chalet or in one of its outbuildings. Just to convey an idea of the US dollar in 1914 and its purchasing power, consider that one school in Tournay, Belgium, charged $200 per annum for full pension and complete instruction by French nuns. There were, however, a few "extras" for piano, singing, or drawing lessons! The Swiss days seemed to have consisted of lessons and tennis with complaints of rain daily and how she missed Donnie Bussey! They went to tea at "the Baron's," and Louise minuted that her present whereabouts were three times as rainy and bad as Lake Toxaway, North Carolina! The Baron talked to Louise in French, and she decided he was quite nice! By late July 1914 Louise was homesick again and still longing for Donnie; fortunately for Louise, World War I entered the picture following the brutal assassination of Archduke Franz Ferdinand June 28 at Sarajevo. However, this incident passed without undue public alarm at first, and it was not until Austria issued its brutal ultimatum to Serbia July 23 that the real panic took control, quickly followed by Austria's declaration of war against Serbia July 28. By August 4, 1914, the war became general, and World War I began in earnest.

With the assistance of Pleasant Stovall, then US minister to Switzerland, and Charles Payson Pressly, vice consul general at Paris, special passports were issued for Louise (and the other Augustans then traveling in Europe) so that they could transit all belligerent

CHAPTER THREE

territory en route to a seaport and home. Louise appears to have gone to England where she "rendezvoused" with Auntie (Mary Lou Phinizy) in London. They stopped at St. Ermins Hotel in late August/early September and likely sailed from Liverpool to New York on the *S.S. Philadelphia* even though their names were not recorded in the passenger listing for this American Line sailing on September 19, 1914. Booking passages in war time probably was difficult, so they may have obtained their accommodation at the last moment.

Louise was then enrolled at Lucy Cobb in Athens (which she apparently enjoyed), presumably remaining there until after her debut party in Augusta circa 1915-1916; this consisted of a large tea at 519 Greene followed by a dance at the Augusta Country Club. Then in the spring of 1917 Donnie Bussey enlisted in the US Army Reserve, applying for a commission at Fort McPherson in Atlanta. He was made a lieutenant following his training, and the couple was married September 20, 1917, at the Church of the Atonement at 11:00 a.m. with a wedding breakfast following at 519 Greene. At that time St. Paul's had been destroyed by the huge 1916 fire, so the Church of the Atonement on Telfair Street was the only practical solution downtown. The bride was given away by her Uncle Bowdre Phinizy, and the best men were Martin Cozart and Howard Ferris. Their wedding trip was to New York and Atlanta with Lieutenant Bussey then stationed at Camp Gordon before his unit went to Europe probably early 1918. Their twin girls, Donald and Harriett, were born July 16, 1918, followed by a third daughter, Mary Louise, arriving September 13, 1920.

Louise stayed on at 519 Greene until her husband returned from Europe in May 1919; they then moved to the house (now torn down) at 409 7th Street given to them by Grandmother Phinizy who also owned the house to the left today known as the Lamar House. When Mary Louise arrived, her great-grandmother, Mary Lou Yancey Phinizy, said, "another little Mary Lou," so this became her name when she was baptized at St. Paul's Church November 21, 1920. While the Phinizy family had not been too thrilled by Louise insisting on her marriage to Donald N. Bussey when she was just twenty and the groom twenty-four (with no large estate or career planned), still her Uncle Bowdre is supposed to have said to his sister, Mary Lou Phinizy, that "at least he can support her!" In the event he really did not fulfill this conjecture very well! But Louise wanted Donnie, and from her diary and his letters it was truly a real love match that endured for their lifetimes.

So to recapitulate a bit, by 1928 the only occupant of 519 Greene was the maiden Mary Lou Phinizy due to the death in late 1926 of Mary Lou Yancey Phinizy, the departure for marriage of Bowdre Mays, Louise Mays, and finally Bowdre Phinizy himself. Initially Mary Lou revealed no sign that she might give up her grandfather and father's home where she was quite comfortable and still with much help. However, the onset of a serious illness (originally misdiagnosed as tuberculosis) appears to have persuaded her to move to the better air

CHAPTER THREE

of Summerville on The Hill where many of her closest friends now lived. As I wrote earlier, Mary Lou's next stage of life is covered under Chapter IV "M.L.P. at 814 Milledge Road." Meantime, in 1933 she sold 519 Greene to Henry W. Poteet and Edward Platt Greelish who used the property for a funeral home.

Circa 1938 the funeral establishment moved to the old Jacob Phinizy house next door and sold 519 Greene to the Augusta Elks Club. At one point in the very late thirties or early forties, Bowdre Phinizy Mays, Sr., my father, was elected the "Grand Exalter Ruler" of the local Elks Club and was interested in showing guests where and how he at one time lived on these premises. In recent years, however, the Elks Club rather trashed the site, covering the beautiful parquet wood floors with commercial carpet or linoleum, adding on a wing to replace the open side porch, painting the handsome leather walls, etc. Then in 1993 a fine gesture was made when William G. Hatcher, Sr. acquired the property from the Elks who had transferred to another location; Mr. Hatcher began renovations retaining and returning to its original state as much of the building as feasible. The project enjoyed success in that the wonderful floors were well preserved under the Elks' decorations and additions; other restorations took place, and items such as the large ballroom mirrors original to the house were returned by me. The home at 519 Green is still known to many older Augustans as the Charles H. Phinizy House; but Bill Hatcher renamed it "The Marion Hatcher Center" in memory of his late wife, and he deserves much credit for his innovative preservation work in rescuing a real Augusta landmark. The Old Phinizy residence is now a popular site for receptions and meetings, so long may this historic property stand and prosper!! I suggest that the house be considered for the National Register for it must be a worthy candidate from old Augusta.

CHAPTER THREE

Mary Lou Yancey Phinizy in her glory at 519 Greene St.

IS LIVING WELL STILL THE BEST REVENGE?

*Charles H. Phinizy ("Cousin Charlie") husband of
Mary Lou Yancey Phinizy*

CHAPTER THREE

Mary Lou Phinizy 519 Greene Street circa 1890

*Bowdre Phinizy as a young man
(sent by Erick Montgomery)*

CHAPTER THREE

Bowdre Phinizy in his prime on the golf course

Harriet Bowdre Phinizy as a young lady

MLP and Tracy Duncan in Paris (1907) calling themselves "The Sponges"

Harriet B. Phinizy and Katie Black in front of 519 Greene Street in cart

CHAPTER THREE

Sam W. Mays, Jr., husband of Harriet Phinizy (L) and Harriet Phinizy Mays (R)

Mary Lou Phinizy and Pendleton King (circa 1911–1912) with MLP in mourning for her sister Harriet

CHAPTER IV

The Private World of Mary Lou Phinizy at 814 Milledge Road

Taken ill in the early 1930s, Mary Lou finally was told by her local physician she had contracted tuberculosis. In those days prior to the introduction of more modern drugs beginning, for example, with the sulfa variety used to destroy bacteria, the usual verdict and conclusion was rest and quiet in the fresh air at a much higher altitude than Augusta. Hence, Mary Lou began to spend time in Asheville, North Carolina, in the western part of the state. She knew Asheville well from prior visits to the King family home located in this medium-sized city surrounded by the Blue Ridge Mountains.

In the summer of 1931, she was at Blossom Cottage, Sunset Terrace, Asheville, on the grounds of the Manor Inn on Charlotte Street. In 1900 Thomas Wadley Raoul opened the Manor Inn in the English style with cottages surrounding where families and their servants would reside on mountain vacations. Meals mostly would be taken at the Inn. Thomas W. Raoul sold the Manor Inn and property to E. W. Grove in 1920 when Raoul became the president of the Biltmore Forest Company. The Raoul family were close friends to not only the King family of Augusta but also with the George Vanderbilts of Biltmore House.

On one occasion, Louise Mays Bussey drove up to Asheville with Rodney Cohen, Sr. to see her "auntie," and as they entered her bedroom Mary Lou experienced a serious hemorrhage from her mouth. This actual event was circa 1931-1933. Genie Lehmann recalls, however, that Mary Lou had at least a touch of tuberculosis in the region of 1919-1921 as she resided in Von Ruck's Sanatorium for a while when Genie's father, Joe Selden, was a patient there. This is news to me, but I write it here as Genie appeared quite definite on the fact. At one stage in the early 1930s Mary Lou stayed in Augusta at Sandy Acres with her close friend Tracy Duncan Cohen in the bed on their back screened porch when she was not in Asheville.

Eventually, she went to Philadelphia to consult the eminent laryngologist Dr. Chevalier Jackson, who was

CHAPTER FOUR

well known by this time for his innovative work with the bronchoscope. Dr. Jackson was a true trailblazer in the use of the bronchoscope to remove foreign objects from the lungs or bronchial tubes. He saved the lives of countless children, animals, and even adults by learning how to extract alien bodies one had swallowed. As Jackson himself had contracted pulmonary tuberculosis at least three times (according to his autobiography) and had been cured, he was accordingly also rather an expert in the disease of the lungs. The Jackson regimen was a diet with plenty of meat and milk combined with a rule of twelve hours rest in bed out of the twenty-four. He also was a convert to the open-air system of treatment for those with tuberculosis.

Mary Lou must have received her diagnosis from Dr. Jackson around 1933-1934; by that time he was the most eminent expert in peroral endoscopy not only in the United States but also in Europe and Latin America. Not limited to the extraction of foreign bodies from the upper air and food tracts, the new procedures were now routine for diagnosis and therapy of orifices below the diaphragm. Dr. Jackson soon determined that Mary Lou, if she once had indeed contracted tuberculosis, must have had what would have been a rather mild attack; there were no bacilli in the sputum. After detailed examination, his conclusion was the development of certain abscesses in her throat and perhaps lungs.

We have learned that the Chevalier Jackson records, files, and all memorabilia are presently housed in Philadelphia at the Mütter Museum of the College of Physicians; however, we failed in locating treatment records for M.L.P. Perhaps all patient files were destroyed after his death in August 1958 at age ninety-two as papers of this class often are judged confidential between the patient and doctor only. So following whatever medical care was rendered in Philadelphia, Mary Lou returned home apparently happy with Dr. Jackson and his suggested remedy and future therapy. As a matter of fact, she appeared to dote on him for the rest of her life! And the good doctor was said to be equally fond of her!

In accord with Dr. Jackson's recommendations, she revised her lifestyle to rest more in the open air and in summer at the higher elevations. If she had not already taken the decision (as is possible), she proceeded with Tracy's recommendation to purchase the old Adams House at 814 Milledge Road. Mary Lou had known the house in her youth when she went to parties there given by the Misses Adams. The Adams family always had owned 814 Milledge Road, a property of around two acres with the second house built on the site circa 1870-1873 when the original 1808 dwelling burned. The second house was built in Second Empire (some now say Victorian) style with the usual high mansard roof and a good deal of intricate millwork. The original brick kitchen from the 1808 house was a separate unit and could now serve admirably as a one-car garage; while the house required some work on the interior ground and second floors to suit the new owner, the location was ideal, and there seems to have been no hesitation in paying the $10,000 pure base price.

CHAPTER FOUR

Mary Lou immediately decided to convert the original second-floor dining room to her bedroom, adding an open-air but screened sleeping porch opening from the bedroom to the side of the house, building a new bathroom to be contiguous to the bedroom, and constructing a small bedroom and bath for Lena Carter Glover, maid and domestic confidant, in an area that was probably a part of a rear porch. Tall bookcases were added to the large open area extending from the front entrance hall, and in the second-floor bedroom, while the back dining room glass windows overlooking the back porch were fully mirrored in the European manner. The dining room with fireplace and mantel in the Phinizy era formerly was sort of a sitting room opening off the more formal drawing room with twin fireplaces at each end and situated across the entire front of the Adams home; or perhaps the Adamses had considered the front long room as their ballroom? To establish the backdrop more clearly, keep in mind a large four-story white clapboard (late Empire) Victorian mansion with a semi-circular driveway in gravel and fronted by a brick openwork wall behind the sidewalk. Mary Lou installed the wall of old brick and ensured that the long curving drive was bordered by large boxwood shrubs of either English or American varieties.

On the third floor a bathroom was upgraded for the two front bedrooms; it remains rather uncertain what other important remodeling happened upstairs although there were several other bed chambers fully furnished. The fourth-floor attic area was untouched and just used for unwanted furniture, pictures, and general bric-a-brac. The Adams house contained a large ground-floor (or first) area in a part of which was sited the "modern kitchen"; installed was an old-fashioned "dumbwaiter" to cart the food upstairs to the pantry. Initially this arrangement continued with Janie reigning supreme in the culinary department. Janie was the long-time cook from 519 Greene.

The house at 814 was furnished almost completely with the furniture and accessories brought from 519 Greene. Mary Lou even found a place in the front drawing room for the twin huge gold-leafed mirrors formerly in the 519 ballroom. These matching Empire mirrors were nineteenth century being 11 feet 2¼ inches in height by 66 inches wide and were hung facing each other in the middle of the long room. Other period pieces included the handsome Empire bookcase/writing desk, Empire sideboard and dining table (which she divided into two sections), a French bow-front inlaid commode, and numerous Empire or American Renaissance furniture pieces. Mary Lou also acquired a reproduction bedstead of graceful proportion in mahogany, queen sized, and probably in the Sheraton style. There was also an old-fashioned single bedstead of Victorian iron on the sleeping porch in complete readiness for the warm fair weather (there was a ceiling fan) and conceivably afternoon naps on the cooler days.

The dining room now contained a pair of interesting Victorian or Empire marble-topped serving tables with mirrors below, an Empire-period cellaret in the sideboard front cavity, and a large high corner Hepplewhite cabinet holding at least a portion of her mother's complete Dresden porcelain collection; this was the output from the world-famous Meissen Factory at Dresden and included not only dozens of plates, large and small, cups, bowls, etc., but also fabulous covered tureens, cake plates on stands, fruit dishes, and other miscellaneous pieces. This porcelain today inhabits the modern residence of Judge Frank Mays Hull in Atlanta.

One noticed on entering the front entrance hall the sweeping curved stairway with mahogany banister leading to the third floor; and set into the curved wall near the beginning of the stairway was a tall niche where the impressive large French Sévres urn glorifying one of the Napoleon Bonaparte victories was positioned. All in all a very imposing and pleasing interior prospect for any visitor.

The health regime of Dr. Jackson was a great triumph so that Mary Lou soon felt herself restored to a salubrious level. To solve the hot weather nuisance for Augusta residents, she found a suitable house on Satulah Mountain above Highlands, North Carolina. She paid about $15,000 for this comfortable summer cottage and separate garage on a fairly large piece of land. There were three bedrooms, an upstairs sleeping porch, two or three full baths, a huge combined living and dining room with fireplace opening onto a spacious screened front porch plus a large kitchen and accommodation off that for her domestic help. The latter consisted of Lena, Janie, and "Son" in residence from early June until October each year. As in the Augusta house, Mary Lou acquired an avid interest in the gardens on her properties. In Highlands her dahlias and rhododendron were well regarded while she added to the beautiful English and American boxwoods in Augusta and constructed a formal garden terrace of old brick, surrounded by roses and azalea to the left side of 814 Milledge Road.

Mary Lou named the 814 Milledge Road dwelling Adams House and bestowed the appellation Caravan on the Satulah Mountain house situated some four hundred feet higher than the then village of Highlands. The real glory of that mountain house was the spectacular view from the porch and side gardens to the three mountain ranges on all sides in the distance; there was some fog at times, but usually one would also enjoy the prospect of the valley down below. On the mostly clear and bright days, there were particularly fine vistas of Sunset Rock on the right and Whiteside Mountain straight ahead across the vale.

While now having solved her housing situation in two climates, for summer and winter, and being in a fine physical state, Mary Lou for the rest of her life rested a great deal: for example, if she were planning to go out in the evening to a cocktail or supper party, she would fully undress and rest and sleep in bed during the afternoon. Should she not be sleepy, she would stay in bed anyway and read. Mary Lou certainly was born with a "gold spoon" in her mouth and never forgot her heritage as a direct descendant of Hamiltons, Yanceys, and Phinizys, although she often allowed that the Phinizy men had "married up." Emily Thomas Clay used to say, "Mary

CHAPTER FOUR

Lou is a Yancey, not a Phinizy!" But Mary Lou well knew that being a Phinizy in Georgia did mean something and never hesitated to say so! This even though local lore and jesters often said she and Tracy Duncan Cohen had been denied hotel reservations on occasion in those less politically correct times!

Mary Lou all her life lived strictly only on income; she could be tightfisted, always complaining about the cost of servants, maintaining her establishments, taxes, etc. However, she would be gracious and provide help to family members or others if she felt the individual required support as a step to making progress. By way of illustration, she gave me a trip to Mexico with a school group one summer and purchased winter clothes for my brother Inman Mays and me when we first obtained jobs after university. But in 1932, when my grandmother Doughty advised that her beloved nephew Bowdre needed funds to start the Furniture Market Inc. and asked her to contribute to a loan in the offing, Mary Lou refused saying, "They have made their bed and now must lie in it!"

She had never really approved of Bowdre's 1924 marriage since he had little visible means of support and never respected or admired Frank Inman Mays, her nephew's wife, until later years when Tracy and others made her realize what a good mother and housewife she had been by mentoring and raising five fine children. Mary Lou finally found at least a modicum of affection for Frankie (as she always called her) and her ebullient personality. Nonetheless she continued to believe

Bowdre and Frankie were spendthrifts and not totally responsible, using as one example the large oriental rug she had given them (originally in the 519 Greene Street house ballroom) that was ruined by water, etc., while in storage at the Furniture Market when they were building the Montrose Court house in 1960.

I believe it fair to state that the three people Mary Lou loved most as the years went on were her old friends from school days—Tracy Duncan Cohen and Sophie Meldrim Shonnard, originally from Savannah—and my father, Bowdre Phinizy Mays, Sr. Mary Lou talked to or saw Tracy virtually every day when in Augusta, had a standing Friday lunch engagement with Bowdre week after week, and visited Sophie in New York City or saw her in the South several times a year in addition from letters and telephone chats. Bowdre at first took her to Greene's at East Boundary for the excellent fried shrimp (taken with lots of hot sauce); later they would lunch at 814 where Lena would prepare a simple but sumptuous repast of grilled chicken, a small steak or broiled quail usually with his favorite potatoes au gratin or an eggplant dish much like the French ratatouille. Bowdre (according to Lena) would impart the Broad Street news and gossip, and they would always discuss "family affairs," past and present, holding little back; obviously here I do not refer to activity in the erotic sense! Mary Lou was quite pleased Bowdre was at last doing well financially and was interested in seeing his children growing as well as taking their place in Augusta or in the exterior.

CHAPTER FOUR

Sophie Meldrim's father, Judge Peter Meldrim, also state senator, the president of the American Bar Association at one point, and mayor of Savannah, had known the mother of Mary Lou as a leading belle in Athens and when as Mary Lou Yancey she married her first husband, Ferdinand Bowdre Phinizy. Peter and Bowdre, as well as Hamilton Yancey, Mary Lou's brother, had all been members of the Chi Phi Fraternity at the University of Georgia and were featured in a 1868 Chi Phi photograph. Mary Lou Phinizy and Sophie were friends as girls, visiting back and forth, and the attachment endured for their lifetimes. Sophie first married the famous Yale football hero Ted Coy and had two sons; they divorced in the early 1920s when Sophie married Horatio Shonnard, called Ray mainly and possessing great wealth. Apart from their New York City residence, there was a "Shooting Box" in Scotland, and as befits a great Southern lady, the new groom presented his new wife with a true Southern plantation in McClellanville, South Carolina, about forty-five miles north of Charleston. At the time there were 953 acres with 350 in rice fields and a manor house of 17 rooms, built 1791-1797, which the Shonnards perfectly restored in 1930 with all of its decorative features. The property overlooked the south Santee River, being around six miles from the Atlantic Ocean and with the Seaboard Railroad two miles away. Among the extensive outbuildings was a guest cottage of two bedrooms with its living room paneled in imported antique English pine.

Sophie offered "Harrietta" for sale through Previews Inc. circa 1940s at $115,000; in 1992 the house was on the National Register and with 7,947 square feet of extensive restorations in 1981-1984 offered for sale with its now 1,016 acres in 4 tracts at $3.95 million. Having visited the house and property in the early 1990s, it is no exaggeration to say Harrietta is a superb example of Southern Colonial or antebellum architecture in an excellent state. I surmise the Shonnards were divorced in the late 1930s; Ray's stepson Peter Coy told me Shonnard became bored with life on the plantation and the lack of any real action on the New York Stock Exchange during the Depression and early 1930s!

I first met Miss Sophie in autumn 1948, my initial year in New York at my first job, when Aunt Mary Lou entrained to the metropolis to visit Sophie who then had an apartment at 675 Madison Avenue where Mary Lou also stayed on this visit. Sophie and her friend Nona McAdoo Park ran a dress shop called Chez Ninon, Inc. located at 785 Fifth Avenue. I later learned that the shop was named for the famous seventeenth-century French "courtesan of quality" Ninon de Lanclos! Seventeenth-century France was really a time of great splendor and extreme ostentation so this truth too might have affected and influenced the decision on the shop name. During the John F. Kennedy presidency one of their most prominent customers was Jackie B. Kennedy; the connection probably arose from Nona McAdoo Park's Washington associations for Nona had been her father's hostess when he was appointed secretary of the Treasury

CHAPTER FOUR

by Woodrow Wilson. This was before William McAdoo married his second wife, Wilson's youngest daughter, Eleanor Randolph, known in the Wilson family as "Nell."

I believe Sophie Meldrim Coy first knew Nona in her early Washington days as the Coys at one time did live in the capital city. Nona's first husband was Ferdinand de Mohrenschildt, secretary at the Russian czar's embassy up to 1917-1918 and one of the many who died (1919) in the influenza epidemic after World War I. The couple then were in New York City. Their Washington wedding, to which the czar's permission was given, had been an important social event in one season.

Another associate at Chez Ninon in the 1960s was Molly McAdoo (I believe sister-in-law to Nona) whom the designer Arnold Scaasi hired away to be directress of his salon due to her contacts with well-heeled social New Yorkers. *Time Magazine* featured a short article on Chez Ninon circa 1965-1966 commenting principally on its interesting dowager owners and their charm. Sophie and Nona went to Paris for the couture shows annually, always stopping at the small Hotel Vendôme just off the Place Vendôme. At this time (1960s) Sophie and Nona shared a large and elegant New York apartment on East 57th Street near the East River and Sutton Place. Sophie was listed now as Mrs. Meldrim Shonnard. The French maid, Thérése, I had first met in 1948, still was with Sophie. Sophie was a real charmer who even at what I considered then to be a rather advanced age (but not now!) used her large expressive "baby blues" and hands to great effect as she focused solidly on her companion or, say, a newcomer. I enjoyed trying out my poor French with Thérése as her English was a bit sketchy but spoken with a delightful French accent. Thérése had been with Sophie for many years (probably hired in Paris in the early 1920s) and always appeared very fond of "Miss Phinizy" and Sophie's two sons with whom she often joked. The story I heard about Ted Coy, Sophie's first husband and father of her two sons, Ted Jr., and Peter Meldrim, is that he became the "great and good friend" of Jeanne Eagels (whose real name was Aguila, Spanish for "eagle") who opened in New York in 1922 in the hit play *Rain* by Somerset Maugham.

During the New York City and Harrietta periods, Mary Lou and Sophie exchanged many visits, with Sophie staying at 814 Milledge on one occasion (in the post-Shonnard marriage) after motoring up from Savannah with a gentleman friend and his chauffeur. Sophie now became a regular summer visitor to Highlands; en route by train from New York to Asheville, Mary Lou and Son would drive over to meet her; if Sophie happened to be in Savannah with her sister Caroline, then she might drive up to Highlands with a friend, for example with Violet or Cheshire Nash, who had a Satulah Mountain house a short walk up from Caravan. Tracy and Rod, Sr. would drive up with Tracy staying on for several weeks after Rod returned to Augusta; he would return perhaps with his mother Nora and Judge Hammond for a long weekend before descending the mountain again.

CHAPTER FOUR

Other Augusta visitors from time to time included Dina Taliaferro, Mary Alexander, Rod Cohen, Jr. and his wife Anne, her Bussey and Mays relatives at different weekends, and also the younger generation in the late 1930s and 1940s including myself and Inman and Ted Mays, Frank Mays, Betty Phinizy, Jim Hull Jr., and Bobby Neely from Waynesboro. Cashiers in those days was just a small village, but Mary Lou liked to drive over to the High Hampton Inn for lunch. It was not "cafeteria-like" in those days! While summering in Highlands, her friends in residence included the Nashes of Savannah with their two daughters Violet (called Little Vee) and Ann, Elizabeth (Sis) Calhoun who had built a home on lower Satulah in the very late 1930s, the Craig Cranstons (also on Satulah), Margaret Rankin from Atlanta (also Satulah), the David Blacks (Marion, the wife, was her Phinizy cousin) of Atlanta with their charming daughter Anne, and several more from Augusta and Florida. Added to the foregoing were some year-round residents (such as the Elliott sisters on Satulah) and their close kin from Scarsdale, New York, the Cunningham family, plus others from Augusta and elsewhere who rented villas at the Highlands Country Club or stopped at one of the hotels.

Marguerite Pressly Kratina and her family rented for several years and were together often with Mary Lou and the Blacks. There were many evening bridge games with the Cranstons, cocktails hither and yon, with a picnic once or twice a month in the late afternoon on Sunset Rock. Lena always made her famous casserole of "jazzed-up" baked beans (much in demand), and while the adults drank their cocktails we saw the sun pass below the horizon before attacking the plenteous supper. Swimming took place in a creek off the road to the Highlands Country Club; there was a pool-like crevice surrounded by rocks with the mountain water very cool and crystal clear. Aunt Mary Lou usually wore a type of life-preserver vest, and sometimes we took a light picnic lunch. Usually the water was too cold for my taste being accustomed to the South Carolina beaches!

Craig Cranston Jr., as I suspected, reports that his parents, being close friends to M.L.P., urged her to buy the Satulah Mountain house. He further recalls her rather extensive entertaining and house guests to also include Jake Lowrey from Augusta, Elizabeth Smart of Savannah, and Sophie Shonnard, who often sunbathed in the long side garden when, Craig reports, "she was not flitting around in theatrical poses!" Craig also jogged my memory of the silver flasks the ladies always carried when gathering for lunch and bridge or at cocktails in the late afternoons. The bridge ladies were M.L.P., Catherine Cranston, Flo Saussy, and Violet Nash, all of whom lived nearby on Satulah. Violet Nash only drank Scotch (rather a rarity at that time) and most others matured corn or bourbon highballs with gin martinis too before lunch or dinner. All conveyed about in their handsome silver flasks usually hand-engraved with initials: we have today the M.L.P. flask in our living room bookcase.

CHAPTER FOUR

Mary Lou continued her strong support of Sand Hills Garden Club as a charter member and agreed to serve as its president from 1938-1940. This entailed making trips to Garden Club of America annual meetings in addition to visits with clubs in the region. The Colonial Dames was another interest, and accompanied by Tracy and sometimes others, jaunts took place to attend meetings around Georgia. On her journeys to New York City, when she did not lodge with Sophie, she always stopped at the St. Regis Hotel, then owned by Vincent Astor who knew Sophie and where she received some special attention.

One trip with Tracy and Jake Lowrey was to New Orleans while en route by automobile to Natchez to see the historic homes. Tracy inserted a poem in her *Out of My Mind* book on this stop when all three travelers decided to stay on in New Orleans and "stuff," so fine and succulent did they all find the eats! On several occasions Mary Lou and the senior Cohens spent long weekends with Frank and Bowdre Mays at their Edisto Beach house enjoying the cool breezes and local freshly caught seafood. This in the 1950s. The only excursions during her 814 Milledge years outside of the United States and known to me were a visit to Canada in the late 1940s (probably connected to the Garden Club of America) and a long three-month tour of Europe in 1957. The latter was her last time to visit Europe and her first since the late 1920s. The tour was carefully organized by Grace Crawford of "Southern Travel" and even included Spain where Mary Lou had never been. Cars and drivers met them everywhere, train travel inside Europe was the mode, and they twice crossed the big pond on famous transatlantic lines: the *Queen Elizabeth* outward and the *Queen Mary* returning.

The party also included Teto Barrett (her first European trip) and Flora Barringer of Columbia, South Carolina. At one time the Barringer family owned the Richmond Hotel in Augusta together with hostelries in other towns. Mary Lou and Teto were roommates on the entire journey and, as per Teto's daughter Mary, having three persons worked rather well in that there always was someone to be with should one prefer at the time solitude. They sailed from and returned to New York where the Harold V. Smiths were their hosts as I believe they stayed with Alice and Harold at their spacious 10 Gracie Square duplex prior to leaving (my brother Inman, however, remembers that M.L.P. and Teto Barrett stopped at the St. Regis Hotel before embarking on the Atlantic crossing as he met them there with Sophie Shonnard and then on to a nearby restaurant to take lunch) and on their return before entraining for the South. On their return Harold V. Smith arranged "Freedom of the Port" so that they flew through US customs, nothing opened and no hassles. Mr. Harold once told me of their return and said he told all the ladies to place telephone calls to the families awaiting their return; he related with a smile and laugh that Mary Lou had called Lena immediately! Mary Lou and Teto (who was much younger and a contemporary of my mother Frank) began this friendship from their Sand Hills Garden Club relationship;

CHAPTER FOUR

such was cemented and indeed blossomed during their European sojourn. The attachment and rapport resulted in much mutual affection on both sides. Mary Lou often used to say, "Teto is the perfect mother," and Teto said Mary Lou was both fun and interesting.

Tracy and Mary Lou lunched together often at each other's home after walking the short distance between 814 Milledge and 2150 Battle Row, using of course Gordon Lane to cut off the corner at Battle Row. They continued to hold hands in public with this act attracting disparaging and risqué comments in certain circles; those in the know realized there was no physical relationship between these two devoted friends and just smiled sweetly! However, long before Mary Lou and Teto became intimate friends, Teto Barrett and "Baby" Hagler would sometimes imitate Mary Lou and Tracy by holding hands while sitting on a sofa at a girl's party! Both Mary Lou and Tracy read widely and invariably supported each other's activities in gardening, writing, whatever the venture. Some would call them snobs and say they disliked the hoi polloi; there may be some truth (or a modicum of it anyway!) to that while one group might say they liked and generally would accept anyone with breeding or money. Money indeed is a great leveling force for as Somerset Maugham wrote, "Money is like a sixth sense without which you cannot make a complete use of the other five." Breeding and money did impress Mary Lou, and very likely Tracy, and one could observe a change in opinion relative to persons who learned what to do and rose in the world becoming wealthy in the process! My father Bowdre and his Auntie once discussed "snobs," and I overheard their conclusion that perhaps they were a bit snobbish and didn't mind it a bit! The difference is that Bowdre had fun with all classes even though his wife Frank generally said he often preferred to be with common folks!

There was one bone of contention in later years that crept into the Mary Lou-Tracy friendship: this was Mary Lou's preoccupation with "facts" for, as she habitually put it, "facts are facts," and one is bound to admit and accept facts! The emphasis on facts became more of a theme as Mary Lou grew older and tended to lose all patience with naiveté as practiced by certain artless mortals. So when Tracy sent Mary Lou a copy of her book of poems, she penned a new poem on the flyleaf for Mary Lou suggesting that facts should be left way behind because it is more gratifying by far to focus on more pleasant exploits! Facts, Tracy wrote, are just "so hard and cold and bare, I find it's nice when we leave fact behind!" Of course none of this would impress Mary Lou who continued her search for the salient "facts" at all times!

Several of the Carter relatives (Lena, Janie, and Son) at various times also worked for Tracy as domestic staff, so this situation also made the two households closer. Both ladies loved dogs, and always had, so following "Sugarlump's" death (circa early 1940s) due to old age, Mary Lou first bought a little black Scottish terrier she familiarly named "Fella" who brought her happiness for many years. I know he was still alive in 1955, as I have seen several postcards addressed to him that year from England and Italy! I presume the Phinizy "Fella" might have acquired his nickname from President F. D. Roosevelt's Scottie who had a similar sounding moniker, "Fala." She next acquired two black Scottie brothers named Mahout (Hindu for "elephant keeper") and Juggernaut (a Hindu belief calling for blind self-sacrifice); the puppies soon were renamed "Hootie" and "Juggy" familiarly, both living to rather advanced ages. Mary Lou never really learned how to handle dogs; they were kept locked up except for short walks on leashes, seldom saw other dogs, and rarely if ever romped or played with children. Hence, Hootie and Juggy were not too friendly with visitors! After the Scotties came a standard-sized poodle, also coal black, and named "Dominique" after the French singing nun then on television. The poodle, nicknamed "Nicky," was something of a terror for visitors (she usually had to be kept on her leash) and would even scratch Mary Lou's arms and legs when on her bed!

Although Mary Lou continued to be a private person but nonetheless someone with much common sense and a practical approach, she accepted in April 1941 an appointment to the Board of Directors of the Georgia Railroad and Banking Company. This was the institution her father, Colonel Charles H. Phinizy, had served as president and director for seventeen years from 1880. She was the first woman to be elected a director and continued to be a member of the board until at her request she resigned after thirty-four years. She was honored at a luncheon upon her retirement at age eighty-eight. In April 1941, her nephew Bowdre Mays went to Union Station to meet the train on her return from New York City. She was then interviewed as her elevation to the Board of Directors had just been announced. When discussing money one of her favorite expressions was "cash on the mahogany," as in "Can they put, say $25,000 now on the mahogany?" This was a measure she liked!

Mary Lou maintained her interest in the Georgia Railroad Bank until her death and was present when the bank's new edifice of some seventeen stories was opened with the Pinnacle Club on the top floors; she gave a short speech praising the executive team for bringing them all to "The Pinnacle"! She once told me none of her heirs would be able to sell Georgia Railroad stock, but at her death she owned none, presumably having sold it later to purchase equities paying higher yields! In honor of her father, M.L.P. endowed the Pinnacle Club library, which has on the paneled wall a brass plaque designating the room as the Charles H. Phinizy Library. At one point she also donated to the club a copy of Ferdinand Phinizy Calhoun's early 1920s book *Phinizy Family In America* and had this placed in a low glass-topped but locked cabinet. This book had disappeared from the cabinet by the early 1990s and could not be located in the club premises when I tried to find it!

Circa 1940s Mary Lou turned the ground floor 814 Milledge kitchen, adjourning pantries, and storerooms into a rather spacious one-bedroom apartment to include a combined living/dining room, kitchen, etc. Bill Trotter rented this through his real estate agency, and over the years she had interesting tenants. One was the daughter of David Dubinsky; she was married to an officer at Fort Gordon. Another was William B. Jones (also known to some as "Willie Boo") but usually the military or medical students studying at Medical College of Georgia. They were all in their turn invited to family lunches, evening parties, or taken to dinner in the later years at The Pinnacle Club. Having someone else resident in the house also gave Mary Lou a greater sense of security. At the same time the main floor pantry/kitchen was expanded with the dumbwaiter blocked off.

Approximately twice a month Lena would call early in the week to invite the Busseys and the Mayses to take Sunday dinner; the Mayses were told to bring two or three children only! There were also family holiday dinners, such as Christmas and Thanksgiving, although in one or two years these gatherings were held at the Bussey or Mays house. In the springtime the Sunday lunches (but always called dinners) were on occasion in the nice weather served buffet style in the rear gardens off the pathway arbor in the right back part. There might be chicken curry and rice or chicken croquettes which Louise Bussey and Frankie Mays thought a fine change from the usual shoulder of lamb provided inside as they said the shoulder was the cheapest fatty part! Miss Dina Taliaferro was usually a guest at these Sunday affairs, sometimes John Walton, Miss Marjorie Innes (a friend from youth), or an out-of-town visitor such as Grace, Countess Gregorini.

Mary Lou's steady and close friends, aside from Tracy, comprised the George Traylors (with Louise Bothwell Traylor a special favorite), Catherine Verderey Cranston and her sister Pauline Verdery, Sadie Cranston Barrett, Mary Alexander, Jake Lowrey, the Landon Thomas Jrs. (M.L.P. took the Thomas-Cassius Clay side in the later family squabble), Marie Phinizy Hull, and William E. Bush. Others included Bertha Barrett Lee and many ladies such as Agnes Beane, Maisie Chafee, Julia Walton Houston, Annie S. Burdell, Helen Jack, Anita Phinizy Wallace, Lib Boardman and her mother Daisy Fleming, Mrs. Joseph Mck. Speer, Mrs. Boykin Wright Sr., the Eugene Murpheys and the Virgil Sydenstrickers, Mrs. Frederic B. Pope (an old friend of Mary Lou's mother), and the mother of Pendleton King, Mrs. Henry Barclay King, she met until their deaths in the late 1930s. Other Milledge Road homeowners Mary Lou saw with varying degrees of intimacy, mainly at Sand Hills meetings, included Mrs. Harry Albright, Mrs. Francis Denny, Mrs. Francis Drury, Nina Cohen White, Frankie Doughty, Miss Langdon, Louise Del'aigle Reese, and Mrs. John Herbert, the final two named being considered non-resident members. All these names will present the reader with the general scene around Mary Lou's life.

Mary Lou was generous in entertaining friends and family: she gave parties to celebrate Tracy and Rod's thirtieth wedding anniversary in 1939, the launch of Tracy's book of poems in 1956, an engagement party

CHAPTER FOUR

for her great niece Frank Inman Mays in May 1947, the same for myself in 1965, and was always agreeable to hosting events for The Garden Club of America or to assist Tracy with a pet project, e.g. The Augusta Council of Garden Clubs. She did have a favorable impact on the civic life of Augusta, even if preferring to remain behind the scenes when asked to participate. Invitations to 814 Milledge probably were rather coveted even though in the last final years Mary Lou refused to recover furniture or repair anything broken; should a leg break on a chair or table to the fourth floor attic the piece would go and an immediate replacement found from the attic or on the third floor! So the many visitors seemed to completely overlook the threadbare or shabby chair coverings or upholstery and concentrate on the silver, china (all English, French, or Dresden), the huge mirrors, and several magnificent pieces of period Empire or nineteenth-century American/English furniture. There undoubtedly was a certain ambiance of charm and graciousness in the totality of the house, surroundings, and contents, all of which enhanced the allure.

As my generation grew to maturity with Mary Lou now enjoying the role more of a grande dame, she started to include the younger people on some guest lists: the Calhoun Withams, Bobby Neelys, The Clay brothers, Jim Hull, Jr., Henry Garrett Jr., etc. She delighted in the Frank Mays-Jim Hull, Jr. 1947 wedding with Marie Phinizy Hull saying how much closer this would now bring these cousins and two friends from childhood. Many of the evening events in the winter were black-tie with white jackets in the hot summer season. Those attending might include the Edison Marshalls, Billy Bush, Judge and Mrs. Fred Kennedy, Grover Maxwell Srs., Rodney Cohens, William T. Garys, Gene Longs, Landon Thomas Jrs., Judge Henry Hammond, Nora Cohen, etc. just to note a few names. When the house of Nora Cohen next door was rented following her death in 1950 to a granddaughter of the writer Mary Roberts Rhineheart, she included this attractive young couple (he was stationed at Fort Gordon) at parties and readily accepted their invitations in return. As I write I can see them now dancing up and down the M.L.P. long living room to the beat of a vibrant polka tune! This in the early 1950s. At that time my father would say that Auntie will go anywhere she is invited!

Mary Lou was particularly magnanimous in 1947 when she offered the newly married Hull, Jr. couple (then temporarily in her basement flat) about a third of an acre hived-off from her property at the back so that their first starter house could be built. Frank's father Bowdre also made a similar offer of the Lake Forest Drive lot he had purchased next to their house. The Hulls chose Milledge Road, and Stockton constructed an attractive old-brick house with two bedrooms. Although Mary Lou's side drive was used for access, still 814½ Milledge Road was private for both homes.

Another indication of her benevolence (and the exact opposite of what some called her tendency to be miserly), was her offer to sell Caravan to John E. Hines, formerly rector of St. Paul's Church in Augusta but

CHAPTER FOUR

later Rector of Christ Church in Houston, Texas, and now Bishop Coadjutor of Texas. It was the summer of 1950 in Highlands when John and Helen Hines came to call and to advise of their plan to build a vacation house on eight acres they already owned. I assume the location of this property was close by or up from Seneca, South Carolina, where Hines was born in 1910. The Hines couple had been loaned the Phinizy house for a time during two summers while he was rector of St. Paul's (February 1937 to January 1941); probably Mary Lou had offered the use of her house during a period when she was away on one of her trips. Highlands, North Carolina was the mountain resort that had appealed to Hines since his youth. Mary Lou, to their great surprise, seemed to have made the proposition that rather than build they buy her house provided she would have the use of it for two more summers. When Hines is supposed to have responded they could not really afford her spacious property, Mary Lou inquired what if she made an offer one couldn't refuse and then received an affirmative answer. They would pay $5,000 in cash and take on a $10,000 mortgage at 2 percent interest per annum. Naturally they could never decline such a bountiful and charitable proposal.

I still don't really know why at this early date in the 1950s she made this decision; the biography of John Hines states she was "in failing health," but this is definitely not the case as she lived on another twenty-seven years; one family rationale is that her butler, chauffeur, and gardener, Son, resigned to work for the Georgia

Railroad, and Lena said she was too tired and could not handle Caravan much more. Perhaps it is true, as the Hines biography opines, that Mary Lou wanted to ensure that Caravan end up with a couple she admired and who were on the way to the very pinnacle of success in the Episcopal Church: John Hines was elected in 1964 the twenty-second presiding bishop of the US church. Hines was controversial in some quarters, even in his early pastorate at Augusta, but many admired his courage and fairness. As Dr. Irvine Phinizy, a strong member of his flock at St. Paul's said, "He always got along amazingly well despite his outspokenness."

I still wonder if Mary Lou, considering her determination to sell Caravan, for about what she paid for it many years earlier, did take advantage of gift tax laws to reduce taxes as she had few deductions? I trust she did!! Craig Cranston estimates the Caravan market value in 1952 at $75,000 and at $900,000 today with its many improvements; my wife says at least $1.2-1.5 million!!

Violet and Cheshire Nash sent Mary Lou a farewell poem in September 1952 deploring her departure:

> "What! Lose you as a neighbor,
> It's in our deepest heart a saber
> To swap you for a bishop,
> Is simply gall and hyssop
> Any kind of ban
> On charming "Caravan"
> Is wormwood and ashes
> To the lachrymose Nashes

CHAPTER FOUR

> So we're hoping next summer when
> You're planning to roam
> That you'll look upon "Cobham"
> As your number two home."

Mary Lou would see the Nashes either in Highlands or Savannah together with Sophie on her visits down South. They liked to discuss history and dwell on the War Between the States as a subject still of distinct importance. One feature of these definitely unreconstructed conversations was in 1952 dealing with President Lincoln's Proclamation of Emancipation in which he only set free the slaves in the rebellious states but not in those states still in the union. The Emancipation Proclamation was effective January 1, 1863, and was, of course, a stab to enfeeble the Confederate states; however, few now know that the slaves in the Union states were not granted then the same treatment. Violet Nash Jr. (called Little Vee) married Olin McIntosh of Savannah and for many years lived on Hilton Head Island in their house on the end of Bram's Point; we visited them there in the early 1970s as arranged by Mary Lou.

When Lynn Alexander, my fiancé and betrothed, came to Augusta in March 1965 to meet the family, Aunt Mary Lou gave us a large evening party at 814 with not only family but my school friends as well in attendance. There also were some of the older friends, e.g. the Rodney Cohens, Teto Barrett, Landon Thomas Jrs., Mary "D" Goodrich, to mention a few names. These evening receptions continued every two or three years when we came to Augusta from our assignments abroad in 1968, 1970, 1972, 1973, and I believe the last in 1974 when M.L.P. was about eighty-seven. My father advised that his auntie began to show some age when, after one of their regular Friday lunches downtown, she drove him the wrong way up Greene Street for a moment before being able to cross to the correct side! Of course at lunch Mary Lou would as usual bring her martini cocktail in a silver flask to drink with ice added before lunch!

We wanted Mary Lou and Tracy to come up to New York City for our wedding June 5, 1965, and this they did to our great pleasure, traveling by train and bringing wonderful flowers to decorate Sophie's apartment for the dinner the night before. Mary Lou that year was seventy-eight. As time crept onward with Mary Lou into her mid-eighties, she appeared to have slowed a bit; Lena's death was a blow in 1968, but she carried on with new staff on a full-time basis in the house and with Moses in the yard and house as butler when "Son" resigned. Teto Barrett assisted a lot with tracking down reliable and dependable persons; Mary Lou probably was not an easy mistress due to a lack of patience and her "facts are facts" approach! Jane Bush Long, the daughter of Billy Bush, paid Mary Lou attention and often had her to Sunday family lunches; so did Skippy Hull Boyd, particularly after her mother, Marie, died in 1974. Frank Mays drove Mary Lou and Tracy to the grocery store several times and reported they were a pair to observe in old tan rain coats and red low-heeled bedroom shoes they always wore outside too!

CHAPTER FOUR

One charming story told me by Ray Raymond, who at one time owned 820 Milledge Road (next door on the right), is that one evening when she was meeting an applicant wanting to lease her basement apartment, the young man was ushered into her bedroom where she was sitting up in bed propped with many pillows behind, drinking a gin martini in a silver julep cup, and reading Hitler's *Mein Kampf*! The medical student too was of course offered a cocktail!

In 1975, when we were in Augusta, aunt Mary Lou informed us she was not having her usual party due to the death of someone I cannot now recall and the rather parlous financial situation of my parents! Lynn and I did see her several times before we went to Hilton Head with our children as usual; on one occasion, prior to lunch at The Pinnacle Club, she asked if we would like her house, so it was apparent she was for the last time putting all affairs in order. She told me once that one would make many wills in a lifetime, and her final one was drawn and signed September 3, 1975. There were several codicils thereafter making revisions as late as September 1976. The final will and testament as probated was rather vintage and typical M.L.P. in that her intention was to reward those who she believed were making something of their lives and to carefully avoid providing more than a bare "safety net" to the relatives who in her judgment had not been responsible. The final estate was worth about $1.5 million with two substantial legacies made to St. Paul's Church and the Augusta YWCA in memory of her parents. M.L.P. had inherited around $250,000-300,000 when she came of age and after her mother's death in 1926; had she sought better advice or even accepted the advice she enjoyed over the years from her banker and stockbroker, her estate would have ballooned far beyond the final total.

Although the bank attempted to provide tax advice to reduce the impact when she died, she adamantly declined to organize irrevocable trusts or simply give money to her family (and some were needy) over the years to reduce the final tax burden and Uncle Sam's take at the end. For example, she retained large amounts in her checking account earning zero interest; in 1977 Mary Lou Bussey, who managed her checkbook in the final months, reports balances averaging $30,000 or more. In the region of the late 1950s and early 1960s there was an officer at Georgia Railroad Bank named William Cassell Stewart who reviewed her holdings, then recommending how she might increase yields. The reasonable assumption is that was the time she unloaded Georgia Railroad stock (paying a low percentage dividend) and went into municipal bonds to a greater degree. This review infuriated Mary Lou's beloved nephew Bowdre Mays who was contacted to provide immediate collateral for a promissory note long outstanding (but paying good interest) with the funds used in his furniture business.

Stewart suggested his children take over the responsibility to guarantee payment as guarantors, but Bowdre would not hear of this and offered a paid-up life insurance policy instead. This little unimportant story is just to denote how Mary Lou could be generous on the one hand and niggardly with the other! It certainly did not infer that she loved her nephew less: perhaps the answer is that by this time her well-worn prejudices really were and had become her life-long principles! Bowdre in truth would have been rather shocked had he read the "last will"; although, by 1975, I think he realized the lack of attention to his physical well-being meant that Auntie would now outlive him. They even then had their weekly Friday lunches, held currently at 814, with Frank joining in from time to time. Dr. Louis Battey warned Bowdre to avoid smoking and take better care of himself—to no purpose. He died September 13, 1975, in University Hospital.

The interesting conundrum in Mary Lou's outlook is why not help her nephew in his declining years if, as she said, his finances were precarious? Was she exacting late retribution for his youthful lack of responsibility or, more likely, she believed his children ought to come to the rescue? During this same 1975 annual visit to Augusta, Aunt Mary Lou also mentioned that my parents "were lit" every night, conveying this bit of data with a strong and firm tone of disapproval and completely overlooking the fact that she herself was a bit "lit" after her gin cocktails before supper each evening.

On returning from lunch at The Pinnacle Club in 1975, and probably the usual turn around Magnolia Cemetery to view the several family plots (two Phinizy, Doughty, and Inman), we, back at 814, escorted Aunt Mary Lou inside to say our goodbyes; there I suddenly burst into tears as I embraced my eighty-eight-year-old aunt saying at the same time how much I admired her strength and loved her. Tears came into her eyes too, and we had a very sentimental fond farewell wondering if we would meet again for we then lived in Brussels and would not normally return until 1976.

When we did drive up from Hilton Head in late July or August 1976, with our two daughters, we saw Aunt Mary Lou the first evening for drinks. Unexpectedly the Baldwins, who owned the former Hull House at 814½, came to call, so we really had no "family talk"; however, the next day or so Aunt Mary Lou said our girls were not in her will but she wanted to give each a remembrance: to Tracy a silver Repoussé sauceboat by Kirk, given to her by Tracy Duncan Cohen and with "Tracy" engraved on the bottom and to Katherine a set of silver creamer and sugar vessels signed "Tiffany" and marked M.L.P. She told us the Tiffany set matched the silver service owned by her mother when married to her first husband, Ferdinand Bowdre Phinizy, and given to Uncle Bowdre when their mother died in 1926. The servants later told Mary Lou Bussey in typical local style that "she is giving things away," so don't accuse us!

Tracy was to pass away next with Mary Lou having been very concerned about her condition for an exceedingly long time. Tracy finally went into the hospital in July 1976 riddled with cancer and died July 25. At the outset Mary Lou was keenly interested in how her closest friend of more than seventy years had left her earthly till; she and Tracy had exchanged silver pieces and pictures for years, and she wanted to retrieve a picture of her mother, a silver basket, and other items. Mary Lou had Elsa, Tracy's companion, bring these to 814 and was quite unhappy when learning later of the house contents sale to be held inside 2150 Battle Row. The comment she made to us that summer of 1976 was, "Genie Lehmann made a clean sweep!" Yet she well knew how Genie had worked hard to cater to Tracy's desires and take care of her household.

Around October 1976 Mary Lou took mainly to her bed and as the weeks rolled by took less and less food even though she still for a time relished her evening cocktail of gin. The reports received by us in Belgium that autumn 1976 said Mary Lou would not eat anything for days; then suddenly she asked Carrie Bell for eggs and bacon. Carrie Bell in disbelief went back to the bedroom to again confirm the request and then had to accept a virtual reprimand in a scolding voice! Whether she ate the eggs and bacon is not known! Carrie Bell Kyler (a relative of Lena's) and Moses Allen still were loyal staff but supplemented by others inside on a 24-hour daily basis. Harriett and Mary Lou Bussey, her great nieces, were managing the household checkbook, and her younger friends and relatives were attentive; although, as the months passed she became rather more reclusive. Mary Lou nevertheless wanted to see Teto Barrett to whom she had been very close since their 1957 trip to Europe. Teto wrote me (after her death) that M.L.P. really wanted to die, particularly after Tracy's death, and we couldn't want her back. Teto said good friends are hard to find, and she would really miss her as she found her fun and good company. Christmas of 1976 is the first I can recall when a note and check (of $25 or $50) did not come with a suggestion we have a dinner out; she was unaware that one course for one person at that time in Brussels might cost the entire gift. Anyhow they say it is the thought that counts!

Having already given my sister Frank Mays Pride a large gold flower stylized pin studded with many full-cut diamonds from the jeweler Seaman Schepps and changing her will in September 1976 to bestow her pearl and diamond brooch on Frank Mays Hull instead of Mary Lou Bussey (as the 1975 will had dictated), she pondered what to do with the handsome diamond and onyx platinum bracelet which belonged to her mother. Some reckon Mary Lou wanted Teto to have it, but being the intimate friend and lady she was, Teto is supposed to have suggested the piece stay within Mary Lou's family. Teto spoke of my brother whom she called "Sam the Man," as he, being the only child then living in Augusta, had shouldered many burdens with his wife Sandra. Teto was fond of this couple. Soon thereafter aunt Mary Lou called Sandra and asked her to come by; Sandra then was presented with an old-fashioned gray suede case containing the bracelet which Sam in 1976 had appraised at $10,000. Sandra proceeded at once to her mother-in-law's house; Frank that same day called Mary Lou to impart her pleasure at this lavish gesture telling her Sandra had never before had such a handsome piece of jewelry. The reply from Mary Lou was characteristic: "Of course

CHAPTER FOUR

she has never had a bracelet like that previously!" When I teasingly asked Teto after Mary Lou died why she had not told her to give the bracelet to Lynn, she replied "You did not need it!" Naturally I was speaking only partly in jest.

Aside from the large cash legacies to St. Paul's Church and the Y.W.C.A., the final 1975 will also dispersed to all living nieces (there was one) and all great nieces and great nephews cash and trust fund bequests. Finally there were minor amounts to be paid to all in her employ at the time of death and to the Augusta Council of Garden Clubs. Handsome silver, furniture, and china items were specifically devised to relatives. No sale was to be held inside 814, and the non-devised items were to be divided equally among her Georgia seven great nieces and great nephews still in life.

Sandra Mays went by to be with Aunt Mary Lou several times; Mary Lou wanted the Bible read to her, and Sandra obliged, sitting on the edge of the bed while she read various passages. As the new year, 1977, came in, Mary Lou still was taking little nourishment; her legs also were becoming atrophied, and she was unable to walk on her own. In the final months she did not even want her usual evening cocktail and obtained the agreement of her physician, Dr. Gray, and Mary Lou Bussey that she would not be transferred to the hospital unless some "operation" was required. In short, she intended to die in her own way at home. The family also felt she wanted to live past her ninetieth birthday on March 27, 1977. On that date the birthday lady was weak and not interested in any visitors; despite this, Skippy Boyd brought champagne and a few others like Stewart Hull to toast her. Mary Lou Bussey told me Auntie wanted to know who kept peering into her bedroom, and Mary Lou told her to shut the door! I wrote Aunt Mary Lou in March to wish her a happy birthday and later found this letter opened in her bedside table drawer. Skippy wrote to us in Brussels that "she loved Bowdre's sweet letter."

A few days before she finally expired on April 22, 1977, she asked Mary Lou Bussey if her old friend Sophie was still alive; Mary Lou called her in Savannah, and Sophie and Mary Lou Phinizy had a final rendezvous by phone even though Mary Lou could by then say little with Sophie mainly carrying the short conversation. Copious tears flooded Mary Lou's eyes, running down her cheeks, during this poignant and touching scene.

Having just lost her usual strong determination to live, she met her end in a private and tranquil manner. The body following treatment at Platt's was returned to 814 Milledge in the old-fashioned way in a closed casket. Sandra Mays was the one who sat with the casket in the living room as many called to leave their cards. There was a graveside funeral next day at the family mausoleum in Magnolia Cemetery with the rector of St. Paul's Church calling the service. As she promised Mary Lou, Teto Barrett had the last dog, Nicky the Poodle, put down as no one in the family wanted this pet. Nicky then was buried by Moses in the back garden of 814.

I rather surmise Mary Lou met her death as an agnostic but hopefully as an optimistic agnostic; this is not

CHAPTER FOUR

only conjecture but as well considers conversations and what I gleaned from others. All the same, I do pray and hope that in her last days she was able to accept at least a degree of faith before she passed away.

After her demise, Sophie Meldrim Shonnard wrote the following to Brussels in a sympathy note:

> I feel I am bereft — I have lost my dearest and best friend. No one could ever take Mary Lou's place. I loved her so much, and I loved Augusta — and I loved her house. And now it is all gone.

When at Hilton Head that summer of 1977, we went to see Miss Sophie with our two girls during a day visit to Savannah. We then lunched at the mysterious Pirate House Restaurant to please the little girls! Sophie was in her charming townhouse at #3 West Perry Street on Chippewa Square in Savannah. Miss Sophie still was very much the grande dame in receiving us on her terrace, beautifully attired as usual and in pearls. Sophie had bravely surmounted serious medical problems with her legs arising from a hip break years back while dancing on Pawley's Island. Although she endured many operations, the hip never really healed comfortably. She even finally had hip replacements and visited Warm Springs (F.D.R.'s spa) for therapy. According to Sally Coy, her beloved and charming daughter-in-law who today lives in Savannah but summers on The Vineyard, Sophie never was without pain. She learned to handle her "sticks," which would be affixed like a bracelet to each arm (Mary Lou called them manacles) very expertly. She never complained and always tried to make those around her happy! As Mary Lou had said after Sophie retired to Savannah from New York in the late 1960s or early 1970s: "All Savannah is at her feet." I detected that Skippy Hull Boyd had already alerted Miss Sophie to the M.L.P. will provisions!

Mary Lou indeed was a loyal and true friend and really cannot be strongly condemned for being faithful to her life-long principles. On balance she made many contributions in her long life to Augusta and to her own blood family. She was one of my early mentors, and I still often reflect and muse on her life and times. Aunt Mary Lou certainly made my life more fruitful and complete.

The legacies earmarked to St. Paul's and the YWCA were not added to any endowment fund but rather paid for what Teto called "nightclub lighting" in the church and a swimming pool for the then new YWCA on Wheeler Road. The latter was dedicated in June 1982 with Mary Lou Bussey and Sam Mays attending the ceremony to represent the family. After much impetus from Margaret Twiggs of the History Commission at St. Paul's, a brass plaque was installed in the high altar area to acknowledge the gift. In 2006, the YWCA building and pool were destroyed with the "YW" unit merged with the "YM" as the "Family Y." However, the new management plans to re-install the Phinizy Memorial Plaque in their new building on Wheeler Road.

CHAPTER FOUR

MLP, Tracy Cohen, Jim Hull, Alice D Smith at our wedding in NY City, June 5, 1965

Tracey and Rod Cohen arriving at 814 to a party

IS LIVING WELL STILL THE BEST REVENGE?

*Sophie Meldrin Shonnard resting at
Harrietta Plantation*

CHAPTER FOUR

Lena Carter Glover and Clarabelle at 814 Milledge Road

Louise Mays Bussey and Inman Mays at 814 Milledge living room

CHAPTER FOUR

MLP & her great-niece Frank Mays Hull in living room at 814 Milledge—probably a Christmas lunch party, circa 1950's

IS LIVING WELL STILL THE BEST REVENGE?

MLP and her great-great niece Frank Mays Hull in front of 814 Milledge Road House

CHAPTER V

Potpourri of Milledge Road Minutiae: Who Was Who on Milledge?

While growing up in Augusta, I thought of Milledge Road as a grand thoroughfare for Augusta: a sort of 5th Avenue or perhaps Park Avenue in New York City. It was only on my first visit to the northern metropolis in 1948 when I discovered 5th Avenue to be mostly commercial below the medium "sixties" while Park Avenue was largely tall apartment and hotel complexes. But Milledge had its character being an old and still premier residential street at the first broad crest of The Hill or in Summerville as one now knows the old "Hill" area. Milledge Road still offers an appealing prospect to the visitor, notwithstanding the rather heavy traffic, as many of the blocks contain handsome homes constructed in the nineteenth and early twentieth centuries.

These blocks range from Kings Way on the south to Country Club Hills subdivision on the north. The heart of Milledge range from lots now labeled 1119 through 606 according to the current street listings. At one point in the past I am told Milledge Road was named "High Street" but am not certain this pertains to the entire street. Indeed this name is still shown as the continuation of Milledge Road (then known as Milledge Street) on the 1874 W. G. Jones map of Summerville. The name Milledge derives from Georgia Governor John Milledge and in the old Indian trading days was used as the continuation of what is now McDowell Street. Today with Broad Street extended west and intersecting with Milledge at that point, High Street probably would be that section of Milledge before and after crossing Broad.

The 1874 map also describes "Battle Row" (which terminates at Milledge) as the old road from Augusta to Summerville; also a rather substantial tract of land on what is now Gardner Street and beyond fronting Milledge is listed as the property of "Crawford and Mays." This particular tract now would include the houses at 656 and 606 and even encompasses a portion of today's Augusta Country Club premises. This discovery sparked my curiosity quite naturally as this land probably belonged to my ancestor (great-great-grandfather) Georgia Governor George W. Crawford whose

CHAPTER FIVE

daughter, Sarah Macintosh Crawford, married my great-grandfather known as Captain Samuel Warren Mays, Sr. They owned property in Columbia County too with Crawford's share inherited by Sarah Crawford Mays.

In studying the background to this "Potpourri of Milledge Road Minutiae," I should also state that in the late eighteenth century there already were plans laid to develop Summerville and The Hill area as an alternative to the very low-lying Augusta in the hot months. George Walton bought 250 acres, John Milledge (later governor) 5,000, and Thomas Cumming acquired his first 10 acres in 1800. Mr. Cumming had been identified as "merchant" at his first purchase, but when in 1818 he purchased 261 acres more, he was newly identified as "gentleman" in describing his occupation! Milledge owned a large plantation to the north of the Walton land and called it Overton, a name still in use today for a street in Country Club Hills, then a part of his plantation. Although not sited on Milledge Road, the original Milledge house is located at 635 Gary Street. The house is now known by the name Milledge-Gary-Setze-Clay in representation of the recent and present owners. Built just following the end of the American Revolution and much altered in the nineteenth and twentieth centuries, it still maintains its peaceful air and sedateness. One interesting fact is that the front of the residence faces downtown Augusta. Originally many of The Hill houses were built apparently with their columnar fronts and porches on several floors facing the city for, in the early years, the views were not obstructed by other construction or evergreens. The Redmond-Hickman House at 956 Hickman Road was built in this manner with open porches on the rear.

Henceforth we will begin at the Kings Way end of Milledge to tackle our "minutiae," which in large part also deals with the "Northern visitors" who began to winter in Augusta during the latter part of the nineteenth century. How did the Augustans interact and relate to these tourists, particularly those who owned homes in Summerville? I am not now aware if any writer has addressed this subject before; nevertheless, I will here outline sparse details known to me at the suggestion of Dr. William S. Hagler who still owns two Milledge Road houses and is a distant cousin. Bryan Haltermann, our local leading preservationist and one of my better muses, wrote that the peak of the winter tourist era for Augusta was circa 1890 to 1930, probably correct due to the onset of the Great Depression but also due to the increasing development in Florida, California, and even abroad in places such as Cuba, Mexico, and Egypt to name a few sites. Nevertheless, in Augusta, the three large tourist hotels, The Partridge Inn, Bon Air-Vanderbilt Hotel, and the Forrest Hills-Ricker Hotel continued to operate for the winter season from December 1st to May 1st until well into the 1930s even though business obviously was well reduced compared to the boom years.

As late as 1924, furnished or unfurnished resort apartments also were available at The Shirley (Greene and 10th Street), the Bowdre (Greene and 6th Street),

CHAPTER FIVE

and the Walton Way (now known as The George Walton) across from the Partridge Inn and Bon Air-Vanderbilt.

One family, which was an early leader in making the trek South, was the Speer family from the Pittsburgh-Meadville area of Pennsylvania. These Speers were the great- or grandparents of our Speers here today and appear to have attracted other friends and even relatives to make Augusta their winter home as will be described in this narrative. The Speer family built Goshen Plantation, originally their country home, outside of Augusta in 1904. Cousins followed (Dennys, Jones, and Kuhns) so by the early 1920s the winter resort trade was in full swing.

Augusta offered the winter visitor a good deal in the form of climate (average December to April temperatures between forty-eight and sixty-eight degrees) and plenty of sunshine, six rail lines serving Augusta, a water route to Savannah, with the train service truly excellent not only to the Northeast but also to the Midwest, Florida, New Orleans, etc. There were direct rail services to Pittsburgh, Cincinnati, and Cleveland, Ohio, and Chicago via Chattanooga, Memphis, Birmingham, and St. Louis through Atlanta. In 1924, twelve local rail sleepers made up daily at Augusta. The motor routes through Augusta were first class with the town being the center of the Atlantic Seaboard highway system for that period.

The winter sports were varied and could be enjoyed virtually all year in a mild climate. The activities included golf played on three eighteen-hole courses by the late 1920s, horseback riding trails, horse shows for jumping over obstacles, and the South Atlantic Tennis Tournament held in March each year on the Augusta Country Club Courts. William Tilden won the men's singles in 1924 with other men and women stars of that era also participating. For a time Augusta provided polo but apparently was unable to compete with Aiken, South Carolina, in this sport played on horseback and then dominated mainly by the very wealthy.

In those days, for the winter influx of visitors, the Augusta Country Club provided temporary membership privileges to non-residents then stopping at any hotel or boarding house in Aiken or Augusta if application was made by a member and endorsed by any member of the club executive committee. The season golf and tennis charge in 1915 was $25 or $18 for thirty days; tickets were purchased by the guest for house charges. In the early resort era days (1890s, etc.) carriages ran between the golf courses and the hotels. Then later in the 1920s there were golf buses run by the hotels on a daily schedule to cater to those who required them. The club charged $10 for the season for non-residents not desiring golf or tennis facilities or $5 for thirty days. The Bon Air stables also were allowed the use of the bridle paths around both the Augusta Country Club's Lake and Hill eighteen-hole courses for their guests, most of whom we can assume were non-resident club members if the visitor wanted sport or social activities.

I am grateful to Levi W. Hill IV who in 2008, as president of the Augusta Country Club, wrote a piece on

CHAPTER FIVE

Henry Clay Frick and his love of golf. Frick, a partner with Andrew Carnegie in the United States Steel Company, came to Augusta in the winter to play golf. Frick enjoyed golf at the Augusta Country Club and quite likely also played here with John D. Rockefeller and President William H. Taft.

Frick loved competition and founded the Frick Cup Tournament first played in 1910. Frick donated a silver cup to the winner, and this century-old club tournament continues as a very popular affair. A handicap format is employed and participants must reside in Richmond County.

On the purely social and festive side, there was much interaction at the Country Club between the Augusta members and the non-residents. By the 1920s some winter visitors had become resident members after owning their local winter residences. The club offered weekly dinner-dances, supper parties, and tea and bridge for ladies.

One important "Augusta Ambassador" from an old and prominent Augusta and previously Baltimore family was Marion Gardner Ridgely, known to some as "Pap." He was one of the initial club golfing members, a perfect gentleman at all times, gallant with the ladies and eager to befriend the visitor with appropriate introductions. Always ready to make up a party and head for the links in any weather, Pap became the perfect native contact; he appears to have been particularly close to Scott Appleby, Alfred Bourne, Julius Setze, and undoubtedly others.

Walton Marshall, manager of a hotel chain that included the Vanderbilt Hotel in New York City and Bon Air-Vanderbilt in Augusta, was another excellent contact who sold Augusta to winter guests and actively supported the Augusta Country Club and its two courses. Marshall knew many well-known personages around the United States and brought these local resort visitors together with prominent Augustans of his acquaintance. In turn, the Vanderbilt Hotel in the East 34th Street and Park Avenue area of New York City was a popular stop for Augusta visitors. Walton Marshall and his wife, known as Vi for Via, came to the Bon Air many winters and were a definite "drawing card." They both were attractive and popular, Marshall being a direct descendant of Chief Justice John Marshall, as per Frances Barrett Zimmerman who knew them and their two sons.

Mr. Andrew E. Martin, local manager of the Bon Air-Vanderbilt for many years, also was quite active in arranging the social and sporting interaction between his winter guests and the local community social and business leaders. There were many functions at the Bon Air, one particularly brilliant entertainment being the New Year's Eve ball given by Mr. and Mrs. Harold A. Richardson, on December 31, 1925. Richardson had opened a branch in Augusta for Munds and Winslow, a New York Stock Exchange member, in the early 1920s. Invitees came in costumes representing some kind of a well-known advertisement. During the summers, Mr. Martin managed the famous Equinox Hotel in Manchester, Vermont, which I believe was his

CHAPTER FIVE

hometown. Eileen Stulb, our well-known local golfer, advises that Mr. Martin's daughter, Pauline, continued to winter in Augusta long after the Bon Air finally closed.

As usual, in speaking of the relationships between Augustans and the winter resort travelers, there were probably several (if not a number) of locals who pursued these tourists, most of whom represented wealth and position; and there may have been a few from outside who also were climbing socially and using prominent Augustans to enhance their own status! In the very early 1930s, 1931 to be exact, a number of winter residents who then maintained homes in Augusta were active in supporting Bobby Jones and Clifford Roberts in the organization of the Augusta National Golf Club. These gentlemen were Scott Appleby of Washington; Henry P. Crowell of Chicago; Francis E. Drury of Cleveland; John W. Herbert of New York City; Alfred S. Bourne of New York and Connecticut; B. B. Taggart of New York City; and William H. Wallace, Jr. of New York City.

In the financing needed for the Augusta National Golf Club, the two largest underwriters were Alfred Bourne and Walton Marshall who as individuals subscribed $25,000 each. Obviously a number of well-known Augustans in addition were very active during the Augusta National's developing stage; these included Thomas Barrett, Jr., Jerome Franklin, Lansing B. Lee, and Fielding Wallace. Only one building lot on excess land was sold to an early Augusta member, W.

Montgomery Harison. It indeed is noteworthy that most of the early Augusta National subscribers lived on Milledge Road or in the near vicinity.

Marion "Pap" Ridgely was a partner in a printing enterprise during the 1920s and probably even before; the company was named Ridgely-Tidwell Company and was active in printing booklets, circulars, etc., all geared to the promotion of "Augusta, the Garden City of the South" as they then named it. In the 1920s and 1930s there in addition was a weekly publication called *Tourist Topics* edited by Marion Ridgely; this weekly paper promoted the winter season activities and contained a wealth of data concerning Augusta. The *Augusta Chronicle* in 1931 reported that *Tourist Topics* rendered a distinct service to the community and fairly exuded good will and cheerfulness in its optimism—much as did its author, Pap Ridgely, whose life was so intertwined with the winter traveler. By the 1930s Pap took over the managership of the country club where, as Louisa K. Smith wrote in 1952, "membership was varied and interesting, as we were also a winter resort, but also strictly guarded"; LKS (as her newspaper column was called) further noted you had to really "belong" in order to be a member with this custom still in effect for many years notwithstanding the hard Depression years and the reduction in tourists. The Country Club with Pap at the helm barely managed to weather the storm and likely would have not come through without the cash infused from Alfred Bourne and Fielding Wallace when needed. Pap now has his permanent recognition in the form

CHAPTER FIVE

of a private room named in his honor in the present clubhouse. His portrait hangs there.

Another additional thought on the Augusta-resort/guest interplay concerns the love matches and marriages taking place over the years with those who first met locally. Such involved eminent Augusta families: W. Montgomery Harison married Kathryn Sawyer of Oshkosh, Wisconsin; Billups Dunbar wed Mary Rowe of Pittsburgh, Pennsylvania; and Lombard Fortson took as his second bride the lovely Janice Bené of New York and Long Island. During the Garden Club of America April 1932 meeting at Augusta while en route to the annual meeting in Atlanta, Landon Thomas Jr. (known as "The Captain") met his future wife Darcy Kellogg of Morristown, New Jersey (no connection to the cereal). Furthermore, some Augusta ladies married into Northern families: Marguerite Wright to James Hillman of the prominent Pittsburgh dynasty while her brother Boykin Wright, Jr. lead to the altar a Harriman and became an important partner in the then New York City legal firm Sherman, Sterling and Wright. Miss Margaret Sheftall, one of the four beautiful sisters, wed George Chester of Milwaukee from a prominent Midwest family. I did hear that Miss Wright and Mr. Hillman first became acquainted at a Virginia resort or perhaps in West Virginia at the White Sulphur Springs Hotel; then each family checked out the other in detail before agreement was reached on the wedding date! Another important union was the Augusta marriage of Alice Davison to Harold V. Smith of Philadelphia and later New

York City. The William H. Barretts and Frankie Clark Doughty had much to do with arranging the nuptial details as close friends of the bride's family. The Smiths continued to make winter and spring trips to Augusta until well in the 1950s, always stopping at the Bon Air where they took a suite.

Finally, a number of Augusta ladies in the Junior Workers and Junior League moreover encouraged contact with winter guests through some popular local business pursuits:

- The Book Shelf (rental library and gifts): run by Louise Hankinson and later Louise Bussey
- Bridge Lessons, Contract and Auction: Catherine Cumming
- Min-Ne-Ya-Ta Tea House at Lake Aumond: Mrs. Bowdre Mays and Mrs. Charles Phinizy, Jr.
- Art Studio, Walton Way: Catherine Jack
- Dancing Classes: Vera Baxter Watkins and The Music Box (Petit family ladies).

Note: There also seems to have been another gathering place called "Fruitland Tea Room" which was frequented by Augustans and the winter visitors. The *Augusta Chronicle* of January 26, 1933, reports on a dinner given there by Mr. and Mrs. De l'aigle Munds who were at the Bon Air Vanderbilt. The newspaper said the Fruitland Tea Room was on Walton Way, but no one now seems to agree with that location; in fact, the site was on or near the old Fruitland Nursery property, then being converted into the Augusta National Golf Club. Cliff Roberts attended the dinner as did Tom Barrett,

CHAPTER FIVE

Jr., future Augusta mayor, and a number of prominent Augustans. Genie Lehmann recalls that Mary D. Phinizy and Frank Mays were running the place—if true, that's news to me!

Another early 1920s venture proposed by the "just twenties crowd" was the "Aumond Boat Club Co."; the amusements were listed in the invitational brochure as "Fishing, swimming, boating, dancing, and cabarets." The officers of the club were Walter Fargo, president; Hollis Boardman, V.P.; H. Gould Barrett, secretary; Scott Nixon, treasurer; and Chas. W. Bowen, Jr., manager. If in fact this proposal became a reality, here would be another venue and resort activity (Lake Aumond) where the younger winter resort guests could hang out (as all now term it!) with Augustans of their generation.

Mrs. Dorothy J. Manice, known as Dot, and her two adopted children, Jean and Fraser, were one Northern (New York) family who came to Augusta in the early 1930s and established a full-time home. John Walton said no one ever saw a Mr. Manice, but Mrs. Manice lived here in one of three houses she built (Bransford, Milledge, and Cumming Roads) from 1933 until her 1966 death. She loved golf and played often, finally becoming the founder of the Women's Titleholders Golf Championship in 1936. Mrs. Manice was a generous contributor to Augusta causes, and her long-time good friend Barney Dunbar was the architect for several of her houses built in the course of "her Augusta years." For the garden of the former Manice and present Chandler house at 803 Milledge, she had English boxwood imported from Saratoga, New York. She is buried at Summerville Cemetery, just a short walk from her last home at 2216 Cumming Road. Incidentally, Mrs. Florence Blanton who sold Dot Manice some extra land on which to build 2216, says that she had been told Mrs. Manice intended to build a bomb shelter underground on this location. There was no talk of another home! She was elected to an honorary membership of the Ladies Professional Golf Association in 1961 according to her Augusta friend and outstanding golfer Eileen Stulb.

Start of Tour

Straightaway let's start our Milledge Road tour beginning as stated before from the Kings Way entrance; first look at the southwest corner of Kings Way, No. 2204, at the small Spanish Colonial house designed by architect Willis Irvin in 1924 for the dowager Frankie Clark Doughty—much more on this classic dwelling of its type in Chapter I for it appears a rather perfect early copy of similar (even if larger) houses built in the 1920s in California and Florida.

Turning now into Milledge the first house on the left-hand corner is No. 1119; the next is No. 1111, former home of Sam and Mamie Martin for many years. Sam E. Martin was vice president of Georgia Railroad Bank for a long period; his wife was a Felder and the sister of Annie (Mrs. Miller) Robertson, and there were no children. A horrendous accident took place one day at No.

CHAPTER FIVE

1111 when Sam climbed up to the roof to install or fix in some way a radio aerial; Sam suddenly slipped from the roof to the ground breaking his neck in the fall—this all in the presence of wife Mamie who was watching! He fell with such pressure that his body was partly embedded within the soft earth from which Mamie attempted to free him. He apparently died immediately. His dates are 1870-1937 and the spouse 1872-1958.

Continuing up Milledge to 1005 is the William B. White house built in 1911 in sort of Italian Renaissance Revival architecture by the leading local architect of that era Henry T. E. Wendell. In the cotton business, Mr. White came to Augusta from Norfolk, Virginia. He married Nina Cohen from a prominent local family who lived on Greene Street where the Whites too first lived. Will White also developed a large real estate portfolio. The house featured a tile roof with wide eaves with an unusual fresco underneath. The site is about 1.6 acres and originally contained beautiful gardens with an emphasis on roses and camellias.

Two large glass greenhouses behind the residence next to the garage were filled with wonderful camellia specimen plants. These particular camellias had been "gibbed" (as they say in Augusta) and had achieved huge blossoms. "Gibbed" is not really a verb, as George Barrett says, but refers to the practice of applying gibberellic acid to the plants in a certain manner so that blooms will come in earlier and in larger sizes.

A second entranceway and driveway is on the Pickens Road side; the Milledge front dual-step cast stone and brick entranceway was added later circa 1935-1936. The house was maintained beautifully together with its spacious gardens containing interesting garden statuary purchased by the original owner until after the widowed Mrs. Nina White died in 1955. Claire and Greg Boulus recently acquired the property and currently are in the process of renewal for this very handsome home, an Augusta landmark. The original oil wall paintings of birds and flowers above the high wainscoting in the dining room are intact.

The gardens of Mr. and Mrs. William B. White were described in 1932:

> This is a garden of perpetual joy, for here at all seasons are flowers in bloom. There are charmingly planned beds of brilliant old fashioned flowers and rare bulbs, enchantingly woody spots of crepe myrtle, bamboo, wisteria and moss, massed with azaleas and bordered with box, also hundreds of handsome camellias of rarest types. A truly fascinating garden made up of many smaller gardens.

Across the street from 1005 are numbers 1004 and 1006, the original Harison homes. The Harisons are an old and distinguished Georgia family whose antecedents are traced back to colonial times. For example, the Reverend William H. Harison in 1852 married a Savannah lady Mary Gibbons Jones, who was a descendant of the owners of Wormsloe Plantation, still one of the beauties of Savannah. It seems that the Reverend and Miss Mary Gibbons Jones first met in Newport at a Jones summer house called Kingscote. Their son, Dr. William H. Harison Jr., married Mary Frances Campbell who was a cousin, but before their wedding, Mary Gibbons Jones with relatives had founded the Church of Atonement, the second Episcopal Church in Augusta, located at 11th and Telfair Streets in the city. There the Reverend Harison, Sr. preached for many years following the official church inauguration in 1851.

The house at 1006 burned at some point, so the current dwelling on this site is somewhat different from the original; next door on the right side, if one is facing 1006, was the original rectory of Good Shepherd Church. Dr. Harison, Jr. had a solid medical education but also was a keen sports figure having been at the forefront in organizing the Bon Air Golf Club as forerunner to the Augusta Country Club where Dr. Harison was club president for twenty years (1900-1920). The Harison family had a large ownership interest in the Bon Air Hotel both before and after the 1921 fire that destroyed the old nineteenth-century building.

As for No. 1004, this house was built for $8,000 in 1922 when the doctor's son, William Montgomery Harison, married Kathryn Sawyer. During the early 1930s, the younger Harison established a children's school through the sixth grade in the backyard where there also was a barn; Mrs. Alex Murphy was the teacher. At various times the students were both local and winter residents including Phil and Gummy Harison, "Red" Boardman, Scott Appleby, Gilbert and Nomina

Cox, Audrey and Sally Hillman, Frances and Mary Anne Grammer, etc. There had been in Augusta some letters distributed warning of kidnappings (all the rage in the Depression Era) and hence the secluded private tuition on Milledge Road. Frances Grammer Stevenson recently told the writer their chauffeur always carried a concealed gun when carting the children around Augusta!

Continuing up the east side of Milledge past Pickens Road, we have Nos. 1000 and 946 until recently usually called the Burdell and Smith houses. This because the Carter Burdells acquired No. 1000 circa early 1920s from the original owner, a Mr. Tinker of Boston, who naturally was involved with the Tinker Toy manufacturing! The house was built around 1913 from the architectural plans of the well-known firm of Henry Preston White also from Boston. The Carter Burdells had formerly built and occupied 2644 Henry Street, also another Wendell design.

As for No. 946, the Smith House, the Charles Shaler Smith family owned the house from 1888 when they came back to their mother's home, Augusta, from St. Louis. The mother was born Mary Gordon Gairdner. Their aunt, Mrs. Artemas Gould, gave them 946 after the death of Mr Smith. Aunt Margaret Gardner Gould was a rich but wonderful philanthropist whose family donated the land on which Good Shepherd Church stands. The former church rectory on Milledge Road was also her own gift as a widow as was money to replace the initial wooden church with its present imposing brick Gothic-Victorian structure. She also contributed

CHAPTER FIVE

to many future parish deficits. The surviving Charles Shaler Smith girls were an interesting addition to Augusta living on in the house as maiden ladies until the 1950s. These were the Misses Anne Gordon, Augusta Eleanor, and Louisa Kirkpatrick (or LKS as she was known) who wrote columns for both the *Augusta Chronicle* and *Augusta Herald*. Their oldest sister, Minnie, had married Bryan Cumming, but as they all frequently were together at parties and Augusta events, one often referred to the ensemble as "four Smiths and one Cumming!" (this bon mot courtesy of their kinsman Bryan Haltermann). Two additional sisters married Messrs. Daniel Davis of New York and James Harper from Augusta.

I well recall the No. 946 "Smith girls" (as they were called) from my youth as they were good friends of my grandmother Doughty; they were rather dramatic, and the LKS articles in the *Chronicle* and *Herald* were read widely and avidly. One is repeated in Chapter I under the Doughty section. Hugh Connolly related that at their 1953 wedding (his bride was Nancy Cumming) LKS, had been unwell for a time, but dressed to the nines she reached her seat at the Good Shepherd Church up front and then turned and bowed low to the congregation!

The grandson of Annie and Carter Burdell currently owns Nos. 1000 and 946. He is the eminent eye specialist Dr. William Schweigert Hagler (Billy) who is also descended on the Burdell side from Sarah Phinizy, first child of Ferdinand Phinizy I, the immigrant from Italy.

Number 920 Milledge is known as Twin Gables, a Wendell architectural production from 1911. The house was built for Francis A. Hardy of Chicago as a winter home. The property was originally two lots that were joined for the house and its spacious surrounding garden. Twin tea houses were positioned to abut the brick walls on the east and add to the outdoor living room concept of lawns, plantings, flowers, and beautiful vistas. Francis Hardy had an arresting background as he was actually born in 1851 in England to American parents from Massachusetts. He came to the United States in 1871 and thereafter lived in Evanston, Illinois, at 1214 Ridge Avenue. Hardy married Mary Pawny Keasly of New Jersey and fathered three children all residing with their servants at the Evanston address. The Hardy business was wholesale opticals.

At some point in the 1920s the Hardy Family sold No. 920 to Mr. and Mrs. Harry Albright. It was after 1924 we know; prior to their ownership of Twin Gables, we believe the Albrights lived on the 2400 block of Williams Street, probably as winter residents. Lib Boardman found their little dog one day away from the house and after returning the pet became fast friends with Belle Albright. Some say Belle initially came to town as a "housekeeper," but we have no hard facts at present.

When in the large house on Milledge, Mrs. Albright employed two white servants named Claire and Walkington who took excellent care of her. Walkington also served as chauffeur and butler. The Alonzo Boardman Family—Lib, Lonnie, and their children—would be invited to take Sunday dinner (in other parts called lunch) and report delicious food always was served. Mrs. Albright was an early member of Sand Hills Garden Club and participated in the April 1932 visit to Augusta and Aiken by delegates en route to the Atlanta annual meeting of the Garden Club of America.

The garden at 920 was designed by Herbert, Pray & White of Boston (who also designed 1000 Milledge) beginning in 1911. This palatial and sweeping expanse had both formal and informal areas including pergolas and fountains. Mrs. Albright lived to an advanced age but became rather reclusive. On her death, the Alfred Battey, Srs. purchased and renovated the house with Mrs. Thérése Battey devoting considerable attention to the large garden which had good bones. She deserves much credit in this respect. The Battey occupancy took place circa early to mid-1950s. The residence is currently owned by the Medical College of Georgia and inhabited by its president. In 1932, the 920 Milledge garden was depicted as follows:

> Having been laid out in 1911 the years have added charm to this lovely garden. Majestic trees shading velvety lawns, bordered with rare plants and flowering shrubs; rose gardens with formal walks leading to rock gardens; miniature pools of tropical fish and lotus lilies; hundreds of rare azaleas; vine covered pergolas showing vistas where one may sit and dream; all these are combined in exquisite harmony and restfulness in this wonderful walled garden.

Across the street from No. 920 is 939, the Emily Thomas Clay house built right on the sidewalk but behind a tall wall of about six feet. This 1932 house resembles a large elegant French townhouse or a small French country home; Lynn Drummond was the architect with the house costing about $16,000 including a slate roof. The land and the rear garden originally were part of the Landon Thomas plot that contains the "big home" (built late 1880s after a fire on the original premises) and a number of smaller out-houses, garages, etc. The old residence was called Cloister Garth (very witty since both words mean the same thing!), and the sizable acreage also embraces an attractive garden with formal and informal aspects. Bryan Haltermann believes that the Boston architect Henry Preston White of Herbert, Pray, & White also worked a bit on the Thomas gardens. The most recent or nineteenth-century patriarch Landon Thomas, Sr. used to say he was the only person in Augusta who had the sun in his face in the morning but also in the afternoon—this due to the fact that he rode his horse in the morning to his office downtown and then back up The Hill to his home on Milledge in the afternoon! This vignette is from his grandson Cassius Clay. The youngest Thomas daughter, Anne, married the well-known Southern author Francis Griswold, whose 1939 novel *A Sea Island Lady* was a best seller nationally. The book was dedicated to Jake Lowrey and "Miss Kate," his mother.

On the southwestern corner of Milledge and Walton Way stood No. 915 until it was acquired for $500 by Mr.

CHAPTER FIVE

and Mrs. Hale Barrett and moved to 508 Berckmans Road at great cost and care in 1966. This was very fortunate in that unless the Barretts had saved the structure, it would probably have been torn down. The house was known as the Gardner-Langdon place due to the names of the prior owners, the Langdons (who also were related to the Cummings) being the final occupants. The house was of pre-Civil War (about 1850) vintage being one of two Langdon dwellings on Milledge; the other is still located on the 800 block and will be mentioned later just briefly.

In 915, until the last sister died in 1962 lived for many years Paul Langdon and his two sisters (known as the Misses Langdon), named Ann (but always called "Nan") and Mary (always called Mazie). Their father, Paul H. Langdon, had obtained the property in 1884 from the Gardners who had rebuilt No. 915 sometime prior to the purchase date. Paul H. Langdon, who died in 1911, was a very successful businessman. He was the president of a local bank and director of local corporations. The only surviving son, Paul Devereaux Langdon, was a jolly sort who sported a monocle when I first met him as a young teenager circa 1939-1940. The scene was Edisto Beach where he and the sisters had taken John Walton's beach cottage for an interval. The trio were trying to catch crabs with lines and nets from the bridge overlooking the creek located just before one dead-ended at the front beach road. As we went crabbing and shrimping in the various creeks almost everyday (depending upon the tides) lead by my mother Frank Mays (and usually Julia Fargo too, plus other house guests), we attempted to advise the Langdons that one had to descend into the muddy creek banks rife with small fiddler crabs if success was to be achieved! Standing in their all-white clothes and straw hats on the bridge and tossing lines from above just wouldn't do! Paul seemed to like the ladies, but Julia reported his kisses were one long slobber!

Paul appears to have been a character: his nickname with his Augusta contemporaries was "Magnífico." He went to New York as a young man (1867-1943), worked for Charles Schwab (I believe this one was president of U.S. Steel), and frequented the Wall Street milieu. Cassius Clay recalled that Paul D. Langdon had studied to become a mining engineer. If the local gossip is accurate, Paul apparently did not marry well (as his sisters would not receive the wife), and the marriage for whatever reason was of short duration. He came back from New York and settled for good with the sisters, still well to do, for Paul is said to have spent most of his assets; this was probably the Depression era. Frances Barrett Zimmerman reports he was rather wiped out but persuaded a taxi driver to bring him and a female companion to Augusta; arriving at 915 Milledge in the middle of the night, the sisters paid the taxi fare but refused the companion entrée and sent her back in the cab! Frances describes Paul as "short, hefty and had a huge bay window"; my own recollections are similar as with the monocle he looked much like the English actor Charles Laughton.

CHAPTER FIVE

Paul often went through The Good Shepherd Church property to the Barrett house (now the Bonnie Thurmond residence in Rockbrook) to visit if they were home; sitting on their porch with a drink in his large hand, he would regale all with his tall tales. Craig Cranston reported Paul was an inveterate gambler who rode the streetcar down to 8th Street most mornings. There was a place there in those days where one could wager on almost anything or play poker, which he did all day, returning to 915 Milledge in the p.m. as though he had been at work! Then he usually played bridge all evening! Hale Barrett told the story of the English sparrows who were building nests in the Langdon house in the eaves or even inside their attic; Paul would find all the small unhatched eggs readily available, hard-boil them, and then wickedly return all to their nests! Hale also believed he would visit his stockbroker's office many days by streetcar or bus for even if his own money was gone, the two sisters probably took at least a part of his advice. Once John Walton told a tale about how either Nan or Mazie made a lot of money investing in the Baltimore and Ohio Railroad stock; the Miss Langdon said she made the investment just because she loved that pussy in the B&O advertisements peering from the Pullman car window. My father in one of his more risqué remarks immediately retorted how much he too had always loved pussy!

The Reverend Allen Boykin Clarkson, the much loved and famous rector of The Good Shepherd Church, in a very religious sense had long coveted the

Langdon property which abutted that of the church; additional land was urgently required for the church and its Episcopal Day School (EDS as it is normally known and which some wags now say means "Everyone Drives Suburbans"). It seems that the last survivor at No. 915 Milledge, Ann (Nan) Langdon did at one time sign some paper devising the property to the church as a memorial to her parents, sister Mary (Mazie), and brother Paul. The story is that she changed her will not long before her death at age ninety-three leaving the property to her attending physician, Dr. Gray. John Walton opined that the reverend perhaps tried too hard in this case as Nan tired of his constant pressure. However, Nan Langdon did will $300,000 to Summerville Cemetery's endowment fund, a very wonderful gesture for this old and private cemetery which badly needed funds. These three last Augusta Langdons are buried there. There also was a legacy to local public radio.

Turning now to the east side of Milledge Road, we have what is the model for the Sand Hill Cottage houses one sees all over The Hill area. This is 914, commonly called the Chafee Cottage and considered the oldest house on The Hill. However, I doubt it was ever owned by a Chafee—although through the 1923 marriage of Maisie Chrystie (first wed to DeWitt Cochraine who predeceased her) to Harry Chafee, the charming dwelling acquired its title. Jake Lowrey in his piece on The Hill's old homes calls No. 914 "a storybook house." A great example of its style, additions here were made with care; the house dates to 1800 or even before when it was owned by Mr. Peter Carnes. The house is built over a brick basement with a kitchen in the garden performing for the house until the late 1940s. Lowrey in 1950 termed 914 Milledge the Chrystie-Fortson house, an appropriate sobriquet for in relatively modern times the house indeed was owned by Chrystie descendants until sold circa 1956-1960 to Mr. and Mrs. Burt Hayes for $25,000 by Mrs. Lombard Fortson, the niece of Maisie Chafee, who had inherited this old historic property. Maisie was descended from Fews and Chrysties whose direct ancestor was General William Few of Revolutionary War fame. Chrysties also were related to the Thomas family by the 1855 marriage of William Chrystie to Emily Howard Harvey Thomas from Augusta.

Maisie Chrystie Chafee (1873-1941) was a popular figure who from an early age spent the winters at 914; later she resided here year-round. She was a social person, liked corn liquor during Prohibition, and was a charter member from 1927 of The Sand Hills Garden Club. She served as the first vice president. Her garden was a showplace which she opened to the winter visitors; at that time the Chrystie property embraced both lots on the left side to Walton Way as well as the lot on the right side. In this large space there were both formal and informal garden areas all greatly enriched by their age and the daily care of their owner. In 1932, the garden was described as follows:

> A garden that is enhanced by age and loving care is Mrs. Chafee's old fashioned garden, planted by her

great, great grandfather in 1784, and today many of the original trees and shrubs still adorn this lovely place. Here one finds a summer house and a sundial, pink and white dogwood, crab-apple, flowering quince, wisteria, climbing roses, jessamine, camellias, azaleas and box wood and single blue hyacinths that "Old Mis' planted and Lil Mis' tended."

Maisie seemingly also loved dogs as the poem quoted hereinafter attests:

> I have a friend, a charming friend,
> Who has a little dog, and when
> The other day out in her yard
> He slipped and nipped me good and hard,
> I could have killed him, so disturbed
> Was I until a voice I heard
> Of tender love and sympathy
> But—
> Lavished on the dog, not me!

This amusing verse from *Out of My Mind* by Tracy D. Cohen who once told me the dog in the poem belonged to Maisie Chafee.

During both the first and second halves of the twentieth century, in almost the identical location, the 900 block of Milledge Road was the scene of two shootings. The first case, in 1910, was the murder of Dr. Charles Hickman, who, according to the newspaper account, became the murder victim by an unknown assassin who

CHAPTER FIVE

had fired three bullets, one of which killed the doctor. Charles Hickman, a prominent local physician, who was trained in the United States, Berlin, and Vienna, apparently was ambushed on the opposite or eastern sidewalk of Milledge just across from the Thomas house at 933 Milledge Road. His assailant was never identified or located despite much detective work.

The second gun instance on the leading residential street called Milledge Road concerned William (Bill) Ficklin of Washington, Georgia, and occurred in the 1950s. Mr. Ficklin's mother, Lucy, then resided on Cumming Road. Seemingly, Ficklin, in a state of mind involving unrequited love on the part of Mrs. Lombard (Janice) Fortson, shot himself, but the bullet was partly deflected by the heavy woolen clothing he then wore. Some speculate Ficklin really was attempting "to just make a statement" and never intended to accomplish more than a flesh wound to his body. The Fortsons then, most charitably I thought, called an ambulance to carry Ficklin to the hospital. This shooting occurred in front of 914 Milledge Road, which is a few feet down toward Walton Way from the spot where Dr. Hickman met his end in 1910.

As I noted previously, the house at 914 is one (if not the oldest) of the oldest on The Hill and was then owned by the Fortsons. No. 914 Milledge is still often referred to by "Old Augusta" as the the Chafee Cottage for Maisie and Harry Chafee resided there for so many years. The 914 gardens as indicated were well regarded and lovingly tended during Maisie's day. She had willed the house to her great niece Janice Bené Fortson on her death, which occurred December 29, 1941.

The new Boone Knox house (2003) on the Walton Way side of the former Chrystie land was designed by architect Al Cheatham and fits in beautifully with the Milledge Road ambiance. This new construction appears to have been there forever and actually much enhances the surroundings. The address is No. 912 Milledge Road; one passerby recently congratulated the owner for the exceptional renovations!

Magnolia Villa condos and apartments now occupy the northwest corner of Milledge Road and Walton Way and known as 827 Milledge. This was the site of a Warner dwelling acquired by Mrs. Frederick Ball Pope in 1917 when as a widow she wanted to move from Greene Street; perhaps the great fire of 1916 also influenced this decision. Mrs. Pope named the house Magnolia Villa; it was the second home on the property, the first having been moved back to 2231 Walton Way. This old house was also a former Cumming/Davis property. The Pope house looked similar to many large suburban dwellings designed and built in the early 1900s; of no particular style but large with several two-window dormers jutting from the roof on front and sides and a porch or porte-cochere across the front. The structure was grayish cement/stucco with white woodwork. Mrs. Pope often spent the hot summer months at the house she also owned in Jamestown, Rhode Island. The spacious yard around Magnolia Villa was rather formal but classic and

CHAPTER FIVE

containing much box, camellias, and shrubs inside the background of old magnolia trees.

Frances B. Zimmerman recalls Mrs. Pope as an elegant, petite, older lady who drove a little electric car with a vase of roses inside on the door post; the electric would not "pull" the Bon Air hill so she would turn around and back up all the way into her driveway. On either side of the front steps she had century plants; one bloomed and visitors came from all over town to see the sight. She and her butler then served lemonade on her porch every afternoon. Mary Wynn Pope's dates are 1846-1936, so she lived to a very mature age; she and her husband are buried at Summerville Cemetery under tombs resembling medieval Gothic architecture. They are quite handsome but urgently need cleaning! Mr. Pope had been a successful cotton broker, so she left many legacies including one important to The Good Shepherd Church. Mrs. Pope had been a close friend of my great-grandmother, Mary Lou Yancey Phinizy, and a sort of godmother to Aunt Louise Mays Bussey. Hence, the family, and particularly Mary Lou Phinizy, deplored the action of her executors in holding a house sale for the public inside the house following her demise.

After the death of Mr. Pope in 1936, the house became the Misses Parker's boarding house for a number of years. Their dining room was well known for good food and many new arrivals to Augusta found these initial accommodations very pleasant and convenient. Al Williams was one bachelor who lodged there in the late 1940s and 1950s and reported the residents interesting and the location a useful springboard for meeting Augustans even though the establishment and its management was sort of disorganized and vague! The house was destroyed and the grounds converted into the series of apartments and condos called Magnolia Villa in the 1960s as alluded to previously.

Across the street from 827 and directly on the northeast corner of Milledge and Walton Way is the splendid antebellum residence (and once the largest on The Hill) commonly known as Gould's Corner. It was built by Mr. Artemas Gould in 1858 as a summer house for there also was a downtown Augusta residence. Mr. and Mrs. Gould were important members and benefactors for The Good Shepherd Church; their niece Julia married the first rector of that parish, the Reverend Edwin Weed. All of the Gould children, three in number, died young, and Mr. Gould following in 1870 with Mrs. Gould continuing to reside in their elegant home until her death in 1898. Now called 828 Milledge, it is an "Italianate design"; the whole top façade and cupola on the roof pinnacle vaguely remind one of the Johnston, Felton, Hay house in Macon which is really more of an authentic Italian Renaissance Revival Palazzo and built of brick. The destruction of the house was avoided over thirty years ago when various Milledge Road residents and perhaps others contributed funds to buy the Gould House and convert the interior into a number of large condos with separate townhomes behind. Mary Lou Phinizy contributed $3,000, while Starkey Flythe recalls Emily Clay and Ellen Thomas gave $30,000 to the Sam Waller Consortium which saved this landmark. I think debentures were issued but do not know if any were even recalled.

The second Langdon home referred to previously is still located to the north of Magnolia Villa and is numbered 819 Milledge. This was originally a Cumming house built in 1826 by Thomas Cumming after his previous Milledge Road home burned. Jake Lowrey wrote in 1950 that 819 is likely the best remaining specimen of The Hill epoch of roomy homes as intended when built in 1826. Of course, 1950 is far back, and we have no word now of later changes or additions. Lowrey had labeled No. 819 as the Cumming-Langdon-Weiss house. Today, however, the 819 Milledge Road residence is owned by Terri and Lyn Allgood who have well preserved this venerable beauty and added a charming back garden featuring both plants and vegetables. This site is now a showpiece!

Now across from 819 Milledge we have numbers 820 and 814, both wonderful antiques and much discussed in other Chapters: 820 in Chapter VI and 814 in Chapter IV. No. 820 (and all of Milledge Road) is on the National Register of Historical Places. This house dates from circa 1810 with W. H. Goodrich, architect and builder, adding the south wing and remodeling the oldest section in the north part. Lowrey wrote in 1950 that there is some evidence the house also includes what had been the summer home of Nicholas Ware whose townhouse is the current Gertrude Herbert Institute of Art on Telfair Street. Mr. and Mrs. Travers W. Paine III obtained No. 920 in 1983 and have beautifully restored what was required so that we now see as much as possible of the original house and garden.

As for No. 814, we should again state that the current owners, Dr. and Mrs. Randy Smith, have devoted much time and attention in re-doing and maintaining this 1870 Victorian — Second Empire residence, the expansive yard, and rear late 1940s guest house of old brick. The present house is the third on the property. The second was built in 1839 by Mr. John Marsh Adams, formerly of Litchfield, Connecticut, and a distant cousin of US President John Adams. When the 1839 home burned circa 1870, reconstruction was immediate. The Adams family and their direct descendants continued to own and live at 814 until 1934 when the property was sold to Miss Mary Lou Phinizy. The first house at 814 (or the lot which became No. 814 Milledge) suffered a terrible tragedy in that the occupant, a Mr. Barnes, was killed by an Indian. The story printed by Dr. C. J. Montgomery in the early 1900s is that while Mr. Barnes was in his home with his two little daughters, "the red savage stealthily crept to the window and shot him dead." One of these little girls married Dr. Louis A. Dugas.

While the first John M. Adams died in 1853, his wife Sarah lived on to 1901; Sarah even recalled attending the Planters Hotel's Lafayette Ball in 1825 as her "debut" where she met General Lafayette himself. There were ten Adams children: one was Harriet who wed Joseph Ganahl, the Augusta lawyer who was once a partner of Boykin Wright. The *Augusta Herald* published a

CHAPTER FIVE

sketch with pictures of 814 Milledge July 8, 1965, under the byline of Caroline Hill Nixon; the then owner and resident, Miss Mary Lou Phinizy, told the writer from the paper that she had an old photograph revealing that the house originally had equal wings with a center entrance. On rebuilding following the circa 1870 fire, she said the right wing was not replaced, but the left wing was extended and ornamented with the current large bay windows. Dr. Randy Smith appears to doubt this scenario for various reasons and never has seen such a photograph. Nevertheless, this is what my Aunt M.L.P. believed as I too heard the story from her but never saw any photo.

To the left of 814 is No. 808, the very handsome residence built 1926 or 1927 by Mr. and Mrs. Francis Edson Drury from the design of an Ohio architect, Meyer and Meyer. The present owner, Al Cheatham, is not certain if Meyer and Meyer was a Cleveland or Cincinnati firm. Cleveland seems likely as the Drury main abode then was at Gates Mills, eighteen miles east of Cleveland. Although the Drurys built 808 as late as 1926 or 1927, I do not think they were unfamiliar with Augusta beforehand. The couple were sometimes winter residents previously, probably stopping in a hotel or rented house. For example, John D. Rockefeller, Sr. who had been a former Drury business associate often wintered in Augusta until 1925 when John D. discovered Ormond Beach, Florida.

Also, Mr. Henry P. Crowell from Chicago and CEO of the Quaker Oats Company bought an Augusta house in 1910 at 2248 Cumming Road and called it Green Court; this is thought to have perhaps influenced the Drury's decision toward Augusta. This may be particularly accurate by the 1920s when both Crowell and Drury were of the very religious bent we know as "born-again Christians." Rockefeller and his wife, Bessie Strong, would stay at the Bon Air Hotel and attend Tabernacle Baptist Church while in Augusta; they gave money to fund "Strong Academy" at the Shiloh Orphanage, now called the 15th Street Comprehensive Community Center.

Drury was born in 1850 to an unpretentious farm family in Michigan and left school at an early age to work in railroad machine shops, hardware stores, and foundries. Drury then patented the first internal gear lawn mower and started to manufacture this item in Cleveland. He next, with the financial help of Rockefeller's Standard Oil Company, developed a clean-burning cooking stove burning kerosene, the by-product of refined oil. This was the predecessor of the Coleman camp stove marketed along with its kerosene. By 1921, Drury's Perfection Stove Company was the premier manufacturer of kerosene oil stoves in the world. Francis Drury was active in the business world into his eighties. In that period of no or very low income taxes, his eventual fortune was estimated as $100 million, and then a dollar was truly a dollar!

Drury was very loving and caring of his second spouse, Julia, his first wife having died of diphtheria. Circa 1912, Drury built a large formal residence in Cleveland

CHAPTER FIVE

on Euclid Avenue at East 86th Street, then known as "Millionaire's Row." The house, known as Drury Hall, has a Tudor look from pictures and is now a conference center for the Cleveland Clinic. One interesting innovation was the drainage trench leading beneath Euclid Avenue to a four-acre formal garden on the street's Southside known as the Oasis. This garden, conceived by a New York landscape architect, is said to have necessitated the removal of five city houses and includes a lake, waterfall, and grotto. Although the Drury couple also had a townhouse in Manhattan, a summer home in the Finger Lakes area of New York State, and seemingly already were coming to Augusta for the winter, they still were considering a more rural country estate away from the city life. Another supposition is that Drury himself conjectured that a country estate could serve as a more immediate conduit to the older Cleveland society still so elusive! Hence, around 1923 or 1924 Drury acquired 400 acres or a bit more from an old farmer at the southwest corner of Gates Mills, Ohio, and engaged Charles S. Schneider, a prominent architect, to develop a copy of the Euclid Avenue mansion but on a much larger scale. The outcome was a forty-one-room manor, very Tudor in appearance and appropriately named Tudor House.

Meantime, Julia Drury traveled and studied art in Europe during much of 1923 and 1924 while the work on the new house and estate proceeded. The entire estate was called Cedar Hill Farm with Tudor House incorporating the latest engineering such as steel beams that would contract or expand under important temperature variations in winter and summer. Furniture came from England for the elaborate oak-paneled dining room including a table to seat twenty-four. There were walk-in vaults for furs and silver, eight fireplaces—each of different marble, a kitchen with electric towel dryers, food warmers, etc., and an organ with an echo chamber permitting the music to filter all through the house! There was a four-car garage with housing above for the chauffeur and his entire family. Tudor House was heated with two boilers, one coal, the other by oil. An elevator ran from the basement to the third floor (Drury bedrooms on the second and guests on the third floors), with an enclosed thirty-two-stair circular staircase from the third floor to a tower commanding a great prospect including a view of Lake Erie to the north (when the day was clear) and parts of Cleveland, eighteen miles away.

Cedar Hill Farm was a real working establishment with sixty-five full-time employees who lived on the premises in apartments with farmhouses for the overseers. The estate had beautiful gardens, and Mrs. Drury had one formal garden moved stone by stone from their Euclid Avenue mansion in Cleveland. The property also included a man-made pond of an acre and a half, an orchard with 350 trees and 600 foot rows of grapevines, just beautiful vistas, pastures with cattle, and fields of daffodils with one million rhododendrons planted in what was known as a "backwoods."

Embedded in several places (a leaded-glass window in the drawing room and in the dining room ceiling) and still there today is the Drury motto in Latin: *Non sine Causa* ("not without cause" for those unfamiliar with Latin!). The farm was reputed to be one of the most modern technology could provide in design and actual construction. The total tab after about two years was $2 million including Tudor House. Apparently nothing could please Julia Drury who continued her unhappy and temperamental attitude. The tale is that one reason for her constant problem was related to the many who declined the important and splendid house-warming affair to which several hundred in so-called "Cleveland Society" were bidden. We shall probably never know the real truth; nevertheless, after about a year and a half, the Drurys left Cedar Hill Farm never to live there again.

Al Cheatham, architect and present owner of No. 808, believes that both the Ohio architect and the Drurys admired the Carter Burdell house at 1000 Milledge and therefore somewhat copied that façade for their new Georgian mansion for such it is; the property comprised 2.38 acres and contains twenty-two rooms overall as there are separate quarters for staff, garages, etc. There is as at 1000 Milledge a portico here on the front exterior with a brick wall of around five and a half feet surrounding the front and a lower wall on the Cumming Road sides of the premises. The entry hall is spacious, running to the rear of the house with palatial dining and drawing rooms to the left and right; the latter really is large enough to be considered a ballroom and contains a grill on the floor to conceal the pipes for the Drury organ. As I wrote previously, Tudor House in Ohio also had an organ.

The Drurys engaged an experienced gardener who lived on the premises full-time, and they both appear to have taken an active interest in horticultural pursuits: Drury himself had been president of the first Cleveland Flower Show in 1925, and by 1932, Mr. and Mrs. Drury both were listed as "Associate Members" of the Sand Hills Garden Club. The 808 Milledge garden was on tour in April 1932 during a visit by Garden Club of America delegates to the annual meeting in Atlanta. The Drury garden was described then as follows:

> Roses, camellias, azaleas, rare shrubs and palms, huge arches of boxwood, a marble fountain from Italy and marble statues of the Four Seasons, from a English estate, give a varied and unusual charm to this garden. One of the most attractive features of this garden is the rare collection of beautiful bulbs bordering the many walks. Shading the gardens are many oaks a century old.

Francis Drury apparently was a jovial man who liked a hands-on approach with his staff or workmen. Money was no real object; once when he ordered an expensive irrigation system for fourteen buildings connecting the Cedar Hill Farm pond, wells, and a huge cistern, his project manager pointed to the cost. The Drury reply was to indicate an open hydrant and say, "The money is coming in just like the water is gushing out!" Francis Drury was a large man weighing close to 300 pounds; in 1932 at eighty-one years old he died in Augusta. Julia Drury died in 1943 at age eighty-four in her apartment at Shaker Square in Cleveland. However, she had initially continued to winter in Augusta for some years; it appears on several occasions she did not open 808 but stayed at the Bon Air Hotel instead.

Money had been left in trust to Drury's surviving son (we do not know whether the son came from the first wife or Julia) and to charity. For twenty years after his death, the Drury estate trustees continued to pay for the Cedar Hill Farm maintenance and to offer employment for the workers as well as pensions to many more older employees. In this regard, even in death, Drury kept his solemn word to the old farmer from whom he had purchased the property. To terminate the Drury saga we should mention that the National City Bank during the Depression sold segments of the Cedar Hill estate but did not discover a buyer for the last 133 acres and buildings including Tudor House. The lot was sold to the Brothers of Holy Cross for a Catholic boarding school in 1945 for $150,000 following much negotiation. Most of the furniture already had been sold at auction after Mrs. Drury died in 1943. The new school was named Gilmour Academy after the renowned late-nineteenth-century Cleveland Catholic Bishop Richard Gilmour. Today, the school enrollment exceeds 600 and now is coed with Montessori, lower, middle, and upper schools. The

Holy Cross Brothers have taken a lower profile with a lay Board of Trustees now in the saddle.

A final interesting historical fact relative to 808 Milledge Road is that William Howard Taft, twenty-seventh president of the United States (1909-1913), spent the winter of 1908-1909 in Augusta for which he had a definite affinity. He probably was influenced by his future military aide Archie Butt, an Augustan who also was serving then as aide to President Theodore Roosevelt. The Tafts stayed at No. 808 Milledge, which at the time was a white wooden clapboard house of the nineteenth century. It was known as the Terrett House. Taft as chief justice of the Supreme Court was in Augusta several occasions, previously stopping with Major Jos. B. Cumming and Mr. Landon Thomas. Mrs. Minnie Smith Cumming wrote that President-Elect Taft's first cabinet and inaugural address were "made in Augusta" at 808. In that epoch the inaugural of course took place in March.

Turn back now to the west side of Milledge where now are situated Nos. 807 and 803. The Jeff and Catherine Knox house is 807, the former rather square brick Howard house from probably late 1930s-1940s has been embellished by the architect Al Cheatham into a fair rendition of an attractive Regency period house, a great new addition to the block. The Bleakley Chandler house on the corner numbered 803 was designed by architect Barney Dunbar for Dorothy Manice circa 1948. There is a charming interior, well-laid out garden all around, and a new separate office-hideaway in the back facing Cumming Road.

CHAPTER FIVE

The two lots, 807 and 803, originally comprised the property where a home was built in 1828 by Henry Harford Cumming who had married Julia Bryan in 1824. The home originally was similar to No. 819 discussed previously in style and appearance, also being then a Cumming home. The entire property area was around three acres. Henry Harford killed himself in 1866, but his wife continued to live in this house until her death in 1879. The house then was sold to Reverend Edwin Weed, rector of the Good Shepherd Church, in November 1879 for $10,000. After his election as bishop of the Diocese of Florida in 1886, the Weeds probably rented or sold this realty. At this time all we know is that the J. S. Kuhn family from the Pittsburgh, Pennsylvania, area were the next owners circa 1906.

We have heard the Kuhns also were cousins of the John Z Speer family of Goshen Plantation in South Richmond County who may have facilitated their move to Augusta for the winter season. The Kuhns employed Henry Wendell, the fashionable architect of the era, to embellish and most likely expand and modernize the residence. A pediment and tall white wooden columns, four in total, were added to the front entrance from the porch to the pediment; a dual stairway with wrought iron railings was installed on the stairs and porch with an addition to the left side of the house consisting of a sunroom below and probably a sleeping porch (with windows all around) above. The interior entrance hall and other rooms were beautiful and garnished with millwork trim and carved moldings. Actually, some of the renovations might have been wrought by Mr. and Mrs. Frank Harvey Barrett, who purchased the estate from the Kuhns in 1916 when the great fire of March that year burned their Broad Street home. It is likely Frank Barrett then was at the apex of his cotton business career with cotton prices high; the family firm, Barrett & Co. Cotton Brokers, at one time said to be the largest in the world, handled over 200,000 bales, then considered a high achievement. Frank was the president of the firm organized in 1905, the same year he married Sadie Cranston, in an important society event uniting two distinguished Augusta families. Their new house was known as 805 Milledge.

We do know the Barretts added the first privately owned swimming pool in Augusta at the rear of their property line next to the Crowell estate. The address 805 embraced gardens much enhanced with a stone walkway and pergola covered in vines leading to a back fountain area and then the large square pool that still exists. The pool surrounds were cast stone and grass with tall electric lights at intervals for night parties and evening swims. To ensure that the pool water was fresh, a special pipeline from the city furnished the large quantity required since at that time there was no chlorine available. A pool house either was built or converted from a small white clapboard out-house near the pool, and two stucco buildings were added to the rear of the property: one as a large garage with servants' rooms above for male staff and a second laundry/sewing house with rooms for the female staff then staying with the family. Both the buildings were later converted into private dwellings, both very attractive, in the late 1930s.

The present owners of the former garage unit, Mr. and Mrs. Finley Merry, have done a spectacular job with more additions and remodeling so that their townhome with a Cumming Road entrance has become much coveted and admired.

The Barrett majordomo for many years was Robert O'Brien; he also served at times as butler, cook, and bartender and was completely devoted and loyal to the Barretts and their many friends and relatives. Robert always was caring and available to the two Barrett children, William Kitchen and Anne; these two always returned this real affection and commitment all their lives.

The Barrett couple, Sadie and Frank, entertained a great deal at home and with a large "tacky party" (costumes) at the country club in 1922 or 1923; most occasions their children were included even though they both were still barely teenagers as can be discerned from the old pictures. There were often supper parties with swimming around the pool with many of the regular resort visitors attending if in town or parties in the mansion during cool weather. For example, in late August 1924, Mary Lou Phinizy gave a swimming/supper party at the Barrett pool for her nephew Bowdre Mays and his fiancé Frank Inman, with the wedding party also attending. Frank Barrett gave Frank the nickname "Frisky" always used too by his son Billy. During the "Roaring

Twenties" the main house was rented some winters and became a "private club" for gambling mainly frequented by non-residents; the Barrett family then leased a small house (near the country club on Milledge Road) for the rental term or as in 1929, a Colonial Court apartment. At this time, Frank Barrett was spending much time in New York City, again often accompanied by his young son Billy.

While it is often said Frank Barrett had a seat on the New York Stock Exchange, the truth is that the "seat" mentioned must have been the New York Cotton Exchange for in the realm of stock and bond trading he worked with Munds and Winslow where the principals included the brothers Theus and Louis De l'aigle Munds; the Munds brothers were nephews to Louise De l'aigle Reese with all related to the Clarks and Doughtys in Augusta and personally well known and very friendly with many Augustans. At one point in the 1920s, Munds and Winslow even had a branch in Augusta; Mr. H. A. Richardson was the manager, being the same winter visitor who gave the large ball at the Bon Air Vanderbilt Hotel New Year's 1925-1926 as discussed earlier.

An Augusta paper also contained an advertisement from "Tom Barrett, Jr. Stock and Bond Broker"; we assume this to be the younger brother of Frank and the Augusta mayor in 1934. He died suddenly in 1934 shortly after taking office. In any event, by the early 1920s Frank Barrett had achieved much business success in cotton broking and was invested in other businesses either directly or through equity and bond holdings; the Barrett lifestyle was extravagant, i.e., a private railroad car on trips to the North and California and an expensive Augusta household to run, the house now called Ivanhoe with a large domestic payroll and entirely filled with handsome furniture and objects. Sadie often displayed her imposing diamond bow brooch that featured diamond and sapphire drops about the size of a nice-sized thumbnail. Without question, the Frank Barretts were the leading Augusta "movers and shakers" of the decade!

But unknown to many, the boom in cotton was tapering off due to the boll weevil and probably other factors. Suddenly without warning in July 1923 the local public was shocked to learn that Barrett and Company was bankrupt—this because the usual buyers of the cotton godown/warehouse receipts had discovered there was no cotton in the storage facilities. This was the old classic deceit or say chicanery perpetrated for years against farmers, brokers, and banks who were owed money for cotton produced, paid for, but not delivered, or who had made loans to Barrett and Company against the warehouse receipts. Ed Cashin's book *The Story of Augusta* states there were 651 creditors due $2,730,887 by Barrett and Company when the final totals were computed; this collapse included the Barrett-affiliated warehouses and the Hill Mixture Corporation which produced a pesticide to kill boll weevils.

Apparently, after the 1923 failure of Barrett & Co., Frank H. Barrett spent even more time in New York

City and probably elsewhere—anywhere but Augusta! We have no information of the legal action, if any, taken against the principals of the company or what was final outcome of the payments due creditors. Frank Barrett most likely was trying to make a "killing" in the booming late 1920s stock market; this was also the "speakeasy era" with gambling and extracurricular activities rampant. I know this from my father who for a short time in 1925 worked with Munds and Winslow as a customer's man in New York City. There was even one story from 1920 reported in the *New York Times* regarding a divorce action brought by a Dr. Frederic J. Barrett (no relation to Frank Barrett) against his wife who apparently was "receiving the attentions of Frank H. Barrett." The wife, Marian, had taken a number of trips with Frank to Boston, etc., and was accused of kidnapping her son from the father's home after she had first agreed not to demand the child of eleven years. Frank Barrett's young son Billy spent much time with his father, thus having early experience in perfecting his future bridge and betting prowess.

Sadie and daughter Anne remained mainly in Augusta. Genie Lehmann stayed many times with her good friend Anne at 805 Milledge; she reports that Frank Barrett would often make unannounced visits to Augusta and surprise them in bed by arriving without warning at night. Genie and Anne were debutantes the 1928-1929 season; Genie comments that Anne's debut party at the Bon Air Vanderbilt Hotel was a lavish affair including even champagne during Prohibition as arranged by Frank.

CHAPTER FIVE

Born in Augusta, November 26, 1884, Frank died much too soon on April 2, 1929, at age forty-five in University Hospital. One perhaps spurious tale or just evil local gossip is that he was afflicted with syphilis (during the time of course prior to the age of antibiotics). His death certificate states the cause as uraemia with arteriosclerosis myocarditis as a secondary cause. He died in Augusta with his home address listed as the Colonial Court apartments. His tombstone reads, "TO LIVE IN THE HEARTS WE LEAVE BEHIND IS NOT TO DIE." His wife, Sadie Cranston Barrett, lived until 1934 at 805 Milledge; her dates are June 18, 1883, to July 16, 1934, and the handsome marker shared with Frank reads, "FOR LOVE IS THE BRIDGE BETWEEN LIFE AND DEATH." She died from "acute dilatation of heart" in her home on Milledge Road.

There are strong rumors and much popular talk that around 1935 Billy Barrett arranged for 805 to burn. He needed funds badly. His sister Anne had married William R. Derry in 1933 and was living away, and no one could really afford to maintain the large estate in those hard times. The winter resort trade was in the main gone, and there was no family interested in renting the house for the winter season. The story originally put out was that somebody in the family "sold the home to the Yankees," a Milledge Road expression often in use to mean burning the house to collect the insurance since most of the large insurers were headquartered up north! Another story told is that Billy hired Spec Redd, Swifty Crawford, Slick Mathewson, or Moon Mullins (separately or together) to perform the dastardly act for a fee, some say $50 to $500 a piece. Billy was said to be out of town the night of the fire that largely destroyed the main house except for the large front columns and perhaps some other huge beams of millwork in the front interior. However, I must stress all of the foregoing could be a just fictitious narration, and if so this writer now makes it clear there is no intention to libel any person dead or alive!

My mother obviously thought Billy Barrett himself was behind the fire and often questioned him over drinks. His constant retort was to just laugh at the absurdity of the idea! The house was insured for $50,000 (about $500,000 or more today), which I assume Anne and Billy collected unless a heavy mortgage intervened! Mother's rationale for Billy to engineer the fire was that she recognized items and vases, etc., (belonging to Sadie and always in the residence) when she went to Billy's apartments or houses in Atlanta or Savannah during his second marriage to Gladys, an excellent bridge player in her own right.

On the other hand, another story appears to absolve the four friends of Billy mentioned but definitely not Billy himself. The second tale was told to Mrs. Florence Blanton by "Jeff," the erstwhile Barrett gardener at 805. As Mrs. Blanton recalled, Jeff told her in the very early 1940s when she moved to the house near the pool, and I quote: "All pretties out and then he light fire." The "he" apparently pertained to Billy. Mrs. Blanton and her husband had bought an unfinished small house in the rear from lawyer Gerald Mulherin who she said had paid $50 for the small portion of property including the pool area. The Blantons extended and finished the house also then adding other land to the original plot purchased from Mulherin. Mrs. Blanton also told Frank Barrett Martien (F. H. Barrett's great-grandson) and myself, when we called on her several years back, that "all property was sold at auction" following the fire. That would seem to indicate a mortgagee/bank was indeed involved. The former Barrett gardener Jeff also noted to Mrs. Blanton that kerosene had been spread around the main home.

John Walton purchased the front columns and also millwork for a minor sum using these items in the Regency-style house he built circa 1935-1936 on Walton Way Extension. This house recently has been extended with the beautiful gardens redeveloped, and even redesigned, by new owners Mr. and Mrs. Charles Falcone of Jupiter Island, Florida, their permanent home at present.

Pieces of handsome furniture from the house were saved from the fire; we had several pieces in our house, and my father seemingly sold items (two small antique sofas with eagles carved into the top molding) to Dr. and Mrs. William H. Goodrich and probably others at the request of the Barretts. My brother Inman had in his Sarasota, Florida, home the bedside mahogany chest/shaving stand that was next to Sadie's bed and then later used by my mother. There also were four Regency-period chairs of mahogany bought by the Bowdre Mayses and used in their homes for years. My mother had the seats covered in needlepoint she made; John Walton had told her these chairs were the finest antiques she owned so she left them to me in their rather decrepit state!

After the fire, it appears Billy Barrett had the idea of selling off segments of the property in separate lots to generate more cash, thus "Ivanhoe Court" at the rear where the Blanton house and others now stand. Billy apparently also had named the main house Ivanhoe at the onset of their residency. Craig Cranston, first cousin to Billy, told me apropos of the fire that he and his father (Sadie's brother) saw from Pickens Road the smoke rising from the Milledge/Cumming Road area when Craig, Sr. cracked, "Billy must be back in town!" Billy had charm and personality, and when in the Georgia Legislature in Atlanta in the early 1930s sponsored a bill to permit Augusta to allow divorces after a thirty-day domicile; the idea of course was to improve the tourism business then declining in Augusta by making us the East Coast Reno! The bill failed to pass!

A final interesting fact from Mrs. Blanton was the obvious small graveyard she discovered early in the Blanton residency in a site near the pool area. There was a tombstone for a child, Elizabeth Murphy, 1799, aged only thirteen days. Mrs. Blanton had this buried later to avoid having anyone using the marker as a stepping stone in future for she had been unable to discover anything definite about the grave or the Murphys.

Located at the northeastern corner of Milledge and Cumming is No. 728 usually called the Forsyth or Dickey House. Now owned by the James Bennett, Jrs., it is said that the façade on the front elevation has been unchanged since 1857. The house is a good picture of the famous Sand Hills cottage; it is believed to have been built in the early 1800s. Col. John Forsythe (1780-1841) was the US ambassador to Spain (1819) and quite a statesman serving in addition as a governor of Georgia (1827-1829), US senator, and US secretary of state (1834-1841). He was against the doctrines of nullification and in 1820 obtained Spain's agreement to the treaty (1819) by which the United States secured Florida. Former US President Martin Van Buren was a guest at No. 728. John W. Dickey was a well-known real estate broker whose wife Helen died in childbirth much too soon; his surviving daughter, the much loved Glenne, married Clayton P. Boardman, Sr. with Mr. Dickey and the Boardmans all living in the house in the late 1920s and early 1930s. Mr. Dickey had a part in the development of the area on the western side of Monte Sano Avenue and named Helen Street and Glenn Avenue for his wife and daughter. NOTE: The present owners of No. 728 are Dr. Laura Irvin and Mr. Eric Smith.

Proceeding down Milledge on the 700 block, we find No. 709 on about three acres now owned by Mr. and Mrs. James M. Hull. This is a large residence designed in the late 1920s by Willis Irvin to be the approximate twin of one he is said to have built in Aiken for the Clark family. There being a divorce, Mrs. Clark wanted a similar house in Augusta but on a smaller scale. The Clarks were family owners of the J. P. Coates Thread Co. of

Ohio or the Midwest; at one point we believe the firm also was known as Coates and Clark. The problem is that we have been unable to date to locate a house in Aiken similar to our No. 709 designed by Willis Irvin. However, we do know that Ambrose Clark (known as "Brosie" to his intimates) lived in Aiken, last residing in a house he called Kellsboro after a horse he owned which won a famous English race. This home was brick, off Grace Avenue, and designed circa 1929 by Scroggs & Ewing for K. B. Schley. The original owner lived there briefly calling the house Habersham. Subsequently, the house became the Aiken Day School, also being called at one period Boxwood Gardens. We have learned, however, that Willis Irvin did build a home in the early 1940s across the street from Kellsboro House for Miss Clark, daughter of Ambrose, who apparently was in poor health.

Architect Al Cheatham in recent years designed the new No. 709 left wing and balancing porte-cochere on the right front when the entire residence was renovated with an attractive "folly" or gazebo built at the back of the property as a focal point. The owners of 709 after the Clarks were Judge and Mrs. Kennedy who obtained the handsome wrought-iron fence from the area of the Augusta City Hall when demolished in the 1950s; this was then installed across the front of 709 between brick posts and has its own history coming from the Benjamin Warren home located before it too was destroyed at the South-East corner of 6th and Greene Streets. To further explain it should be recorded that in the 1950's when the wonderful old City Hall

CHAPTER FIVE

sadly was torn down, other surrounding properties also were lost to Augusta. The current Mrs. Frederick Kennedy surmises the late judge and his wife paid about $40,000 for the property circa 1938-1939.

This present No.709 property originally extended to the Cumming Road corner and up that road to where Montrose Court now begins. These were about six or seven acres belonging to Inverness, the home of Joseph B. Cumming, who was known as the "Major" for his service to the Confederacy. The area began at the northwest corner of Milledge and Cumming Roads to be exact. Major Cumming died in 1922 and his wife less than two years later. Thereafter the part of the estate where No. 709 stands now was sold to Mrs. Clark. She only purchased the tract on the stipulation that the old house, Inverness, be destroyed. Inverness was constructed following the Civil War around 1869 on what was called the "Burnt lot" where the Thomas Cumming house once stood prior to burning. Inverness is the Scottish town from where the American Cummings originated. The family had supported the Stuarts until the defeat at Culloden in 1746.

The home at 709 Milledge is a handsome town residence of a classic American style, and the current owners should be congratulated on their taste and efforts in bringing the original Clark estate fully up to speed. The surrounding gardens and lawns are all well tended adding much to the beauty of the property which in the rear resembles a spacious parkland. There is an appealing guest cottage, the same style as the main mansion, as well as a large "play house" for the teens and younger set situated in the back on side parts of the property.

To the right of No. 709 is No. 707 which we shall call the "Wallace" house as in the Augusta heyday of 1920s-1930s as a resort, the house was owned by and used as a winter retreat by Mr. and Mrs. William H. Wallace, Jr. Mr. Wallace, or Billy to his friends, was a first cousin to Fielding Wallace, a prominent local year-round resident. Billy had a French wife, Jeanne, and in those days had a seat on the New York Stock Exchange and usually summered at Juan Les Pins on the French Riviera. Otherwise, the Wallaces lived in New York City or on Long Island. Billy Wallace was an early supporter/underwriter of Augusta National and one of the first members. The house is a very early Sand Hills Cottage totally renovated circa 1910 by a Hardy family member from Chicago. To the rear of the old dwelling, a large drawing room was added the entire width of the structure. This addition containing a sizeable fireplace and mantel is certainly one of the dwelling's finest features. The original owner was Mr. James Gardner whose land extended north to Gardner Street.

The Wallaces usually gave "garden parties" during their visits in the cool, sunny weather, probably spring in Augusta; on one such occasion, in the early 1930s, Frank Mays stopped by the Barrett home at 805 Milledge to pick up Sadie Barrett as had been arranged. Frank said "Miss Sadie" (as she called her) came down the front steps beautifully attired in her large leghorn straw hat, gloves, and flowing chiffon dress on backwards. I

CHAPTER FIVE

don't recall if this position necessitated a change before proceeding to the function! Caroline Hull Eve, whose late parents, Frank and Marie Hull, were great friends with the Wallaces, said the Wallace couple gave her a garden party at No. 707 when she was sixteen.

Dr. and Mrs. Howard Hudson presently own No. 707 and are to be congratulated for their stewardship of a Milledge Road gem with a long history in old Augusta.

On the opposite eastern side at No. 708 Milledge we have the very interesting and old Summerville home dating back to circa 1826-1830 with changes and nineteenth-century-plus later accretions. The house on the southeast corner of Milledge and Battle Row usually is known as having been occupied in past times by James Penman and son Gordon Gairdner, the Stovall Family, or Groats, who came from the Massachusetts area in the 1950s. Mr. Groat opened a Broad Street bookstore for a few years. The Misses Smith (related to the Gairdners/Gardners) and discussed under "946 Milledge" previously owned No. 708 at one time (circa 1915) and maybe much later until the Groats acquired the realty. At one point, probably around 1937-1938, the Rudolph Kratina family of Dresden, Germany, lived at 708 on their return to the United States from abroad. Marguerite Pressly Kratina's mother had been a Stovall, a close relative of Pleasant Stovall, appointed minister to Switzerland by President Woodrow Wilson. Her father, Charlie Payson Pressly, had a US diplomatic career mainly in France and once retired lived also at 708. The Kratinas left Augusta in 1941 moving to Ansley

Park in Atlanta. Fredric Kratina, son of Marguerite and Rudolph, their sole child, graduated from the Medical College of Georgia in 1952 and has enjoyed an interesting but varied US military and medical career in the US and in Japan. He now lives in Gainsville, Florida.

On the opposite side of Battle Row and Milledge at No. 704 is the house built in the last century during its first decade by the Stearns family. Wendell again was the architect of this rather Italian or Spanish-style residence. George R. Stearns was one of the original incorporators of the Bon Air Golf Club in 1899; this later evolved into the golf links of the Augusta Country Club. The 704 property embraced an entire block, backing up to Gary Street with Gardner Street on the north side. At the rear is a "carriage house" which was sold separately to Jake Lowrey probably in the 1940s-1950s and made into an appealing maisonette. This is still there but with other later additions. Mr. Stearns was the president of Riverside Mills, came from Massachusetts, and settled in Augusta for the rest of his life. His son Richard was killed in an automobile accident with a Walton Way Tram in the late 1920s. A Ricker of the Forrest-Ricker Hotel Rickers was in the car at the time of the Christmas tram accident and also killed. The rumor is that much Christmas "cheer" probably contributed to the horrific accident. The Stearns grandson, Lieutenant Richard Stearns, Jr., was awarded the Distinguished Flying Cross, having flown thirty missions over Germany in World War II.

CHAPTER FIVE

After the Stearns, the big house eventually became the home and writing base for the prolific historical novelist Edison Marshall. He had first seen Augusta during World War I and met then his future wife, the beautiful Agnes Flythe, from a prominent local family. They lived first in Oregon, then at Beaufort, South Carolina (very quiet for writing), before moving to North Augusta, there buying the house formerly owned by the John Herberts who built later their Cumming Road Tudor mansion circa 1929. Olive Sydenstricker, then a real estate agent, sold 704 Milledge to the Marshalls for about $22,000 right after World War II. For a time during World War II, the Marshall family also lived in Coral Gables, Florida, and Havana, Cuba, while Edison, Jr. was in the Coast Guard.

The successful novelist named 704 "Breetholm," which is a Nordic term having to do with a wood, say a calm or beautiful wood, and a word used in his well-known novel *The Viking*. *The Viking* was sold to Hollywood and became a very profitable movie, at least for the studio and producers. Nevertheless, Edison Marshall also became quite prosperous himself due to book sales and royalties, etc., in addition to wise stock market forays over time. Cassius Clay visited the Marshall writing room at 704 and told me he made frequent use of reference books as he wrote. His other well-known books include *Yankee Pasha*, *Benjamin Blake*, *West with the Vikings*, and many others (say forty to fifty in total), most of them translated into other languages including the Scandinavian tongues where his historical novels seemingly were extremely well received.

His "Heart of Little Strikara" was honored with the O. Henry accolade as the best story of the year in the 1920s. Another title I just discovered is *Cortez and Marina* based on the "romance" of the Spanish conquistador and the Aztec Indian in the sixteenth century. Some so-called cognoscente still titter or poke fun at his large output although there is no more accurate observation than the apt phrase: "There is nothing like success!" He made a lot of money from his work.

As a former military man, Edison Marshall fostered a friendly relationship with Fort Gordon and always knew its top commanding officers. For some Marshall home receptions, a soldier in full dress appropriate to the occasion stood near the house entrance to announce the guests in a sonorous voice. Edison's brother-in-law Will Flythe was a Hearst News employee covering the White House and thus would accompany President Dwight D. Eisenhower on his frequent Augusta visits to rest and play golf at the Augusta National Golf Club. During these sojourns, the Marshalls would entertain the White House press corps with a cocktail party at 704 Milledge.

Edison's literary agent was Paul Revere Reynolds who too liked to visit Augusta. Edison on these visits would invite the Authors Club of Augusta to hear Reynolds discuss current literary trends with marketing of their works also an important topic! Pearl S. Buck (cousin of Dr. V. P. Sydenstricker) also visited once when she as well spoke at the Authors Club.

CHAPTER FIVE

Edison Marshall, Berry Fleming, Hervey Cleckley, and others formed the "Attic Club" to discuss literature and similar interests. Edison profited from his friendship with the Georgia-Pacific financial genius Owen Cheatham, and the Marshalls easily became key social members of the "Milledge Road Set." On his sixty-ninth birthday in 1963, Edison sent a select group his photograph (taken by Morgan Fitz) standing over a table displaying all of his books. On the copy sent to his neighbor at 814 Milledge, Mary Lou Phinizy, he wrote in his own hand, "To Mary Lou Phinizy, my true companion, on my sixty-ninth birthday, while meditating my works, I thought upon those who have made possible their performance: those in concert with me and comrades who have given me access to their thoughts and personalities; a few who have presented me with brilliant ideas for novels, and a generous many who have recognized the sincerity of my efforts and have not deprived me of their support."

Edison Marshall's writing program was a very focused regimen divided into four three-month annual segments: three months research and planning for the themes and pace of the novel, three months of daily consistent writing, three months to work with his editor and publishers to bring out the new book, and finally three months vacation. This data from Joan and Cassius Clay who, as I wrote, saw his writing room on the second floor of No. 704; the furniture included a large desk or writing table on which rested a sizable lazy Susan containing a set of the Encyclopedia Britannia, one of his principal reference works.

In recent years the current owners, Caroline and Will Morris IV, have done masterful work in maintaining and lavishing attention on the house and grounds at No. 704.

Moving ahead past Gardner Street on the left-hand side are the country club tennis courts partially facing Milledge Road. At one time, there were several small houses located on this land; one was owned by the club and designated No. 671 Milledge in the 1940s-1950s. I have a hunch that Alfred Bourne gave this property to the club, and at 671 lived the Marion Ridgely family beginning in the late 1930s for some years. Pap Ridgely then was managing the club on a full-time basis. No. 671 might also have been the house Mrs. F. H Denny occupied after selling No. 606 Milledge to the Alfred Bournes.

Crossing over now to the east side of Milledge we find Nos. 656 and 606. The home at 656 was built in the 1920s by the Benjamin Franklin Jones family. I am told they came from the North, possibly the Pittsburgh area, and were friends or even cousins with the Speers, our very early transplants to Augusta. The Jones were connected to the former Jones & Laughlin Steel Company, which in recent memory merged with others or declared bankruptcy. The house is a typical Southern Revival manor house with high columns across the front and wings extending from each side. The construction is white wood clapboards. Mrs. B. F. Jones is listed in 1932 as an associate member of the Sand Hills Garden

CHAPTER FIVE

Club with her house and garden at No. 656 portrayed in this account:

> It would be hard to find anywhere in this country a modern home and garden more thoroughly American in type and atmosphere than the attractive residence and grounds of Mrs. Jones. In the more formal part of the garden is a large circular pool. The breadth and sweep of the main garden gives an added touch of charm and restfulness.

The Jones rented No. 656 for some years to J. Gordon Gilfillan of LeRoy, New York, a charter or very early member of the Augusta National Golf Club. This in the early 1930s, i.e. after 1932. J. Gordon Gilfillan is listed by the Augusta National as one active during the club's formation. This probably means he contributed at least $5,000 to the initial underwriting in 1930-1931. He died January 6, 1945. Mr. Gilfillan began his business career with Watkin Products Company but was president of the Jell-O Company when he came to Augusta for the winter; he was married to the great aunt Agnes of Herbert Lorick III and was, therefore, Herbert's great uncle. The Gilfillan chauffeur filmed the first Masters Golf Tournament in 1934; Herbert now has these films and has loaned them for the current Augusta National members to view on occasion. We have not done a title trail search, but by the late 1940s the Swints were the owners and year-round occupants of No. 656.

The house at 606 on the same east side of Milledge was a Henry Wendell design for the Frank H. Denny family of Pittsburgh circa 1909. There appear to be some similarities with the Wendell house at No. 920 Milledge in this large somewhat resort-style winter residence but perhaps less formal a structure than Twin Gables. Bryan Haltermann terms it "Dutch Colonial Revival" and reminding one of a "seaside resort cottage"; I agree, thinking of old Cape Cod or Martha's Vineyard. In 1920, Mr. and Mrs. Alfred S. Bourne bought this large house and the extensive gardens from the Dennys as a permanent winter home; their summers were spent in Washington, Connecticut, or in the Thousand Islands, New York. At the latter, on Dark Island, Commodore Frederick G. Bourne, then president of Singer Sewing Machine Co., had built a summer and hunting lodge named the Towers. The architect was Ernest Flagg (who later was the designer of the Chrysler Building in New York City) who modeled the Bourne residence on Sir Walter Scott's Woodstock Castle in Scotland. Frederick was Alfred's father. This 1896 twenty-eight-room mansion on seven acres is to be renamed Singer Castle and will be open for guided tours. The new owner is a German investment group.

In 1950, the Bournes sold their No. 606 residence called Morningside to Mr. and Mrs. Henry Garrett with thereafter a large section of the property/garden hived-off to create a new cul-de-sac Bourne Place and other lots on Gary Street behind and fronting Milledge Road. Over the period of their long residency in Augusta, the

CHAPTER FIVE

Bourne family made many worthwhile contributions to the community and to golf in particular. Alfred was not only a charter member of the Augusta National Golf Club but also one of two initial vice presidents; he gave the Wallace house to the Augusta Country Club in 1929 and was a principal benefactor during many lean years in the 1930s and 1940s. Knowing some of this, I was very interested in meeting Kenneth Bourne in Bombay, India, in 1968; this was Alfred's grandson who was then probably in his thirties and managing the Singer Sewing Machine operations in India. My employer, AFIA/Cigna, then was insuring the Singer India businesses. Kenneth and his wife paid a visit to Augusta in 1997, so we met again when Ann and "Red" Boardman entertained in their honor.

The Alfred Bournes were regular churchgoers at Reid Memorial Presbyterian when in Augusta. One could always establish their presence by the vintage 1935 Lincoln Town Car parked outside; the automobile was perfectly maintained with custom leather roof over rear passenger compartment and moveable glass partition separating the driver's front seat which had the usual convertible top. The Bourne uniformed chauffeur with leggings would be standing alongside.

The current PGA Senior Golf Trophy is named "The Alfred S. Bourne Trophy" in his memory and is still awarded yearly to the Senior PGA winner. As Eileen Stulb wrote in the Augusta Country Club Centennial history in 1999, Bourne provided financial help when the first National Men's PGA Seniors Championship was established and played at the Augusta National Golf Club in 1947. He also gave the trophy.

Mrs. Alfred S. Bourne in the 1930s was an active member of the Sand Hills Garden Club and often allowed the public to visit her spectacular acreage. While much of the expansive Bourne gardens have now been lost as explained, the following account will convey to the reader a true picture of them in 1932:

> This beautiful garden includes among its many lovely features a fascinating waterfall, which cascades its way down broad terraced steps, bordered with box and azaleas, into a marble pool; sunken gardens with graceful fountains; and above one of these gardens, 'High set on a Heaven-kissed hill,' the Temple of Love, enshrined in a location of beauty and delight beyond description.

The landscape architect had been Rose Standish Nichols. And with this elegant description we end our Milledge Road ramble.

CHAPTER FIVE

Frank H. Barrett house at 805 Milledge Road

IS LIVING WELL STILL THE BEST REVENGE?

Lombard & Janice Fortson in 1935

CHAPTER FIVE

October 1928, in front of Barrett House, 805 Milledge Road. Augusta Debutantes 1928-29
Left to Right: Betty Wallace, Genie Selden, Anne Barrett, Natalie Merry, Harriet Alexander, Lib Ridgely

IS LIVING WELL STILL THE BEST REVENGE?

*Marriage of Anne and William Derry, Jr., Athens, Ga.
October 29, 1933
Left to Right: Joshua Derry, William Derry, Jr., Anne Barrett Derry,
Sadie Barrett, and (Billy) William K. Barrett.*

CHAPTER FIVE

Original entrance to 805 Milledge Road prior to later embellishments.

IS LIVING WELL STILL THE BEST REVENGE?

Taft Terrett Cottage then located at 808 Milledge Road/corner Cumming Road

CHAPTER FIVE

"Inverness", originally situated on lot Milledge Road to Cumming— now numbered 709. (Circa 1867)

Edison Marshall at 69 in 1963

IS LIVING WELL STILL THE BEST REVENGE?

Eileen H. Stulb and Bowdre P. Mays at her 1999 book signing "Centennial History of Augusta Country Club

CHAPTER VI

Miss Tracy and Mr. Roddey: A Window into 2150 Battle Row

"She was a show-off but a cute show-off," so opined my father once when referring to Tracy Duncan Cohen years ago; Bowdre P. Mays, Sr. had known Tracy all of his adult life and even before in his childhood prior to Tracy's arrival in Augusta for permanent residence after her wedding to Rodney Cohen, Sr. in December of 1909. Tracy was the schoolmate and close friend of Bowdre's Aunt Mary Lou Phinizy, with whom he lived at 519 Greene Street and where Tracy came to visit often. I became conscious of Tracy during my grammar school years beginning with a first summer visit to Aunt Mary Lou's house in Highlands, North Carolina, at about age eleven in 1938. We were at one period both guests, and I recall that with "Miss Tracy" (as I always called her) there I was given my own room and no longer was placed in Aunt Mary Lou's room or on the screened porch upstairs! There were two singles in my aunt's bedroom on opposite sides of the room.

Miss Tracy told me she always had been interested in the Bowdres, and I was the third one she had known: Uncle Bowdre Phinizy, Aunt Mary Lou's brother, and my father, named for his uncle, being the others. She was very fond of the Bowdres, she said.

As I grew up and interacted with Miss Tracy and her family through the years, I found in Tracy much more than just spectacle: this because she was creative, well read, a poet who was published, a local newspaper columnist, a gardener of some note, a captivating and appealing hostess, always providing excellent edibles, and finally a person who, over the years, really did make several important contributions to the improvement of life in Augusta. This then is the "Tracy and Roddey Story" as I know it from personal observation and research done in Augusta and Macon since 1992.

Anne Tracy Duncan was born with the traditional "silver spoon" well placed in her mouth: on her mother's side she was the granddaughter of Colonel William Butler Johnston and his wife, the former Anne Clark Tracy, after whom she was named. Both the Johnston and Tracy families were prominent pioneering citizens of Macon, Georgia. Johnston had wide banking,

CHAPTER SIX

retailing, and railroad investments, all giving him substantial wealth and leverage throughout the state and even the South by the late 1840s. Johnston also played an influential role in the development of the city utilities, including the gas works, water works, and the ice plant.

The Tracy family originally came from Connecticut, Anne's father being a lawyer, the second intendant or mayor of Macon, and then elected Judge Edward Dorr Tracy of Superior Court. In August 1851, Anne Tracy and William Johnston were married, departing soon after on their honeymoon, which was to be a year-long Grand Tour of Europe. The Johnstons had diplomatic introductions, which provided many special invitations to balls and other functions; for example, in Paris they attended balls at the Hotel de Ville and Tuileries Palace when Louis Napoleon was president before the Second Empire. Then they stayed in Italy the winter and spring of 1852, journeying as far south as Naples and Pompeii; their visit to Pompeii was of particular interest. Many purchases were being made as they traveled in France and Italy: porcelain, china, paintings, and sculpture for the grand new house they intended to construct when they returned to Macon.

A little girl was born to them in Paris on August 23, 1852, but died the same day. Anne's recovery consumed much time, so their Grand Tour extended to two or three years. By 1854, the Johnstons were back in Macon and awaiting the birth of their second child. It is very sad to relate that of the Johnston's six children (four girls and two boys), only the two last infant girls, Caroline (named for Anne's younger sister) and Mary Ellen survived to maturity. Caroline was born in 1862, Mary Ellen in 1864, and both came of age in the new mansion where construction began circa 1856-1857. Caroline Johnston was the mother of our heroine, Tracy, who was born in 1888.

Before proceeding further with our word portrait, we must digress a bit to provide the reader with a short depiction of the enormous mansion the Johnstons built at 2 Georgia Avenue on land once belonging to Anne Johnston's late father; his house was relocated to Cherry Street. T. Thomas and Son of New York drew the plans for the house in 1855; it was to be an Italian Renaissance Revival Palazzo of 18,000 square feet comprising rooms on four levels. The roof was crowned with a three-level cupola rising over eighty feet above the ground. The interior technical achievements, very "high-tech" in the 1850s, probably were quite unique and not duplicated at any other private home in the United States from that era. The home had three bathrooms with hot and cold running water, a central heating system, and a voice speaker tube system, walk-in closets in the bedrooms, a large in-home kitchen, and a cooling system to ventilate the home in hot weather. As the architect said, his plans would be splendid for a house in New York or other large eastern city!

In 1857, a local paper estimated the total cost, excluding equipment, to be about $100,000; at that time the cost of new housing construction in Macon would range

CHAPTER SIX

from $6,000 to $12,000 relative to a more normal residence! The Johnston mansion was about complete by late 1859 when Anne described it to her sister-in-law as "My Fairy Palace." At first they lived in the basement area as the house was not fully furnished and on another occasion with an aunt nearby. However, by the end of the Civil War in 1865, the Johnstons began to live in the entire house, which also was populated by several Tracy and Baxter (Anne Johnston's brother-in-law was Dr. John Spring Baxter, a widower) nieces and nephews. One interesting feature of the house was 1,200 square feet of floor space dedicated to the "picture gallery," as the family called it. This was a most splendid room where much of the art acquired by the couple on their Grand Tour was displayed and where large receptions took place. The clerestory ceiling was thirty feet high.

It is said William Butler Johnston was opposed to secession but submitted under pressure, as all his interests were in Georgia, and there was really no other choice. Nevertheless, Johnston was rather intimately involved with the Confederacy, being assistant treasurer of the Confederate government, and as such was the receiver of all Southern Confederate deposits. The Macon Depository was the most important after Richmond.

Macon suffered little or no vital property damage during the 1861-1865 war, although there was a Union cavalry advance near Macon and some shelling of the city. General Howell Cobb pushed the Union cavalry back in early August 1864, but meantime Macon was filled with refugees and wounded soldiers from the Atlanta area. After Atlanta fell to Sherman in September 1864, there was some consternation relative to Sherman's intentions, but the Union army began their March to Savannah in December, and Macon was ignored.

Colonel Johnston seems to have rapidly adjusted to the surrender in April 1865, and he signed his amnesty agreement and had pledged loyalty to the Union by July 1865. He was then elected president of the Central of Georgia Railroad, which the war had destroyed. By mid 1866, Johnston had secured over $1,000,000 from New York investors to put the railroad back in operation. From all accounts, the Johnstons appear to have emerged from the Civil War (or the War Between the States, as many in the South persist in calling it!) fairly well off, their home undamaged, and with both the will and capital required to move forward. This is contrary to the situation of many other families who lost much as they were more in the direct line of fire, one could say.

The Johnstons arranged receptions for their Tracy nieces (who had resided with them following the deaths of their parents in 1863 and 1868) in their elegant home after their marriages in 1879 and 1883—Susan Tracy first to Dr. Appleton Collins and Georgia Tracy to George Wadley, whose home was at Bolingbroke, near Macon. Then on January 23, 1883, the Johnstons' oldest daughter, Caroline (but always called Carrie), married George W. Duncan, who is listed as a colonel in a book of biography entitled *Georgia's Public Men 1902-1904*. He was born 1852 in Greenville, South Carolina, and it is stated that his father, Perry

CHAPTER SIX

E. Duncan, signed the order of succession separating the state from the Union. A Colonial Dames publication, however, lists Tracy's Duncan grandfather as Archibald Duncan, stating he was an important officer. Initially, the Duncans, following their winter wedding and reception which undoubtedly took place at the palatial Johnston residence, lived with her parents in the family home. Then in January 1885, the Johnston's first grandchild arrived and was named William Butler Duncan. He was born at the residence some thirty-two months prior to the death of his grandfather Johnston. The widow, Anne, continued on at the home until her own death in 1896.

The Duncans remained at the Johnston mansion until about 1895 when they built a new house on College Street for their family. By 1902, three more children had been born, George W., Jr., Anne Tracy (September 13, 1888), and John Baxter. There is no further mention of the first-born William Butler, so it is assumed he died in early childhood. Colonel Duncan was engaged in real estate business in Macon and was regarded as one of the city's most popular businessmen. Grandmother Anne Tracy Johnston's estate was at last settled and apportioned by 1901; the two Johnston daughters were the principal beneficiaries. Carrie took cash and the upper portion of the 2 Georgia Avenue property, while the younger sister, now Mary Ellen Johnston Felton, retained the home and the lower end of the same property. Carrie Duncan subdivided her property for future development; Mary Ellen had married William Hamilton

Felton in November 1888, and thereafter the Feltons stayed on in the Georgia Avenue home.

In 1895, William Felton was elected a Superior Court judge, at that time the youngest in Georgia. Their first and only child, William Hamilton Felton, Jr., was born in 1889, about a year following the birth of Tracy Duncan. The Johnston-Feltons and their descendants lived on in the famous old mansion with, to be sure, some renovations and modernization over the years, until 1926 when Judge and Mary Ellen Johnston Felton died. Mary Ellen had resided in the house her entire lifespan. The house is now owned by the Georgia Trust, having been conveyed to them by the Hay Family who purchased it in 1926. The Felton Jrs. then built a handsome Federal-style house in the Vineland district at 2417 Clayton Street. The historic house is now opened for visits and well worth the detour!

Now turning back to the Duncan family, Tracy was six or seven years old when the family took possession of their new residence on College Street. Although born in and living in the most famous house in Macon for the first part of her life, Tracy said later when revisiting No. 2 Georgia Avenue circa 1960s, she had left feeling so sorry for her young cousin about her age, William Felton, Jr., who was to remain in the old house while she went to a brand new home just constructed! At that time, Tracy also spoke ruefully of the ugly late Victorian architectural style Ma Duncan had chosen! But when growing up in the College Street house, she probably was proud of the new structure which appeared to cater

CHAPTER SIX

well to her family needs. Tracy was positioned in the Duncan household between her two brothers, George W., Jr. and John, who was born with a harelip. When ten years old, Tracy accompanied her mother and younger brother, John, on a trip to New York City, presumably to see a medical specialist relative to John's condition. While in New York, Tracy wrote her absent father a letter, which is now quoted mistakes and all:

New York, December 18th, 1898

Dear Tardoo,

I want to see you very much. New York is not as large as I thought it would be. We got to New York late Friday afternoon. Saturday morning mother took John to Dr. Wire's and it was so cold we liked to have frozen. & in the evening mother bought me the cunningest little red reaper with soldier straps and little brass soldier buttons. Yesterday we went to Brooklyn and saw Mrs. Ripley and Mrs. Heldges & a whole lot of people. We went over on the elevator railroad & crossed the Brooklyn Bridge. I had a very nice time & a good dinner. It is so cold up here that I had to put on my little shirt yesterday & this morning too. I ate two great big blue plums for breakfast. Tardoo there is the biggest fat man there I ever did see. Tardoo, this evening we went around town. Mother went to Altman and bought her a jacket and then I went and bought me some writing paper & some stamps & some envelopes and a pen then we got on the street car & came home. Mrs. Belmont you know died over in Europe and they are bringing her home across the street from us. You know the Belmonts are very rich. There is a carriage here that runs with electricity and it hasn't any horses and it has rubber tires & it looks just as funny. I wish you could see it. Tardoo, John's saying the lessons now but he is not most through. Tardoo, John and I sleep in the same bed. Tardoo, you must write to me soon. I inclose (sic) a letter to brother. Good by (sic) from your loving little mustard. When you write direct your letter Tracy Duncan 187 Madison Ave., New York City, N.Y. c/o Miss. Patterson

Apparently her nickname for her father was "Tardoo." Tracy certainly showed precocity in her writing and observations on events in New York. This was an early indication of her way with words still to come.

Tracy first had tuition in Macon schools and then at Wesleyan College (for women only) followed by enrollment at Mrs. Lefebvre's School. The latter was a finishing school which all young ladies of quality would attend for a few years, as few ladies in that age attended a university to secure a degree. At Mrs. Lefebvre's school, located at 122 West Franklin, Baltimore, Maryland, occurred one early major event in Tracy's young life: she met Mary Lou Phinizy of Augusta, another boarding student, and they appear to have rapidly developed what girls then called a "crush" on each other. They became lifelong friends and soon were exchanging visits between Augusta and Macon. The second seminal event in Tracy's future took place on

CHAPTER SIX

a visit to Augusta, where Mary Lou introduced Tracy to her future lifelong partner and husband, Rodney Sneed Cohen. But that was in the future, even if not too distant. First Tracy became a Macon debutante, introduced by her parents at a ball, and she joined a party of school friends, including Mary Lou, on a chaperoned trip to Europe in 1907.

The group of about six or seven girls was guided by Miss Emilie D. Huntley, likely a teacher at the Lefebvre school on whom many of the students also allowed they carried a "crush." The party sailed on the *S.S. Kroonland* of the Red Star Line (believed to be connected to the White Star Line) June 1 from Jersey City to Dover, England. The tour was about three months with much time spent in England, Scotland, Holland, Belgium, and France; they were long in Paris and also visited Loire Valley chateaux. In both Paris and London, the theatre was a nightly attraction with both plays and musicals enjoyed. In those days, travel was much slower but quite thorough. As an example, in England and Scotland, they followed the usual tourist trail from Dover to Canterbury, the Lake District (staying at Lake Windermere), Warwick Castle (where Tracy left her hair "switch," which I assume is a wig of sorts!), Furness Abbey, Durham Cathedral, Edinburgh, Scott's mansion "Abbotsford," York, Lincoln, Ely, Cambridge, and on to London, etc. Then the party attacked the continent.

While in Paris, Tracy and Mary Lou had some masculine company, too, for there are pictures taken with North Winship and Will Burt, both from Macon and members of what they called the "Log Cabin Club." These gentlemen were traveling in Europe at the same time and rendezvoused July 28, 1907, in Paris. Then there are snaps with a "Benjamin" and a "William," and one evening they went to a show and cabaret with "Lewis, Mr. Barrett and the Russian Count." Mr. and Mrs. Edward Mare Barrett (just married and from Augusta) also met Tracy and Mary Lou in August 1907, again in Paris. Anne Tracy Duncan was appointed "historian" for the trip, but if she authored a report such has not been discovered. The two girls nicknamed themselves "The Sponges" as they managed a few "freebies," i.e., some rides or whatever; included with this chapter is a charming snapshot of "The Sponges" in Paris! This was Tracy's first European sojourn but the second for Mary Lou.

We must now address pertinent facts on our hero of this piece, Rodney Sneed Cohen, who also was born with the proverbial silver spoon. He was the only child of Leonora Sneed and her husband, Cornelius Henry Cohen. Leonora, usually called Nora, was from Richmond, Virginia, and born in 1864 while Henry was born in Charleston, South Carolina, on April 7, 1854. Nora was betrothed soon after she came of age to a man ten years older (so the story is told) as Richmond and probably her own family still were suffering from the aftermath of the Civil War and reconstruction, so it was considered advisable to move on. There were Sneed relatives apparently already in Atlanta and Savannah (and probably also Augusta) with Cohen relations residing in

CHAPTER SIX

Richmond, Savannah, and Augusta where Henry (as he was called) had a legal practice. Henry graduated from the University of Georgia circa 1873 and was a member of the Phi Kappa Society. Nora Sneed Cohen was a perfectly beautiful lady with dignity, charm, and even erudition according to the standards of that era. Their son, Rodney, was born October 20, 1883, and grew to adulthood in Augusta, becoming a handsome and popular member of his generation.

In that perhaps more narrow-minded and prejudiced time, one did not speak, as most do now, of "our Judaic-Christian heritage." Rather the Hebraic culture or a person descending from such suffered a definite stigma; however, in the Cohen case the family was not really hurt in the social sphere, having already achieved a certain financial and intellectual success. Even though Nora is said to have had Jewish blood of 50 percent and her husband fully Hebraic in background, the family moved mainly in Christian circles and may have been sometime communicants (although never regular churchgoers) of St. Paul's Church, the original Episcopal Church of Augusta. However, the Henry Cohens seemed to have been always uninterested in religious matters, either Christian or Jewish, even though their son Rodney was christened at St. Paul's Church in October 1883 and confirmed there in 1899.

It is believed the Henry Cohens lived first in the Greene Street/Telfair Street areas, then the best local address in the city for residences, and later circa the early 1920s they decided to move to The Hill to a wonderful old house, constructed about 1810 and now listed on the National Register of Historic Places. Nora named the house High Gate for the tall wrought-iron gates they installed at the entrance to the driveway. High Gate consisted of about 1.63 acres, so there was sufficient space for Nora to pursue her love of gardening. Many shrubs and flowers from afar mingled with native specimens: boxwood (old English and American varieties), camellias, azaleas, bamboo, tea olives, dogwood, oaks, magnolias, and evergreen trees were all represented in the plantings mixed in with iris, lilies, and other flowers depending on the season. The house located on the crest of The Hill at 820 Milledge Road indeed became a showplace.

Rodney attended local schools and then went away to VMI, class of 1903. He lingered two years in Lexington, Virginia, while studying at VMI and then obtained his law degree from the University of Georgia in 1904. He appears to have joined his father's legal practice after his time in Athens at UGA. Meantime, Rodney most likely attended the "at-home" reception given by Mrs. Charles H. Phinizy and her daughter, Mary Lou (probably then a debutante), in 1905 or 1906 at 519 Greene Street where there was a ballroom and dancing mentioned on the printed invitations. It could have been here that Rodney and Tracy Duncan first met or perhaps later in Grovetown one hot summer as both the Cohen and Phinizy families maintained country houses in that town. The Cohen house was called Cohen Crest.

CHAPTER SIX

The local anecdote is that Tracy was playing a wide field with numerous beaux at the time and even several years onwards, so that the idea of a very early marriage was not too appealing with Rodney or the others wooing her from Macon or from elsewhere; for instance, North Winship, Sam Dunlap, and Howell Erminger from her hometown, to mention a few names. But eventually as per the story Tracy in later life told her close friend, Genie Lehmann, Ma Duncan made it clear to her daughter that a decision on marriage should be taken sooner rather than later. One reason was, notwithstanding the good time Tracy was having with many in pursuit, the Duncan fortune seems to have been somewhat diminished (in part due to her education, trip abroad, other travels, and debut); hence, by 1908 or 1909, Tracy determined to accept Rodney's proposal for there was we must assume a great physical attraction; she also had found Augusta and the friends made courtesy of Mary Lou quite agreeable and knew the Phinizy family at 519 Greene Street to be a decisive and positive force in her introduction and ultimate transition to life in Augusta. The religious differences did not seem to be a major obstacle, so in the end the wedding date was set for December 8, 1909, at Christ Episcopal Church in Macon.

There were several prenuptial affairs given to honor Tracy, Rodney, the bridal party, and even all out-of-town guests during the days preceding the wedding scheduled for nine o'clock p.m. on the eighth of December. The entire wedding is described in the two local newspapers as an event of signal interest considering the social prominence of the young couple and their wide family circle; the papers reported the occasion as of state-wide importance, and the ceremony one of the most "brilliant, elaborate and beautiful seen in Macon in many years!" One innovation was the boys' vested choir who led the bridal procession, singing at their entrance and during the ceremony. The choir consisted of nineteen boys, one of whom was named Jack Bowdre! The bride was attended by two pages, Mary Lou Phinizy of Augusta as maid of honor, and six bridesmaids, while the groom's best man was Judge Henry Hammond of Augusta, with his groomsmen and ushers numbering ten. Included among the groomsmen were Austin Branch, Estes Doremus, Archie Blackshear, and Coles Phinizy from Augusta. The out-of-town guests from Augusta embraced Miss Marguerite Wright, Mr. and Mrs. W. K. Miller, Dr. and Mrs. Asbury Hull, Miss Mary Hull, Miss Mary Harison, Mrs. Charles H. Phinizy, Mrs. Harriett Phinizy Mays, Mr. and Mrs. Henry Cohen, while there were Sneed and Cohen/Moses family connections from Atlanta, Savannah, and Richmond.

Following the church ceremony, there was a reception at the Duncan home on College Street. Here there again were elaborate and gorgeous flowers everywhere in all rooms thrown wide open to welcome about seventy-five guests who all were seated for an elegant supper at small tables. The bridal party had their own circular table elaborately decorated with lilies of the valley, candles, and streamers. At a late hour, Tracy and Rod left

CHAPTER SIX

Macon in their own private railroad car hooked onto the Atlanta train for a "northern destination" unknown to their friends! Tracy in later years told the story that the private car contained two bedrooms, and they used both their wedding night!

By early 1910, the young married Cohens were at home in Augusta, perhaps initially with the senior Cohens at their residence 1024 Greene Street and later at a house in the same area (in 1914 they were listed on 11th Street). By 1920, the Rod Cohen Jrs. resided at 1030 Greene Street. Tracy already knew many of the younger set from her prior visits, so there was no real homesickness; in this respect Mary Lou Phinizy was helpful, for the two still were rather inseparable friends. In later years, some wags would say Tracy talks only to Mary Lou and Mary Lou only to God! Amusing to some but a great exaggeration is the true fact! When Rodney Sneed Cohen, Jr. arrived October 16, 1912, Mary Lou Phinizy was asked to be his godmother. Rod, Jr. was christened at St. Paul's that same month.

North Winship from Macon evidently was back in the picture courting Mary Lou in this early post-wedding period of 1910-1911, and there were house parties in Grovetown at Cohen Crest or at the Phinizy country place known as Sans Souci. On one party occasion, Tracy and Boykin Wright, Jr. were discovered in a clinch on the Cohen Crest verandah by Nora Cohen. The story always told in Augusta is that Tracy told Nora, the mother-in-law of whom she was very fond, that if she told no one, then Tracy would never mention the ongoing relationship

Nora had with Judge Henry Hammond! Nora and Henry had been great and good friends for many years! This probably occurred about 1913 or 1914 or maybe a few years later when Rodney had been called to military duty and became a captain in the American Expeditionary Force in Europe in 1917. There was a training assignment in Chattanooga, and Tracy accompanied her husband for at least a portion of the time. However, Rodney does not appear to have been sent to Europe before hostilities ended November 11, 1918.

One of the permanent and early accomplishments (apart from the birth of their only child, Rod Jr. in 1912) of Tracy and Rodney was their purchase in July 1921 of the rather large house and garden at 2150 Battle Row, just off Milledge Road on The Hill in the Summerville area. I have read that Tracy first saw the property circa 1910 when she moved to Augusta as a new bride. She coveted this site, and finally the Thomas Loyless family was ready to sell to the Cohens who they believed would protect and preserve the fabric and grounds. The price was $21,000 for what some say had been about twenty acres but which was reduced in size in the early years of the Cohen ownership to a little less than two acres. Following the chain of titles to 2150 Battle Row, we find that Rodney, Sr. transferred the entire property to the "Tracy D. Cohen Estate" December 24, 1941, for "love and affection." According to Margaret Loyless Mell, who grew up in the house, the Cohens first named the house Dunomovin but then later converted that fanciful sobriquet to Sandy Acres.

CHAPTER SIX

The old clay tennis court was made into the sunken boxwood garden (all the box grown by Tracy), a rather formal area with the box bordering the flowerbeds. There was a spot called "an outdoor living room" with an open brick fireplace, a water garden on various levels encompassing five pools, a rose garden, and a secluded path known as the "Long Walk" adjacent to the eastern property line. Throughout the grounds were masses of tea olives, lilacs, evergreens, camellias, and trees: magnolias, oaks, dogwoods, and chinaberry with some trees and arbors swathed and garlanded with jasmine and wisteria vines. Nevertheless, the general layout of the grounds remained as before under the Loyless ownership. The house was actually two dwellings stuck together in the early part of the nineteenth century and always known as the Sand Hills Cottage style; still, the house was spacious with, say, 4,000 to 5,000 plus square feet, a guest cottage, garages, and another sheltered garden behind the house and down from the back porch.

Inside Tracy carefully arranged their furnishings, adding over the years inherited pieces from Macon and the Henry Cohen home. There was a large entrance hall and master bedroom on the ground floor, a long living room, a library with bookcases everywhere, a dining room of good size, a spacious rear porch which was screened at some stage, and various other rooms, including bedrooms on the second floor reached by a staircase from the library. Tracy and Rod remained in this house the rest of their lives, celebrating their fiftieth wedding anniversary here December 8, 1959. One silver mint julep cup to commemorate this important milestone was given and engraved as a gift from Rod, Jr. and his law associate Ed Slaton, while there is another engraved "Mr. Roddey."

As the Cohens worked on their new property with principal focus on the garden, Tracy converted Rod to her love of gardening. In particular, he took a great interest in their cultivation of roses and gradually became a great supporter of Tracy's gardening talents. She often termed herself "Head Gardener"! This early 1920s attention to the beauties of the garden and general horticultural pursuits turned out to be the perfect background when Tracy in 1927 was invited to become a charter member of The Augusta Garden Club; then in 1929 the club became a member of The Garden Club of America, and the name then changed to Sand Hills, as there was a Virginia Club with the Augusta name in its title already a member of The Garden Club of America.

From the start, Tracy took an active role among the twenty-six regular resident members. She was president of Sand Hills Garden Club when, as she said, Sand Hills "put the big pot in the little one" and invited the five hundred delegates to stop in Augusta and Aiken for a two-day visit prior to the 1932 annual meeting of The Garden Club of America held in Atlanta. The "500" arrived by special train and a festive program of meetings and tours of Augusta/Aiken homes and gardens were arranged in glorious April weather with everything in full bloom, as there was a late spring that

CHAPTER SIX

season. As one part of the program on the final day a "High Tea/Supper" with music and spirituals was held at the Old Medical College, which Sand Hills had adopted as a needed restoration project in 1931. Tracy was the "leading light" in pushing this worthy objective and clearly showed herself as an early advocate of historic preservation. The Old Medical College, circa 1835, was an excellent replica of a Greek temple but had deteriorated as an unused building for some years while the surrounding yard was overgrown with weeds, etc. The restoration work appears to have stimulated much interest in the Augusta community, and many sent checks (including many doctors who had studied there in years past); others contributed services in kind and some worked on the building for reduced pay or for nothing!

The hard work paid off eventually, and circa 1933 Sand Hills held an international camellia show in the restored building; there were exhibits from near and far to this first in the world all-camellia flower show opened to the public. These all-camellia exhibitions continued for many years with numerous local grafters developing new and improved varieties of blooms. Tracy's well-earned recognition of her long involvement and support of the Old Medical College came in 1961, when the history of the Old Medical College was written and published by the Augusta Council of Garden Clubs, Inc. (founded principally with impetus from Tracy in 1948). The dedication to Tracy reads as follows:

> "In Grateful Appreciation and Affection
> We Dedicate This Book To
> **Mrs. Rodney S. Cohen**
> Whose Vision That This
> Historic Building Would Be Restored
> As A Cultural Monument To
> Augusta's Past and Be Preserved
> As A Cultural Center For
> Augusta's Future
> This Has Been Brought To Fulfilment
> By Her Selfless Dedication and
> Infectious Zeal Which Inspires Others"

Tracy's picture and a plaque were installed in the old building with "Tracy" spelled incorrectly as "Tracey"! In the latter portion of this piece, there will be further mention of Tracy's own fine and continuing involvement with the Old Medical College preservation ongoing challenge. Meantime, before one camellia show in the mid 1930s held in the old building, there had been a severe winter frost damaging many camellia plants already in full bloom around Augusta; Tracy's own entry, therefore, consisted of large camellia blossoms turned brownish by the cold arranged in a copper vase reflecting some of the colors emanating from the blooms, and she won one of the top prizes! She always was creative in the most appealing and original way.

As one moves on into the 1930s and beyond, Rod Sr. continued with his legal career, succeeding to his father's practice following his death in 1924, while Tracy

CHAPTER SIX

focused on (a) her husband and son, (b) her writing of articles and poetry, and (c) her never-ending activities as "Head Gardener" at 2150 Battle Row extending to include her constant garden club and Old Medical College endeavors.

(A) Family: Tracy loved her mother-in-law, Leonora Sneed Cohen, always called

Nora; she had been a beauty in her youth and continued as a handsome lady until her death in 1950 aged eighty-six. Tracy insisted that Nora be buried in her beautiful pearl earrings which she had worn always. Inscribed on her tombstone at Summerville Cemetery is, "She was beautiful and through life's day walked with flowers all the way." Tracy, no doubt wrote this description of the stately and gracious Nora, who also was a great fan of her only grandchild, Rodney Jr., whom she continued to spoil. Circa 1939, at age seventy-five, she motored up to Highlands, North Carolina, with Judge Henry Hammond at the wheel for a long weekend visit with Mary Lou Phinizy. Nora and Henry continued over the years to be great and close companions; they were "an item" as they term it these days! The drive up from Augusta took much more time than normal, for they tarried and picnicked on the way, stopping several times to bathe in the inviting mountain streams as the car had no air conditioning. At dinner that first night, I sat across from the judge, who by then in a quite mellow mood began to recite verses he knew from Hamlet; and he declaimed these passages as though he was delivering a lecture, i.e., with much animation and ardor. It was obvious the whole company, including Tracy and Rod Sr., were enchanted with this fascinating older couple.

One Christmas in the late 1930s or 1940s, Tracy decided she wanted a "Pink Christmas"
instead of the more traditional green and red; so she had the surround of the front door painted pink, decorated a pink tree, and used pink linen for the Christmas dinner table. All this of course long before others began to revise the holiday color palette fairly frequently. In the 1930s, there was available plenty of help; Tracy entertained beautifully with much imagination, and her table combined good simple foods most people wanted with a touch of innovation and uniqueness. Pickled Jerusalem artichokes with cocktails and creamed as a vegetable in winter were favorites, as were chicken croquettes! Once Tracy wrote Mary Lou Phinizy, then in Highlands for the summer, that one hen yielded twenty-nine croquettes! Most evenings, Tracy and Rod, Sr. dressed for dinner, she in a long dress and he in his black tie, even if they dined without guests. They lived the good life, even if there might have been no real excess of money.

During the late 1920s when Rod, Jr. was a teenager, Tracy and his godmother, Mary Lou Phinizy, took him on a trip to Europe. Rod, Jr. was most certainly pampered and well thought of, not only within his family but also among his peers. He was growing to be a handsome man, notwithstanding one rather traumatic episode during his early grade-school years: Rod Jr. came home one day with a black eye or some slight facial injury to tell Tracy some rude and crude boy had called him a Jew,

CHAPTER SIX

so they scuffled, with Rod Jr. holding his own quite well. Tracy said, "Well, you are a Jew, and so is your father, but I am not!" We are not privy to other family conversations on this subject, but the entire family continued to be active communicants at St. Paul's Episcopal Church. Rod, Jr. even taught my Sunday school class at the Good Shepherd Episcopal Church for a brief time in the late 1930s, probably prior to his second marriage.

Rodney, Jr. followed his father to VMI, where he joined the class of 1933; he stayed in Lexington two years only before transferring to the University of Virginia Law School for an additional period, then to the University of Georgia Law School in Athens, but he did not graduate. However, he later passed the Georgia Bar examination and began to practice law with his father. While in Charlottesville at UVA, Rodney shared one of the famous housing units on the quadrangle designed by Thomas Jefferson. Rodney shared this school accommodation with a man from Staunton, Virginia, named Monroe, but Rod always called him "Money" as he was said to be very well-to-do!

At some point, probably while in Athens, Rodney met a pretty girl from Thomson, Georgia, and eloped with her. His parents evidently disapproved violently and had the marriage promptly annulled, for Rod, Jr. as yet had no means to support a wife. Stewart Hull, who knew the girl and was a friend of Rod's, says, "All she got was a set of china from Tracy," who clearly was behind the marriage dissolution. Meantime in 1936, the parents were visibly delighted when Rodney, Jr.

asked Anne Robertson to marry him; the engaged pair were cut from the same cloth, with both sets of parents moving in the same general social circles and both regular attendees of St. Paul's Church. The wedding was scheduled at St. Paul's in February of 1937, but as the bride's father, Miller Robertson, died suddenly January 1, 1937, the wedding was held at the Robertson's Henry Street home with only family and very intimate friends present on the scheduled date. Isabel Robertson (later Maxwell) was the flower girl to her Aunt Anne.

The 1930s culminated with Rod and Tracy's thirtieth wedding anniversary on December 8, 1939. Mary Lou Phinizy entertained in their honor with a lavish evening party at 814 Milledge Road for family, the wedding party, and close friends from Augusta and Macon. On this stellar occasion, Dr. John Duncan, Tracy's brother, then living in Atlanta, made a wonderful toast, followed by his wife, Blanche, and Edison Marshall. These jolly and festive poems broadly convey their history together as man and wife and set the tone for the celebration and perhaps one apogee in their long marriage. The poems are as follows:

1. "Thirty years ago tonight
   Mother was there and Father was tight!
   And I was feeling quite all right
   Thirty years ago.

   Friends had gathered from far and near
   To see a bride without a peer

CHAPTER SIX

Dressed in a gown of satin and white
God! Wasn't she a pretty sight!

The wedding itself was a gorgeous thing
The groom didn't even forget the ring!
And wasn't Ma Duncan having a fling
Thirty years ago.

The groom all smiling and debonair
Was easily the best man there,
And the toast he drank to his bride that night
Made me know Miss Tracy was right.

For sister and I have always been
A damn sight closer than kissing kin,
And thirty years is a right long span
To live with any lawyer man.

So — here's a toast to Rod: "True Blue" —
The finest man I ever knew"

Even little "Johnny Jones" was there
On isle No. 3 — with a vacant stare
An usher he was in this pomp affair
Thirty years ago.

Estes Doremus — bless his soul
Was drunk as a cooter at the old punch bowl
While Father ushered him in and out
Having no idea what 'twas all about.

His Honor, the Judge, was also there
Resplendent as always, with snow white hair
His speech an epic of wit and charm
And could he make one, when he got warm!

The private car on the old side track
Caused <u>lots</u> of comment, and a few wise cracks.
Atlanta bound with a bride and groom
And who could ask for a better room?

A lot has happened since that night
Some good, some bad, but still all right
As the youngest brother, all I can say:
"Thank God she's alive, and with us today!"
– Dr. John Duncan (Tracy's youngest brother)

2. All of this poem could not be
Without the help of M.L.P.
She loved the bride and knew the groom
And introduced them, none too soon.

The friendship of dear Mary Lou
Mixed with Cupid's ballyhoo
Made this wedding then come true
Here's a toast to her – Toodlehoo!"
– Blanche Duncan (Tracy's sister-in-law)

CHAPTER SIX

3. To Rodney and Tracy

> A Mistress of Arts,
> In the best that life brings,
> A poet of parts,
> With hummingbird wings,
> A hummingbird bill for life's golden honey,
> A luminous quill for the trenchant and funny;
> Long-wedded to Roddey
> Of athlete body,
> And mind calm and spacious,
> And manner most gracious,
> He loves to grow roses,
> Thus his soul he discloses'
> And the dark rose he's grown,
> And has kept for his own,
> Is as haunting, enchanting,
> As any the wild winds have sewn,
> Or Memory's summers have blown.
> - Edison Marshall (Noted writer, neighbor and friend)

(B) <u>Tracy's Literary Activities:</u> Always a history buff and an enthusiastic reader all her life, Tracy also composed poems and wrote feature articles through the years for various publications. The latter included the *Atlanta Journal*, Garden Club of America bulletins, *Reader's Digest*, and during the late 1930s a newspaper column for the *Augusta Chronicle* under the nom de plume of Anne Howe. The column usually appeared on Sundays on the editorial page and was entitled "Here's How by Anne Howe." The Anne Howe topics dealt mainly with the social and civic life of Augusta and reflected her own firm interest in the community she grew to love. Examples of the "Here's How by Anne Howe" columns taken from the 1939 *Augusta Chronicle* follow:

The Augusta Chronicle
Sunday, October 8, 1939
Community Chests

    This is the season of the year when Community Chests all over the country are opened up and aired. They have been completely cleaned out and are waiting to be refilled.

    Faith-Hope and Charity-It takes lots of both faith and hope when it comes to Charity; nine times out of ten-Here's How:

How sweet and rare it is,
The way that we share what is,
Spent at a Charity Ball

Mrs. Big Wig has taken a table.
The tickets are five dollars per,
She hems and she haws,
She does it because
Being seen is important to her.

CHAPTER SIX

She buys a swank dress for the party
As do many others that go.
For it just wouldn't do,
Not to have something new,
To wear to a Charity Show!

Beauty shops do a land-office business,
They're busy from morning 'till night,
Giving facials and curls,
To matrons and girls,
And setting their ringlets just right.

The gentleman, too, catch the spirit —
They all have the time of their lives,
Swapping crisp paper dollars,
For white ties and collars,
And bouquets for sweethearts and wives.

Then there'll surely be wine at the dinner,
And cocktails galore they'll all take—
Oh the lids off that night,
They must be gay and bright—
It's done for Sweet Charity's sake...

But the blood money spent for the ticket,
The five dollars paid at the door—
Will have to include,
Music, floor show and food,
Or else they won't go any more.

> So they sit back serene and contented—
> They've answered the clarion call.
> How sweet and how rare it is,
> The way that we share what is
> Spent at a Charity Ball!
>
> Let's turn over a new leaf.

The Augusta Chronicle
Wednesday, December 13, 1939
Christmas Gifts

Let's all be sensible about Christmas this year. Let's get away from gadgets and doo-dads. Let's look the situation squarely in the face and realize once and for all that nobody in the world wants a combination can opener, screw driver and billy goat-bit! They don't want a flossy cover for their telephone or a little brown jug that plays a tune when you pick it up.

They really don't!

There's too much unhappiness in the world — people are too serious minded — too wary and too wise to be interested in that junk. Let's be practical.

CHAPTER SIX

Let's burn up everything in that drawer where we keep the unsuccessful offerings of our friends — the bridge prizes and assembled Bazaar purchases. The chances are there's not one single thing in the entire drawer worth wrapping up. Burn them instead! You don't want them. and neither does anybody else! Louise or Eleanor would rather have a ten-cent can of baked beans than that purple pincushion with the dancing doll on the top. Believe it or not. They don't want that little handkerchief bag made in the image of a man's night-shirt, or those lipstick towels; they don't want scalloped wash-rags or hair-pin-holders, or heart shaped sachets that have lost their first youth. Your friends probably have as many "seconds" as you have — they can keep sending them as long as you can. Break away from this nefarious habit. It's all wrong. It destroys the spirit of Christmas. Burn the mess. Come clean. Give sensible, practical, or even frivolous things — but let them have a personal touch. Let them be something that it gives you pleasure to give — that expresses you — your taste — your affection. You know you are humiliated and ashamed sometimes of the atrocities you send forth, with chirpy little "Best wishes for a Merry Christmas." That sort of thing doesn't make for a Merry Christmas. It makes your friends mad as H--- and what's more when next Christmas rolls around, "the elephant remembers."

The shops are full of a variety of lovely things within the price range of all. Exercise a little ingenuity. The simplest things can sometimes be the sweetest. Candles for instance are among the nicest of all Christmas presents. You can never have enough candles. Give two candles, four, six, eight, or a box. Everybody'll be pleased. There are white ones, green ones, or those soft creamy things that come in all sizes and shapes. Search the shops for the heavy kind that burn slowly and have the least amount of drip. Candle light is so flattering. Give candles. It's Christmas. Be Christmasy.

Another safe bet is food. If you've made catsup, jelly, pickles, marmalade, mincemeat or fruitcake, what about sharing them with your friends? If you haven't, there's still time — and there are so many darling little pots and jars and bottles and dishes to put them in. you can get the most enchanting cellophane papers — in the shiniest brightest colors. You can get ribbons to match or contrast. You can dress up your food-y presents to look like a million dollars. It's fun. It's economical, and everybody's happy!

What about a fruitcake this year? Christmas without a fruitcake seems like a play without Hamlet. But there are fruitcakes and fruitcakes, the same

CHAPTER SIX

as there are Hamlets and Hamlets. Here's the best fruitcake in the world. It will make one enormous cake, two smaller ones (big cakes themselves) or any number of little cakes to give as presents. It's the favorite recipe of a very famous Southern house-keeper. Here's how:

Black Fruit-Cake

4 lbs. raisins
3 lbs. currants
1 lb. citron
1 lb. pecans
1 pt. bottle Maraschino cherries
1 pt. molasses
1 lb. flour
1½ lb. sugar
1 lb. butter
1 doz. Eggs
1 tumbler whiskey
1 tumbler sherry wine
1 cup milk
3 teaspoons baking powder, sifted in flour
2 light tablespoons cinnamon
2 light tablespoons nutmeg
1 teaspoon mace
1 teaspoon cloves
Pinch of salt

To Make:

Prepare fruit the day before (wash and seed currants and raisins, cut citron, nuts and cherries). Then mix the fruit with flour. Use hands or spoon in stirring and tossing them up and down. You will find the fruit will take up all the flour. (Save out about 2 tablespoonsful). In another large bowl prepare your batter, creaming butter and sugar, adding eggs, the two tablespoonsful of flour saved out, molasses, fruit, spices and liquor — tasting from time to time to avoid excess of spice. Stir well, then bake in a very slow oven. It will require from 3 to 4 hours. Grease your pans thoroughly. Cake should be well done, but not allowed to dry out. That luscious moisty taste is what you want.

Get to the kitchen. Get busy. Only two weeks more to go. It's such a nice bustling time. Hustle about. Avoid that top drawer. Don't open it. Once you're in, all is lost. You'll find something that will do for John, Jenny or Sue. You'll slip back into the old place — and so will the presents a few years hence.

CHAPTER SIX

The Augusta Chronicle
Sunday, December 24, 1939
Tomorrow's Christmas

Tomorrow's Christmas
Down in the kitchen,
Everything show is
Rollin' 'n pitchin —

Turkeys to steam,
Hams to bake —
"Do Goodness help me
Ice this cake."

"Janie, watch out;
Goose gotter be done —
Put the big pot
In the little one."

Up in the Library,
Miss Ravenal —
B'lieve it or not
Is working like ----.

Papers and parcels,
Litt'rin the floor —
People all opening' 'n
Shutting the door.

IS LIVING WELL STILL THE BEST REVENGE?

House chock full
To overflowing' —
Young folks, old folks,
Comin' 'n goin'.

Postman arrivin'
Lop-sided with mail —
Puppy dog got a
Slant to his tail.

He loathes fire poppers —
Poppin' about.
Got under the bed —
You can't get him out!

Up Up Up —
In the Arctic snow,
Old Santa Claus is
Rearin' to go.

Sack all packed —
Reindeers out side,
Prancin' 'n dancin' —
Ready to ride.

Tomorrow's Christmas!

The "Tomorrow's Christmas" column showed above it a charming picture (probably snapped in her own

CHAPTER SIX

kitchen) of a white-coated butler, a cook, and an aproned uniformed maid tending to their chores and captioned, "Puttin' the Big Pot in the Little One."

I remember the summer of 1939, when staying at Mary Lou Phinizy's house in Highlands, North Carolina, Tracy would on some days type away on her portable so her "Anne Howe" columns would meet the newspaper's deadline. These weekly columns written for the *Augusta Chronicle* were very popular and much anticipated by most subscribers. Reflecting the Cohen ongoing and reading activities, the lending library and sales records from "The Bookshelf" shop show that aside from the Rod and Tracy book transactions, orders were given to send various books to Tracy's mother, Mrs. George Duncan, at 290 College Street, Macon, this is in the late 1920s and early 1930s. The Bookshelf was first owned by Eliza Phinizy and Louise Hankinson, then later by Louise Mays Bussey, herself a great reader. The location was Albion Alley (in front of the Richmond Hotel) and later on Broad Street in a very narrow storefront near the Imperial Theater.

The Tracy Duncan Cohen writing activity culminated with the 1956 publication of a book of verse entitled *Out of My Mind* and published by Exposition Press in New York. This was her first book and contained seventy-five poems written throughout the years and each apparently the account of an episode in the author's life. Many, she said, "were jotted down on the backs of old envelopes." When interviewed on publication, Tracy related she had "hundreds more" when discussing her new forty-eight-page slim volume of verse dealing with various events as life passes on.

The subjects vary, including humor and witticisms, with some sadness as World War II was underway when a few were written. Dogs always enchanted Tracy and were the inspiration of several poems, i.e., "Little Butch" deals with one who attended the University of Virginia (having been born in this state) and later enjoyed a new wild life in Athens at the University of Georgia; another was "John" who was reared as a sort of a human child; "Mr. Tippy" the dog became an epicure and had his day; and a wonderful melange of four verses about "Mr. Peter" and others. In later years, Tracy had other dogs: Lilibet (named for Princess Elizabeth of Great Britain) and Cinderella, her Manchester terrier who birthed three black and tan pups rather unanticipated!

One funny dog story involving Tracy happened when Jake Lowrey asked her why she didn't have Lilibet marry like her namesake in 1947; Tracy without missing a beat asked Jake why he did not marry, and those knowing the facts will find this bon mot wisecrack quite amusing! The charming friend who consoled her little dog after he had nipped Tracy "good and hard" was Maisie Chafee and not Mary Lou Phinizy, as Tracy told me one day. The book was dedicated to "Mr. Roddey," her spouse of forty-seven years, and there are several verses where he is the subject.

To launch the book locally, there was on February 12, 1957, an autograph party in downtown Augusta at Davison's Department Store. The paper reported that

CHAPTER SIX

the fourth floor "was fairly blooming with camellias ranging in color from white to crimson and in size from mammoth to petite—presenting a magnificent sight in their containers of shining silver." In this milieu, Tracy signed her book (I presume for all paying customers at $2.50 a copy) for two hours and then repaired to 814 Milledge Road where Mary Lou Phinizy entertained at a luncheon to honor the author, close Augusta friends, and all out-of-town guests. The latter included Ambassador and Mrs. North Winship (former envoy to many foreign countries as well as Canada and South Africa) and other Macon friends; her Felton cousins also made the trip from Macon for the occasion, as did relatives from Bolingbroke and Washington, Georgia.

Tracy did me the honor of sending a copy of her book for Christmas 1956 when I was then working in Hong Kong. She wrote this inside on the foresheet:

"To Bowdre Mays — A homey touch for a young man in a strange land, with my love —

Tracy D. Cohen, Christmas 1956"

Around this time, Mary Lou Phinizy was strongly focusing on "facts," as she called them, when discussing or debating almost any topic. So Tracy sent Mary Lou a copy dedicated to her as hereunder. This was apparently Christmas 1956, even though no date is noted:

> "Leave Fact behind and come and go
> With me up lovely paths I know
> That wind aloft through shining woods
> To avenues of Escape where gala moods

Infect the air, and dancing feet
Lead far and farther from Fact's street,
So cold and hard and bare, I find
It's nice when we leave Fact behind.
My Love and Merry
Christmas!"
Tracy D. Cohen

(C) <u>Horticulture/Gardening Pursuits:</u> during the April 1932 visit to Augusta of the large contingent of ladies en route to The Garden Club of America's annual meeting in Atlanta, the Cohen garden at Sandy Acres was on the tour; in the visit schedule there was a picture of the boxwood garden under which Tracy had penned a verse:

"In my garden I've boxwood and roses,
Peach trees that are rugged and bare,
The woodbine entwines around the Jassamine vines
And I've old fashioned bulbs here and there.

But it isn't so much of a garden,
And it's hardly worth coming to see,
Except in the Spring when the birds they all sing —
Then it looks mighty pretty to me."

Tracy was president of Sand Hills Garden Club twice, 1930-1932 and 1960-1961, and over her long life in Augusta continued to support all worthwhile gardening activities; highlights in her horticultural and cultivation

CHAPTER SIX

career including her restoration endeavors are enumerated here to supplement that which was discussed previously:

- Restoration of the Old Medical College building and grounds as an ongoing project for Sand Hills Garden Club.
- First large public all-camellia show opened at Old Medical College premises; other fundraisers also housed in the building through the years.
- During World War II, she persuaded General Van Fleet, a guest in her cottage at Sandy Acres, to encourage the military to lease the building for the U.S.O.; even though no rent was paid, the U.S.O. made important improvements to the building.
- A trailer ambulance was equipped and given to the Borough of Erith, Kent, England, by Sand Hills during the war years.
- In the 1950s, "Waltz Night" was founded in the Old Medical College; this helped begin the city interest in the Augusta Symphony.
- In 1960, at Palm Beach, Sand Hills won the $10,000 Founders Fund Award for saving the Old Medical College building from the wreckers; this gift permitted many improvements to the front apron and grounds of the historic structure.
- Assisted in the organization of the Garden Club of Georgia in 1928.
- Proposed the formation of the Augusta Council of Garden Clubs in 1948. Thus the preservation

of the Old Medical College became a community-wide project.
- Aided the restoration of "Ware's Folly," home to the Gertrude Herbert Institute of Art, with matching funds from Sand Hills Garden Club.

Undoubtedly there were many other worthwhile civic and gardening ventures involving Tracy; as a charter and founding member of Sand Hills Garden Club, Tracy wrote long ago: "We now stand ready and willing to help landscape the moon...if and when...?" Such neatly sums up Tracy's approach! As the reader easily can discern, Tracy Duncan Cohen made a real difference for the better in Augusta.

In her later years, Tracy's interest in the Old Medical College never faltered, so in the autumn of 1970 another dream was realized when she secured the installation of the old animal water fountain (originally at Walton Way and 15th Street) in the Medical College yard. The fountain has three water spouts from three sides of the obelisk, and on the fourth is a plaque telling how such fountains were erected in forty-four states and also in Mexico City to cater to animals. The presenter was the National Humane Alliance (founded in 1896) with the fountain erected in Augusta in 1907. Water flows into a large basin (for horses) and thereafter feeds into four bowls at the fountain base for dogs and other small animals.

World War II, followed in 1950 by the Korean War, brought the Cohens some heartache and fear; a bit of trepidation arose when Rod, Jr. was called to active duty

CHAPTER SIX

November 25, 1940, as a captain commander of A Btry 214 AAA. He had been serving in the National Guard. Later Rod, Jr. served at Fort Stewart for further training and then was posted with his unit to the West Coast (Long Beach, California) following the Pearl Harbor attack. His unit became part of the West Coast defense strategy. Subsequently Rod, Jr. was assigned to Camp Davis, North Carolina, as a gunnery officer and instructor at the anti-aircraft school. I am now told Camp Davis no longer exists. Rod, Jr. returned home after hostilities ended with the rank of lieutenant colonel.

The Cohen Jr. marriage also was coming to an end; but around this time (late 1940s) Grandmother Nora Cohen, deeded a small plot from her 820 Milledge Road property to them, and they ordered a small house constructed in 1946. Their new address was 824 Milledge Road with access to the new home then by the main Highgate entrance driveway. Anne Cohen provided most of the construction money from a legacy given by her Aunt Mamie Martin. The land was .59 of an acre.

During the Korean Conflict, Rod, Jr. served as a lieutenant colonel of S-3 108 Brigade Georgia National Guard. General Joe Fraser was commander. Rod's unit was sent to Fort Bliss, Texas (El Paso), after initial training at Fort Stewart. Then his detachment went to Philadelphia to command all anti-aircraft units on site. Then apparently back to Fort Bliss and afterwards shipped to Japan in a "holding command." While in Japan, there was an unintended accident whereby a bullet from Rod's pistol struck an army captain. Rod later was discharged and returned to Augusta to practice law with his father. General Van Fleet is said to have competently assisted Rod, Sr. and Tracy with the "shooting incident" in order for Rod, Jr. to leave Japan and come back home expeditiously. Sadly, Rod, Jr.'s marriage to Anne Robertson soon finally ended. He then remarried for the third time to Donna Lamb Smith who had been the wife of a Colonel Smith. The Smiths, it seems, had known Rodney since the World War II days when the colonel had been one of Rod's artillery instructors; during the Korean strife they all were at Fort Bliss, Texas, where Rod, Jr. stayed in a cottage behind the Smith's home while Colonel Smith was posted to Korea.

The Cohens were very fond of their new daughter-in-law, who was mature and gave every indication of imparting a very stabilizing influence on Rod, Jr.'s life in Augusta. Tracy hosted a large and sumptuous afternoon reception to introduce Donna to her lady friends and, I imagine, Augusta society. 2150 Battle Row was filled with flowers, including large camellia plants in full bloom throughout the party rooms. The local paper reported that "Camellias and Candlelight" were the dominant notes at the large reception when several hundred guests were invited to call from 5:00 p.m. to 7:00 p.m. Pink camellias were featured in the drawing room, red for the library, and all white displayed in the dining room. Only lighted candles were used throughout the house. The time must have been circa 1952 (when they were married) or winter 1953. Unfortunately, in 1959, Donna died suddenly of a massive heart attack in her

CHAPTER SIX

bathroom at their Partridge Inn suite where they then were residing. She was only fifty years old.

From the commencement of World War II, Tracy followed events carefully; Tracy was as always a wide-ranging reader heeding carefully all the war news on a daily basis. During the summer of 1940 when in Highlands we played a sort of fantasy game wherein everyone present could make a wish where one would prefer to be. Aunt Mary Lou Phinizy wanted to be on the Left Bank in Paris eating roast duck and drinking champagne, but Tracy wished to be at a family lunch at Buckingham Palace with the King, Queen, Prime Minister Winston Churchill, and the two little princesses! Through their friendship with General Van Fleet at Fort Gordon, both Cohens continued to have military contacts and always supported the United States war effort where possible.

Tracy during the war years and after in the 1950s and 1960s continued her family orientations and contacts with close family friends in addition to the younger generations as they came along. For example, her nephew George Duncan lost his parents at an early age, and he came to stay at Christmas and on other occasions. George went on to Annapolis, finally graduating around 1948 or 1949. It is very sad to relate, however, that George died circa 1954-1955 in a naval plane crash. Tracy also began to have one or two small tables of the younger people at large dinner parties (always black tie), and we all had a lot of fun sitting apart in the library from "our elders" in the Cohen dining room pretending to be "grown-ups" in our teen years! Various persons on some of these occasions included Frank Mays, Betty Phinizy, Cassius, Landon, and Harris Clay, etc.

Tracy generated much goodwill and showed her basic kindness and thoughtfulness in various ways. One example in my family was in 1959 when Ted Mays became engaged and needed to give an engagement ring to his fiancee. Tracy gave him a diamond ring that had belonged to her, knowing Ted was only just in the embryonic phase of his career. When I brought my betrothed, Lynn, to Augusta in March 1965 to meet everyone, Tracy and Rod had us over to a wonderful small gathering complete with a wedding cake featuring figures of a bride and groom on top. Tracy also accompanied Mary Lou Phinizy to New York City for our wedding June 5, 1965, carrying loads of gardenias and roses from her garden (all packed in ice) for the rehearsal dinner party given by Sophie Meldrim Shonnard the night prior to the ceremony. The ladies traveled by train with all these flowers! When I once asked Mr. Rod, Sr. how he had managed such a happy marriage for about fifty-six years at that time, he replied, "I always allowed her freedom to accomplish whatever she wanted to do!"

Keeping in touch with her Johnston-Felton relatives in Macon also was an interest. It was noted before that Tracy and Mary Lou went to Macon with both Rodneys circa 1960s to visit the Johnston Mansion, the Feltons, and lastly the Burts at Bolingbroke, where the Burts' home was named Great Hill Place. When the last owners, the P.L. Hay Foundation, opened the Johnston

CHAPTER SIX

house to the public as a museum, Tracy apparently had some interest in returning to the house certain original furnishings she had in Augusta, provided the name Johnston-Felton-Hay house was employed. I understand such was not agreed upon then; although, now the current owner, The Georgia Trust, generally uses all three owners in the title. Tracy did at some point donate furniture to the Colonial Dames for their house in Savannah; I understand these furnishings comprised French period furniture inherited from the Johnston family and which presumably came from the mansion in Macon.

In July 1956, Tracy's namesake and godchild Anne Tracy Felton came to visit with her parents, Mr. and Mrs. George Felton of Macon, and Tracy gave the four-year-old a "debut party" at Sandy Acres where the hostess and "debutante" received the guests standing by an oil painting of the first Anne Tracy (Tracy Cohen's grandmother after whom she was named and the great-great-grandmother of the "deb"). Tracy continued to see the Feltons and their three girls even if infrequently in later years. One daughter Polly Felton Morrison and Tracy's third cousin, or as they say first cousin twice removed, wrote me she often stopped off to see Aunt Tracy (as they all called her) when driving from her home in Columbia, South Carolina, to Macon. On one trip, Tracy was having a lunch party, and Polly was made the bartender and told to make martinis for the small group of ladies. Polly recalls Aunt Tracy saying, "Light on the vermouth, Polly!"

When our first little girl was born in Singapore July 12, 1966, we wrote Tracy we were naming her Tracy, and she seemed delighted to have another namesake. We first brought our little Tracy to Augusta in 1968, and Tracy and Rod, Sr. gave us a lunch party at 2150 Battle Row. Although still early May, it was like an early summer day, and we all sat on the back screened porch. Our Tracy behaved well as Tracy Cohen presented her with an antique coin silver spoon engraved "Tracy." Our small Tracy also received later from Mary Lou Phinizy a beautiful repousse silver sauce boat which had originally belonged to Tracy Duncan Cohen, made by S. Kirk and engraved "Tracy." This 1968 visit was our last occasion to meet Mr. Roddey, Sr., who died September 23, 1968. As Rod and Tracy were close companions, his loss really was a blow even though he was just several weeks shy of eighty-five years.

I transited Augusta in early December 1968 en route to New York for the company annual meeting where I was to speak on Southeast Asia; and while in Augusta, I saw Tracy once. She appeared somewhat preoccupied and wanted to plan a winter trip to Vienna and other parts of Austria; she spoke specifically of spending Christmas in Vienna. Mary Lou Phinizy was worried and inferred to my father that Tracy was in no condition then to make such a trip, which in any event never took place. Nor were there any other future long sojourns away from Augusta. Mary Lou spoke on the telephone each day with Tracy

CHAPTER SIX

and on many days walked down Milledge Road and into Gordon Lane to reach 2150 Battle Row to take lunch. First the martinis and then luncheon either hot or cold depending upon the season. Tracy usually employed a good cook, and at one point her servants were blood related to one or more working for Mary Lou. Freeman was the Cohen gardener, and one former tenant in the Cohen Cottage tells stories of Tracy ordering him to "cut down that S.O.B." or "move (a chair perhaps) that broken S.O.B." The tenants had rented the Cohen guest cottage as a newly married couple. Tracy even with age said exactly what she thought (usually!) and never was a person to mince words! She also often liked to use swear words and profanity to lend emphasis!

The second family tragedy came all too soon: the death of Rodney Cohen, Jr. from lung cancer in April 1973. Tracy had known he was seriously ill at least from January 1973, when she told a visitor one cold and snowy evening of her son's malady. This visitor was Dr. Russell Moores, who due to the unusual weather in Augusta had walked all the way from his home on Kings Way and Milledge Road. Rod, Jr. had been particularly devoted since his father passed on in 1968; and what a devastating loss when any mother has to lose a child, in this case the only one! The natural and normal order of life is just destroyed. The card Tracy sent to all those offering her sympathy probably very well reflected her feelings and is quoted here:

IS LIVING WELL STILL THE BEST REVENGE?

Mrs. Rodney S. Cohen
2150 Battle Row

"In life's vale of shifting shadows
Two things stand alone —
Kindness in another's troubles
Courage in your own."

For some reason, I have the idea that Tracy took this piece from something Madame Chiang Kai-Shek said during the early part of World War II when she was visiting the United States. On Rod, Jr.'s cemetery marker is engraved onto the stone:

Rodney Sneed Cohen, Jr.
October 16, 1912 – April 20, 1973

"How many fond hopes lie buried here"

He was interred next to his last wife, Donna.
There was to be one final disaster when after her son's death it was discovered he had, while in the hospital and probably on his deathbed, revised his will leaving properties placed in his name years ago by Rod, Sr. to a girlfriend! Rod, Sr. perhaps quite naturally felt his son and their heir would not pre-decease Tracy when he made the cessions. Mary Lou at once called Hale Barrett, who due to other pressing matters turned the matter over to Wyck Knox, then a fellow colleague in the Hull, Barrett legal firm. One meeting was held in the Cohen dining

CHAPTER SIX

room with Tracy, Mary Lou, Genie Lehmann, and Wyck presiding. The attorney advised the legal positions relative to the wills and codicils in Georgia, and they discussed the best course to take, for Tracy required the income from the real estate under contention. Mary Lou was very vocal in her opinion to take strong legal action and immediately employed an epithet to strengthen her point! ("Don't give the Goddamn bitch a dime," this dignified old lady is reported to have snapped!) In the end, Wyck Knox negotiated a compromise whereby the friend in question kept one piece of real estate in the 15th Street vicinity, with the remainder returned to Tracy. This included the Partridge Inn.

It appears to a certain extent Tracy lost some of her natural zest about this time; of course, in September 1974 she was eighty-six and may have just "given up" a bit. But she did attend the May or June party Aunt Mary Lou gave during our annual visit from Brussels and before moving on to Hilton Head for vacation with our two girls. I recall this evening affair vividly because Tracy arrived rather late and dressed (so Mary Lou said) in a black lace nightgown. It certainly looked to me like an evening dress, but when I said so, Mary Lou shot right back that she knew what it was as she had one just like it! I drove Tracy home that night and much enjoyed our conversation about the guests and the party.

Tracy did like to shock, I guess, and once in earlier years answered the front door entirely starkers (as the British say) when the three Bussey girls came to call at a pre-arranged time! During these last years, Tracy was lucky to have a close younger friend and admirer in Genie Lehmann who was most supportive. Genie for years had found Tracy's spirit and creative touch an inspiration, having been infatuated and taken with her since her girlhood in Chattanooga. Then Tracy as a young wife had spent some time there while Rod was in military training during World War I. Their relationship deepened also because of the King connection where Elizabeth Cashin King (Pendleton's mother) was Genie's great aunt. Genie in these final years, and particularly following Rod, Jr.'s death in 1973, assumed much of the domestic day-to-day burdens and assisted with Tracy's financial affairs. Genie was named Tracy's executrix in her last will and became the principal heiress to almost everything after the bequest of a Broad Street property (known then as now as the Sunshine Bakery) to George Felton and the main cash legacy of $25,000 to "my faithful friend and servant Elsa Landenburger" who had been of great comfort and service to both Tracy and her late son. Aunt Mary Lou commented, "Genie made a clean sweep." I say she well deserved all of it!

Either in October 1974 or 1975, Tracy and Mary Lou were joint hostesses for the Sand Hills Garden Club autumn meeting and luncheon at Mary Lou's house. Betty B. Bowring wrote us in a letter from her then home at Martha's Vineyard: "A splendid affair." It was probably the last time the two old friends entertained together.

In September 1975, Tracy once again showed her kindness and affection for my family, this when my father died September 13, 1975, after a short hospitalization.

CHAPTER SIX

Lynn and I flew directly to the United States from Belgium via Washington and London; the funeral took place the day after our arrival. Mother said Tracy wanted our family to come take supper that evening, and she accepted. Mary Lou tried to dissuade Tracy, saying she was not up to having a crowd to dine, but had no luck. Tracy said she had ordered the best and largest roast beef she could locate, and Chick Lehmann was coming to carve it! So there but please come!

Tracy received all of us in early evening sitting in a small French chair in her living room but dressed in nightgown and robe. It appeared she had already started the cocktail hour. When I leaned over to kiss her, I asked, "How are you, Miss Tracy?" and she peered up as though I had made such an asinine remark. Her expression clearly said, "How in the hell do you think I am at eighty-seven sitting here in my condition?" But immediately, very quickly, she made a truly beatific smile and said how joyful it was to see me! Later Tracy told me she was glad my father had died as he had nothing to live for; I found this statement very heartless, although she followed it by saying, "It has been a very long time since I have been sorry about the death of anyone!" This sort of took the sting from her initial remark. It was a rather melancholy evening but with plenty to drink and eat, kind of for me a final remembrance from the past. Tracy refused to eat much, and Mary Lou fed her roast beef like she was a child. Teto Barrett was jolly as usual; she and Frank (my mother) talked about their teen years and what the future would hold, Mother saying she would be as "poor as a church mouse!" That expression had come from her own mother, Frankie Doughty. The whole evening was somewhat surreal, at least for me.

In summer 1976, we went to Hilton Head as usual to vacation with the children. We planned to visit Miss Tracy when we went up to Augusta; in the interim we heard she was quite ill and called Aunt Mary Lou, who advised she was "eaten up with cancer" in the hospital "where she would be more comfortable." Those quotes were her exact words. I asked to be kept informed and in late July heard through Skippy Hull Boyd that Miss Tracy died July 25, and Aunt Mary Lou said to inform us not to interrupt our vacation to attend the funeral. Looking back, I now wish we had followed our first inclinations and gone. Tracy would have been eighty-eight years old September 13, 1976, and apparently was ready to go. The night of the funeral, I called Aunt Mary Lou, who was at home with Ann and George Felton, Tracy's cousins from Macon, and her closest surviving blood relatives. I was told the funeral service had been well attended for Tracy had many friends from several generations and was very popular in various quarters. As James M. Hull, Sr. once commented apropos of Tracy in her hey-day: "She had the cutest mouth in the world; every time it opens something wonderful comes out!"

So with the passing of Tracy Duncan Cohen, we reach the beginning of the final end to an interesting era: Mary Lou Phinizy, being one of the few then remaining. Tracy spent the bulk of her life as an Augustan, having moved here to live in early 1910 as a young wife. Both

CHAPTER SIX

Rod, Sr. and Tracy were contributing human beings and always added much to the civic and social life of the community. Tracy was an individual way ahead of her time; her quickness of mind, unfailing commitment, and keen insight allowed her to truly make life a real partner in her daily endeavors. The initial restoration and preservation of the Old Medical College is without a doubt a magnificent memorial, testament, and tribute to Tracy and continues to be (we hope forever) a site of immense public pride. I trust that the reader will enjoy not only this glimpse of another time but also hope this piece will serve to enhance and perpetuate for future generations the facts relative to one of the early owners of 2150 Battle Row and its gardens now being restored as they were in "the Cohen days." Miss Tracy and Mr. Rod would be delighted with the present charming owners of their Sandy Acres who are interested in preservation and now devoting copious and plentiful time and effort to bringing all up to speed.

IS LIVING WELL STILL THE BEST REVENGE?

Rod Cohen (L) and Tracy with her new baby Rodney, Jr. (R)

CHAPTER SIX

Tracy with her favorite flower (L) and The three Tracys pictured in the Battle Row House (R)

CHAPTER VII

**Frank and Bowdre:
The Way They Were**

They said it would never last when their engagement to marry was announced in the early summer of 1924. The announcement was June 28, 1924, and their wedding date was set for September 3, being still late summer in the Deep South. Both Augusta papers and the two important Atlanta newspapers carried flowery announcements with detailed descriptions of the young pair's forebears and antecedents. Well, it did last until Bowdre's death September 13, 1975, some fifty-one years and six children later! All Augusta seemed somewhat skeptical because, they said, "both had too much already" for a firm foundation to a marriage; there is some truth in this for both had looks, breeding in that they were members of prominent Southern families, charm, personality, popularity, and were even considered to be very wealthy. This, then, is their story.

Frank Clark Inman was a posthumous twin born November 27, 1904, her father having died suddenly August 28, 1904, as a direct result of a congestive chill caused by a sudden drenching rain while motoring to Augusta from his summer home at Golden Camp, eight miles from the city. Her twin brother, John Walter Inman, Jr., lived only until December 27, 1904. Her father came from Atlanta to set up a cotton business in Augusta, where he met and married a young local belle, Frank Crowell Clark, whose mother was the sister of the leading local doctor, William H. Doughty, Sr. Frank was the third Inman daughter, with older sisters Cordelia Dick Inman and Ruth Doughty Inman (named after their paternal and maternal grandmothers). She had one older brother, Walker Patterson Inman, born in 1900 and named for his grandfather who lived in Atlanta.

Her mother remarried in 1907 to her first cousin, Llewellyn Goode Doughty, who was a widower with one daughter, Jean Doughty. The Llewellyn Doughtys then had two children, a little boy who died unnamed and a pretty little girl, Mary De l'aigle, who lived only sixteen months. She was named for Mary Clark De l'aigle, the aunt of Frankie Doughty. "L. G.," as Frank called him, also was a cotton factor and apparently

CHAPTER SEVEN

very well-to-do. They all lived in a large house at 1012 Greene Street, now destroyed but later used by the Knights of Columbus during my youth, as I remember seeing it often. The house was yellow brick or stucco with white columns.

The Inman family formerly had lived at 443 or 445 Broad Street, as news articles mention both numbers. Frank was christened at St. Paul's church April 14, 1905, with Mr. and Mrs. James R. Gray of Atlanta as sponsors. Mrs. Gray was Frank's Aunt Mary (May) Inman.

Grandfather Walker Patterson Inman in Atlanta died in 1907 and left $150,000 (equivalent now to approximately $1.5 million to $2.25 million) to his Augusta grandchildren in trust, with the trust to be terminated in part at different ages, say twenty-one and twenty-five. By the time of Frank's marriage in 1924, her own share of the principal had grown to $150,000 or up to even $300,000, as per Pat Walsh. Keep in mind also that due to the premature death of her two Inman sisters, Cordelia and Ruth, she had inherited one-half of their matured capital, with the other half going to her brother, Walker. In any case, she had been considered one of the richest girls in Augusta, always having first a pony (General Mutt) and cart and then later a car (Teto Barrett recalled a blue Kissel), the first colored shoes (other than black, brown, or white) in Augusta, and clothes acquired in New York and Paris during her 1922 European trip with her mother and the Billy Whites, including Cornelia White and Elizabeth Burdell in the same party.

After a short time at Tubman High School in Augusta, Frank was sent to Briarcliff Manor College in New York and later to Oaksmere on Long Island, both being finishing schools. Although she always said she begged to go instead to Virginia to school with many of her friends from home, her mother insisted on Briarcliff, where her elder sister, Ruth Inman, had excelled before her terrible death at age eighteen in an automobile accident in 1920 near Augusta.

In her teen years, Frank was spoiled by her mother who, over the years, had lost six children to too-early deaths. Nevertheless, Frank was extremely popular and gregarious, having numerous suitors from Augusta, Atlanta, etc. One of her early teen beaux was Walter Fargo, and then Howard "Bully" Fortson was crazy about her, according to Sam, his brother. Chubby Grant was one suitor from Atlanta. About the time she was dating Bully, she began to know Bowdre Mays from some of the weekly dances at the Augusta Country Club. Bowdre had known her sister, Ruth, who was closer in age, and while he had spent much of his youth away at school in Virginia, he still came to Augusta for vacations and when school closed down. He began to write her and so began their courtship, even though he had been spending a lot of time previously with Martha Stelling, who he always said was the best dancer in Augusta. For every date, he sent Frank a corsage of Parma violets centered with red roses.

Bowdre, named Bowdre Phinizy Mays for his uncle Bowdre Phinizy, essentially was an orphan, with his

CHAPTER SEVEN

mother, Harriet Phinizy Mays, having separated from his father, Samuel Warren Mays, Jr., shortly after his birth August 22, 1901, at 519 Greene Street. He never really knew his father well; he died in June 1906 and his mother in 1910. He was christened at St. Paul's Church April 11, 1912, with his uncle Bowdre Phinizy as sponsor/godfather. So Bowdre was mainly raised by his grandmother Mary Lou Yancey Phinizy and always called her "Mother," copying his own mother (Hattie), her sister (Mary Lou), and brother (Bowdre), who also lived at 519 Greene. The fourth floor of 519 Greene had been turned into living quarters for Hattie and her children, Mary Louise and Bowdre, once she returned from Thomasville, where they had been living, and separated from Sam.

Shortly after his mother's death, Bowdre was sent at age nine to Warrenton, Virginia, to the Stuyvesant School, sometimes also known as the King School, for the King family owned it. Mr. and Mrs. King were worthy mentors and very fond of Bowdre, whom they treated as a member of their family; he even spent some vacation periods with the Kings when his grandmother and aunt might be away in Europe or on other trips.

After excelling at Stuyvesant School, where he won several silver cups for "General Excellence" in 1914 and the prestigious "Stuyvesant Cup" in 1916, there was a short period in Athens at the University of Georgia, where he seemed to have played and enjoyed a wild life with his fraternity brothers of SAE; Richard Russell, one of his classmates, later became a prominent United

States senator from Georgia. Although the details are a bit murky, Bowdre and Tracy Mathewson were later jailed in Savannah, as it seems Bowdre had signed his grandmother's name to a check (or checks), and Judge Peter Meldrim had called Uncle Bowdre Phinizy asking "what to do with them." The reply was jail for a few days until Uncle Bowdre could travel to Savannah. When he arrived, Uncle Bowdre told his nephew he had one choice: take $500 and get lost (or some say $5,000, but even $500 at that time was worth fifteen or twenty times more in purchasing power) or go at once to V.M.I. in Lexington, Virginia, for four years. Bowdre fortunately chose V.M.I., although the story is that Tracy told him to take the cash! It was September of 1919. He graduated in 1923 from V.M.I. Bowdre appears to have been a veritable "Big Man on Campus," as, according to the V.M.I. yearbook, the 1923 *Bomb*, he left V.M.I. with honors and activities as follows:

- Cadet, 1st Lieutenant and Adjutant Battalion Staff;
- Business Manager, Dramatic Club;
- President, Cotillion Club.
- Cadet, Orchestra, where he played traps;
- President, Georgia Club;
- Leader, Final German Ball;
- American Political Science Association member;
- ???? Member;
- H-1 Quartet Leader.

He was obviously considered very popular with the ladies and had developed into a handsome man, looking much

CHAPTER SEVEN

in the style of F. Scott Fitzgerald and that early twenties generation. Two of the girls he invited to V.M.I. for school affairs, called "hops," were Margaret McGowan and Martha Stelling, both from Augusta. Both had photographs in the 1923 *Bomb*, as they were sponsors for the first Thanksgiving and Christmas hops respectively. Following graduation from V.M.I., Bowdre was offered a teaching job at Stuyvesant School in Warrenton, Virginia, by the King family, and he seemingly began there the autumn of 1923.

That same year, he began to pay attention to Frank, and by 1924 began to "rush her," as the lingo of that era would say. One evening about that time at 519 Greene, he was pulling his grandmother up to the third floor in the hand-operated elevator when she said she had learned he was "rushing" Frankie Doughty's daughter and wondered if he wanted to give her a ring. They arranged to go to Schweigert's to pick one out, and by spring 1924, the two were engaged formally with a diamond ring. Frank was not yet twenty and Bowdre not yet twenty-three.

They both were considered then as two of the most attractive and sought-after persons in Augusta. She was vivacious, popular, pretty, athletic, and very stylish with her New York and Paris clothes, and he was handsome, charming, and outgoing, well-liked by all. One defect not really noticeable was a glass eye, for the original was lost as a little boy when he threw a firecracker; it did not immediately explode, but when he went to investigate, the cracker suddenly fired off into his eye as he leaned over. Frank was born with a birthmark but of a most fortunate kind: a white natural streak in her dark hair, something I am told was very sought after in that epoch.

The Doughty/Inman ménage had built a new house at 2321 Kings Way circa 1916-1917; I do not believe this was a direct result of the great Augusta fire of 1916, as their Greene Street block was not affected. It is believed that Wendell was the architect, for the style appears to be his, as per Starkey Flythe. So Frank spent her early preteen and teen years on The Hill, while Bowdre, when in town, still resided at 519 Greene. Frankie Doughty was directing the "spring cleaning" (winter rugs would be rolled up and stored for the summer, hot weather slipcovers fitted on large upholstered furniture pieces, and summer grass rugs laid down) when Bowdre's Aunt Mary Lou arrived for a visit with Frank's mother. As they could not conveniently sit in the living room, they sat on the lower steps of the front hall staircase leading upstairs. Unknown to them, Frank was listening unseen at the top of the stairs on the second floor.

Aunt Mary Lou said that Uncle Bowdre would have come if Frank had a father, but as that was not the case, she had come—Frank's stepfather and cousin, Llewellyn Doughty, had died in 1921. Apparently the decision to visit was made by Mary Lou Phinizy and Bowdre Phinizy without the knowledge of their mother and Bowdre's grandmother, Mary Lou Yancey Phinizy, who had reared him following his mother's death in 1910 when he was only nine. "Auntie," as Bowdre called her, said that while they were very pleased at the engagement, they

CHAPTER SEVEN

wanted Frank's family to know that Bowdre had no assets or income of his own and had just begun to teach in Virginia. He would be only twenty-three if the marriage took place as planned in September.

Frankie Doughty said the couple seemed determined to marry and that Frank did have her trust fund, which would be under her full control at age twenty-five. Frank heard all this and at once wrote Bowdre in Warrenton, who in turn blasted home that his Auntie and Uncle Bowdre should stay out of his nuptial plans. I surmise that is what Mary Lou Yancey Phinizy, who he still called Mother, also believed as she thought the engagement rather perfect in all respects and probably had given up in that regard relative to her own daughter and son, Mary Lou and Bowdre Phinizy!

One of the Atlanta papers wrote a charming piece about Frank and Bowdre after their engagement was announced in June 1924. I am quoting this in its entirety, as it does seem to encapsulate the bright future this betrothed couple would have: "Just think of the two most attractive people in the world, I believe, getting together on things matrimonial." She held in her hand the wedding invitation of Frankie Clark Inman of Augusta, daughter and granddaughter, niece and great niece and several different kinds of cousin to some of Atlanta's most distinguished families of society and civic advancement, and continued: "Ever since Frankie Inman was a little bit of a girl, she has been captivating people, old and young, by her prettiness of face, figure and manner. And, in this last, don't you think she greatly resembles her mother, one of the most fascinating women I have met, ever? By the way, didn't you say that her mother was that belle, Frankie Clark, before she married Walter Inman of Atlanta?"

"Well, in my own memory, Frankie Clark's daughter has revived the memory of her mother's social reign. And I have had good opportunity to watch her visiting here as the guest of her Inman relatives or her schoolgirl friend, Ada Peebles. Then, in the brief number of summers of her young lady hood at famous resorts, she has been one of the accounted belles. 'And now she is to marry Bowdre Phinizy Mays.' Is there a girl habitué of Georgia Commencements who does not recall the handsome bridegroom, an S.A.E.? Later Bowdre went to V.M.I., where also he was among the most popular of young cadets, maybe he was an officer. One's memory gets so hazy about things. Nice, isn't it, that Bowdre, with such a reputation for attractive personality selects anything but a foil in these for a life partner?"

The wedding at 9:00 p.m. on September 3, 1924, was described in the Atlanta and Augusta papers as a brilliant affair at St. Paul's Church, followed by a large reception at Augusta Country Club, where the bridal party of twenty-five was seated for supper followed by dancing. The news reports state that the "entire" club was transformed into a bower of green interspersed with cut flowers and shaded electric lights. Over the bridal table was suspended a huge bride's shower bouquet of white roses from which ribbons fell to the table, etc.

CHAPTER SEVEN

Included in the bridal party were four girlfriends Frank had met while away at finishing school and also four out-of-town friends of Bowdre, who actually had few close Augusta friends due to his many years spent in Virginia. The maids from Augusta were Louise Ferguson, Julia Fargo, Anna Eve, Dorothy Merry, Grace Stafford, and Isabel Cozart as matron of honor; the maid of honor was Edith Rambo (called "Happy") from Knoxville, and other out-of-town bridesmaids: Suzanne Hanckel of Charlottesville, Eleanor Atkins from St. Louis, and Bernice Baker of New York. Groomsmen were John Mason of Rocky Mount, Cobb Torrance from Atlanta, Charles Farwell of New Orleans, Emmett Casey of Lynchburg, and Stewart Walker, William Cozart, Purvis Boatwright, Henry Carrere, Jr., John Jackson, and Henry Robertson, all from Augusta. The little Bussey nieces, twin girls Donald and Harriet, plus smaller sister Mary Lou, were all flower girls, and their father, Donald N. Bussey, at the last minute substituted for best man Buxton Ridgeley (from Baltimore) who became ill and could not come. Teto Barrett once told me that "Frank had some wild girls down for her wedding!" One of her close friends, Anne Campbell, was away then from Augusta visiting John Walton in China. Frank's brother, Walker P. Inman, gave her away.

Mother once said that the wedding cost $10,000 (about $100,000 in today's money), but I doubt that figure, for such seems too much considering the purchasing power of the currency then; probably more like $5,000 (today $50,000), which in 1924 was a very important sum indeed. The wedding bouquets for the bride and bridesmaids were made and sent by the florist formerly housed in the brick building just across from the entrance to Magnolia Cemetery. This was always the shop frequented by Bowdre and his family. Frankie Doughty was not satisfied with the end result, so late in the day of the wedding she had her Walton Way florist make a new bride's bouquet, paying $25.00 herself for the rush job. The pictures of the wedding party appear to confirm the analysis from the mother of the bride.

The book kept to record wedding gifts listed 353 items, including two silver services, a complete chest of flat silver for twelve and included every possible piece then known, plus serving pieces, numerous silver goblets and ice teas, two silver pitchers, silver ice creams and sherbets, silver butter plates, numerous pieces of individual flat silver items, silver dishes and bowls, plus many china and glass items. Some presents were not listed at all, for such were held for their honeymoon visit to New York. One story is that Frank asked several of her bridal attendants to write thanks-you notes; this backfired when relatives were addressed in Atlanta and Augusta as "Mr. and Mrs." Instead of "Aunt, Uncle, or Cousin." Many of her Inman relatives from Atlanta had attended.

They were driven to the Phinizy country house at Grovetown at a late hour by Son, the family chauffeur, accompanied by his sister, Lena, to cook breakfast before they departed by train for New York on their honeymoon the next day. Grandmother Phinizy had

CHAPTER SEVEN

decorated the marriage bed with pink bows, and we can assume, I dare say, there were welcoming flowers in all the main rooms. I believe there was an impromptu farewell party at the Bussey house at 409 Seventh Street before train time so that the newly married couple saw the entire bridal party again the next day. The night of the wedding, Grandmother Phinizy had slipped $1,500 in an envelope into Bowdre's pocket to pay for the honeymoon and, I assume, to launch "the newlyweds." He told me once he had not known how he was going to pay until that happened.

Honeymooning in New York and also visiting Atlantic City, which was more attractive in those days, Frank probably was "showing" Bowdre around, for I doubt he had ever been further north than Washington/Baltimore. Frank, of course, who had gone to finishing school nearby, had charge accounts at Best & Co., I. Miller for shoes, and likely other stores, knew people residing in New York City, and also had relatives there, i.e. Louise De l'aigle Reese and her nephews De l'aigle and Theus Munds. Uncle Bowdre Phinizy had arranged their reservations at the old Vanderbilt Hotel, 34th Street, and the first morning Frank locked the door to the bathroom and could not open it from inside for some reason; the engineer finally had to come and take the door off its hinges so the bride could leave! Bowdre said he was not intending to enter while she was inside, and suggested she not lock the door in the future!

While in the metropolis, it is likely they met Frank H. Barrett and the Munds Brothers, who had a seat on the New York Stock Exchange known as "Munds and Winslow." Although much older than they, the newly married were very fond of "Miss Sadie and Mr. Frank," as they called the Barretts, who owned the house and the first swimming pool in Augusta at the corner of Milledge and Cumming Roads. Frank Barrett called Frank "Frisky," and that name always was used by his son, Billy Barrett. It is probable that during this trip Bowdre was offered a job as a broker/customer's man at Munds and Winslow. I do not know when he accepted the offer, for he was due back in Virginia at the Stuyvesant School in Warrenton to teach the fall term, and return to Warrenton they did to a rented house which Frankie Doughty had visited during the honeymoon with her driver and a seamstress to sew and prepare curtains, etc., to make all quite pleasant and livable.

Frank also had a new Cadillac, which she drove daily to collect Bowdre each afternoon from school, blowing the car horn loudly when he didn't appear quickly! I doubt Frank was content in Warrenton, for by Christmas 1924 and early 1925, they were back in Augusta, where Grandmother Phinizy gave a large reception for the bride and her new granddaughter-in-law on the afternoon of Friday, January 9, 1925, at 519 Greene Street. Thereafter, it is not now clear when they went to New York City where Bowdre was to be connected with Munds and Winslow: either the spring of 1925 or the autumn, it is surmised. Probably the latter, as their first child, Ruth Inman Mays, was born July 23, 1925, dying the next day, having lived only thirty-six hours. She was

CHAPTER SEVEN

buried in the left-hand back corner of the Inman-L. G. Doughty plot at Magnolia Cemetery on July 25, with the Rector of St. Paul's Church officiating. There is no marker.

Grandmother Phinizy paid the rental on their first home in Augusta at 2330 Kings Way, which was occupied later by the Irvine Phinizy family and is almost directly across the street from Frank's premarital home at 2321 Kings Way. Grandmother Phinizy said "not to tell daughter," i.e. Aunt Mary Lou or "Auntie" to Bowdre!!

In New York City, they rented a small one-bedroom apartment in a building on Lexington Avenue located on the block directly across from the rear entrance of the present Waldorf-Astoria Hotel, which was built in the early 1930s. Their building later had become the Shelton Hotel by the time I first went to New York City in 1948. The apartment rent of around $250-$300 monthly was more than Bowdre's salary, and he also did not like the wild "Wall Street life" led by many of his colleagues, being himself a recently married man. Julia Fargo did visit them once, sleeping on the sofa in the living room during her stay. Money seemingly was no problem, for when Frank asked for cash and maybe Bowdre hesitated a bit, her rejoinder always was, "I'll pay you back!" What the time in Wall Street did teach Bowdre was something about the inner workings of the stock market; it was the era of wild speculation on all sides, and as it turned out by the early 1930s following the 1929 crash, his philosophy had become "Buy blue chips and leave them alone." But that lesson was learned too late, as we shall see!

By late 1925, the couple again was back in Augusta, for they attended the Richardson family's fancy dress ball at the Bon Air-Vanderbilt Hotel on New Year's Eve. This is confirmed by a picture appearing in the *Augusta Chronicle* on Sunday, January 3, 1926. Frank and Mary "D" Phinizy attended dressed as Coty powder puffs (as this was in accord with the party "advertisement theme") while Charlie Phinizy, Jr. and Bowdre were attired as regular sailors in white. There is in existence a wonderful photograph taken of the two couples together clothed like twins.

Around that time, they bought a Willis Irvin House at 2817 Hillcrest Avenue, which then was about the limit of the West Augusta residential area. This was a small Tudor-style house (apparently Tudor being the rage in the twenties) to which circa 1928 they had Willis Irvin add a sleeping porch on the second floor and a den with fireplace directly underneath on the first floor. It was said they paid $10,000 for the house from where their next two children, Bowdre, Jr. (1927) and Frank Inman (1928), were born.

They were now in the latter half of the twenties decade, a "party couple," for the most part, and leaders of their "crowd," which included Anne Campbell and Lombard Fortson, P. J. Boatwrights, William Cozarts, Henry "Legs" Gardner, Charlie Phinizy, Jrs., Mike Mells, Stewart Walker, George Wrights, Alfred Martins, Henry Carrere, and, later into the 1930s, others

CHAPTER SEVEN

including Martin Cozart, Clayton Boardmans, John Walton, Joe Mathewson, etc. Frank's close lady friends also included Julia Fargo, Henrietta Alexander, Anna Eve Fleming (known as "Willie"), "Dimp" Stafford Roberts, and Anna Pride Wilkins. All these names are mentioned just to indicate a small sampling. Amaryllis Pride Phinizy, the second wife of Charlie Phinizy, Jr. who admittedly was known as the president of the Mayses Fan Club (aptly named by Jim Hull, Jr.), said that all of the activities of the "crowd" always revolved around Frank and Bowdre.

One notable party they gave was a large fancy-dress dance at the Augusta Country Club around Christmas 1928, and there were many house parties during the summer at Wrightsville Beach, North Carolina, where a cottage was rented for several months each year on the beach. Almost every night, the house party walked or took the streetcar from the cottage (cars were not permitted on the beach road in those days) to Lumina Pavilion for dancing to one of the big bands. A silver pitcher was taken to the Augusta Country Club one night filled probably with corn whiskey and never seen again! For most of this period, however, Frank only drank champagne, usually the New York State dry variety.

Frank was one of the original Junior Workers (predecessor to Augusta's Junior League), and with Mary "D" Phinizy once ran a tearoom called "Minneyata" during the winter season for the winter visitors largely from the North. This was located on the hillside overlooking Lake Aumond on property belonging to either the Forest Ricker Hotel or William E. Bush, who was then developing the present Forest Hills area. The tea house burned down one night, taking with it silver and china used in the business (afternoon tea only at $3.00 a head for tea, sandwiches, and cake), but they did collect $500 in insurance money, which they promptly used to throw a party and not to replace their lost silver, china, and small furniture pieces! The date must have been circa 1930 to 1931, for I recall driving out to see the scene of the fire. Bridge with the ladies and at times poker at night with men included was also an important activity at the early stage, for house servants were numerous.

Bowdre pursued several business activities following their return from Virginia and New York. The initial venture, we surmise, was a 1926 business with a young engineer named Sig Cox, who had worked with the J. B. White department store in their appliance section. Air conditioning then was in its infancy, so they started offering air conditioning (mainly for fresh meat market cases) and sold refrigerators, also known as Frigidaires. Sig Cox, Inc., is still thriving today as an air conditioning contractor.

Another business with enormous potential was a Buick dealership called Georgia Motor Sales, Inc., a partnership formed with Walker P. Inman, Charles H. Phinizy, Jr., and Donald N. Bussey around late 1927. Frank apparently supplied whatever capital investment Bowdre required in these ventures, as by 1929 the trust set up by her Grandfather Inman finally terminated

CHAPTER SEVEN

wholly with a portion of the capital disbursed as early as 1925 when she was twenty-one.

There also was a chicken-raising venture and a passive $5,000 investment in a local food-processing business (name unknown), with the latter declaring bankruptcy as per Frank's late-life recollections. Her mature inference is that Bowdre had a healthy respect for work at that stage; while there is probably some truth in her assertion, the other side is that both were very young with little experience or sense of responsibility and at the same time were focusing on having what they all called a "good time!" Uncle Bowdre, "Master of the *Augusta Herald*," the local afternoon daily newspaper, called his nephew often for golf and other rendezvous, but Bowdre seems to have avoided him. With his education and mental ability, he no doubt could have succeeded his uncle (who died much too early on February 8, 1931) had he asked for a position and showed the appropriate aptitude during his namesake's lifetime. Bowdre certainly had a literary bent and could have easily dominated the "Broad Street milieu."

Aunt Mary Lou said she and Uncle Bowdre were at the savings bank, then located on the lower side of 8th and Broad Street, in 1927 to sign some papers following their mother's death, and saw from a window their nephew on 8th Street going to Warren Bothwell's office when Uncle Bowdre mused, "I wonder if he will ever grow up!"

They led an extravagant lifestyle, bringing two nurses for their first two children when lunching at 519

Greene Street and ordering baby clothes from a shop in Richmond, Virginia, that even Cornelia Barrett said she could not afford! Frank had her brother, Walker Inman, drive her almost new Cadillac to sell in Florida around 1925 (probably when they went to New York), but there was a serious accident with no insurance, so a $4,000 asset was lost. Willie Washington (Grandmother Doughty's chauffeur, butler, and handyman) said he often found unopened dress boxes and other boxes as well in the car when he was washing it, as Frank always demanded a clean motor; and Frank was very generous with her friends who were needy by often slipping gifts of money into their handbags. Frank always engaged a "drawing room" on trains to New York or elsewhere and insisted on a private room, her own linen and pillows, and trained nurses during all hospital stays! The latter around the clock, of course! A trained nurse always accompanied her home with the baby for a week or more. Perhaps at the end, she had settled for just a practical nurse to come home with the new baby.

Frank and Bowdre were in New York around 1928 when the Walker Inmans also were there, I believe, on their honeymoon. Bowdre and Walker had purchased matching derby hats from Brooks, and one night, returning from somewhere in a taxi, Frank pitched both derbies into the street for fun as they sped on to their destination, laughing uproariously in the cab. Why, Alice Inman who told me this story, never knew! Sounds a bit like shades of the Scott Fitzgeralds to me! Circa late 1920s or early 1930s there was a loud party at 409 7th

CHAPTER SEVEN

Street, the Bussey house—music and probably dancing until a very late hour—when some neighbor called the police who arrived promptly. Mary Lou Bussey said Mary D. Phinizy finally told the policeman, following some conversation and continuing noise, music, and general merriment, "You can't arrest a Phinizy!" To this the cop without a blink replied, "I'm about to arrest a bunch of them!"

Suffice it to say, they lived way beyond their immediate income, spending about $25,000 a year when their receipts were say $10,000-$12,000, both rather sizable amounts in the late 1920s and early 1930s. Many still accuse Bowdre of spending Frank's money; the more accurate truth is that they both spent it lavishly! However, the records show Bowdre began to sign promissory notes to Georgia Railroad Bank as early as November 1927 ($20,000), then $5,000 on July 1, 1929, and a note to Mary Lou Phinizy for $10,000 in March 1930. There was about a $70,000 stock market loss in late 1929-1930, so that by late 1930 and early 1931, the position was rather bleak indeed with the full descent of the Great Depression, which was rather worldwide in scope. It is likely Bowdre had resorted to speculative practices in his stock trading (probably buying on margin) so that when the final crash came, he did not make a killing as a few did by having sold "short" sometime prior.

They felt themselves ruined. They had to give up 2817 Hillcrest Avenue, and they began to sell some assets (for example, Frank sold her diamond pin to Mrs. Harry Albright. From pictures, this contained some large diamonds, and when she tried to buy it back in the 1940s, Mrs. Albright refused). When their fourth child, Walter Inman Mays, was born July 6, 1931, Bowdre visited University Hospital and took Frank's diamond engagement ring to sell. Some important silver items also were sold, many of which she recovered from Henry "Legs" Gardner in later years. One embarrassing incident occurred when Ruben's Store on Broad Street had in their front window for sale Frank's handsome sterling silver dresser set engraved with initials "F.I.M." She had them buff off the hand-engraved initials at once when told of this!

In 1934, Bowdre sold the house inherited from his Grandmother Phinizy at what is now 415 Seventh Street and known today as the Joseph Rucker Lamar Boyhood Home. Formerly the address was listed as 530 Seventh Street and had been the residence of his grandparents when they first came to live in Augusta from Athens, circa 1875, for the house was purchased in that year for $10,000. The house had been rental property for many years, and the address in 1875 was known as 51 McIntosh Street.

By the time their fifth child, Stedman Clark Mays—always known as Ted—arrived June 14, 1932, the family had moved to a rented house at 2817 Lombardy Court, with the rent presumably paid by Grandmother Doughty. She also bought Frank a previously owned (as the dealers now specify) four-door A Model Ford for her personal use. Bowdre now rose to the occasion and, having met Abe Fogel on Broad Street while arranging

CHAPTER SEVEN

to store some furniture following their departure from Hillcrest Avenue, decided upon a joint venture: a store on Broad Street dealing in both new and used furniture. As capital was required to obtain inventory and premises, etc., Grandmother Doughty again came to the rescue, loaning Bowdre $8,900 as a five-year loan dated May 30, 1932, at 8 percent per annum. She sold profitable stock she held in Maxwell Brothers Furniture Company to be able to make the loan. Fogel also made his capital investment, and the firm was incorporated as The Furniture Market, Inc.

The business proved to be quite successful, so that by the early 1940s, Bowdre was taking $1,000 or more per month from the business just to support his family, whose number had increased to seven with the birth of the last child February 8, 1937. This was Sam Warren Mays, who was named for his paternal grandfather and born almost exactly ten years after the eldest living child and present writer. Bowdre also had to pay off his promissory notes, which were returned fully paid by the Georgia Railroad Bank in February 1943, and the loans from Frankie Doughty and Mary Lou Phinizy. A legacy of $25,000 from Uncle Bowdre Phinizy finally was paid around 1944 in accordance with his will.

By 1933 to 1934, the Mays family had moved to Lake Forest Drive, now listed as 2914, to live with Grandmother Doughty. In preparation for this, a sleeping porch with windows all around had been added to the second floor, and later another small bedroom was built on the left side of the upstairs for myself. Two bathrooms only in the house, but there was a sink and fireplace in one of the upstairs bedrooms. Grandmother Doughty really kept us from being declassed during the early difficult period, as she was totally unselfish, even spending her capital to see that her daughter and Mays grandchildren never lacked new clothing or summer vacations, etc. In 1934, and probably 1933 too, there was Sullivan's Island, and in 1935, she rented John Walton's cottage on Edisto Beach, so that we could vacation several months while she was away in the Orient on a Garden Club of America trip. She liked Edisto Beach so much that in 1935-1936, she bought a cottage rather newly built called Silencia, which became then the Mays summer home from about June 1 until after Labor Day in September. Unfortunately, Silencia was totally destroyed in a 1940 hurricane, which devastated that section of the coast in South Carolina.

Frank had inherited the Edisto property after her mother died in February 1939, so with the insurance proceeds and additional funds from Bowdre, another larger cottage was acquired further up the beach on a huge lot fronting the Atlantic. Such was not only larger but more comfortable than the first Silencia, for the identical name was employed. Here the Mays continued to summer until about 1959 or 1960, for twenty-five years in total. On occasion, Frank would rent the cottage for part of July and August. She disliked that month at the shore but loved May, June, half of July, and early September.

CHAPTER SEVEN

As Bowdre's business prospered in the 1940s and 1950s, they bought the lot next door to the right side of the house on Lake Forest Drive and redid the entire house, adding a fireplace to the downstairs bedroom and updating other aspects. Bowdre also replaced her engagement ring in the 1940s with a handsome new platinum creation set in the Tiffany style with two large old-mine diamonds of over two carats each on both sides of a large sapphire he purchased from Billy Burdell of Schweigert's who made up the ring. The diamonds were derived from an earring of his grandmother and were generously given by Auntie (Mary Lou Phinizy). Frank also picked out at Cullum's a mink or sable fur piece for Bowdre to give her one Christmas to wear over the favorite gabardine suits and matching "beanie hats" she ordered again from Best & Company in New York City. During this period, Frank and Bowdre took trips to Pompano Beach, Florida, and the Isle of Palms with Glenn and Clayton Boardman, visited Jacksonville to see Henry Carrere and his wife Olive, and spent several weekends in Spartanburg with "Ferg and Boat" Boatwright. There was also at least one trip together to New York City. To summarize, it is clear that following a shaky and unsteady start, Bowdre did succeed in his business as a merchant; he had much help at the beginning, but then he did turn all around by paying all his debts, educating five children through university, and again becoming more active in the social life of the city and country club and serving on the Board of the Augusta Library. As Clayton (Tater) Boardman once told him, "Each of your children is worth a million dollars!"

He also was Grand Exalted Ruler of the local Elks (B.P.O.E.), then housed at 519 Greene Street, his old home. He found this position useful for business purposes, and because this permitted him to make new friends, such as his older cousin William T. Gary, Jr., Dr. Henry Michel, Warren Walker, Wesley Killebrew (city attorney in that era), and many others. The Elks Club dining room in the 1940s and 1950s also served good food in what had been the Phinizy house ballroom. Their fresh lump crabmeat au gratin was a house signature dish. Frank and Bowdre both now took a new interest in food; chili parties were a favorite, then "goulash," a pork, veal, and tomato vermicelli concoction learned from the Telfair Street Alexanders who always had a well-laurelled kitchen. Frank's goulash became a tremendous favorite we still enjoy. Her granddaughter Carol Hull Palmer even printed her recipe in the latest Junior League cookbook. They also liked foods like wild duck, quail and doves, grilled sweetbreads with bacon, globe artichokes, and broccoli and small yellow squash with her famous hollandaise sauce. Leg of lamb was a favorite with plenty of Tabasco on everything, such as scrambled eggs, grits, soups, etc. Tomato aspic also was spiced up with Tabasco and served often with fried chicken. Codfish cakes and grilled tomatoes for breakfast or supper with eggs and grits was a staple.

The fact is that one way or another, the good life truly had continued even in the darkest days of the 1930s.

CHAPTER SEVEN

There were always servants—a cook, nursemaid, and yardman/butler—no matter the reduction of income. Grandmother Doughty was the original "safety net" until Bowdre's business really achieved success by the late 1930s. A typical Frank buffet table for cocktails prolongé might include a whole Smithfield ham, whole roast turkey, beaten biscuits, tomato aspic with avocado and fresh asparagus, plus Charlotte Russe or instead of the turkey, fried chicken cooked at home with Frank's goulash noted before to provide something hot. At Edisto Beach, Frank employed a local woman, Earnestine, to cook each summer; crabbing and shrimping in the local island creeks was a daily occupation, with all the household and guests invited to participate. Earnestine and Willie Washington boiled the crabs and shrimp and picked all to make deviled crab, succotash and gumbo soup, crab au gratin, and shrimp prepared for cocktails, salads, or sautéed with grits. Wagons stopped behind the house early every morning selling fresh fish (flounder, black fish, or croaker usually) and fresh island produce such as corn, okra, butter beans, tomatoes, and field peas. Thus Frank would order the usual hot Southern lunch, usually with rice (lunch then called dinner), with the seafood served at supper with a salad.

A very happy family event was the 1947 engagement of Frank and Bowdre's only daughter, Frank Inman, to James Meriwether Hull, Jr., her third cousin on the Phinizy side, since Jim's mother and Harriet Phinizy Mays were first cousins. Frank was only nineteen and Jim twenty-four, still in law school at the University of

Georgia. Aunt Mary Lou gave them an elegant black-tie supper engagement party in May attended by all members of the connected Mays, Hull, Garrett, Inman, Neely, and Phinizy clans. The Hulls were also related to the Walker Inmans on Alice Inman's side. This was interesting, for all these families had known one another all their respective lives. Close friends of the couple and prospective wedding party members were also present.

The wedding date was set for September 3, 1947, being the twenty-third wedding anniversary of Frank's parents. Big Frank insisted on the Good Shepherd, where her children had all attended Sunday school, while Cousin Marie pleaded for St. Paul's, where both families had been so long closely identified. Big Frank of course won, but in retrospect, I believe Cousin Marie was right. The size of St. Paul's would have also assisted as many guests were unable to find seats in the much smaller Good Shepherd. They did compromise in one sense: both Good Shepherd's and St. Paul's rectors presided at the wedding service in front of a large crowd, including many (and some joint) relatives on all sides from Athens, Atlanta, and South Carolina.

A reception immediately followed at 814 Milledge Road, where Mary Lou Phinizy had moved her bedroom for the duration to the second floor. The entire wedding party was seated for supper on the enclosed porch off the downstairs bedroom at a beautifully decorated table loaded with silver, crystal, candles, and flowers. Guests greeted the hosts, Frank and Bowdre, in the double living room, the majority of the furniture removed, with

CHAPTER SEVEN

the senior folks, bride and groom and wedding party standing nearby adjacent to the two huge wall mirrors brought from the ballroom at 519 Greene. There was a real receiving line, in the sense that you spoke to everyone, contrary to the current practice where at a large wedding one cannot even greet the bridal pair without much effort! Although many apparently assumed Auntie was defraying the reception costs, the truth is that Bowdre paid all the bills! The assumption annoyed him!

Then the guests departed the main house for the side and back gardens (by both front and rear stairs) that had been specially lit for the occasion with strings of lights. There was champagne punch poured and food tables installed in several locations dispensing chicken salad and other tasty morsels including Smithfield ham, roast turkey, beaten biscuits, aspics, etc.

At a late hour, the bridal couple departed for their honeymoon to Nassau, but not before big Bowdre pressed $100 into the bride's hand as a small special honeymoon gift to his beloved only daughter.

Frank was delighted with the arrival of their first grandchild in December 1948, Frank and Jim Hull's first child whom she wanted to name Mary De l'aigle. This was vetoed—I think principally by Jim who wanted to continue the Frank family appellation. As the little girl grew, and Jim III came along in 1951, Frank came to see them both at their 814½ Milledge Road home almost daily and often rode them out in her car for treats. She told them to call her "Granny," which they began to translate as "Dandy," and this was copied by all the future grandchildren. When the other grands came along, she was interested in them and would organize birthday parties with the backyard decorated with balloons and favors. However, she always said a mother tends to be closer to the progeny of a daughter. But she constantly had time for all of them when they came to visit and liked to tell them about her youth and the "old days."

Inman Mays, the second son, who has a fine way with words, sent me the following, which serves well to illustrate Bowdre's interests and innate personality and distinctive character:

> Words — BPM was always interested in the spoken and written word...he loved interesting, different expressions, especially from uneducated blacks and others he came into contact with. He was a voracious reader, reading two or more novels weekly plus all the weekly news magazines, etc. He had good taste in literature and enjoyed good writing from good authors (Faulkner, Hemingway, etc.). He told me he knew Hemingway was a winner when he first read his short stories in the 20's. He was a close friend of Berry Fleming for many years and they used to sit and discuss literature and writing, and Fleming evidently had high regard for his opinion, since he asked BPM what he thought of some of his unpublished stories. At one point in the 40's and 50's, Bowdre wrote a weekly classified ad in the

CHAPTER SEVEN

newspaper, "The Second Hand Man Says," which always included at least one slightly esoteric word, such as "conundrum" which was not only amusing but became the talk of Augusta!

People — BPM loved all kinds of people from all walks of life — blacks, uneducated rednecks, men, women, children and dogs. He liked to hear different language, thoughts and ideas from everybody, especially jokes, gossip, etc. Since he was well read, he could hold his own in discussing all kinds of topics, even with so-called intellectuals (Berry Fleming, John Walton, etc.). He was a kind, sensitive person who would never intentionally hurt anybody's feelings but did like to hear the latest news and gossip about one and all.

Personality — BPM had a wonderful sense of humor and a charming personality which appealed to men and women at all times and could charm one and all, no matter the subject or who he was conversing with. He liked young and old, and the feeling was returned. He liked some of his unusual and interesting friends (John Walton, Henry "Legs" Gardner, Jake Lowrey, etc.) as well as a wide spectrum of others, i.e. Clayton Boardman, Mike Mell, Moon Mullins, Joe and Tracy Mathewson, Billy Barrett, etc., and they were all fond of him. By the way, who was Count Giovanni Gregorini? [This query answered in the King Family Chapter Number VII]. BPM told me GG used to embarrass him when he came into

The Furniture Market, saying "Bowdre, Darling, I have a juicy morsel I must tell you"

Inman is he sweetest child we got Frank and Bowdre always said!

Bowdre was a natty dresser; 1920s pictures show him in plus fours or knickerbockers with a jacket and tie. He always owned a tuxedo and white tie/tails, for these clothes were more often worn in his era. As he moved into the 1930s and 1940s, a local tailor, Mr. Skoge, made him at least one three-piece suit a year (costing about $75.00), the Christmas gift of Auntie (Aunt Mary Lou), from the best English or Italian suiting materials. His shirts, ties, and perhaps other items came from the Terry/Juden Shop in New Orleans. Such were ordered from a Terry/Juden salesman who visited Augusta several times a year. The Terry/Juden style was in the manner of Brooks or J. Press. Across his vest and in a vest pocket, he wore a gold chain fastened to the fine gold pocket watch with his full name engraved on the back, a gift from Frank. The widow of Sam Mays, Sandra Hutchinson, now has this watch, while I possess a handsome pocket cigarette case in silver with gold stripes on the front, also a present from Frank. The case is initialed "B.P.M." In the late 1940s, he went back to New York City with P. J. Boatwright to the World Series. They went to Brooks on Madison Avenue and were fitted for sports coats; the tailor told Bowdre one arm was a trifle longer than the other, something he had never heard previously.

CHAPTER SEVEN

Into the 1950s and 1960s, some of the younger generation came into Bowdre's orbit: Stewart Phinizy Garrett, Billy Calhoun, Lowrey Stulb, and others of that ilk. Charlie Phinizy III always liked to talk about his late father and what those good friends had done in business and play over the years. Billy Calhoun told me on my return to Augusta what a good mind Bowdre had. And following his death in 1975, "Red" Boardman wrote that Bowdre always had time for him going back to around 1938 when Red was twelve. A favorite bon mot, or, perhaps better said, a happy expression from Bowdre was the following: "Don't expect too much and always be kind." This quote comes from his much-loved only daughter, Frank, and seems quite representative of his personal philosophy, life-long behavior, and attitude.

The last notable party they gave for a large crowd was cocktails and a buffet at the Old Government House on Telfair Street in the 1950s. That is the old Murphey house which had been restored by the Junior League and which they knew from the time of the Murphey occupants, who Frank said liked to entertain "young people." The Murpheys were known as Dr. Eugene and "Miss Willie." Dr. Eugene was not only a noted doctor of medicine but also a poet and bird lover. There will be more on the Murpheys in Chapter VIII. For a while during this period and beginning in the late 1940s, Frank and Bowdre would go on occasion to the regular Saturday night supper dances in the original country club building; here they also would encounter many of the younger generation and some of their own contemporaries. With the Clayton Boardmans, they would "ride out" often on a Saturday afternoon all over Augusta to see new and old sights, and especially new real estate developments opened in the 1950s in surrounding areas, such as West Augusta, for example. Sometimes they would pause to see relatives or friends at their homes. They always carried a well-stocked bar on the back seat: a small ice chest plus all the usual accouterments—all strictly verboten today. However, their "ride-outs" always took place in daylight, and they drove slowly! Once or twice, they went to Clark's Hill Lake to see or sit on someone's boat, and one at least annual stop was the Masters Golf Tournament, where they would take up a position on the eighteenth hole near the clubhouse and "picnic"! This was quite easy in those days of small crowds and when tickets readily were available.

His last years were marred by ill health (Dr. Louis Battey said he refused to take care of himself—i.e., he would not give up cigarettes or eat properly), the break with his original Furniture Market partner, Frank's horrendous fall at Hilton Head in 1974 (their fiftieth anniversary year), and the divorce of Frank and Jim Hull. However, he was very pleased when Frank married Cad J. Pride from Greenville in 1971 and moved there with Carol Hull, her youngest child. He also launched the Richmond Furniture Company on Broad Street, but I do not really believe his heart or spirit was focused on business by that time. Nevertheless, it did give him a way to occupy each weekday morning and managed to get him away from his house. He died September

CHAPTER SEVEN

13, 1975, much too young, having just celebrated his seventy-fourth birthday on August 21. The cause was acute heart failure complicated by an intestinal volvulus.

"Inman," as Bowdre often called Frank, lived on to the grand old age of over ninety, another twenty years after her husband. At first she seemed happy and continued to see some of her friends and go about, but then she suffered another fall in her kitchen and, after this second stumble which fortunately did not involve broken bones and traction as had occurred in 1974 at Hilton Head, she became much more reclusive, gave up her car, and ceased to play bridge or see many people at all no matter the occasion. She stopped smoking and "taking drinks" before supper, and even objected to anybody engaging in either custom in her home! What a change from the gregarious Frank of old! Or was it really? John Walton once told me she basically was a rather shy person, although such was not the world's view, as she gave all indications over the years of being a great "party girl" when in public. I think one should probably adopt a "middle view": she never liked organizations for ladies or meetings, she did like certain people and parties, but she was at heart a rather private person who was devoted to and loved Bowdre, the true love of her life, preceded only by Bully Fortson, one could opine. She was a good mother in most respects who wanted to do, and did, the correct thing always. Even Aunt Mary Lou, who never was a great fan, admitted this. Although Frank essentially was totally uneducated in a studious way, she was a very genuine person with loads of common sense, a popular person who had been madly generous with her friends, and one who never catered to anyone as some well-known local figures did. She usually said exactly what she thought but without hurting anyone's feelings knowingly. The key word in describing her indeed is Genuine with a capital "G."

Frank always loved dogs, and "Bing" (named after Bing Crosby), a wire-haired fox terrier, and "Mr. Mays," a cocker spaniel, were favorites. She read a lot in the 1940s, 1950s, and 1960s; one favorite author was Somerset Maugham, and her musical tastes extended to encompass light opera, such as "Butterfly" and all the Broadway musicals she'd enjoyed on her several trips to New York City.

It appears obvious that the loss of her fortune in the early 1930s had an important impact on her life and outlook thereafter until she died. But she finally did rise to the occasion and made a new life for herself and immediate family. Around 1959 to 1960, the Edisto Beach cottage and Lake Forest Drive house were sold, and Frank and Bowdre built a small house of old weathered brick at 704 Montrose Court. This was a new area developed on some acres following the teardown of an old home facing Cumming Road and with property running back to Gardner Street, which abuts the country club. She was delighted with this fresh new house and devoted much time to the rear garden and all her box and other plantings. One lacuna was the lack of any dining or breakfast room. Bowdre kept complaining about "nowhere to eat"; one rejoinder she gave

CHAPTER SEVEN

was, "Neither does Lib Boardman have a dining room"! Another mistake was the rather massive brick fireplace in the small den, and I believe she later agreed with this. Tracy Cohen wrote her a note she saved following drinks and supper in the new abode, saying "how smiling and shiny" it all was. Tracy and Frank had a great rapport at all times. Tracy's complete note read as follows:

> Such a lovely little party —
> The house so shining — the garden so smiling —
> You and Bowdre eat Bumble Bee for breakfast Easter morning and have a happy day.
> Love from Mr. Roddey and T.D.C.
> (Note: Bumble Bee must refer to some dish she sent over with the note for Tracy often gave funny names to special foods.)

Tracy and Frank often would compare rings, Tracy's with diamonds on each side of a beautiful pigeon's blood ruby and Frank's the same design but with a sapphire!

Looking back, it is difficult to understand how, following Bowdre's death, she wanted to lead a single solitary existence; in her youth she had been fun-loving and indeed very people oriented. She was a good athlete who played hockey at school in New York, golf later in Augusta, and finally championship badminton in the 1930s. She and Lib Boardman were considered one of the finest (if not the best) ladies doubles partners in Augusta. They won many matches and even local tournaments. She was well coordinated. The falls in 1974 at

Hilton Head and later at home seem to have been the main catalyst for her virtual retirement from all society. This was largely because she never fully recovered her walk, refusing to complete the intense rehabilitation needed. She simply lacked that discipline. Eventually her legs atrophied, so she became confined to a wheelchair or bed, although for some years she could walk with help or a cane from bed to a chair in her den to look out at her garden or watch TV soaps. She was still interested in food and ate her Southern "dinner" daily at 2:00 p.m. with appetite. Snacks, sometimes of "piece lean, piece fat" with toast and orange marmalade and at night dishes like turkey or chicken hash with grits or tinned red sockeye salmon (it had to be red sockeye) with copious lemon squeezed on top also taken with hot grits. She liked to have Eggs Benedict sent over from the country club. She grew to enjoy her routine and did not like to have such interrupted by visitors, although in the early years a very faithful few continued to drop by, including Anna Wilkins, Dottie Baxley, Mary Lou Bussey, Alice Inman, and, more rarely, Gene Boardman Claussen and Caroline Eve. She even refused to see Lib Ridgely Dohm, her first cousin, on her last visit to Augusta from Dallas in the early 1980s. This hurt Lib a lot, she told me when I tried to make excuses in Dallas in 1985.

Her youngest child, Sam, was attentive with his wife, Sandra, and their children, and Frank and Sam had lunch together at 704 Montrose once a week. She went to their home for some occasions, such as Christmas dinner, and in the early recluse days, she drove to Greenville

CHAPTER SEVEN

with Mary Lou Bussey for Christmas with Frank Pride. She continued to be intimate with Amaryllis Phinizy via telephone calls or when Amaryllis came to Augusta. She spoke occasionally with Julia Fargo (who she would tell me had become a bit "ga-ga") and with Julia Butt Slaton, her second cousin on the Doughty side in Atlanta. A terrible blow was Sam's too-early death from cancer in April 1988. To lose a child must always hurt one deeply, but to lose Sam, who had been her mainstay and had reached the pinnacle of worldly success, was a relative disaster. After this, if possible, she withdrew even farther, nor did her temper improve relative to her keepers, who as time went on to became more and more difficult to recruit and train to suit her demands. She remained, in essence, a young girl by arguing always with servants like Willie Washington, who had known her from girlhood on Kings Way. and those that followed up to the end, "just like a child," so long ago had said Bowdre! The strange part is that many still laughed with her (and probably also at her) and remained her devoted helpers.

Her temper was short lived indeed. She grew up believing that servants and nurses were easy to hire and quite prepared to run to and fro 24/7 all year long! She had a bell and never hesitated to ring it! By a stroke of great luck, back in the early eighties or late seventies, Elizabeth Ray agreed to work during the week and, at first, shared the task with others. This continued until Mrs. Ray finally stayed at 704 Montrose five days a week with others assuming the weekend slots. Mrs. Ray was in charge and actually became quite fond of Frank, whom she called

"Mrs. Mays" always. "Big Frank" talked to "Little Frank" in Greenville often on the phone, and Little Frank made the drive to Augusta at regular intervals to see her mother and check on the help and household all managed by Mrs. Ray. This included all the hirings and firings, which were copious!

The above was the approximate status when I retired and returned to Augusta in 1992. Jim Hull, Frank's grandson, had taken Sam's place as her steward, brought her lobster and cooked it himself as well as roast beef sandwiches which he ate with her, and developed a fine lovable rapport and understanding with his grandmother, who opened many past vistas for him. Her last public appearance was to Millen for his wedding and reception in December of 1982. She and Amaryllis Phinizy sat together arm-in-arm without drinks at the reception on a beautiful warm night by the swimming pool and had the entire crowd come up at intervals to pay court! Frank looked handsome clad in a luxurious silken fabric dress of off-white with a mink collar, worn originally by Frank Mays Hull at her second wedding, and her daughter, Frank Pride, created an audible stir and murmur of awe and approval from the crowd seated in the church when she advanced down the aisle so beautiful and elegant in her evening dress. She looked like a celebrity from afar! Jim resigned (having done yeoman service), however, when I arrived, for by that time his own business needed complete focus. Frank, I detected, did not like his departure as Chief Steward, feeling I would not necessarily cater to all her whims and ways to spend her

CHAPTER SEVEN

modest income! But we worked it out, and Frank became quite fond of Lynn, who dropped by often to sit on her bed and tell her "the news," as she called the local gossip about people and places we had been.

I also found that during her long years of self-chosen idleness, she had become quite introspective in analyzing and dissecting the past relative to parts of her life:

- Her mother, Frankie Doughty: Frank wished she had been much sweeter during her mother's lifetime. She felt that at one time her mother had favored sisters Cordelia (or Dede as she called her) and Ruth Inman. I doubt that was ever done intentionally.
- Her marriage: She felt she had loved Bowdre more than he had loved her but said that in his own way she knew he loved her always; she tended to dwell on his business failures (and not the ultimate success) and on what she termed his "cutting-up" with Mary "D" Phinizy while she and the children were at Wrightsville Beach one summer. Frank and Mary "D" had been close friends for many long years, including the period following her marriage to Dr. Harry Goodrich, so she may have learned of this rather late or had just chosen to ignore it previously. Nonetheless, their intimate past relationship was broken for years prior to Mary "D's" death in 1988. Frank to the end often said Mary "D" could charm the birds and the bees from the trees and that Charlie always had loved her! I think she missed seeing her. She said

that once Julia Fargo was taken home by Bowdre from some party while she was out of town, and when he tried to kiss her goodnight, Julia then recoiled, saying, "What would Frank think?"!
- Her extravagance with money: How she had gone wrong, blaming it partly, I feel, on being sent to school in far away New York at an early age and having no one to teach her simple, common-sense rules about income and principal. It was too easy in the past to call John K. Ottley, the trust officer of First National Bank of Atlanta. The fact is, she, on occasion, really tried to live within her income and always found such difficult to the final days of her life.
- Her religion: Although not attending church each week, she said she believed in God and heaven and said her prayers. She enjoyed one visit from Donald Fishburne of St. Paul's and was still interested in St. Paul's, where she had been christened, had attended Sunday School regularly, and was married. I once inquired whom she first wanted to see in heaven. She replied, "My mother and Sam." I next asked about Bowdre, and she said she also wanted to see him, too, but after her mother and Sam!

Frank's inert lifestyle proved to be very unhealthy after so many years; she contracted pneumonia in early 1992, when fluid had to be drained from her lungs. This was a painful experience in the hospital for some days. On November 27, 1994, we celebrated her four

CHAPTER SEVEN

score and ten (ninetieth) birthday in her bedroom at 704 Montrose Court. Flowers were placed and balloons hung with birthday cake and French champagne served. She took a few sips of champagne, her original favorite drink, and accepted gifts, including a $100 check from Mary Lou Bussey. She gave the check to Mrs. Ray to hold privately and not for me to deposit to her checking account. This was a typical "Frank maneuver" to squirrel away cash on the side, and we all laughed with her! As we departed, Frank said this had been one of her best ever birthdays!

But then again in late 1994, she lost interest in food (as per Mrs. Ray), and eventually the second bout with a bronchial pneumonia infection began. Pneumonia was the immediate cause of death on February 9, 1995, in Doctors' Hospital, as stated on the death certificate. She had been under an oxygen mask since arrival in the emergency room several days before, and arrangements were made for Elizabeth Ray to stay in her room through every night. She was with her when her heart and breathing just stopped the night of February 9. All of her children and grandchildren, including the Inman relatives in Augusta, attended prayers led by the St. Paul's minister at our house in Conifer Place before driving in a procession behind a police motorcycle escort to Magnolia Cemetery, where the coffin covered by the handsome pall of St. Paul's awaited, with a large mantle of beautiful white flowers. The Episcopal burial service was given by the rector of St. Paul's assisted by the associate rector of Good Shepherd Church. Included was the Bible reading of Ecclesiastes 3 we had requested, beginning "To everything there is a season, and a time to every purpose under the heaven, a time to be born, and a time to die..." Then Frank's coffin was entombed in the Phinizy-Mays mausoleum in the tomb drawer directly above Bowdre. United again forever.

To a large extent, Frank and Bowdre's lives are a fair example of "Living well is indeed still the best revenge." They did contribute to the Augusta scene no matter the decade when active and left behind their many descendants (five children, twelve grandchildren, and twenty-one great-grandchildren) who still often cherish their memory and celebrate their lives. As Teto Barrett wrote me after Frank died, "she made many people very happy." So did Bowdre, so this may be considered an appropriate secular epitaph for both.

<u>Special Note:</u> For anyone interested in further pursuing the Frank and Bowdre era, there is a large and great collection of photographs taken by Scott Nixon in his teen and later years and donated by his son, Cobbs Nixon, to the Augusta Museum of History. Bowdre is shown with other Augustans at V.M.I. and Frank is in many photos with Teto and Gene Baker, Hollis Boardman, Anne Campbell, Julia Fargo nicknamed "Mama," and her cousin Walter Fargo, "Dimp" Stafford, etc. - B.P.M.

CHAPTER SEVEN

*Frank Inman honored Debs of 1922 with a party held at Augusta Country Club:
Left to Right: Martha Stelling, Julia Butt, Julia Fargo, Elizabeth Fleming, Frank Inman, Anne Campbell, Margaret Nixon, Louise Martin, Pegram Williams*

Bowdre P. Mays
circa time of his marriage, 1924

Frank Inman
at the time of her marriage, 1924

CHAPTER SEVEN

Bowdre & Frank Mays (L) and Mary "D" & Charlie Phinizy, Jr. (R) 1925 "Roaring Twenties" Ladies dressed as Coty Powderpuffs

At Hillcrest Ave. house circa, 1930, a Bachrach picture

CHAPTER SEVEN

The complete Mays Family on Lake Forest Drive circa 1940

IS LIVING WELL STILL THE BEST REVENGE?

Bachelor's party at Bon Air Hotel circa 1936. Clayton Boardman between
Frank & Anna Wilkins, Bill & Mary Dunbar standing with
Bowdre & Louise Phinizy

CHAPTER SEVEN

Mays Family progeny at Sam and Sandra Salmon wedding November 2, 1963 at the Old Government House

CHAPTER VIII

The King Family in Augusta and Europe: A Cursory Sketch

I first heard about the King Family from Augusta when as a boy of about eleven or twelve (1938-1939) I took lunch on a Sunday with my parents and other relatives at 814 Milledge Road. Our hostess, Aunt Mary Lou, introduced me to a slight but bright little lady dressed all in black and then sitting next to one of the living room fireplaces in the chair normally favored by Mary Lou Phinizy. This was, she intoned, the Countess Grace Gregorini who held out her hand as I went over and sort of bowed before her; I took her hand to shake firmly, knowing by that time from my father that no one wanted a tepid or "wet fish" response! At that period in Augusta, most local ladies did not usually shake hands, so I remembered this and assumed it must be a European custom. The countess was then visiting from her home in Bologna, Italy, and my interest was first piqued by this encounter and what I subsequently heard and read over the years concerning the Kings and their descendants. So here now I will recount the story as I know it, all culled from various interviews, articles, and writings.

Although the facts concerning the founder of the King family in Augusta may be well known to some, I still will lay out salient details to set the stage for this overall depiction. John Pendleton King was born April 3, 1799, near Glasgow, Barron County, Kentucky. He was the son of Francis King, formerly of Virginia, and Mary Patrick from Pendleton District, South Carolina. Soon the family moved to Bedford County, Tennessee, where he first began his tuition; one account stated his education commenced at age nine, but in light of his future precocious development, I suspect he was taught at home or elsewhere long before age nine. He boarded at the school during the week and returned home on the weekends by horseback. When sixteen, he was provided with a "stake" of money by his father and also a horse on which he rode to Columbia County, Georgia, the residence of a maternal uncle. From there to nearby Augusta, where in 1817 he enrolled at Richmond Academy. Here it is said he completed his studies or academic courses and then studied law in the office of

CHAPTER EIGHT

Major Freeman Walker, a prominent local lawyer and mayor of Augusta several times.

Walker came from Virginia and was a leading local citizen with many interests; he was elected to the United States Senate in 1818, the year when our protagonist, John P. King, was accepted by the bar. The Walkers appear to have been very "top drawer," so King must have been very alert, capable, and had much going for him to have been taken in by Major Walker. King, having been admitted to the bar prior to his twenty-first year, seems to have done well in legal work, particularly since Major Walker passed over his own important legal practice to him once he left Augusta for the US Senate.

One story is that King sold "lightard" (kindling wood) door-to-door on the Augusta streets; even if not apocryphal, this must be something he did as a student to earn pocket cash, for he seems to have had a "golden touch" when it came to the accumulation of wealth. Also, King must have amassed wealth rapidly, for by the end of 1821, he sailed to Europe for an extended stay of two years; he probably considered this his "grand tour" to study the world, people, the general manners of men and women, etc. He met General Lafayette in Paris, and they were together on the same ship during the return ocean transit. When Lafayette came to Augusta in 1825, King is said to have made a welcome speech, although it is also well known that Nicholas De l'aigle welcomed the general in French as he arrived in Augusta, the marquis replying in the same tongue.

King now returned to his local legal practice and appears to have had a major aptitude for the law; his business was again successful so that in 1829 he retired to focus on his large estate and business interests. Money seems to have come to him easily! In 1831 or 1832 (the written accounts differ), he was named by Governor Lumpkin as judge of the Court of Common Pleas (City Court). He was appointed to the Constitutional Convention of Georgia in 1833, his debates with William H. Crawford adding to his reputation, and then that same year was appointed to the United States Senate. He was re-elected by the Legislature in 1835 but resigned in 1837. He was the youngest United States senator of his time and served with figures such as Calhoun, Clay, Webster, etc. Andrew Jackson was president, as was Van Buren for a time. Apparently he patently disliked the political life and seems to have been a very strict constitutionalist. Alexander H. Stephens said, "No like abandonment of politics from personal disgust has ever occurred in the history of the United States." King never again was involved in the political life.

Judge King took the management of the Georgia Railroad in 1841 and became president of the Georgia Railroad and Banking Company, a position which lasted until 1878. Thus for thirty-seven years, including the difficult Civil War period, he headed and passed to his successor a then flourishing bank and railroad. He also had other commercial interests, including King Cotton Mill, named for him, and supported the Augusta Canal construction in 1865. He was a prominent shareholder

CHAPTER EIGHT

in the early days of the Augusta Factory. The King family continued to live at the higher elevation at their estate in the Sand Hills, where a train "whistle-stop" was in effect to collect him each day for the ride to and from downtown Augusta; summers were passed in the mountains of Western North Carolina, and his library and reading are said to have been very close companions before and following retirement.

Mr. King, in 1842, married Mary Louise Woodward, the only daughter of Mr. and Mrs. John Moore Woodward of New York City. He was forty-three and she but twenty-three. King was apparently quite wealthy by then, and we assume Miss Woodward was rather "top-drawer" New York herself. The Kings had three daughters and one son. The eldest daughter, Minnie (or Minna as she was always known in Europe), had formal names variously reported as Mary Sands and Mary Livingston; the second was Grace Sterling King; the third Louise Woodward King; and the only son, Henry Barclay King. In order to provide a clearer picture for the narrative to follow, the birth and death dates for the King parents and progeny are as follows:

- John Pendleton King: 1799-1888 (as per his tombstone even though another account says 1887); he died of congestion of the lungs at almost ninety.
- Mary Louise Woodward King: 1819-1890; she died in Paris, but her stone is on the family plot at Summerville Cemetery.
- Minna King (as we shall call her): circa 1843-1931.

- Henry Barclay King: 1844-1931.
- Grace Sterling King: 1846-1875.
- Louise Woodward King: 1849-1878.

The Augusta Family:

John P. King obtained control of the old Bugg Plantation on the Sand Hills, the site of the present-day Pendleton King Park, although at its zenith the entire estate contained much more land; in the King Estate heyday, the entire acreage extended to include what is now called Kings Wood subdivision, the Johns Road Extension area around Pendleton Camp, and also encompassing the territory where St. Joseph Hospital and the Veterans Administration Medical facility now stand. In short, a very huge tract. Here an imposing house was built; see the photograph contained in this book as such was reprinted from one taken before the fire that destroyed much of the main house circa 1914-1915. The Bugg Family private cemetery still exists in the park. The Kings appear to have been members of St. Paul's Church (at least at some stage), for St. Paul's rector, G. Sherwood Whitney, gave the Episcopal Church service when Pendleton King (son of Henry) died in 1919. As the family grew and the Civil War approached in 1861, the story in Augusta is that the King ladies were sent abroad to Europe to remove them from the unpleasantness. Henry, the sole son and familiarly called Harry, also went and began his college education at Oriel College, Oxford, at some point for he graduated with honors in 1867. Katherine H. Cumming reported in

CHAPTER EIGHT

her reminiscences that "Mrs. King, Grace and Lou" returned home to Augusta around December 1864 after being detained in New York for about a year prior to obtaining the permit to travel South. Minna and Harry remained in Europe; Mrs. Cumming also reported Harry then was left at Oxford in school.

Grace Sterling King married John Berrien Connelly of Burke County. They were the parents of Louise King Connelly and Grace King Connelly, both born in the early 1870s; however, tragedy struck when both parents died much too young, their mother at age twenty-nine in 1875 and the father later passing away. Then their mother's sister, Louise Woodward King, who never married, died in 1878 but only after having been acclaimed in Georgia and abroad for the enactment of a state law to prevent cruelty to animals. She also established the Louise King Home for Widows in Augusta. Louise King, in another rather heart-rending blow, further died at twenty-nine, the same age as her older sister!

Unfortunately more appalling adversity yet was to come to the two Connelly sisters! In 1891, when she was only twenty-one, Louise King Connelly was drowned in Lake Olmstead (her tombstone states "At the Foot of the Lake") as the result of a boating accident. She and Henry Cumming Lamar were together, and somehow the boat overturned and his arm was broken. There seemed to be in this terrible event an incongruity of fate that Lamar, considered a celebrated athlete at Princeton, could drown and fail to rescue Louise Connelly, who could not swim. Lamar had run a 104-yard pass in a football game with that particular feat unbeaten for years. The couple seemed to have smashed into a factory weir connected to one of the mills on the Augusta Canal; perhaps this broke Lamar's limb, thus impeding the rescue of Louise. A photograph of the memorial stone placed on the canal bank is included in this book showing the date of the drowning as March 10, 1891.

After these disasters, it was quite natural that Grace King Connelly was distraught and bereft, particularly at the loss of her sister, for she was now entirely alone except for her Uncle Harry in Augusta and Aunt Minna then living in London and also Paris. It was decided, therefore, to send her to visit Aunt Minna, now Marchioness of Anglesey. Grace then was about seventeen; what then took place will be amply discussed under the English, Italian, and French family headings.

Now left in Augusta was the Henry Barclay King family. As mentioned before, Henry graduated from Oxford in 1867 with honors at age twenty-three. It is not clear what business endeavor he ever pursued; suffice to say he never appeared interested in commercial ventures, nor did he possess the entrepreneurial streak of his illustrious father, who did not die until 1888. His great niece by marriage, Genie Lehmann, speaks of him as sort of an introvert and perhaps rather like some of the English gentry he had known in Englan, but certainly not in the manner of King Edward VII! I don't think he much increased the family fortune in his lifetime; rather I take it over time he reduced assets and the

CHAPTER EIGHT

size of the Sand Hills estate by selling land adjoining the original premises after the main house burned circa 1914-1915. While they intended to rebuild, they never did but rather lived in one of the subsidiary houses nearby. All that remained of the original large home was the kitchen, and several rooms were added to this to make a small comfortable cottage/guest house in use for many years thereafter.

The remaining family members continued to spend the hot weather months in the Asheville, North Carolina, mountains, and here they were in contact often with the George Vanderbilt family, then building Biltmore Castle, and also with the Seldens, for Harry at last married in 1884 at age forty Elizabeth Cashin. Elizabeth Cashin King's sister had married John A. Selden, and their son, Joe Selden, married Jennie Lee Walton, the mother of Genie Selden Lehmann. So Elizabeth C. King was Genie's great aunt, and their one child, John Pendleton King, her second cousin. As grandfather John P. King died in 1888, and John P. King II was born in Asheville July 9, 1889, Pendleton, as he always was called with no suffix attached to his surname, never knew the great man. From the time he was a bit more than one year old, Pendleton had a nurse of French nationality, so he grew up using both English and French with equal facility, becoming completely bilingual. This was to prove to be of immense utility to him in the years ahead and particularly during World War I. Pendleton did know his Grandmother King, who it is said lavished copious affection on him until her death in Paris on

November 19, 1890. When time for schooling arrived, he attended kindergarten in Asheville and Monte Sano School in Augusta followed by Richmond Academy; then in 1905 Sewanee Grammar School and continuing at Sewanee University until 1909, when he entered Oriel College, Oxford. Here he took his degree, Bachelor of Arts, in 1913. Pendleton, as a freshman at Oxford, lived in the same rooms at Oriel occupied by his own father as an undergraduate, then later at the "Old Parsonage" with Oriel friends.

Pendleton made his initial visit to Europe as a small child in 1892, crossing the Atlantic subsequently sixteen times in total. He visited not only England and Scotland, but also France and Italy, stopping with his Aunt Minna, Marchioness of Anglesey in Paris and Nice, and with his first cousin Countess Grace Gregorini-Bingham in Bologna. One interesting friend who started as a freshman at Oxford the same year as Pendleton (1909) was the Russian prince, Felix Youssoupoff. The Youssoupoff family was probably the richest non-royal family in the Russian Empire, and Felix matriculated as Count Elston, a title of his father. Although Felix attended University College (or "Univ" as all termed it) and Pendleton Oriel, they in the early autumn days of 1909 were and remained friends during the following three years, but particularly at first it seems when Felix's English was so poor they spoke to each other in French which both knew as if a native tongue because, as Pendleton wrote, "I could talk only United States"! Once when his father wanted some cows shipped to one

CHAPTER EIGHT

of the Youssoupoff estates, Felix sent this telegram to a farm: "Please send me one man cow and three Jersey women"!

Felix was assigned a suite of rooms at "Univ" looking onto The High (which I assume is High Street). These large rooms were called "The Club" for, no matter the resident, many students would "hang out" there as one now says. At present, these same rooms have been named "Youssoupoff Rooms" to acclaim the famous past occupant. As described by Pendleton, Felix led an extravagant, luxurious lifestyle, particularly after the first year when he was allowed by "Univ" to obtain his own "digs." He then rented a house on King Edward Street with two friends, hired a Russian chef, a French chauffeur, an English butler, and a French valet. He also was much entertained by London society but must have studied enough as Felix left Oxford in 1912 with his Bachelor of Arts. However, prior to this, he began to play cricket, polo, and to hunt—this when he joined the Bullingdon Club and began to see less of Pendleton, who was in Vincent's club. Once Pendleton drove into London with Felix in his Delaney-Belleville, whose interior contained sable robes for cold weather! There was a minor accident in Kensington High Street, but the bobby let them off. After Oxford, Felix stayed in London for another year enjoying the good life with his best friend Jack Gordon. He leased flats in London and really was a member of "le tout Londres" at that period. Felix signed a long-term lease on one flat, paying rent years in advance so that when he left

Russia after the 1917 Revolution, he still had intact a place to live.

Felix returned home to Russia sometime in 1913 and was married in February 1914 to Princess Irina, niece of Tsar Nicholas II and only daughter of the Tsar's sister, Grand Duchess Xenia, and Grand Duke Alexander. There is no known record of any communication between Felix and Pendleton following Oxford; however, after Felix and his cohorts killed the Russian mystic, Rasputin, the night of December 16-17, 1916, Pendleton was the author of an article published in the *New York Times* magazine January 14, 1917, covering the murder. Pendleton took the position that Felix Yousoupoff was not the sort of person to commit "a 10-20-30 cent murder." He defended him for the rationale that the affair does not accord with his character even though he could have been involved in "intrigues" resulting in the death of Rasputin. Felix, he wrote, was "gentle, wistfully humorous, gracious," and he leaves it up to the reader to decide if it is possible to associate him with a brutal murder.

Well, we learned the facts after Felix himself told how he plied the "Mad Monk" with poisoned food and wine while a gramophone upstairs was playing "I'm a Yankee Doodle Dandy." When Rasputin failed to die after eating and drinking the poisoned wine, tea, and cake, Felix shot him at close range in the heart. Later, another of the conspirators fired additional shots into Rasputin, and his body was thrown into the icy Neva River. But to give Pendleton his due, there have been many doubts relative

CHAPTER EIGHT

to the full honesty of all the various published reports on the murder, even including the admissions of Felix. For example, Serge Obolensky, a cousin of Felix, had his doubts that he had personally committed the crime as he was a "gentle soul." Obolensky wrote that it was difficult to picture Felix as he described himself acting in such a cold-blooded manner. Obolensky opined it was more likely that Tesphé, the Abyssinian servant who Felix had smuggled out of Jerusalem to St. Petersburg, was the one who prepared the poisoned drinks and finally finished the monk off. Many accounts of the events of the night and early morning hours of December 16-17 are contradictory depending on whether one is defending or accusing.

Now returning to Pendleton, after he took his Oxford degree in 1913, he was hired by the *Augusta Herald* and assigned to the Recorders Court. He wrote a series called "Morning with the Recorder," in which he outlined the scenes of blended poignancy and comedy so legion in a police court. Then in the latter part of 1914, he left for Washington, DC to take the foreign service examination, but not passing it he went on to New York City. He lived near Washington Square in Greenwich Village where he wrote plays, one called "Cocaine," and acted in others. Before the United States declared war on April 6, 1917, Pendleton attended lectures at Columbia on military tactics, completed a drilling course, and took the examination to join the Officers Reserve Corps. He entered May 12, obtained his commission as first lieutenant of Infantry on August 12, 1917, and went immediately to Cambridge, Massachusetts, for training by French officers. He was seconded in September of 1917 to the staff of General Clarence Edwards, then commanding the 26th Yankee Division, and sailed late that month to France via Liverpool. After a few days in England, he was given a short leave that he spent in Paris with his aunt, Lady Anglesey. On October 30, he went to his assignment in the Vosges, near Nancy, and later took part in the advance on Chateau Thierry and St. Mihiel. He was cited for bravery and awarded the French Croix de Guerre. Lieutenant King was liaison officer between the French and American division at Chateau-Thierry.

After the Armistice in November 1918, President Woodrow Wilson, then in France, dined with the 26th Division on Christmas Day accompanied by Mrs. Edith Wilson and General Pershing, among other dignitaries. It would be interesting to know if Pendleton and the president had time to discuss Augusta where Wilson had lived as a youth! Pendleton departed France on March 14, 1919, was discharged from the army April 9, and arrived in Augusta April 21. He was taken ill in late May, became much better, but then suffered a relapse, the cause of death being a cerebral hemorrhage May 28. He was not yet thirty. This death was a tremendous shock to the entire community.

Newspapers in the South, in New York, and at Oriel College, Oxford, paid him genuine and sincere tributes. He was buried at 6:00 p.m. just at sunset in the family plot at Summerville Cemetery. The Episcopal church service was read by the Reverend Whitney of

CHAPTER EIGHT

St. Paul's. There were many relatives and friends from elsewhere present, and the pall bearers were Messrs. Lawton B. Evans, Landon Thomas, Henry Cumming, Bowdre Phinizy, Lansing Lee, Eugene Verdery, Jr., Fred Eve, John Harper, Dr. E. E. Murphey, and Archibald Blackshear. Published later was a small book dedicated to this life of so much promise but cut so short and his extremely untimely death. Following are a few of the expressions of condolence sent to his parents and printed in the memorial booklet:

> Pendleton has had a wonderful life; his conduct is luminous with bravery, fortitude, tenderness, joy. I for one am glad there will never be for him defeat or tragedy.
>
> Henrietta B. Alexander

> It is a consolation to think he had a happy and prosperous life, and died full of honour, in a cause he knew was the greatest he could have made his sacrifice for. We all have to die but to few is it given to die in honour and glory, beloved and mourned by all. What a blessed ending he had to his brave young life, full of success and the sense of having done his duty nobly and unselfishly in the crowning glory of a lovely and beloved existence. No sorrow or suffering was for him — no regrets, no disillusions. His race well run, his victory won. What more can we wish for those we

love? We must feel thankful that our dear one did not fall on a distant battlefield, or be wounded or mutilated to find perhaps a nameless grave; but his name will live and be honored among his own people in our own Southern land.

          Mina Anglesey

On the threshold of his enlistment as a soldier, in his own poetic language he realized that at the end of the misty road we tread there was a terrifying figure, and he saw that shape distinct and felt no awe, but strange, exalted joy instead, and went to war. Though he did not die on the field of battle, his willingness to do so was attested by a devotion and valor that justly earned the high honor awarded him as an American officer in the greater war the world has ever know.

          J. C. C. Black

Our country has lost a gallant son, his fearless, brilliant war record will never be forgotten. His splendid courage, his unusual intellect, his fine character will be an inspiration to those that knew him. His memory will live forever!

         Marguerite Wright Hillman

His presence in every gathering was a ray of sunshine, always sparkling and delightful, and his brilliant mind was a challenge.

          Bertha Barrett Lee

CHAPTER EIGHT

I think he had the most vivid and charming personality and was the finest gentleman (in the highest sense of the word) that I ever knew. I have never ceased to miss him, and I can't realize yet that it isn't some hideous dream — that he can't really be lost to us and to the world.

Mary Lou Phinizy

As time goes on his place is not filled and we miss him more and more. He has truly made a blank in my life.

Edith Vanderbilt

I want to express on behalf of the officers of "C Mess," Hdqs. 26th Division, the deepest and most heartfelt sympathy for you at this sad time. The tragic death of your son John Pendleton was a tremendous shock to all of us who had been associated with him through the trying times of our service in France. His friendly character, his cleverness, his unending store of wit and his unfailing courage endeared him to everyone of us, and his presence at "the Mess" cheered many a dark hour.

Nicholas Biddle

I make no attempt at consolation. The case does not admit it. Only an irrepressible expression of my boundless sorry for you, not unmixed with personal grief, in no small degree, of my own.

Jos. B. Cumming

Our dear boys are spared all further suffering and sorrow, and with that thought we must try to comfort our desolate hearts.
                    Carolyn P. Cumming

I am inexpressibly shocked at the news which has just reached me of Pendleton's death. I find it almost impossible to realize such dreadful tidings of the lad whom only a few days ago I say in all the gay joyousness of is splendid youth and vigor.

Since his return it has been the constant comment of all those who had met him that he, almost alone of those who have come back, had seen the great conflict in Europe in its true meaning and purport, and those of us who delighted to be numbered among his friends found a new gratification in a maturity and soundness of judgment which we looked on as the natural development of those high gifts with which he was endowed.

I recognize only too keenly that there is nothing that can be said that can in any wise mitigate your grief at this dire loss of a son upon whom so justly was centered all your hope and pride, sorrow there may be some sad solace to you ini the sympathy of one who so greatly loved and admired your dear dead boy.
                    Henry H. Cumming

Apart from your pride in his patriotism and achievement, I want to say that we share in the

CHAPTER EIGHT

universal grief, but rejoice that his traits were those that will live forever in the hearts of all who knew him.

                       Constance Cabell Wright

Pendleton was a poet of some parts and wrote one amusing piece during the Taft Presidency as follows: On Prohibition

ODE OF INVOCATION
(A despairing cry)
To The Hon. W. H. Taft

O, High Official, whom the Fates endow
With might still, on a crumbling throne:
Arise! And bend thy beetling brow;
Frustrate their purpose with thine own,--
Their fiend's design! Do not allow
This Law! No man can help us now
      But thou.
Of Winter climes we once were first.
Then, wouldst thou see thy favorite fall
And all her laughing throng dispersed
By Prohibition? For of all
The pangs with which mankind is cursed
Thou knowest that by far the worst
      Is thirst.
We call thee in the last despair
To quell this high conspiracy.
Our women have let down their hair.
Think of the terrors of the Sea
With nought but WATER everywhere—

IS LIVING WELL STILL THE BEST REVENGE?

>How ill did the Titanic fare
>>Out there.
>And even so should we go down
>If House and Senate close the gate
>That brings relief to sage and clown.
>The young and strong would Emigrate
>And leave the Old to keep the town
>In misery, and sit aroun'
>>And frown.
>O, Taft! Thou canst not be the same
>Old Taft we knew, that one of old,
>If thou wilt not prevent this shame!
>The power if thou canst not hold
>Then use it now and go for Fame,--
>Augusta, Georgia'll take the blame,--
>>Withhold thy name!!
>>>J.P.K.

Former President Taft wrote the following to Pendleton's father seemingly after his death:

>I thank you for sending me the very bright verses, which you find among your son's papers, on a prohibition bill during my incumbency. I have had a copy made of it and I return the original with thanks for the opportunity of reading it. Your son didn't send it to me I think.
>>Sincerely yours.
>>>Wm. H. Taft

CHAPTER EIGHT

For the Henry Kings, the premature death of their only child was a total disaster and cataclysmic. Mr. King then seemed to have devoted much time to the conception and creation of a permanent memorial to their son. They still maintained the house named Woodward in Asheville on Merrimon Avenue, so at their two residences he toiled on his last will and testament, finally contriving a long document with which he felt his ultimate wishes as the testator would prevail always. And then as time passed, codicils were added as conditions changed regarding relatives or new ideas on bequests were conceived. The key memorial provisions desired above all that the memory of his son, Pendleton, be preserved; to accomplish this, the trustees were directed to dispose of the estate called Sandhills as follows:

- Pendleton Camp, already established by Mr. King, he wanted to be a "living memorial" to his son, and in his first codicil dated December 24, 1921, extended the rights to live in the cottages in perpetuity to the descendants of World War veterans;
- Pendleton King Park, a public domain, to be established. No cutting of plants, flowers or trees, and no boisterous athletic games to be played; The City of Augusta leases the park from the King Estate Trustees for $1.00 per annum. Mayor George Sancken was instrumental in opening the park in 1969, with the formal dedication December 3, 1969.

- Sandhill Park to be established upon the death of his grandnephew, Giovanni Gregorini-Bingham with no male heir; this to comprise 100 acres and a strip 100 feet wide for an approach road to what he called the "old estate," i.e. "the old Sandhills tract." This park was to be used as a resort for the residents of Pendleton Camp and to be its adjunct; meantime the area and its houses was to be used by Giovanni and any male heir; Mr. King was following here the English law of primogeniture meaning that the first born, or usually a son, is to inherit.
- On Sunset Avenue, a cemetery to be provided for the residents of Pendleton Camp.

It now appears that only Pendleton Camp and Pendleton King Park were created. The facts are rather obscure, but strong suspicion points to the important factor that Mr. King, and even the trustees after his death on January 25, 1931, sold off land over the years to generate adequate income for living expenses. The will is quite clear that Mrs. King as the widow (she died in 1938) is not to be denied sufficient income. Giovanni Gregorini-Bingham only died in 1952 or 1953, and Sandhill (the will spelled this in the singular) Park was not officially formed. However, we do know that after Mrs. Henry King died in 1938, their niece, Countess Grace Gregorini-Bingham, and her son, Giovanni Gregorini-Bingham, took legal advice on how to break

CHAPTER EIGHT

the will. Both New York and Augusta attorneys appear to have been instructed.

During World War II on April 24, 1943, the *Augusta Chronicle* reported that the U S Alien Property Custodian filed claim to the trust property left to Giovanni Gregorini-Bingham, an Italian citizen of a belligerent country. I assume that after the war Giovanni and his mother, who was a United States citizen, were able to secure the release of his trust from the Alien Property Custodian prior to any title change or liquidation. The final denouement apparently was a decision against them following World War II when it is presumed they were rather "hard-up," as they say in Augusta. Meanwhile, both before and following World War II Countess Grace and her only son, Count Giovanni Gregorini-Bingham, occupied the reconstructed remains of the old King house during their frequent visits to Augusta. In any event, both Pendleton Camp and Pendleton King Park are very wonderful additions for Augusta and, as intended, are and will remain appropriate memorials to honor Pendleton, the war hero.

One final interesting feature related to Henry King's precise instructions in his will (Codicil No.2) was that at his funeral there was to be no religious service, no singing, no flowers at the grave site. He calls his instructions "unorthodox" but says he cannot "consent, without a protest, to pass into the great beyond with my last act that of a hypocrite." His last words on his funeral:

> To thine own self be true,
> And it must follow, as the night the day,
> Thou canst not then be false to any man.

The above is the well-known and famous quote taken from Shakespeare's Hamlet.

The English Family:

In a sense, this section might be reported under the "French Family" as Minna King actually lived so much and so long in France; however, her two husbands were both English, and she did live in England, particularly when younger and first living in Europe circa 1860, and was always usually known after her second marriage as the Marchioness of Anglesey. As reported previously, Minna, eldest child and daughter, did not return to Augusta toward the end of the Civil War with her sisters and mother. She was then about nineteen or twenty and likely took some schooling in England and perhaps France to perfect her French language skills. Katharine H. Cumming said she was "with friends," and another reference to Minna in a May 1864 letter to her mother in New York could conject that Minna then was in Paris. We are uncertain when or if she ever came home to Augusta; my purely surmise is that she returned at least once to visit her father, who had great hopes this charming and attractive well-educated (by the standards of that day) daughter, possessing looks and red hair to boot, would marry up (if possible), but most definitely "well"!

CHAPTER EIGHT

This was also the era when trans-Atlantic marriages were beginning to burgeon in the "Gilded Age" following the Civil War. Anglomania began after the Prince of Wales (later Edward VII) visited New York in 1860; this first exposure to American ladies created in him an enthusiasm that endured to the end of his life in 1910. If the lady was good-looking, the prince saw to it that all doors were ajar; one of the early marriages of an American girl into the English peerage with the Prince of Wales himself helping to convince the Duke and Duchess of Marlborough to permit the union of their younger son, Lord Randolph Churchill, with the beautiful Jennie Jerome of New York, took place at the British Embassy in Paris in 1874. Money naturally also had a place in English aristocratic unions—this with or without Americans as gentleman did not toil and depended upon their landed estates to generate income. Because of the rule of primogeniture, younger sons, daughters, and even an eldest son could be needy depending upon economic conditions; this actually became the urgent case commencing circa early 1870s with the agricultural depression and rapid industrialization ongoing in England.

The pertinent factor to focus on in all of the above is that the father of Minna, being ambitious and a real go-getter, was quite prepared to back her to the hilt in achieving an impressive marriage. We presume Louise Woodward King, as her mother, was equally enthusiastic and zealous, as she herself was a woman of the world and knew London and Paris certainly were then well on their way to becoming the brilliant social capitals of that epoch. But it is unusual to note that Minna did not marry until June 25, 1872, when she was about twenty-nine, rather old for a first-time bride at that time; she was married (so they say) for love to the Honorable Henry Wodehouse, younger brother of the 3rd Baron (later first Earl) Wodehouse. Another report states that the Honorable Henry was a brother of the first Earl of Kimberley so the baron apparently assumed a new title when made earl. The well-known old mining town of Kimberley, South Africa, was named for the earl.

Minna then was called "the rich and vivacious Mary Livingston King, a daughter of the American railroad and banking tycoon, John Pendleton King." She was said to be related to the well-known New York Livingstons. Another maiden name attributed to her at this early period was "Mary Sands King" of Sandhills, Georgia." But as I wrote, we will continue with Minna, the name she preferred and which, on occasion, also was spelled Mina. The Honorable Henry was posted to the British Embassy in Paris as second secretary where the wedding took place. Unfortunately, he died the next year, 1873, while on diplomatic service in Athens, Greece. It is not known if Minna was with him, but if he was stationed in Athens one can assume she was. Then probably back to England, where the young American widow Wodehouse would have had access to top aristocratic and even court circles. For example, Sir Philip Wodehouse, likely a relative by marriage, was British governor of Bombay and

CHAPTER EIGHT

received the Prince of Wales when he went to India for his Durbar in 1875.

One interesting digression is the fact that while in Paris, the Honorable Henry and "Minnie" (as those close then called her) Wodehouse were intimate friends with Robert Ormond and Edith Snell Maugham, the English parents of Somerset Maugham, who was born at the British Embassy in Paris in 1874. He was born at the embassy on British territory to avoid French citizenship, and thus future liability to serve in the French military. Robert Ormond Maugham was solicitor to the British Embassy with his legal office across from the embassy on Faubourg St. Honoré; this friendship continued long after Henry Wodehouse, who'd died merely fourteen months after his marriage. Minna was Edith Maugham's fond and affectionate friend, remaining so until Edith died of consumption in early 1882, still in Paris. It would be interesting to know if the Maughams initially introduced Henry Wodehouse to Minna!

It is not clear exactly when Minna met her second husband, Henry Paget, son of the second Marquess of Anglesey. Henry would have had the courtesy title of lord, having been born in 1835 to the second marriage of the second Marquess of Anglesey. Henry's grandfather, the first marquess, was known as "One-Leg," having lost his leg at the famous Battle of Waterloo in 1815. One-Leg was a particular favorite of Queen Victoria, who ordered a state funeral when he died in 1854 at eighty-six. In 1851, at the opening of the International Exhibition in London's Crystal Palace, One-Leg, with his artificial apparatus in place (the new limb was articulated at the knee and joints), entered arm-in-arm with the Duke of Wellington, his old comrade in war. One-Leg also had served the crown as viceroy/lord lieutenant of Ireland and master-general of the Ordnance at cabinet rank. In addition, he received the dignity of field marshal and was made a knight of the garter in 1818. One-Leg had two marriages and children by both wives, all of whom carried the surname Paget. One-Leg by succession had become Earl of Uxbridge and then by creation of the Prince Regent (later George IV) the Marquess of Anglesey in 1815.

It is clear that beginning in the eighteenth century until well into the twentieth, the Paget family was very influential and prominent in British court circles; for example, one son of the first Marquess, Lord Alfred Paget (1816-1888) by his second wife, was Queen Victoria's chief equerry and clerk marshal. Lord Alfred also was named to be her representative in the entourage with the Prince of Wales on the 1875 journey to India. Lord Alfred had six sons, three of whom all married Americans; and one had two American wives! These sons were Arthur Paget, who married Minnie Stevens in 1878, then Almeric Paget married Pauline Whitney in 1895 and (after her death in 1916) remarried five years later Florence Miller of New York. Finally Sidney Augustus Paget wed Marie Dolan in 1906. Almeric later was created First Baron Queensborough for political service and with Pauline lived at 38 Berkeley Square in London, then a good address indeed. Arthur Paget was

CHAPTER EIGHT

the great friend of Edward as Prince of Wales, a boon companion really. Minnie Stevens brought a dowry to Arthur of US $100,000; an English pound then equaled five dollars, and I am told a general rule by which to consider the inflation over the years is to multiple by thirty-three. After his accession to the throne in 1901, Edward VII created Colonel Arthur Paget a knight so that at last Minnie Stevens Paget had the title of "lady"! She always remained a favorite hostess of King Edward even though in theory the title was conferred for Arthur's military deeds!

Pagets also married with some of the fine English names, e.g., Villiers, Wellesley, Cardigan, Wyndham, Capel, etc., and several Paget daughters married nobles, such as the Duke of Richmond, Earl of Strafford, Earl of Sandwich, and one son a daughter of the Duke of Rutland. So considering all this and the preceding paragraphs, it is rather obvious the introduction of the animated and lively Minna King Wodehouse to the English court and aristocratic circles was a given for even an American widow of her standing. Minna's father furthermore had many European connections that had developed over the years from his commercial and political relations.

Thus Minna King Wodehouse remarried June 26, 1880, to Henry Paget, Fourth Marquess of Anglesey, who must have just recently succeeded to the Marquisate, the hereditary rank above earl, count, and baron but below duke, for the Third Marquess, Henry's half-brother, moreover died in 1880 leaving no male heir. Henry, to repeat, was the grandson of One-Leg as were his Paget cousins, sons of Henry's uncle Alfred, who of course was a later son of One-Leg by his second marriage. This was mentioned previously. Minna was thirty-seven and Henry forty-five. She was Henry's third and final wife; there was one son born to Henry's second wife, Blanche, who died in 1877, but no issue from Minna's marriage. J. P. King provided a dowry of $200,000, for those days a very substantial principal, but we do not know on what conditions these funds changed hands. To safeguard the future welfare of his daughter, there well could have been conditions that this fortune would not be absorbed into the husband's estate so that the original capital was not fully under his control. This seems logical in this case based on Henry's prior marriages and the existence of the stepson. As the reader will see, Minna to the end of her life gave the appearance of independent wealth and always dictated her own lifestyle.

The Fourth Marquess of Anglesey controlled three properties or residences: Uxbridge House in London, the mansion of Beaudesert Hall in Staffordshire, and Plas Newydd, Isle of Anglesey, Wales, known as the official "seat." The new marchioness as a bride must have known well all these homes and many other English stately homes, for this was the era of frequent weekend house parties; guests would bring their maids, valets, and large quantities of luggage; at times there were shooting weekends when the ladies would join the "guns" for lunch, sometimes served outdoors in fine weather. Servants then were plentiful and cheap, but

CHAPTER EIGHT

still the cost to maintain all three establishments would have been huge. Minna certainly was exposed to all the English "top drawer" circles of this period, including the "Marlborough House set" of the then Prince and Princess of Wales (later Edward VII and Queen Alexandra). However, I have never seen her name noted as one of the many lady friends of the prince in any books on this epoch, even though John Walton, from Augusta, thought she was! Notwithstanding the English abodes available to Minna, she appears to have maintained a residence in Paris, even after her second wedding in 1880, probably preferring France to her husband's family seats in England and Wales.

One family story told by Genie Lehmann in Augusta is that Minna in her usual high-spirited way incurred the wrath of Queen Victoria (by slapping the marquess at the opera or in some public location), who then made her persona non grata at court. In any event, even in the early 1880s, the Angleseys spent much time in Paris, another possible reason being financial and tax considerations for the marquess. The date is confirmed by a Somerset Maugham anecdote he was fond of telling about the end of Minna's marriage to Lord Anglesey; this is quoted from an article he wrote in 1962 for *Show Magazine* and again appeared in a biography of the Maugham family authored by Robin Maugham, nephew of Somerset:

> One evening, the Angleseys were giving a dinner at which the Russian ambassador was to be

the guest of honour. The guests arrived and Lady Anglesey greeted them, but Anglesey did not appear. Lady Anglesey thought he was still dressing and she apologized to the Ambassador. They waited and still he did not come. At last she sent a footman to his room to tell him that their guests were assembled. The footman came back to say his lordship was not in his room and gave her a letter, addressed to her, which he had found pinned on the pincushion. In it he told her that he was leaving her for good and had started for England with Madame de So-and-So...How the dinner proceeded, I do not know. It must have been a grim affair. When all the guests had departed and only my mother remained, she tried to console Lady Anglesey, who throughout the evening had put on a bold front.

"He'll come back to you," she said. "After all, Madame de So-and-So is as ugly as sin."

Lady Anglesey gasped. "If she's ugly, he'll never come back."

She was right. Lord Anglesey remained with his French mistress for the rest of his life.

But this story does indicate Minna's obvious wit, sophistication, and quickness at repartee.

As Somerset's mother, Edith, died January 31, 1882, just after the birth of her sixth son in Paris, this story would give the definite impression the Anglesey couple was living in Paris at least part-time subsequent to

CHAPTER EIGHT

their 1880 nuptials. The other factor is the apparent early breakdown of the Anglesey marriage; a divorce in that era was quite a stigma. They must have decided to keep up appearances, even if living largely apart until Henry, the Fourth Marquess, died in 1898. He then was succeeded by Minna's stepson, who became the Fifth Marquess at age twenty-three; he was another Henry, known as the "Dancing Marquess" who spent a huge bundle on jewels that he is said to have displayed on his own person! He died in 1905 with no issue at age thirty.

It appears from all accounts that Minna, Marchioness of Anglesey, was now establishing herself as one of the most prominent American expatriates in France, which she vastly preferred to England. While she probably did not really entirely penetrate the "gratin," as the French call their top aristocratic society, neither was she subject to their constraints and limitations. Nevertheless, as an attractive and well-to-do American with a fine English title, Lady Anglesey found many doors wide open, particularly in artistic and probably political circles, including some aristocratic drawing rooms. For example, the French Marquis Boni de Castellane (who married Anna Gould for her wealth) writes of an 1896 visit with Minna and Princess Doria, with whom Minna was then staying in London, to the Kent estate of Knole, owned then by the Sackville family. Boni, in his memoir *How I Discovered America*, describes Minna as follows:

> The Marchioness, who presents one of the most interesting personalities of her day, is perhaps

better known in Parisian society than in that of London, and she has been able to transform herself into an aristocrat worthy of the Court of the Sun King. She looks the part, and plays it to perfection. One associates her beauty with the era of brocade, powder and lace, just as her keen wit belongs to the same period.

So this is most likely an odds-on accurate depiction of Minna in the early 1890s: someone you instinctively would want to meet to discuss the world both past and present!

A long time prior to her husband's death in 1898, Minna settled into her estate, called the Hermitage, at Versailles, the Parisian suburb about twelve miles from the center of Paris. She was pictured as "lovely, eccentric and wealthy enough to indulge her many passing enthusiasms," one of which was to be an important buyer of eighteenth-century French antiques. She was one of the first Americans to focus on this period, which had been out of favor since the French Revolution a hundred years before. Minna worshiped the eighteenth century and purchased large lots of both furniture and fabrics of that era, including porcelains and objets d'art, etc. This while others then concentrated on the dark Victorian pieces and Second Empire, so that unsigned pieces not having been owned by Marie Antoinette were readily available. What Minna liked she purchased, and all that could not be used in her villa, the Hermitage, she kept in her cellar. American travelers also began to collect

CHAPTER EIGHT

antiques, and I have read that her drawing room was a meeting place for some of the more perceptive collectors. This brings up the question of whether Minna herself acted somewhat as a "dealer" with certain visitors!

In the late 1880s, Minna appears to have struck up a friendship with the Misses Elsie de Wolfe and Elizabeth Marbury who summered in France for several years before renting on a three-year lease a small but quite charming "pavilion" on Lady Anglesey's estate. The pavilion was one of the separate buildings in the grounds. It was 1899, and Minna now was the "Dowager Marchioness." Elsie de Wolfe then was an actress and student of the eighteenth-century decorative arts so embraced and championed by Minna Anglesey, who too was fond of the painted woods and light colors of the epoch. Elizabeth (Bessie) Marbury owned and ran Elizabeth Marbury Enterprises, a theatrical and literary agency that was most successful in representing the authors on the US productions of their works. She also had Democratic Party connections that extended to Washington, DC and came from a prominent New York family. Following the 1902 expiry of the Anglesey pavilion lease, the de Wolfe-Marbury menage rented a larger house in Versailles at 69 Boulevard St. Antoine and subsequently, after two or more years, they purchased and restored an old villa at 47 Boulevard St. Antoine. This house always had been called Villa Trianon, a name they continued, and the deed was in Marbury's name by the summer of 1905.

Minna Anglesey continued to be a role model for these friends who were brought into her intimate circle; Minna was far ahead of her time in some respects and pushed many to follow a more health-conscious regimen including a vegetarian diet. Minna was a very forceful defender of Captain Dreyfus in that famous case that divided France on the question of whether he was a traitor or the victim of a savage anti-Semitic intrigue. At the Paris Exposition of 1900, Minna was enthralled by the twining shape of art nouveau and bought the complete salon of art nouveau furniture on view. She planned to have it placed in her Versailles villa when the exposition closed. She then sold de Wolfe-Marbury some eighteenth-century carved and painted wall panels of wood for their Villa Trianon salon and main hall, indicating that indeed she did dabble on occasion as an antiquary. Lady Anglesey finally died in 1931 at an advanced age, around eighty-eight, and was buried in the famous Paris cemetery called Pere Lachaise. Her mother, Mary Louise Woodward King, also had died in Paris in 1890 while on a visit to her eldest child. As her stone is on the family plot at Summerville Cemetery, it is assumed her body or ashes were returned there.

Minna appears never to have returned to Augusta, but we assume her 1931 death was after that of her brother, Henry Barclay King, who died January 25, 1931, as she was a beneficiary under his will. I have found no reports or writings from Augustans who often were in Europe from, say, 1900 through the 1920s, relating to Lady Anglesey; there were many persons

CHAPTER EIGHT

taking European tours (and undoubtedly some from her own generations or even later generations) who knew the King family well. A few Augustans even resided in France for extended periods, and in those days before air travel and frequently jetting hither and yon, a meeting with such a well-known resident of France would have been a treat. The one exception I found is a 1914 meeting by Mary Lou Phinizy with the marchioness in Paris. Mary Lou called her "Aunt Minna" in her letter. Nevertheless, Aunt Minna continued to be close, or so we believe, to her Italian and French nieces and nephews, as discussed in the ensuing portions of this narrative.

Elsie de Wolfe remained a Minna Anglesey disciple to the end. She had secured full control of the Villa Trianon over time, so that in January 1933, she sold the house and its furnishings to Paul-Louis Weiller, but only with the caveat of occupancy until she died. Bessie Marbury had died in New York City in the same month. By this date, Elsie was Lady Mendl, as she became after her 1926 marriage to Sir Charles of the British Embassy in Paris. He had been created a knight in 1924 for "services to the Crown" according to the Smith biograph of Elsie. I have not to date been able to read any of de Wolfe's own writings, which may provide further input on the close friendship with Lady Anglesey. Elsie died in the Villa Trianon in 1950, was cremated at Pere Lachaise Cemetery, and her ashes interred underground in a white marble urn on the Columbarum lower level.

The Italian Family:

Earlier in this King saga, we wrote of the decision to send the young mourning Grace King Connelly, deprived of both her parents and only sibling, to Europe to visit her Aunt Minna, Marchioness of Anglesey. The year must have been 1891 or 1892 and about the time Grace would want to make her debut. The story told in Augusta is that she accompanied Aunt Minna and the Marquess of Anglesey to a ball in Vienna at Schönbrunn Palace, the Hapsburg summer home, and here she met Count Ugo Gregorini of Bologna, Italy. She apparently became immediately smitten and was found by Aunt Minna in flagrante delicto with the count. Aunt Minna, after reviewing the circumstances and the Gregorini antecedents, ordered a quick marriage which then took place. I assume the newlywed Count and Countess Ugo Gregorini began their married life in Bologna where in some periods there was a villa in the outer suburbs and either a townhouse or flat in the city. There were three children born to the Gregorinis, two daughters (Minnie, named after Aunt Minna, of course, and Adela Louise) and one son, Giovanni, the youngest child, and named John (Giovanni) after his great grandfather King. We do not know which was the elder girl but assume it was Minnie, nor do we possess information relative to their education or early lives.

At some point, a wealthy relative on the Gregorini side named Bingham left the family, I guess specifically Ugo, some money on condition that the name "Bingham" be hyphenated and appended to Gregorini.

CHAPTER EIGHT

So the new appellation Gregorini-Bingham as the surname was definitely in use by the 1920s-1930s. Pat Walsh of Augusta said that the hyphenated name was not to his knowledge used in Augusta, except perhaps for legal documents following World War I.

It appears quite likely that Grace Gregorini and her children were in close contact with Aunt Minna Anglesey all through the ensuing years, both at Versailles and in Italy. Do recall also that Minna was friendly with Princess Doria of that famous Roman family which dates back hundreds of years to their origins as high admirals and almost despots of Genoa. One Doria vanquished the Venetians, and Andrea Doria worked with one pope and became the greatest sailor in Europe. Hence, Aunt Minna's French and also her Italian connections doubtless, too, were in the picture. In 1920, Minnie Gregorini married a Prince de Beauveau-Craon, whose family seat was the Chateau de Haroué situated at Haroué, near Nancy, France. The other daughter born to Grace and Ugo Gregorini was Adela Louise, always known as "Baby" in the family. Baby seems to have married very young someone that her parents did not exactly approve of and this first marriage was later annulled by the Vatican; we have no precise dates here. The only son, Giovanni Gregorini, never married.

Baby Gregorini (or Adela Louise Montanari prior to her annulment) married a second time to Prince Pietro Colonna of the old Roman dynasty. The prince was governor of Rome under the Mussolini regime with his complete title as Prince Don Pietro Colonna; I have also seen Pietro spelled as "Piero" but believe such is a printing error in this case. His wife is not to be confused with Princess Isabelle (or Isabella) Colonna, married to Prince Marc-Antonio Colonna, an assistant to the papal throne and another scion of this old noble house. Princess Isabella was of Syrian origin (maiden name Sursok). Both the Prince and Princess Marc-Antonio Colonna possessed large wealth and entertained extensively at the Palazzo Colonna; they were also very close friends of Galeazzo Ciano, Mussolini's foreign minister who was housed in the Palazzo Chigi nearby. The Colonna family is an ancient one, still numerous, distinguished, and vigorous after more than a thousand years—probably longer, back to the Roman Empire. Colonna means "column," and the famous "Colonna Colonna" still stands majestically in the Piazza Colonna. The family name derives from this column featured on their arms or crest. The family has given cardinals and popes; during the Middle Ages, a large region in the vicinity of the Piazza Colonna was under their strict control and held with a chain of towers and fortification. This includes the Corso of today.

Another Colonna, Prospero, was mayor of Rome; he died in 1937. According to John Walton of Augusta, toward the end of World War II, Baby Colonna's sons joined the Allied Forces and entered Rome with the Army of Liberation. Her husband, Prince Pietro Colonna, appears to have died circa 1938. Baby Colonna and her children never came to Augusta; in the 1950-1960s when one Augusta couple who were related on the

CHAPTER EIGHT

Connelly side attempted to call on these Colonnas, they were rebuffed, as the tale goes.

We have no further details on Count Ugo Gregorini; however, his son told friends in Augusta Ugo sired illegitimate children. Giovanni created the impression that they were legion and used to say that in going about the streets of Bologna, he would see urchins who he could tell were the count's offspring! The taking of a lover in those days was no big deal, provided the parties came from the same social strata; what was not acceptable was for one of the parties to be of a lower social strata. So, according to Giovanni, his father was guilty of the latter behavior.

On the other hand, Countess Grace Gregorini and the Marchese Guglielmo Marconi (1874-1937) became great and good friends at some juncture. In Italy a marchese (marquess) is the rank next above a count and next below prince, so presumably this liaison was considered very comme il faut. Marconi was the famous electrical engineer and inventor from Bologna. Marconi invented a system of wireless telegraphy with the messages called "Marconi-grams" in the early years. His first patent was secured in 1896 in England where Marconi had schooling following his student days at the University of Bologna, founded in 425 A.D. and the oldest in Europe. Marconi had an Irish mother, and with an Italian father probably grew up completely bilingual. Marconi served in both the Italian army and navy and won the prestigious Nobel Prize for Physics in 1909. Marconi gave Grace beautiful pearls that she unfailingly wore and a most unusual brooch of a petrified Egyptian scarab surrounded with diamonds and perhaps other precious stones encrusted thereon. Genie Lehmann of Augusta reports Grace never took this pin off and even attached it to her nightgown! In Egypt, the scarab is sacred to the Sun God, was used in religion as a symbol, and featured in much Middle Kingdom jewelry. Many wore it as a good luck charm, as seemingly did Grace Gregorini. Marconi was nominated by the King of Italy to the Italian Senate in 1937, the same year he died. There is "Gregorini gossip," which cannot be substantiated at all, that Grace's son, Giovanni Gregorini, was actually Marconi's son! Pat Walsh of Augusta wrote that, based on a picture he saw of Marconi, he perceived a resemblance to Giovanni. However, he had never seen a picture of Count Ugo, nor has anyone now in Augusta.

In the 1930s, Grace, accompanied by her son, Giovanni, were making various visits to the United States, usually to escape the winters in Italy. After crossing by ship to New York, they went South and lived as already reported in the remaining portion of what had been the main King house before the fire in 1914. Apparently a blowtorch was being employed to take off old paint, and the wood, being old and very dry, caught fire. Only the kitchen, laundry room, and a few other sections were saved and remodeled to be habitable quarters for the Gregorinis. As per the provisions of his great uncle's will, this portion of what is today Pendleton King Park belonged to Giovanni for his lifetime. This is probably the crux of the legal action Giovanni now launched, as

CHAPTER EIGHT

he wanted to break the trust and take complete control and ownership immediately. In New York City in the mid 1930s, we hear of Grace and Giovanni stopping at the Ritz Hotel before traveling to Augusta; they were in touch with Mercer French, whose aunt was Maisie Chafee, a prominent Augusta resident, and who often visited her. Giovanni crossed once on the Acquitania and met his mother, who already was in New York, and then came South by boat. The French family was prosperous and well known in New York City.

Their last trip before the start of World War II appears to have been the winter or spring of 1939. As Grace had lost her US citizenship when she married (citizenship rules being vastly different then), she sought to have it reinstated and such was accomplished on this final trip to Augusta prior to the outbreak of war in September 1939. Why they went back considering the international situation is not known; maybe Giovanni could not get admitted for an indefinite stay or there were reasons we don't know about. But as long as Mussolini had power, there was a certain mantle of protection covering them due to the Colonna connection and perhaps even others. Pat Walsh of Augusta wrote that "Giovanni was not in anybody's army. He wasn't army material. He just was not disciplined enough." We don't know if the Italians hasseled Giovanni about not serving Italy during the early years of the war (Italy did not really enter until 1941), but in any case the Gregorini troubles seemed to commence with the break between Italy and Germany in 1943. According to Grace, their names were on a roster of hostages to be sent to a concentration camp in Germany. This is when they went into serious hiding; the same thing happened in Rome when many of the Italian leading families still in the capitol took refuge in neutral embassies, Spain, etc. We don't know where Grace hid in Bologna or elsewhere, but Giovanni was supposed to have spent time in a monastery posing as a monk. Another time he simulated a patient in a hospital. Some thought Giovanni's conduct during the war was not exactly exemplary and were harsh on him!

As the Germans retreated up the Italian peninsula, they occupied the Gregorini villa and caused much damage. When Dawson Teague of Augusta visited and stayed with them in the early 1950s, they stood on and showed him the wooden floor and tile under which silver and valuables had been hidden; they were then living in the villa. Immediately following World War II, they resided in what had been the stable, as the main house had been seized, probably by the then Communist city government in control of Bologna—this latter fact from Cassius Clay of Augusta as he visited them in the very early post-war period. He told me Grace seemed very ancient, but I would estimate her age then around seventy-four or seventy-five. But to a very young man at that time three score plus ten indeed was old! By the time Dawson Teague arrived, they had taken back control of their villa, which Dawson said was an easy stroll from the town center. Giovanni, at that time, had a dog called "Pulcho" ("flea" in Italian) who had a sort of ruff made of his hair around his neck. Giovanni died in late

CHAPTER EIGHT

1952 or early 1953 of stomach cancer, but prior to his illness again had accompanied his mother on several trips to Augusta right after World War II. I met him myself twice, once circa 1939 at John Walton's house on Walton Way and again around 1946 or 1947 at a party given in the old Thomas House at Christmas time when we all were home from school.

According to Pat Walsh of Augusta, people here thought Grace and Giovanni Gregorini were hard as nails and used people shamelessly. However, on the final visits to Augusta made by Grace, she was accompanied by her daughter, who was then Lady Humphrey Gale. This was Minnie, whose first husband was Prince de Beauveau-Craon. Pat Walsh wrote that on these trips to Augusta with her mother "she was truly a lady in every sense of the word. She was so gracious and perfectly lovely." We write more about this Minnie in the next section relative to the French family. No one now in Augusta knows when Grace, Countess Ugo Gregorini, passed away. But it was in Italy where she presumably was buried with her husband and only son. Today only the Colonna descendants remain in Rome, Bologna, or elsewhere. I found among the papers of Mary Lou Phinizy a wedding invitation from "Donna Adele Luisa Colonna" to the marriage of her daughter Mary Elena Colonna on January 18, 1956, in Rome. This discovery probably indicates Grace still was alive then and remembering old Augusta friends. "Donna Mary Elena" married the Count Marco Bucci Casari. The Bucci family gave their address as Piazza Farnese 44, Rome, while the then Colonna address appears to be one of the Colla Rome residences or palaces. This find was one of the usual double-sided European nuptial summons from both sets of parents but with no mention of any reception.

The French Family:

Minnie (Minna) Gregorini, also called Maria in Italian, age twenty-three, married Prince Charles-Louis de Beauveau-Craon on March 27, 1920, in Bologna. The prince was about forty years old then and died circa 1942 at the family estate, Chateau de Haroué, located in the province of Lorraine, twenty minutes south from Nancy. We know there was an only son, and if there were daughters we possess no details. Their son, Prince Mark de Beauveau-Craon, joined the Free French during World War II and was sent to Maxwell Field near Montgomery, Alabama, to train and become a pilot. This was about 1943. The prince was short on cash, so he came to Augusta to determine if he could get some money to tide him over. What funds his maternal grandmother Grace Gregorini might have had apparently were impounded by the Alien Property Custodian (even though Grace was again a US citizen but in Italy). So the prince was unable to touch any of these assets, and an Augusta group of friends (of Grace and the Kings), including Mary Lou Phinizy, John Walton, et al, made up a purse of around $1,500 to put him in solvency. The prince repaid them promptly when family monies again were available.

CHAPTER EIGHT

Following the end of World War II, Prince Mark married a Patiño from the fabulously wealthy South American family who had emigrated permanently to France once their tin-mining holdings in Bolivia were nationalized. The couple had two daughters: Minnie and Diane de Beauveau-Craon. Both seem to now live mainly in Paris, where some of them at least are part of "le tout Paris," so one gathers from the papers and journals who report on those in the "public eye" (as the French would say!). We hear that Prince Mark and Miss Patiño long ago parted company; however, one interesting fact is that another Patiño lady, sister to Prince Mark's wife, eloped with the English Sir James Goldsmith (then an unknown) even though the Patiño family strongly opposed the match. The Goldsmiths had a baby girl who was raised with the two de Beauveau-Craon girls, as her mother died under very mysterious circumstances.

Dawson Teague of Augusta visited the Chateau de Haroué twice, once about 1965 with his wife and one child, and on one earlier occasion. He was received by Minnie (now Lady Humphrey Gale) and some of her French de Beauveau-Craon grandchildren for, by this time, it was after the death of Prince Charles-Louis in 1942. Probably when World War II was over, Minnie remarried to Sir Humphrey Gale, who served with General Eisenhower in Paris at Shape and then later with the Foreign Office, NATO (when the move was made to Belgium), and perhaps at the United Nations. At one point, the Gales lived in London at No. 8 Cheyne Walk, Chelsea, and then later on retirement occupied one of the "Grace and Favor" flats at Hampton Court Palace. From the news reports, we can gather that the widowed Lady Gale actually started the fire in the early 1990s, when one of her many candles caught a drapery. There was quite a conflagration which ensued, and it appears Lady Gale also lost her life at this time. We have no hard details on this very tragic end to the charming and lovely Minnie Gregorini-Bingham de Beauveau-Craon Gale.

It is a real pity I have been unable to discover more facts on the current King descendants in France or in Italy for that matter. Minnie de Beauveau-Craon went to France to live in 1920, so her great aunt Minna Anglesey was still living in Versailles; did Aunt Minna help in making this match? Was there interaction with Prince Mark as a child, and what about her niece Grace Gregorini and great nephew Giovanni in Bologna, as well as the Colonna family in Rome? Were these Europeans, and particularly those residing in France, known to the American writer Julian Green, born in Paris in 1900 to American parents who originally came from Savannah, Georgia? Green spent his early life in the South and graduated from the University of Virginia; he wrote in both English and French and was the only foreign member of the Academie Francaise. I did write to both the Anglesey and Beauveau-Craon families in England and France for assistance with the help of the British and French Consulate Generals in Atlanta: no response to date. In 1965, when Dawson Teague mentioned the family Gregorini to Somerset Maugham in Cap Ferrat, the old author acknowledged the connection. He definitely

CHAPTER EIGHT

knew Lady Anglesey in France, and through this devoted friend of his mother most likely the Gregorini-Binghams and Colonnas in Italy. So I must now end these sketches as such do encompass all information extant and at present known to me.

One rather entertaining postscript is the letter sent to the editor of the *Augusta Chronicle* in February 2003 indicating how strange stories can grow over the years as they become less factual and even filled with gross inaccuracies. The reply to the *Chronicle* is also included, but I do not know if such was ever printed:

Deceased Fiat Leader Lived Here:

> In the Jan. 27 *Chronicle,* you picked up the story of Fiat leader Giovanni Gregorini Agnelli. You missed the fact that he lived in Augusta during the 1930s. His mother was a sister to Mrs. Henry B. King, who owned the King Mill, the Georgia Railroad, the Georgia Railroad Bank and a lot of miscellaneous real estate.
>
> Their only son had died around 1919 of the flu. Mr. King died around 1931. Mrs. King, who was an Italian countess, had her sister join her here with her son Giovanni. When Mrs. King died, she left her huge estate to her nephew, who then took the proceeds from the sale of all this and bought Fiat motors in Italy.
>
> My uncle and I worked Mrs. King's flower gardens for her and, at 80 years of age, I can still

hear his mother calling him for the evening meal. It was almost like a song as she would call out, "Giovanni Gregorini.

I hope this will refresh the memory of others in the area and get them to come forward with associated details of this interesting story.

Lindsay L. Wood
McCormick, South Carolina

RE Death of Gianni Agnelli": Letter of 2/11/03 (think this is date) from L. L. Wood

In reply to Mr. Wood's letter, as I noted on the phone, I think he has the facts wrong. This is because:

1) There is no relationship by blood that is known between the King, Gregorini and Agnelli families.
2) Gianni Agnelli's mother was named Virginia Bourbon del Monte, and she was ½ American in that her mother was Jane Allen Campbell married to Carlo Bourbon del Monte. The latter was granted the title of Prince of San Faustino by Pope Pius IX. Hence, his mother was not sister to Mrs. H. B. King as Mr. Wood writes.
3) Giovanni Gregorini is another person whose surname is Gregorini and not Agnelli; his mother was Grace King Connelly (maiden name) married to Count Ugo Gregorini

CHAPTER EIGHT

who fathered two daughters and the one son discussed here.

4) Grace Connelly Gregorini was the niece of Henry King, so Mrs. H. B. King was her aunt by marriage. Mrs. King was Elizabeth Cashin prior to marriage.

5) Grace Connelly Gregorini was the Italian countess and not Mrs. King.

6) The Gregorinis always lived in Bologna and not Turin, which Fiat and Agnellis still call home. However, it is quite possible both families did know one another socially, being from Northern Italy and with each family having an American connection as explained above.

7) While the King family did own shares in the Georgia ventures noted by Mr. Wood, they most certainly did not own them entirely. Fiat in Italy, as far as I know, had nothing to do with the King Family and their estate.

8) Fiat was founded in Turin in 1899 by Giovanni Agnelli, the grandfather of Gianni Agnelli. Gianni's father was Edoardo Agnelli, who died in a plane crash in 1935 in Genoa.

My data comes from family knowledge (as we were friends for years), my meeting once with Countess Gregorini in Augusta years ago and on several occasions with her son, Giovanni Gregorini. This after World War II on their visits to Augusta. Giovanni never married, but there are Gregorini descendants today in

France and Italy, we believe; also having been requested to write a short history of Pendleton King Park, I have been gathering information. Finally, I am now in touch with the great-niece of Mrs. Henry B. King.

Please do <u>not</u> publish my name or address if you print this; however Mr. Wood ought to know the facts, so kindly inform him.

Sincerely yours,
Bowdre P. Mays

<u>A Final Note to the Reader:</u>

    The facts, comments, opinions, conjectures, and stories set out in these sketches may be candid and frank but are not intended to hurt anyone still alive or to besmirch the memory of those dead, whether family relations or friends. I wrote to honor and record mainly for posterity the fascinating tale of the King family in Augusta and Europe. After the "French Family Section" was finished some time ago, the writer learned that Prince Mark (Marc in French) died in 1982 with the Beauveau-Craon family then becoming extinct on the male side.

    The author of "Crowning Glory", Richard Jay Hutto of Macon, Georgia, also advises that Minna Anglesey's body was taken back to England by the Anglesey family and then buried in the Paget Cemetery on the island of Anglesey beside her husband.

B.P.M. June 2013

CHAPTER EIGHT

Augusta Canal Stone on Louise King Connelly and Henry Cumming Lamar drowning, 1891

IS LIVING WELL STILL THE BEST REVENGE?

King Family Home (now burned) in the King Park

CHAPTER EIGHT

Pendleton King in World War I uniform

IS LIVING WELL STILL THE BEST REVENGE?

Count Giovanni Gregorini, son of Grace and Ugo Gregorini

CHAPTER EIGHT

The Dower Marchioness of Anglesey, formerly Minna King of Georgia, and Harry Melville, visiting Elsie and Bessie in Versailles just before the turn of the century. Elsie credited Minna Anglesey with introducing her to French antiques and vegetarianism. COLLECTION OF TONY DUQUETTE

Minna King Anglesey, circa 1900 in Versailles

CHAPTER IX

John Walton and Pat Walsh: The Best of Friends

I first recall John Walton from about 1935 when Grandmother Doughty rented his front-beach cottage at Edisto Beach, South Carolina, so that my parents and the then four children would be able to have a summer idyl during June and July at the seashore. That was the spring/summer Grandmother traveled to the Orient with her close friend, Nina White, on a Garden Club of America-sponsored trip to California, Hawaii, and Japan with later side visits to China and Korea (then a Japanese colony). My parents, however, had become quite friendly with John several years earlier when he had returned to Augusta from France; while they all on both sides were Augustans, there was an age difference, so aside from being aware of each other much earlier in life, they were not close. Also one of Mother's best friends during teenage years was Anne Campbell who knew John perhaps better due to their separate Johns Road residency at one stage and the visit Anne made to China in 1924 while John lived there with his mother and stepfather.

I think my parents first saw him after France, circa 1932-1933, at a supper party given by Louise Del'aigle Reese at her Meigs Street winter residence then more frequently at other Augusta functions and parties. John, Frank, and Bowdre soon became fast friends: they asked him to be a godfather to their last child, Sam, born February 8, 1937. They were often in and out of each other's houses as I grew up and always saw or entertained John's mother, known as "Miss Julia," on her visits to Augusta from Austin, Texas, after 1936.

Pat Walsh I knew far less well. I first recall seeing him at one of the Saturday night dances at the country club when very late in the evening he did his "soft shoe" routine in the ballroom of the original clubhouse. He then was with his close friends I think, Craig Cranston and Heard Robertson. Then on another club occasion, he introduced me to a distant cousin, Marion Coles Phinizy, with whom I guess he had a date. When I was discharged from active duty in the army in February 1945, I worked for several months at the Augusta Arsenal as a messenger awaiting the commencement of the summer term at the University of Georgia. Pat then had a responsible

CHAPTER NINE

position in the Arsenal Finance Department and being on my delivery route, I saw him frequently in the same office where my Doughty cousin, Betty Councill, also was employed.

When I told Genie Lehmann of my plan to include a chapter on John Walton (who was a cousin on her mother's side) and requested input, she suggested I expand a bit also including a section on Pat Walsh as the two were very close friends in their adult lives. This I was happy to do, particularly since in later years Lynn and I were in fairly regular touch with Pat after our December 1983 visit to San Francisco where he had moved from Augusta. We returned to Europe in 1984, living then for six years in Athens, Greece, and during this period corresponded at some length; then there were many telephone calls and letters following our return to the United States in 1990 and my retirement in 1992. Pat had an exceptional memory and provided a good deal of "Augusta data" on many of the subjects covered in these chapters even including my own family! We never met in person after 1983, but he told Augusta friends how much he liked Lynn!

John Moore Walton was born in Augusta on July 28, 1898, being the sole child of Maurice (pronounced Morris) J. Walton and his wife, Julia Scales Jackson. Both parents came from prominent local families; one Walton ancestor was the well-known American patriot George Walton, a signer of the Declaration of Independence. Maurice was the youngest child of five born to his parents, William Augustus Walton and his wife, Elizabeth

Adams Moore. There was an older brother, John Moore Walton, so "our John" must have been named for his paternal uncle who also seems to have practiced law with their own father, William Augustus. Unfortunately, John's father died very suddenly when he was about forty-seven years of age in 1913; they were living at 1206 Greene Street where he passed away in the night. His two physicians gave the estimated diagnosis as an "attack of acute dilation of the heart."

Maurice Walton was a successful businessman, owning real estate, and had been president of the Merchants Bank, vice president of the Chamber of Commerce, as well as a director of various associations. Maurice and Julia were married in 1897; by the time of his premature death in 1913, all the members of his immediate family had died, so the survivors were only the widow Julia and fifteen-year-old son, John. Mary Lou Phinizy used to say John had occupied his mother's bed until he was twelve; I doubt this unless Julia and Maurice had given up a joint marital bed soon following his birth in 1898!

Mary Lou Bussey's father, Donald, was a Greene Street contemporary of John Walton when they were growing to young maturity; Donald told her that Maurice Walton had asked "Donnie" to teach John how to hunt and fish. Does this request sort of indicate Maurice himself was too busy with his business endeavors to spend much time with his only child? John attended the University of Georgia in Athens 1916-1917 and the University of Virginia in Charlottesville from which he graduated with a degree in law. He was a Chi Phi fraternity member.

CHAPTER NINE

John apparently had to register for the military draft September 12, 1918, in Augusta; he and his mother then were living at 934 Johns Road. He stated he was a "law student" employed with Irvin Alexander and then described as "short and slender, with blue eyes and light brown hair." One of his friends in Augusta, George Barrett, a later lawyer, always called him "Demi-John," as per George's eldest daughter, Mary Robertson, who as I did also saw a lot of John growing up (he always had time for the younger generations) and in the ensuing years following her own marriage. John did not serve in the US military in World War I, but was not so lucky during World War II as will be explained further ahead as we continue to review his life.

After graduating from the University of Virginia in 1919, when John was twenty-one, he and Johnny Evans (later the father of Helen Evans Blitch) went on a trip to Europe. When they returned, probably in the autumn of 1919, John requested the permission of his mother Julia to allow him to go and live in Paris. She agreed, and so John went to Paris in about 1920; Miss Julia had arranged for him to live in a pension run by the widow of a Protestant minister at 51 Rue Claude Bernard. Her name was Madame Foustaire (pronounced "foo-stare"); John stayed on in this pension until some date in 1923, and during those years also made arrangements for Adele Petit (who came to Paris to study piano under some famous pianist) of Augusta to stay at the same pension. These were apparently very happy years for all concerned.

At this time, John had no capital of his own so he was wholly dependent on his mother's allowance; this was likely barely adequate to cover his living expenses. However, we do know he was writing book reviews for the *Chicago Tribune* (this paper has made several attempts to become established with a regular Paris edition but seemingly has never succeeded even though there was a Paris edition in the early twenties) to earn a little extra cash and also may have had some connection with William Bird and the Three Mountains Press which published a work or more by Ezra Pound. At this stage of his life, John did have aspirations to become a writer so this is another reason for his work with the *Chicago Tribune*, and the articles sent for publication in the *Augusta Chronicle*. Articles published in Augusta carried bylines of both London and Paris, and following I am copying two of the 1922 Paris features sent to Augusta:

I.

MAINTENON
The Chateau

Few foreigners who come to France go to Maintenon. That is why I went. The Chateau of Maintenon is not even mentioned in the guide books and its existence in no way adds another burden to the weary traveler. Before the exhausting summer is over the ubiquitous Americans feel as if they must do something desperate the next time a cathedral, or a palace, or an art gallery is mentioned. The parties usually start at Naples with the same baggage

CHAPTER NINE

handicap and the same delicious course with Paris as the ultimate goal. These races might be called potato races except that the potatoes are left out. Their omission is easily explained. In such a race there is grave danger of dropping the potatoes and the Americans have no time to stop and pick up anything. The object of most American tours on the continent is to see how many cities can be visited in three months. As I understand the rules you are permitted to count the places with railroad station in which you exited between trains for half an hour. Just the other day I was talking to a gentleman who was utterly aghast at the useless number of days that I have spent already in Paris when the whole of France lies around as yet unseen. This particular gentleman in his travel lust had something of the thirst of the American Indians for scalps. He recounted boastfully his rush through Italy where he spent the night in Florence whence he departed early, rode for an hour on the Grand Canal of Venice, and had lunch in the Milan cathedral!

Feeling that I needed a little change from the city, I looked about me the other day for some quiet community near Paris. The village of Maintenon is on the outskirts of Paris with express trains passing by that land you on the great shed of the Gare Monteparnasse in half an hour. So at the earnest solicitation of my friend, Mademoiselle Mochelet, I boarded one of those expresses. At present the Chateau is private property inaccessible to the general public and had it not been for a permit obtained for me by the Grand Mademoiselle I would have been compelled to admire from afar. After alighting from the train I went immediately to the imitation hotel on the main square directly opposite the Chateau gate. No time was lost in seeking the garden where I afterwards spent several very happy hours browsing around.

Maintenon is not a very large Chateau, but it is exceedingly well proportioned. It has something of the intimacy, the homelike simplicity of Malmaison which makes that spot, beloved by Josephine and Eugenie, the favorite also of the Paris Sunday excursionists. Low turrets projecting at every angle, and the moat filled with clear water, lend to the place quite a medieval atmosphere. In the limpid morning air the garden was beautiful. Small and unpretentious with long narrow beds of geraniums and salvia laid methodically on the great, damp, green, carpet. At the command of Louis XIV Le Notre, the famous landscapist of Versailles and Chantilly, undertook the arrangement of the part of the garden contiguous to the Chateau. The parterres, the two or three faintly traceable terraces and the pools, show clearly the result of his workmanship. This is about the simplest garden that he laid out in the environs of Paris, the least formal. Farther on Nature has been allowed to take her course and it is miraculous how wonderfully the two widely divergent types blend into one harmonious whole. It reminds you of the Louvre, the great repository of all French art. There

CHAPTER NINE

are to be found the flighty canvasses of Watteau and his school, perpetuating the empty frivolities and artificialities of the Bourbon courts there are the more recent works of Millet whose great privilege it was to illustrate the majesty of manual labor. Thus if we are observant can we read history on every side without opening a book, for each generation has left its impress in every field of human endeavor.

Now for a bit of the history of Maintenon. The Chateau once belonged to the powerful Noailles family. The picture gallery is paneled with life-size portraits of this family done in oil. Many generations stand proudly before you garbed in the latest style of the age to which they belonged. The Marquis Jeanne de Noailles who was killed at Crecy in 1415 stands, sword in hand, at one end of the long narrow hall. He is very striking in his shining armor. Facing him from the other end is the famous Louis Antoine. Cardinal de Noailles in his flowing red robes. Madame de Maintenon and her little niece occupy the middle panel and they are the only intruders. It is easy to picture in minds eye the wonderful widow in this long gallery receiving a visit from His Majesty the King. In the early part of the century which witnessed the battles of William of Orange, Marlborough, and Turenne in Flanders, when the vacant Spanish throne was offered to Phillip of Anjou, grandson of the French king, and Bourbon ambitions knew no limit, there was an unknown woman in France who is considered today as one of the most remarkable women the world has ever produced. For she combined brains with beauty, something rarely found. Madame de Montespan, the king's mistress, entrusted to this woman, the widow Scarron, the education of her sons. It was in this way that Madame Scarron was thrown with the king whose children she trained so well. When the children were old enough to be emancipated from their governess Louis wished to show to Madame Scarron his appreciation of her services. He was always interested in the welfare of beautiful ladies. For years the poor widow had been longing for an establishment of her own, and the king found this out. No Louis XIV never did things half way. He was God's representative on earth, and he said that the power to tax is limited only by the king's pleasure. It is easy to do things nicely when others pay the bill. So in the year 1674 the king bought the Chateau and started LeNotre on the grounds. He had in the previous year conferred upon the widow Scarron the title of Madame de Maintenon, had legitimated his offspring, and introduced their governess at court. Shortly after she was installed in her new home Madame de Maintenon wrote to a friend, "My heart is fixed here." What a delusion! For heart are rarely fixed anywhere if the same body possess much brain power. Maintenon seldom saw its charming proprietress. We cannot follow the widow to court where she struggled for ten years for her ascendancy over

CHAPTER NINE

the king, and finally forced the wicked monarch to marry her, and return to the church and end his days in respectability instead of the sensuous senility that seemed eminent. For those deeds belong to the annals of Versailles and not to our modest Maintenon.

The last time that Maintenon figured in history was when the feeble Charles X, the last of the Bourbon kings, fleeing from France after the July Revolution, stopped here for the night.

The Aqueduct

Near the Chateau is the aqueduct of the Grand Monarch. Crumbled and vine covered, it seems to belong to the Roman campagnia rather than to modern France. Of all the foolish schemes of Louis Quatorze this was the most calamitous. The king wished to bring the waters of the Eure to Versailles that the countless fountains might play. There was not sufficient force from this stream to supply the gardens and the project was finally abandoned for another. But this was not until after 10,000 workmen had been engaged for months in constructing the aqueduct and 50 million francs had been expended. The treasury was drained to the last sous and in the swampy bottoms the workmen died of malaria. Why look any farther for the cause of the great cataclysm that over ran France? Today the gigantic arches of the aqueduct stand as monuments to the unknown who died uselessly, and as a memorial to the folly of the Sun King. It never fails to arouse great interest and admiration. How strange that the remainder of the wholesale injustices and wickedness of the past have for us all such a strong appeal!

Monsiour Lussac

Before I left Maintenon I became quite a friend of one hotel properitor. That worthy individual had no better occupation than to lean over his desk in the little lobby and talk at length upon the state of the country, the coming election, and anything else that occurred to him. In France the last report in conversation is no longer the weather, it is the brutality of the Boches. But my friend generally found wide scope in the doings of the neighbors-men never gossip and in imparting all the information available on the few guests beneath his roof. His apology for idleness was the explanation that Maintenon is neither here nor there. It is too close to Paris to be a good place for travelers. The thought of a wayside inn only half an hour from the city is ridiculous so the little hotel is never full.

One day I was talking to the proprietor-clerk as usual when one of the guests passed. My friend beckoned to me and leaned way over the desk with all the gravity which he employed when there was a choice morsel forthcoming. He motioned to the stranger going out and then said: "That is Monsieur Lussac."

CHAPTER NINE

To his consternation I registered blank and he was forced to go into details. "Monsieur Lussac comes from Senlis and is here only for his vacation. You know that Senlis was in the line of the Boches and that the city was completely destroyed. The bombs set fire to several buildings in different parts of the town and soon everything was gone, even the beautiful cathedral. My cousin, who lives in Senlis, told me of the dreadful time the people had and of the wonderful work of Monsieur Lussac. You know Monsieur Lussac is one of the prominent citizens, but he is not like most of the prominent citizens — I wish you could hear my cousin tell of the work of that man for the relief of suffering and the rebuilding of homes for the people. No body makes any fuss over Monsieur Lussac and it is a good thing, for he does not want it. He is not that kind at all: My cousin says that it is a funny thing how you don't hear of Monsieur Lussac in Senlis until somebody gets in trouble; then you are sure to hear his name. For they all call on him when ever there is distress, and organization and work to be done for charities. The whole town turns to Monsieur Lussac right away.

He has many interests but none of them surpass the interest in his fellow citizens. And they don't seem to know that they do it. Now isn't that a fine position to have made for oneself in a community?"

After this tale-which was told at length-was finished, I went up to my room, puzzled by what I had just heard. Some how it all seemed so familiar to me.

I felt as though I could have interrupted him and have finished it as well as he did. Surely Monsieur Lussac of Senlis was a stranger to me. I went over again every work that the proprietor has said and I racked my brain. All of a sudden when I saw the great flames leaping from house to house and licking the walls of the church completely enveloped, it came to me like a flash. I had solved the mystery, a veritable Sherlock Holmes I was right. I had known Monsieur Lussac before, but it was in a different city and even a different country. And they call him there William H. Barrett.

> John M. Walton
> Paris, France

II.

PUBLIC CONVEYANCES

In Paris, getting about is the simplest matter in the world, even for the man who has no car and cannot afford a taxi. Manhattan should learn the art from Paris, this facility of moving crowds. The Sunday throngs that approach to Chantilly, Versailles and the other neighboring chateaux do not create the congestion that occurs twice daily in little old New York. But the problem confronting the two cities is by no means the same, nor is it solvable in the same fashion. For the failure of Manhattan to handle her millions is attributable principally to her huge office buildings downtown that enable more people to work and live in one square inch than is say four or

CHAPTER NINE

five blocks of sprawling Paris Naturally these toilers *stop* at the same hour and all rush for the same street cars, subways, and busses. Paris has no skyscrapers. Here is another argument against them—she avoids mad rushes, the trampling and fainting of women. Interborough Rapid Transit Co. strikes and constant elevation of fares.

It is not necessary to speak French to get about in Paris. Every thing is labeled and usually there is an alternative in getting close to one's destination. The street cars present to me the nearest thing to a problem. They retain still many secrets that my inquiring mind has not yet fathomed. For instance, why should they have large letters on the front? There must be some plausible explanation. These capitals do not appear singly nor doubly: sometimes they are *even* triple. "A" "M" and "F" "M" are frequently rounding the corner. In spite of yourself, it is annoying to board a car marked "A. M." when you know perfectly well that you have had lunch long ago and it is late afternoon. Then too, there is "B.C." The first time I saw one of this variety I felt that the letters were misplaced – they belonged on some cars that some of us have seen in Georgia. But these letters do not interfere with the directions which are also placed on the front. The system of boarding cars is both novel and just. In busy neighborhoods on bussing corners one always finds on the lampposts little tickets of this tissue paper with numbers on them. These are to be torn off, one for each person. When the car arrives those who have stood longest are rewarded first by getting on as their numbers are called. Then too there is the first and second class. The car is divided in the middle and the front is for the first class passengers. Though France is a republic there is nowhere that you cannot by paying a little more be in a higher class than somebody else. The French are very brazen about these the same today and Democracy is the bag of gold at the rainbow's end. Speaking of paying, the fares of the Paris cars are regulated by arbitrary sections or divisions of the city. Whenever you cross one of these lines late another district you pay more than if your entire route should lie within one section. Even at that the system is more just than the ten cent fare of which some of us have heard. But then in France labor is cheaper by far than in America and many of the street railway employees are women. The conductors job seems to be an easy one. All those conductresses dress alike in black with a kind of overseas cap and one varieties of horns, small but shrill, which she toots with a vengeance whenever she is ready for the car to start. They are very efficient- women always are good at small things. And no one can blame them for stopping at small tasks. They have discovered that they are not paid for what they do. Who wants to work for nothing?

But let us go on to the subway, another easy method of getting about. The Paris subway system is generally acknowledged the best in the world. There is none of the uncertainty of direction of New York

CHAPTER NINE

and there are no green lines to follow there is none: of the hopeless tediousness of the London underground, none of the impossibility of getting to places. You can not only get everywhere by using the Metropolitan and the Nord-Dod-the two main subway lines-but you can have the satisfaction of knowing that your direction is right. For there are plain charts and lists of station on all the walls for the men who can read. You do not move as rapidly as in New York. There you can console yourself amid the confusion by remarking upon the velocity of the train.

Then finally there are the busses that ply the Grand Boulevards. Huge cumbersome things that rattle along carrying some thirty odd persons at a time. And usually they are odd. But really this is the most effective and agreeable means of transportation in Paris for purses that are thin. And for everything there are tickets, sometimes two and sometimes three. The printers guild no doubt flourishes in France. At first all this red tape is irritating: then you wonder where the profit lies for the corporation that supports all these distributors and collectors of tickets: then you accept the situation automatically. It is extraordinary how quickly we all adjust ourselves to foreign conditions and customs.

Ed Pinaud

Frequenters of barbershops need no introduction to Mr. Edward Pinaud. He is the hair tonic gentleman whose attractive advertisements embellish the walls of our most select tonsorial parlors. He it was who gave me one of my rudest shocks in Paris. The Place Vendome is familiar to all who have been here. For years and years it has stood, this square, with the same facades facing it, the same column of victory in the center surmounted by an iron statue of the Emperor Napoleon I. The column was erected to commemorate his military glories and is an exact replica of that of the Emperor Trojan in Rome. It is true that in the seventies the commoners in their fury tore down the column and destroyed the statue; but later it was restored and another statue, a reproduction of the original now looks down upon what? Napoleon is advised to see Ed Pinaud's hair tonic! Never can Paris laugh at America's grotesque, ubiquitous sign boards. I have never been so surprised as to see there in capitals the name of Ed Pinaud. One would think that the strategic position of the Place Vendome would be its greatest security against vandalism; for it is just between the fashionable Rue de la Paix and the more fashionable Rue de Rivoli. But not so. That is the great advantage to such as enterprising individual as Mr. Pinaud. Close beside Mr. Pinaud is the banking house of Mr. J. Pierpont Morgan. I once had a conversation with one of Mr. Morgan's able corps who told me in his righteous indignation that the city would not permit his firm to change the façade of the building. They could alter and moderate the interior, but the front must retain

CHAPTER NINE

some resemblance to its former self. I suppose he wanted to replace this dingy old exterior with a nice new skyscraper in white marble. Skyscrapers and hair tonics are all right, but for everything there is a place and the Place Vendome is hardly worthy of these honors.

Opposite Mr. Pinaud is the Hotel Ritz. And that is not the only name that familiarly greets again the stroller of Broadway and Fifth Avenue. Tecia the pearl firm, is in Paris; Cartier; Hanan's shoe store; Brentano's book store; the Equitable Trust Co.; and the Banker's Trust; Wanamaker's; Gimbel's; and other department stores; Worth; Louise and manifold modistes and so on ad inifinitum. Of course, the steamship lines great and small abound and countless tourist agencies lead by the redoubtable American Express Co. magnificently enshrined at 11 Rue Scribe. Often you can wheedle yourself into thinking you are in New York. And it must be the same to the Londoner and the Roman for Paris partakes of a little of everything.

The most frequently recurring sign in Paris is "Patisserie" or "Pastry Shop". We have no such institutions in America and I regret that in this grave matter we are woefully deficient. Congressman Vinson must be urged to propose a bill in the house, for even Dr. Land at the corner of Twelfth and Broad does not substitute. He who has been dealt the privilege of a real French pastry in a patisserie will search Webster in vain for a definition of the word "delectable". These are tarts and puffs, éclairs, and cakes mercilessly displayed in windows before which wistful passerby of al ages stand and sigh. I know that it seems childish to those at home, but nevertheless it is true. I am reminded of Miss Pynchen who kept her little shop with the bell on the door that rang when you opened it to enter the House of Seven Gables in Old Salem. She, poor thing, was vainly striving to attain to some such height as the French patisserie. Always even till my dying day, will I regret that we in America have no patisseries. And I am forced to the conclusion that after all there are many things of greater import than a naval program and an Association of Nations.

Then too, there are naturally many boulangeries and boucheries (bakeries and butcheries). The bakers are vendors of that firm, crisp French bread which everybody enjoys–French rolls. Occasionally one sees a sign "Boucherie Chevelein." Or Horse Meat shop. I am told that this announcement is required by law and that nothing else is obtainable within. Of course horse meat is not the delicacy in France that snails are, on the contrary, it is eaten only by the very impoverished and today has lost its war popularity. Poor old animals! After years of strenuous service on crowded streets and boulevards, after narrow escapes from flitting taxis, aged and decrepitates neurotic quadrupeds meet with such a miserable and ignominious finals. The way of the transgressor is not the only hard one.

CHAPTER NINE

The tobacco shops of Paris aspire to no such pretenses as our cigar stores that cluster around the Albion and the Confederate Monument. They are generally narrow little rooms right down on the streets as crowded as an Eastern bazaar. The sign of the "Tabac" is two cornucopias placed one on top of the other and painted red. In the tobacco shop one always finds stamps for sale one of the few places, if not the only one outside of the post offices. But "voltare" money will not buy tobacco, for it is not really money. It is made for the convenience of the transportation companies, this carriage money, and has a street car on it a prosaic substitute for Louis Napoleon or the figure of the Republic of France.

In the subways, on the cars and in every place the law permits one sees extensively advertised "Byrrh," and "Dubonnet". These beverages evidently corresponds to our "Cocoa cola" at founts in bottles. I am not competent to compare them with our "dope" It is certain that they have not the hold on the population that cocoa cola has obtained below the Mason and Dixon line. Often I have wondered just what success the promoters of this beverage have met with whether they live in marble palaces constructed after the style of that of Mr. Asa Candler on Druid Hills in Atlanta and if they do, whether they are so benevolent as he is reported to be. Somehow I rather doubt it. The French are by no means the world's most capable instructors in all things desirable. Even America, the newborn babe in the national family, has already met some excellent paces for the old world.

The Eighteenth Amendment

My reference to the so-called "soft drinks" makes apropos here a few words on one of the most vital questions is in the life of our nation: The whisky question. Technically the question exists no more; it has to all intents and purposes been set at rest in the most effective way at the hands of the American electorate. By constitutional amendment. As a result we have an anomalous situation. In France everybody drinks and nobody is drunk. In America nobody drinks and everybody is drunk. This is of course, an exaggeration, but anyway the result in America today is deplorable. The constitution of the United States a document which some of us choose to consider impeccable is violated daily before our very eyes. Mr. Bryan and the hosts of good people, who assisted in the passage of the amendment were no doubt actuated by the noblest of motives; but they are too big and broad to deny today that for some reason havoc has been wrought. Whether we should have prohibition or not is to my mind a petty issue lost in the appalling calamity, the levity with which Americans of the highest type disregard the fundamental law of their land. I ignore the prohibition question. I refuse to discuss it. There is but one real question, one alternative: shall we repeal the eighteenth amendment or

CHAPTER NINE

shall we uphold and enforce it with accustomed rigor of the law. Either course would mean the preservation of our self-respect, the triumph of American government. Any other course would be the first step on the downward path, the subversion of the constitution. As it is here it is intolerable. We must set and act quickly for the safety of all those things which we hold nearest and dearest.

John M. Walton
Paris, France

Pat Walsh wrote that one of John's greatest sorrows was that he was not mentioned in his father's will. Maurice Walton left everything to his wife for her lifetime, and, "if she is not survived by issue" to various relatives; four or five were named in his will. In addition, Mr. Walton had a large (for the time) life insurance policy of which Miss Julia also was the beneficiary. John said it was the largest life insurance policy anyone in Augusta ever had up to 1913; it was thought to be around $75,000. The foregoing is the prologue to what must have been word from Miss Julia circa 1923 that she intended to follow Dr. William Richardson Houston to China and marry him there. John returned to Augusta in 1923, and just prior to her departure for China to join Dr. Houston, Miss Julia took John to Judge Barrett's office to draw up the necessary documents to settle on John what remained of the funds she had received as the sole life insurance beneficiary. Miss Julia from all accounts had been left well-to-do by Maurice Walton with other assets plus real estate holdings, so this transfer very likely presented no real problem to her.

John said this was $60,000, which in 1923 probably was equivalent to say $600,000 today. The $60,000 was John's initial capital and all he had to live on until Miss Julia died in 1952. John apparently felt his mother had abandoned him and for a time was rudderless! He went to North Carolina and Virginia to visit relatives on the Scales side as Miss Julia had sold the Johns Road house when she made the decision to move to China. Pat Walsh then said John too left for China (also in 1923) so he managed to cram a lot of activity into that one year!

Now before dwelling further on the John Walton life saga, it is advisable to bring into this narrative a clearer word picture of Julia Walton and her second husband, Dr. William R. Houston, both fascinating persons of charm. Miss Julia I saw in her later years on visits to John from Texas; she was as well described by Jane D. Chandler in her 1986-1987 monograph "Dr. Murphey and His Friends": "small, attractive and extremely feminine." She tended to be a bit intellectual but definitely not a "bluestocking"; she was also Dr. Houston's intellectual companion as well as his wife, and the doctor from all accounts had a huge intellect. Pat Walsh wrote that Miss Julia was more intellectual than the average Southern matron; she read all the latest books, including non-fiction, and was very cognizant of the political scene both here and in Europe. Pat said, "She was a real charmer."

CHAPTER NINE

The Houston clan came originally from Virginia; William R. Houston came to Augusta in 1897 at age twenty-four to teach English and elocution at Richmond Academy where his uncle, Colonel Charles H. Withrow, was principal. Houston was a graduate of the University of Virginia and had been born in Hang-Chow, China, in 1873 of Presbyterian missionary parents. After teaching for several years, Houston switched and decided to enroll in what we now call the Medical College of Georgia although the new changed name is Georgia Health Sciences University or Georgia RegentsUniversity. By 1906, the "new" Dr. Houston was an associate professor of clinical medicine at MCG as well as in his own outside practice of internal medicine; he was well known for his medical expertise, intellect, and vision. He departed to Europe in 1916 with his friend, Dr. Henry Michel, to practice medicine in French military hospitals. The US vice consul general at Paris, Charles P. Pressly, who was also mentioned in the Milledge Road section, assisted the two Augusta doctors in securing their French wartime jobs. Dr. Houston was stationed in Lyons.

On returning to Augusta to private practice, Dr. Houston was elected to the governing board for the University Hospital and continued his work at MCG, when suddenly in 1922, at one of the pinnacles of his career, Dr. Houston accepted a position to come to China and teach medicine at the Yale-in-China Medical School in Hunan Province. The city was Changsha, the local capital of Hunan and situated on a tributary of the famous Yangtze River. We should explain that in this piece we shall endeavor to employ the older Yale or Wade system of Romanizing Chinese words as such is the form with which I am most familiar, particularly with place names. The new post-1949 system, following the Communist takeover is known as the "pinyin," being now the closest to an international standard. This is also related, I believe, to making the Mandarin Chinese dialect the primary lingua franca of the entire huge country.

Changsha today is known as "Tanzhou," and the river on which it is a port is called "Xiang"; however, as I said, we will continue to call the city Changsha. When in 1922, Dr. Houston was asked why he was leaving Augusta, one of his favorite retorts was that he was tired of discussing the barbarics of the Barretts and the finances of the Phinizys! This bon mot from the late Teto Barrett. Another valid reason probably was that he was fond of China and certainly spoke one or more of the local dialects in his youth when living in that country; a further rationale relates to the fact that his one-time college roommate was Dr. John Leighton Stuart, then the president of Yenching University (as Yale-in-China was known locally) and located in Peking. It is documented that the Yale-in-China Medical School was in Changsha, and it also is quite possible that the entire Yenching University had for safety reasons moved to this same large city by 1922 due to the very troubled political situation in most of China at that period.

In 1956, the Yale-in-China Medical School was renamed Hunan Medical College. The reader should recall

CHAPTER NINE

that following the revolution of 1911 that brought down the Manchu/Qing dynasty and formed a new republic, the country was very unsettled with local warlords controlling large swaths of territory. One of the "Fathers of the 1911 Revolution" was Sun-Yat-sen (1866-1925); he was out of China and in Denver, Colorado, when to his surprise the army in Wuhan revolted with the last Manchu monarch ousted. Thereafter, even with the imperial power collapsed, conditions did not permit a peaceful and organized progress to a modern and democratic future. By the time Dr. Houston, Miss Julia, and John Walton arrived in 1922-1923, Sun-Yat-sen and other well-meaning persons had turned to the Soviet Union for advice and organizational assistance with their Nationalist Party known as the "Kuomintang."

At this early stage in the 1920s, ChiangKai-Shek (a native of Chekiang Province near the coast), and MaoTseTung (born in Shaoshan Village, Hunan Province), were at least nominally working together when Stalin sent Mr. Michael Gruesenberg as his "ambassador" or advisor to the "Kuomintang/Communist Alliance." The restructuring was accomplished on broadly Bolshevik lines with a number of Russian advisers working with Gruesenberg whose nom de guerre was Borodin. Borodin actually was a Lithuanian Jew so, after most of the noble Borodin family had been killed in the 1917 Russian Revolution, he took this surname. Madame Borodin was in Changsha as well; Pat Walsh reported that John was commanded to give her French lessons too for he was already engaged in giving a class in conversational English to students at the Yale-in-China institution commonly known as Yenching University. One interesting fact perhaps little known now is that in the past century several great American universities founded educational enterprises in various parts of China as sort of branches or joint ventures. Many US missionary teachers were involved with the objective to provide a modern education in English while, at the same time, indulge in conversion activities leading to Christianity. For example, aside from Yale, St. John's University in Shanghai was a "branch" of the University of Pennsylvania as well as Harvard. During my career in the Orient, I worked with many and employed Chinese graduates of these "branches" of US universities and even remember attending in Hong Kong the annual dinner/dances given by St. John's alumni living then in the British colony after all of mainland China was finally captured by the Mao Tse Tung faction in 1949-1950.

By 1927, the military forces of Chiang Kai-Shek had broken with the army/Party of MaoTseTung and ChonEn-lai in what was called the "Northern Expedition" and ended by the 1930s with Chiang Kai-Shek controlling about two-thirds of the total population of China. However, at this time, the communist factions still were strong in the Changsha/Hunan region, and there was unrest and probably fighting between them and Kuomintang supporters. Foreigners had to make a hurried departure, and thus Dr. Wu (as the Chinese called him finding "Houston" difficult to say), Miss Julia, and John had to give up their "Lotus

CHAPTER NINE

Life" in 1927. They had all apparently been residing in a large compound with other foreigners but in separate houses; Pat Walsh joked that life in Augusta was great training for life in a compound where one sees and entertains many of the same people constantly! The Houstons returned to Augusta; John Walton went directly to France, landing at Marseilles.

One report has John then proceeding to Paris while another infers he stayed in the Marseilles area and almost at once bought a peasant's cottage on the coast at La Ciotat, a pretty village between Marseilles and Toulon but also quite close to Cassis on one side and Bandol on the other. Today, La Ciotat is very likely around twenty miles from Marseilles. Houses rise in tiers above the bay of the same name, La Ciotat having been a port since ancient times when it was called "Citharista" as an outpost of Marseilles. The population in the 1980s was about 25,000, today probably much more but also far less in 1927. Aside from the "Vieux Port," there is now "La Ciotat Plage" north of the harbor, created as a resort with hotels and villas lining the beach. John forthwith had the entire interior of the cottage gutted and replaced with modern facilities of his own design.

Here John lived very happily from late 1927 until some date in 1932; during those five years he was host to American tourists, who came rather frequently, as the Riviera had now become more of a summer than winter resort if we can designate La Ciotat as part of that region. With his excellent French language ability and, at the time, strong US dollar income for the dollar-French franc exchange rate was most favorable, John also enjoyed local social life with some of the residents in La Ciotat and others who lived in the neighboring towns. John had always been able to readily pick up and master all and every foreign tongue, a gift with which he was born.

During the summer 1932, Miss Julia visited John and confided in him that things were not going well between her and Dr. Houston. She asked him to return to Augusta; apparently, this was about the time when Dr. Houston was "gaslighting" Miss Julia. Today we probably would term it "playing around," but I am using Pat Walsh's terminology to add some 1930s flavor! John immediately did as his mother requested and always regarded it as a stroke of good luck that he sold the cottage just before F.D.R. took the US dollar off the gold standard and thereby devaluing the currency.

Having left China rather precipitately in 1927, the Houstons and John had entrusted the packing and shipping of their household goods to close friends; all came through in fine condition. The Houstons on their Augusta arrival lived first in an apartment at the George Walton and then later in a house on Walton Way. Dr. Houston resumed his medical practice and also held public posts, including chairman of the Board of Health. It was reported from Pat Walsh that he was considered the "society doctor" of Augusta and also attended the winter resort moguls stopping at the Bon Air, Partridge Inn, etc. The Chandler research concludes that the Houstons were members of the "fast set" in

CHAPTER NINE

Augusta! The Doctor and Miss Julia both were magnetic and appealing in conversation and must have been much in demand socially. Dr. Houston had escorted Landon Thomas, Jr. as a young man to Germany as a sort of combined tutor-mentor; this was likely when Dr. Houston still was teaching at the Richmond Academy, but later he became close friends with the Thomas family. Another special companion was the author Berry Fleming once he returned to Augusta from France and New York.

One true and fascinating story is about a party given by the Allen girls in their house on Greene Street. Numbers on Greene changed through the years so the Allen girls are listed in the Old Social Registry at both 613 and 701 Greene in different years. The occasion for the party was the baptism of their monkey; the ceremony was performed just as if the monkey was a child of one of the first local families! The monkey was dressed in a beautiful christening robe, someone acted the part of the minister, there were godparents, and most importantly there was the party after the ceremony! John Walton's grandparents (Scotch Presbyterian) or other Walton relatives living then across the street were shocked! These Allen ladies were Celeste (Lessie), Elizabeth (Lizzie), and Lucy who became the wife of Archibald Blackshear (Archie), a well-known local lawyer. During the boom days before and in the 1920s the men returning from their Broad or Reynolds Street offices, often would stop off at the Allens for an afternoon toddy en route home. Another Greene Street lady living nearby at No. 415 and 453 was Miss Marie D'Antignac

Allen who on occasion joined the Allen sisters at their home or also entertained every afternoon at her own "salon." At a later stage in their lives, but still known as the "Allen girls," a move was made to a small house on Bransford Road where Barney Dunbar continued to be a regular and frequent visitor to the afternoon cocktail hour long after the Houstons had left Augusta.

Male friends of Dr. Houston included Dr. Henry Michel and Dr. Eugene Murphey, all three medical comrades, intellectual companions, and drinking buddies! Many friends after the return from China also greeted him with his Chinese sobriquet, Dr. Wu! The good Dr. Wu is said to have considered the usual Chinese words of greeting "Have you eaten your rice" much more logical than "How are you?" Circa 1935, the Houstons determined to move to Austin, Texas; Dr. Wu's Augusta lady friends apparently made Miss Julia decide they had to move on! Dr. Houston's brother, Hale, lived in Austin and found them a house on 13th Street where they resided for the rest of their lives. Dr. Houston continued to practice general medicine for around ten more years but would spend several months each summer in the cool mountains at Cashiers, in western North Carolina. Miss Julia would visit Augusta to see her son for one of these months. All continued in this happy vein until Miss Julia died in Austin early 1952. Dr. Houston passed away around a year and a half later in August 1953. Both were buried there. The *Augusta Chronicle* reported February 8, 1952, that "Mr. John M. Walton

CHAPTER NINE

has returned from Austin, Texas, due to the illness and death of his mother."

When Lynn and I were in Austin in 1992 for a wedding, we rang Pat Walsh in San Francisco to find out the address where the Houstons lived until their deaths. He directed us to 1404 W. 13th Street, by now a very built-up area similar perhaps to Augusta's old 15th Street when they arrived circa 1935. So we had just a feel of their life in a university town where they had been so content. My wife, who spent four years in Austin at school, considers Austin the nicest city in Texas. Austin is hilly and built amidst many lakes and streams. There are a lot of greenery and trees around.

When John, true to his mother's wishes, came home to Augusta in 1932, he in due course built a small home at 2418 William Street. It had a Regency clean-cut look and originally was white clapboard; one entered directly into the living room all paneled in pine stained a light brown. Without further ado, I should state that according to Pat Walsh, John Walton didn't trust his stepfather, Dr. Houston. They were friendly on the surface, and John admired the Houston broad intellect; nevertheless, it appears he resented him as a stepfather. John would say often, "If Mother could have just had an affair with Dr. Houston and got him out of her system!" When I once asked Pat Walsh what he really thought of the Dr. Houston-Miss Julia relationship, he wrote, "In 1946, I think it was, when I met Dr. Houston and saw them together for the first time, it was obvious that she was deeply in love with him and any past sins of his (including 'Gaslighting' according to John) were forgiven."

In the region of 1933-1934, John was motoring with Anne and Berry Fleming en route to Charleston, South Carolina. When reaching the tiny crossroads of Adams Run they saw a sign stating "Edisto Beach 20 miles"; as they had plenty of time, they drove to the beach and met a resident and the only real estate salesman around named McGowan Holmes. The Augustans of course knew the McGowans from their city (McGowan Holmes was first cousin to Henri McGowan, Sr. from Augusta), and after some discussion John Walton paid $800 for a basic but comfortable beach cottage facing the Atlantic. The purchase might have been something of a whim, but John after his five years on the French coast, still wanted the sea and thought Edisto would be an ideal place to vacation. In those days, the roads from Adams Run and on the beach were unpaved, and there was no electricity then serving the beach. It is likely, too, that the unexpected visitors already knew that Edisto Island was still the location of several old and handsome plantations some of which even then were used in season for hunting and sporting activities.

John Walton in his first years back in Augusta became friendly with "Bunny" (Francis) Calhoun who I believe assisted him in getting whatever license in the early 1930s may have been needed to sell real estate. I hope there was some success but have no real facts. He was very social and enjoyed all Augusta had to offer in these 1930s Depression years; his friends and invitations were legion

CHAPTER NINE

and embraced the very old, young, and medium-aged adults as well as the teen-aged. John had a copious fund of stories, was very well read, and had been highly educated from both academics and travel. He was popular, more so now than ever before at a younger age in Augusta, and considered by many "good company." He saw a lot of his father's first cousin, the widowed Jennie Lee Walton Selden, her daughter Genie Selden Lehmann, and the latter's young girls. He taught French to one daughter, Jennie Lee, and helped the senior Jennie Lee during some bad financial times. While he could be generous, as I infer, he also had a bit of a close-fisted reputation at the same time and never picked up a check in a public place with alacrity; John also had the bad tendency to smoke the cigarettes of others as he normally carried no smokes.

John was out a great deal, moving equally well across all strata including some of the winter resort residents. He apparently agreed with the old Chinese of his day who generally eschewed exercise! However, he told Mary Barrett, then in her early teen years, that every guest has a very solemn duty to work to make a success of a party; the guest, he said, has the obligation to entertain, the same as one's host.

During the 1930s, John also concerned himself with support for cultural activities in Augusta. In particular, he took the lead in converting the Young Men's Library into the Augusta Public Library after having been president of the Young Men's Library where he instituted the first "rental shelf." He was a trustee of Summerville

Cemetery and the Gertrude Herbert Institute of Art. John was very instrumental in prevailing upon Mrs. Herbert to purchase and endow the old Ware Mansion as the Gertrude Herbert Institute in memory of her daughter. In short, he really contributed in a lasting manner to the local environment. He was a good fundraiser for the Young Men's Library, then housed on Telfair Street in the old Richmond Academy Building, and convinced others to become involved, including Celeste Cheatham and my father who had the Elk's Club and other business associates from the Broad Street area make cash donations.

After the Barrett house burned at 805 Milledge circa 1935, John purchased the four unburnt front columns and other millwork and built a second Regency house on Walton Way Extension as it was then known; I believe the road still was dirt on that section which was then outside the city limits. The Walton Way No. is now 3106, and John probably finished his new house in 1936. While the front façade indeed is imposing from the street on this six- or seven-acre property, the white wooden clapboard house was quite simple: one entered the front by the double staircase with wrought-iron railings directly into the living room. The dining room was to the left with a handsome carved wooden archway separating the two nice-sized rooms with a small kitchen off the dining room. Behind and off a corridor opening from the living room were two bedrooms and two baths.

The Francis Calhouns lived on the left on a large property; it is likely John acquired his acreage at a very

CHAPTER NINE

low price, and construction costs then for his type of house probably were modest indeed. Here John lived happily until 1942 at the height of World War II when he was drafted into the US Army at the mature age of forty-four! He then sold the Walton Way house to Louie Brooks, a wealthy Jewish man born in Augusta. Brooks had gone to New York where he achieved some financial success and married B. Altman's niece who was also B. Altman's heir. John at that point left Augusta to go through basic training.

While John was not exactly army material, still he possessed the necessary discipline to complete basic training in Texas, if my memory serves. Then suddenly the army decided to discharge anyone drafted over thirty-six with the automatic draft ages reduced from eighteen to forty-five to eighteen to twenty-five, a large drop. On one of his "leaves" to Augusta prior to final discharge, I remember seeing John in his uniform at our house regaling those present with his entertaining tales of army life as a buck private! Apparently, John was serving with a number of very much younger men, many of whom had little real education; he would write letters for some of these comrades in arms and provide advice where indicated. These were quite amusing reminiscences.

After his final honorary discharge in something like 1944, John came home to Augusta and rented an apartment at the George Walton where he remained until May 1950. Next, he bought a brick house at 3036 Lake Forest Drive, built originally as a combination residence and garage in the rear of a large house facing Park Avenue; however, there always was a private entrance to 3036 from the street behind, Lake Forest Drive. Before buying 3036, John took my father to see the house in search of his opinion. My father said it reeked of Germanic efficiency and orderliness, so John added a small portico or stoop at the front to soften the façade. The house had two bedrooms and bath up a narrow and steep staircase and a large attractive dining/living room downstairs. There were casement windows and bookcases everywhere. John, in due course, had the garage converted into another room for Miss Julia; this addition became a den following her death. As Pat Walsh moved with John into this house in May 1950, we should now introduce him more fully into this narrative.

At the George Walton Apartments, when John Walton returned from "the Wars," were several other bachelors, some of whom had resided there for sometime. These included Pat Walsh and Walter Fargo; at that period, there was a dining room serving meals on the ground floor, and many of the residents would gather there after the work day. John mingled with this group for drinks, and perhaps too for supper if hungry, as in some of these years he went, every weekday at least, to the Alexanders' to take lunch (or "dinner" as the Augustans termed it) as a paying guest, I do believe. The "Alexander meal" would have been a substantial one. Pat and John soon became good friends and began to spend much time together although each had their own separate apartments. John's wide circle of friends soon opened bright

CHAPTER NINE

new vistas for Pat whose previous crowd had been much more circumscribed.

Patrick David Walsh was descended from Juriah Harriss, a landowner in Columbia County and with other properties in Richmond County; his grandfather, Robert Yerby Harriss, Jr., or Bob as he was called, was the marshal or constable of Summerville before the village became a part of Augusta in 1912. Bob and his wife, Barrett, lived at 401 High Street which then was a part of lower Milledge Road. Disaster struck in October 1892, when the marshal went to curb a domestic disturbance at a black family's house and was shot by one Henry Ramsay. About one-half of Bob's face was blown away, and he died near midnight the same night. Some wanted to lynch Ramsay, but Solicitor Boykin Wright promised that justice would be done, and the mob then dispersed. Ramsay was tried (charged with murder), found guilty, and sentenced to hang in January 1893. Barrett died in Atlanta in June 1941, and she and her husband are interred on the Harriss plot in Summerville Cemetery. As the marshal's father had married Sophia Bryan, he and Major Joseph B. Cumming were first cousins. The first son of the Bob-Barrett marriage was named Joseph Cumming Harriss and always called "Cumming." Pat Walsh's mother was named Joe Harriss, born in 1886, and married Patrick D. Walsh April 20, 1908, at the Sacred Heart Church in Augusta. Patrick worked for the *Augusta Chronicle* then owned by his uncle, Hon. Patrick Walsh, who was born in Ireland in 1840 and for whom he had been named. He also is known as Senator Walsh having served in the US Senate in the 1890s, in the Georgia Legislature, and as Augusta mayor.

Our "Patrick David Walsh, Jr." was born July 2, 1915, in Augusta; there was a sister, Agnes, and another infant boy who lived only a few hours. In September 1919, the parents moved to Atlanta where the father Patrick started work at the *Atlanta Constitution*. Our Pat was but a boy of eight when his mother died of pleurisy and only twelve when Patrick, Sr. passed away. Hence, Pat was really raised to maturity by his maternal grandmother with whom he thereafter lived in Atlanta. Expense seemingly always was a consideration, with grandmother Barrett just managing, for with the death of her husband Bob (the marshal), she faced the prospect of raising five children with almost no money. Pat attended Atlanta schools and later Augusta Junior College here (now known as Augusta State University). Pat spoke with sort of a slow drawl but without any stammer; on occasion one felt he might not quite get his words out!

He never appeared interested in any church, Catholic or Protestant, and spent most of his adult life in the Protestant milieu. This may have been partly due to his Grandfather Harriss's (and initially his Grandmother Barrett Harriss's) antipathy to the Catholic Church that had refused to marry them due to their age difference of twenty-four years. For this reason, they had been married by the Church of the Atonement (Episcopal) on Telfair Street in Augusta. Barrett was the original surname of Pat's grandmother (she did not use Bridget, her

CHAPTER NINE

given name) who always made it clear she was no relation to the "cotton" Barretts, meaning the prominent Barrett family of Augusta of which some members were closely identified with Cotton Row. Pat wrote that neither the Harriss nor Barrett clans approved of their marriage.

Pat never really appeared much interested in the Walsh side of his family; it is likely the Harrisses surely considered his mother's marriage something of a mésalliance, although at that period it certainly was the Walsh tribe that had the assets and even position in Augusta. Pat's father never participated, however, in these assets for in 1899, the Hon. Patrick Walsh died with no children leaving all to his widow! On the other hand, the Harriss kinship group still could look back to some glory and revel! In addition to the Bryan/Cumming connection, there were other decendants of Juriah Harriss in Columbia County near Appling where the Old Harriss Cemetery is located. The Pollard Family, now well known in Augusta, did a splendid job in restoring the Harriss Cemetery for they also are Juriah Harriss descendants. As another example, Pat wrote of the Savannah Casey-Meldrim clan and said Sophie Meldrim Shonnard's sons, Ted Coy, Jr. and Peter Meldrim Coy, would be his third cousins. There seemingly was no contact between such family connections for Pat wrote, "As my Aunt Julia Harriss used to say, we were everybody's poor relations." He went on to state that Ted and Peter Coy's great-grandmother, Caroline Harriss Casey, is buried in the Harriss Cemetery noted before.

IS LIVING WELL STILL THE BEST REVENGE?

During all of his mature life in Augusta, Pat showed a real consuming interest in the facts pertaining to all the families considered prominent in local so-called "Society." He soaked up all the particulars and often could expound to one relative on rather obscure details not even known to that particular family member with whom he was then conversing. The friendship with John Walton opened many new doors and launched him significantly onto the Augusta scene. Pat in his low-key, non-controversial way was popular; he was an excellent listener and willing to consort with all kinds of people and age groups. He knew how to fit in beautifully and probably made himself useful to John around the house where he was in charge of the kitchen when no cook was around.

While Pat wanted to treat and hob-nob with the so-called rich and well born, I do not believe he was a snob in the normal definition of that term. He was a great reader and certainly educated himself to a high level through the written page and by his close association with John Walton and John's friends. In the autumn of 1945, Pat took his first annual trip to New York City with John; they went to plays, ate well, and continued these motor trips about every year with one night spent on the road each way. Once they stopped in New Castle, Delaware, and another time at Southern Pines, North Carolina, where Pat visited with one of his Harriss relatives. In New York City, John introduced Pat to his friends Adele Petit and Anne Campbell Greene who then were living in the metropolis.

CHAPTER NINE

As already noted, when John Walton had purchased the house at 3036 Lake Forest Drive in 1950, at that juncture both John and Pat gave up their George Walton Apartments and transferred to this new abode. By this time, if one thought to invite John or Pat separately, you did not do so except perhaps under the most unusual circumstances. The pair of them had become a friendly couple who shared their lives and friends. Pat still was employed in the finance area in a government post at the Augusta Arsenal and then later at Fort Gordon. I imagine the home expenses were shared. Jane Chandler has the recollection of being invited by John for drinks late one afternoon; during the cocktail session, she and Bleak were urged to stay on for a potluck supper and had to await Pat's return from work at Fort Gordon to prepare all the food!

The Walton cottage on the beach at Edisto was completely destroyed in the 1940 hurricane; as the lot too was washed away totally, rebuilding on that property was impossible. Hence, aside from visits to friends with cottages on the Atlantic Coast, the regular trips were the autumn visit, usually by car, to New York City with perhaps stops along the way to see John's cousin Katherine Moore Hall in Maryland or other relatives in Virginia. The annual monthly summer visit of Miss Julia to Augusta was another event, with many friends entertaining John's mother or John inviting people to see her at the Lake Forest Drive house. Neither John nor Pat followed any regular exercise regimen, so their life was mainly very sedentary and perforce rather unhealthy, particularly for John who was older by seventeen years. Pat did his first trip to Europe in November 1952. While in Florence, he called Grace Gregorini in Bologna and was informed Giovanni, her only son, was quite ill; Giovanni then passed away in late 1952 or early 1953. John, as far as I know, never returned to Europe but continued to talk to Pat about his life there in the 1920s and early 1930s. My brother Inman Mays wrote me apropos of the Walton-Walsh household in the late 1950s that he was there with our parents when he and Pat went into the kitchen to replenish drinks; then John came storming in, apparently irate that Inman and Pat were together chatting—was this a tiny fit of jealousy? John also laughed about the very frequent Pat hand-washings in the course of a day, but now all doctors recommend this action to all.

Al Williams was a bachelor friend in the 1950s until he married Barbara at age thirty-three. Al often took lunch at the Lake Forest Drive house on Sundays; Mary Alexander might be there but never a large group. After drinks Pat served lunch, which he mostly prepared. Al recalls that John either before he was drafted or following his discharge from the army took a sort of "war job" at the Lombard Iron Works to do his part in the war effort. His good friend Lombard Fortson probably arranged this position. Another tale is that finally Pat convinced John, who had never carried a wallet, to do so now that credit cards were being used and a handy receptacle was required for a Social Security Card and driver's license.

CHAPTER NINE

John promptly lost his first wallet the second week he carried it!

In the region of the early 1960s, John experienced some heart problems; I have not heard that he underwent some type of heart bypass (not so common then as now), but he did avoid the steep stairs at home by moving into the downstairs bedroom originally constructed for his mother. Here he would receive a few visitors while his health returned to an improved level. However, late 1962 or early January 1963, he came to the Chandler house to bring some magazines where he suffered severe shortness of breath and had to lie down. Jane Chandler called the ambulance, which conveyed him to the hospital emergency room. While I believe he did return home after this attack, he once again returned to the hospital where he died Saturday, February 9, 1963. Graveside services were conducted by a Presbyterian minister on February 10 at 4:30 p.m. at Magnolia Cemetery where he was buried next to the imposing tomb of his father. On February 13, 1963, the *Augusta Chronicle* published on its editorial page a fine tribute on the specific offerings and contributions John Walton made to the benefit of all Augusta following his return from abroad. The editorial read as follows:

John M. Walton

To anything that concerned itself with the cultural ennoblement Of Augusta, John Moore Walton was a patron with perseverance. His was a single-mindedness of purpose that the city long enjoyed and will sorely miss. It was a consuming, yet unpretentious, dedication to the arts that was based upon an appreciation he had gained of the finer things in life in years spent in China and France.

This admiration he felt for the artistic was in its entirety neither confined to the graphic nor to the performing arts. He had a keen and appreciative taste for good literature and played more than a passing role in the conversion of the Young Men's Library into the Augusta Public Library.

In the long years that he spent here, after his return from abroad, John Walton, to quote an intimate friend, was "up to his ears" in cultural and literary events. At one time he was president of the Young Men's Library Assn., and instituted the first "rental shelf" by which the public could "take out" the institution's books. He served as a trustee of the Young Men's Library Trust Fund, a trustee of the Summerville Cemetery, of the Gertrude Herbert Institute of Art, as well as of the endowment fund which sustains it.

Only those extremely close to this modest man could have known that it was by his unflagging enthusiasm for Augusta's cultural progress and his complete sincerity in that attainment that he persuaded Mrs. Gertrude Herbert to purchase the old Ware mansion and endow it to her daughter as a mecca for all lovers of the graphic arts.

CHAPTER NINE

If the expression "hard to replace" may, in truth, be applicable to any man, it must assuredly apply, so far as Augusta is concerned, to John M. Walton whose death Saturday brought an end to a fruitful life.

Now it was the turn of Pat Walsh to find himself rather rudderless for some period of time. Shortly after the funeral, he appeared in tears at the William Street home of Mary and Heard Robertson; he continued to cry and sob as he indeed had lost what had been his compass in life for around twenty years. Mary says today he seemed almost inconsolable and ever so disconsolate. As one must eventually adjust, so Pat did over a period of time, but he mourned for a long interval, probably more than for any of his own blood family.

Pat was the executor of the Walton will and also was bequeathed everything, but only after the various cash bequests were paid; there was one further stipulation by which Pat Walsh was only the "life tenant" for a certain property John owned at 950 Broad Street with John's Moore relatives inheriting in fee simple on Pat's death. However, properties at Walton Way and 15th Street (northwest corner) and the house on Lake Forest Drive were devised outright to Pat. The "washed-away" beach lot at Edisto was left to John's godson, Sam Warren Mays, together with a cash legacy of $2,000; the beach lot over the years built up again with sand dunes, and Sam sold the property some years later for $4,000. The Walton family flat silver and a handsome Pembroke table went to

Genie Lehmann while forty-four pieces of silver forks and spoons, being Miller family silver, all marked with the letter "M," were bequeathed to Helen Duncan Derry, daughter to Anne Barrett and Billy Derry. Among other cash bequests, John's old friend from Augusta, Paris, and New York City Adéle Petit received $5,000 with a second godson, Gil Willis of New Jersey, left $1,000.

In the spring of 1964, April or May, Pat decided to sell the Lake Forest Drive house and proceed for an indefinite stay in Paris, which was to be his new base. The sale was made for $18,000 to Mr. and Mrs. Walter Fargo, both of whom even before their own marriage had been friends then and also tenants at the George Walton Apartments. No. 3036 Lake Forest Drive was worth about $150,000–$175,000 when we moved to Augusta in late 1991. Mary Robertson thinks Pat wanted to try a new lifestyle and also had an urge to relive, as it were, the John Walton early 1920s experience when he determined to move to Paris in 1964. Pat lodged first at the Hotel St. Anne and later rented an apartment on Rue Rivoli. When we were on our honeymoon in June 1965, we called him from Cap Ferrat, so he was in residence then. Later that year or early 1966, he appears to have returned to Augusta but then decided to move to San Francisco, which he did in early 1969. We know that Christmas 1968 was his last one in Augusta for he wrote that year was his final Christmas dinner with Marie and Craig Cranston, having been with Craig's family for many years. The Cranston eldest daughter Catherine is his godchild.

CHAPTER NINE

Both the Chandlers and Mary Robertson are in agreement that Pat was not terribly happy in France as he did not have John Walton's facile language ability nor the extrovert personality to meet new people and get around as his mentor did in the 1920s. Without John he probably still was somewhat "lost." I surmise that Pat, even after forty years, still was hoping to find in Paris some offhand reference to John and his period of the early 1920s. John was writing newspaper articles then and, in addition, might have had some work with one of the printing presses then in vogue and printing first editions on watermark paper. The William Bird "Three Mountains Press" was mentioned earlier in this piece. Pat continued to hope that in somebody's memoirs of Paris in the twenties he might come across a remark about John, who did say he had met Gertrude Stein. However, Pat wrote in March 1990 that so far he had not.

In San Francisco, Pat obtained another government job in finance, but we have no details. He did return to Augusta at least once, for Nina Blanchard's funeral in Augusta 1969; nevertheless, he kept in close touch with Augusta by means of letters and through the frequent use of the A. G. Bell invention. There were long weekly chats with his widow friends, including Margaret Fargo, for example, with long letters written to the Hugh Connollys, Heard Robertsons, and Craig Cranstons among many others.

By early 1987, when we were living in Greece and began our correspondence, Pat's San Francisco address was 447 28th Street; he had a roommate, Al Dulay, who he said was of Asian origin. This apparently is the same Al who drove him to the Fairmont Hotel in December 1983 to join us for dinner. Maude Gary Doris and the Hugh Connollys met Al during visits to their accommodation but inferred that Al soon disappeared and did not take much part in the conversation with Pat and his guests. In one of Pat's letters to me, he did write that Al felt the black population wanted to be the only minority and get all the sympathy in this country! When we invited Pat to visit us in Greece or stay chez nous after we moved to Augusta in 1992, his reply was, "The only trip I'm looking forward to is crossing the River Styx. I understand it's quite pleasant on the other side." Pat wrote once in 1987 that he did have a yen to go to Paris again but doubted if he ever would go.

As happens to almost everyone, the problems of older age began to afflict Pat. For example, in March 1989 he had bypass heart surgery, but he did recover well after an operation performed March 10 and a stay of about three weeks in the hospital. This serious operation obviously prolonged his life, but he seems to have died rather suddenly on April 28, 1996. I write "suddenly" as our daughter Katherine was married February 17 of that year, and we had talked about this on the telephone, for Pat said he had to decline our invitation due to age. He honored us in any case by even sending a present of silver candlesticks. Pat had seemed in good spirits when we last spoke, so his death surprised many of us here even though he was in his eighty-first year. We had a

CHAPTER NINE

group at our house to celebrate his life and then later a cocktail session at the Hugh Connollys from where, drinks in hand, we walked to Summerville Cemetery nearby to formally dedicate the stone marker a number of friends had ordered. The Harris plot has very impressive stone coping all around but no other markers, so Pat is remembered by his Augusta cousins and connections with a proper monument:

Patrick David Walsh, Jr.
July 2, 1915 – April 28, 1996

Near the Harriss plot are the tombs of John Walton's Moore relatives and grandparents, William Augustus and Elizabeth Moore Walton. Very fitting, although several of his Augusta friends said Pat would not want any of this as a remembrance, most of us disagreed and still firmly believe he would be quite pleased at our gesture and small tribute to his life. He was a very kind and understanding person with many devoted and fond of him. His ashes as per his instructions were consigned to the Pacific Ocean. We have no hard facts relative to Pat's will. However, he had sent French Moustiere China to his goddaughter Catherine Verdery Cranston Whitham, who lives in Richmond, Virginia.

Pat lived almost thirty years in San Francisco; until I obtained the facts recounted here, I had not realized what a long time it had been. He told his cousin and friend Craig Cranston before leaving Augusta that considering his lifestyle it was the best course for him. Hence, he must have been happy there to linger so long, although we really know so little about his life following Augusta. What a change from associating with and pursuing the well-to-do and well-born in Georgia to the ultra-liberal and hurly-burly of the West Coast! As the French are fond of saying: "Chacun á son goût." The Americans these days also often opine, "It takes all kinds."

CHAPTER NINE

The local Augusta celebration of the life of Pat Walsh at Summerville Cemetery, 1996

CHAPTER X

The Alexanders of 1027 Telfair Street: The Real "Lucinderella"

Well into the 1930s there remained in downtown Augusta some very nice residential pockets notwithstanding the great fire of 1916 and the late 1929 flood due to breaks in the levee. Telfair and Greene Streets still offered attractive accommodation possibilities, and one such dwelling was the 1847 house 1027 Telfair at the corner of 11th Street. While this abode was usually known as the Alexander residence, that family never owned it; rather it was the property of the Craig Family (John Craig originally) whose daughters later married into the Alexander and Cranston families.

IS LIVING WELL STILL THE BEST REVENGE?

William Craig, the only son of John Craig, came into possession of the property on the death of his father, and as trustee under his father's will, he maintained the house during his lifetime as a refuge to any Craig relatives who wanted to live there. The Craig estate paid all the expenses related to the house maintenance, i.e. taxes, insurance, utilities, etc. The occupants dealt with the other items such as food and servant wages. During the period from 1900 to about 1945, all of the Alexanders and related Cranston and Craig descendants all lived at number 1027 at various times.

This very unorthodox arrangement was the basic theme adopted by our local noted writer Berry Fleming in his 1967 novel entitled *Lucinderella*. However, the novel really does not deal with the true residents of number 1027, which he called The Homestead, or any of the Alexanders known to me as the author modified all names and details to develop his own plot built around a lady called "Lucinda Fannin" who returned to live in Augusta at "The Homestead" after some success in New York as a writer and experiencing psychoanalysis. The head of that household was called Uncle Brownell.

The second Episcopal Church founded in Augusta, Church of the Atonement, was across the street from the Alexander/Craig home on the corner of 11th (Kollock Street) and Telfair. This church opened for services in 1851; the building was deconsecrated circa late 1970s and became a mission. This landmark has now disappeared from the street.

CHAPTER TEN

The Alexanders of 1027 were an interesting family but should not be confused with the Irvin Alexanders of Hickman Road or E. Porter Alexander, famous Confederate general and president of the Georgia Railroad and Banking Company (1878-1880), even though they may indeed be related. Mr. Thomas W. Alexander, a cotton factor with office (Alexander & Alexander was the firm's name) at 731 Reynolds Street married Helen Duncan Craig (but always called "Nellie"); their dates are Thomas 1862-1918 and Nellie 1863-1939. The couple had five children: Bishop (1890-1948), Mary (1893-1970), Jessie (1895-1957), Henrietta (1898-1955) and Tom (1900-1959). Bishop married a Jackson from North Augusta, Jessie married Jack Taylor (father of Ashby and Helen), and Tom married Louise Sehler; Mary and Henrietta never wedded. But early in the lives of these progeny a terrible crisis came upon the entire Alexander family as a result of their father's "trading bogus warehouse receipts" as Craig Cranston terms it.

Money usually was borrowed from a bank, in this case Georgia Railroad Bank, a very normal practice in those times. However, there was a certain timetable in that events had to happen (sales and prices set, etc.), but in the Alexander instance, as he later admitted, there was speculation and eventual ruin when the bank called his loan and found that the cotton was gone (the bank's collateral) from the warehouse.

Mr. Alexander on July 6, 1906, wrote the bank that he was leaving at once for New York City to secure a loan, thereby allowing his firm to pay all creditors. Apparently the New York loan did not materialize as Mr. Alexander had hoped, so Alexander and Alexander Cotton Factors was bankrupt. He already had been in negotiations relative to the loan but felt the trip to New York essential to accomplish his objective for, as he wrote the bank before his departure, the letter conveying all facts regarding the financial status, indeed bankruptcy, of the firm would not be delivered should he attain success. Mr Alexander's July 6, 1906, letter reads as follows:

Alexander & Alexander,   Augusta, Ga. July 6th, 1906
   Cotton Factors,
731 Reynolds Street.

To Georgia R.R. Bank,
        Augusta, Ga.
Gentlemen:

   I am leaving for New York this afternoon with a view of perfecting a loan. If I am successful in so doing this letter will never reach you otherwise it will bring to you the unexpected announcement that the firm of Alexander & Alexander is bankrupt. Should the pending negotiations for the loan above referred to be consummated A & A will have ample assets to pay their creditors otherwise it will be impossible for them to do so. The responsibility of the existing condition of affairs is <u>entirely mine.</u> My brother and partner has no idea of the involved condition of the firm and <u>particularly he has no knowledge</u> of

CHAPTER TEN

the cotton hypothecated with you: It is absolutely and utterly useless for me to endeavor to excuse myself to you or to try and tell under a smiling exterior the Hell on earth I have been through during the past year. It is simply the old story of wishing to make money too fast. The trouble began with comparatively small speculation on the wrong side the Sully year and subsequent endeavors to recoup losses all of which proved disastrous until now the climax has come. God only knows the regret and remorse that overwhelms me. I have today executed a bill of sale of my interest in the firm to Bishop who innocently suffers from my fault. There are approximately of bills receivable and accounts that will enable the firm to pay a large percentage of its indebtedness.

Could some arrangement be made for Bishop to carry on the business I think the best results could be obtained.

Yours truly
T. W. Alexander

Once the Georgia Railroad Bank received the Alexander letter, their management called a special meeting of the finance committee for 3:30 p.m., July 18, 1906. Those present were Messrs. Jacob Phinizy, Latimer, Tobin, and Bothwell; agreement was reached that the following advertisements were to be published for ten days in the *New York Herald* and *Augusta Chronicle* on July 22, a Sunday. Also 2,000 copies should be printed and placed in the hands of the chief of police for distribution throughout the country. The notice read as follows:

A REWARD
Of
ONE THOUSAND DOLLARS. ($1000.)

Will be paid for the arrest and delivery to the Sheriff of Richmond County, Georgia, of THOMAS W. ALEXANDER, charged with various felonies and Misdemeanors under the laws of said State, who Absconded from Augusta, Georgia, July 7th, 1906.

Description: Age forty-four or five. Height: Six feet one inch, blonde type. Figure: Broad shouldered, Erect, well proportioned and inclined to be stout. Greyish blue eyes, bald with small fringe of light sandy Hair. Known to have been in New York City (and Probably at the Waldorf-Astoria) Sunday evening July 8, 1906.

OR

A REWARD OF $500.00

Will be paid for his arrest and detention at any place in the United States until requisition papers for his return to Georgia can be obtained.

OR

A REWARD OF $500.00

Will be paid for his arrest and detention for extradition in Any place in Canada, Great Britain or the Continent of Europe or elsewhere.

**Georgia Railroad Bank,
Augusta, Ga.**

CHAPTER TEN

The history of the Georgia Railroad and Banking Company written by Joseph B. Cumming in 1971 contains an account of the following change which without doubt came about as a result of the Alexander & Alexander failure:

> In 1906, a substantial loss was sustained by reason of the Bank's being inadequately protected in a line of credit with a cotton factorage house, so in September of that year nine of the principal cotton factors met with the Finance Committee of the Bank to discuss the Bank's security, and an agreement was reached permitting inspection of warehouses by the Bank to count bales and check the amount advanced to the owners.

Both Pat Walsh and Craig Cranston , Jr. confirm that Mr. Alexander was convicted and spent some time in the slammer due to improper trading in the cotton warehouse receipts. Pat actually wrote he served his sentence in the "Georgia penitentiary." From then on the Alexanders always regarded Jacob Phinizy II, president of Georgia Railroad Bank 1897-1924, as the great villain in the case for they often premised that Phinizy took a personal interest in prosecuting their father; the children felt he went above and way beyond the call of duty as the bank certainly could have given Mr. Alexander more time to satisfy the loans. Whatever the actual facts, the situation obviously had a most traumatic affect on the minds and feelings of the entire family and most especially the children as they grew.

Pat Walsh wrote that Mary, being the oldest girl and a young teenager in 1906, was considered to have been the most affected psychologically by the scandal. He said "she was an embittered woman" and that she and the other ladies always continued to revile Jacob Phinizy even after he was long deceased, 1924 being the year of his death. The Alexanders were pretty hard up financially after the failure of the cotton firm, and that is why they were still living in the house at 1027 Telfair when in my early youth I drove with my mother Frank to visit her good friend Henrietta Alexander. This must have been around 1937 or 1938.

Of course, I had known Henrietta long before from her visits to our house in Augusta, at Edisto Beach, and even before at Wrightsville Beach, North Carolina, when she came to stay with my parents. The Telfair Street house was rather dark inside and mysterious; I was taken up to the second floor to meet Aunt Jess (or Jessie), an old lady then bedridden and I now believe the widowed sister of Henrietta's mother. Aunt Jess (1847-1938) was the widow of Francis Stovall. I think our visit was to pick up some plants for our garden as Mary and Henrietta were helping Frank decide how to build and develop a new flower-cutting garden. I recall large round flower beds in the Alexander front yard at No. 1027 all filled with bright flowers and of varying varieties.

I rather think Frank and Henrietta initially were often thrown together at the Frank Barrett house at 805 Milledge as Sadie Cranston Barrett and the Alexander siblings were all first cousins. Thus their friendship

CHAPTER TEN

began; contract bridge was also a factor and much played in those days with both ladies and on occasion with men at nighttime supper parties. Though Henrietta was some six years older than Frank Mays, by the late 1920s and 1930s the age difference was less important for there were other mutual interests, including the Junior Workers/Junior League, and Anna Eve Fleming (called "Willie"), who was Henrietta's first cousin once removed (or second cousin) and Frank's close friend, plus the entire range of rather "Roaring Twenties" attitude and its at times irresponsible behavior (at least to some folks!).

There were private "Tacky Parties" at the country club, the club's weekly dinner dances, frequent swimming parties at the Frank Barrett's private pool, and no one had much to do at home as servants were cheap. These were the country-wide prohibition of alcohol days although no one ever had any difficulty in securing alcoholic beverages. Frank liked champagne but gradually moved on to gin and matured "corn," if I read it correctly. Close friends (or intimate friends as they then termed it) now called Henrietta "Ebba," and I have seen a small photograph of several ladies, including Ebba and Frank, sitting I believe on the Telfair Street house porch holding bridge hands. At parties Frank said Ebba on occasion would seem inebriated quite early in the evening with all wondering why, as most were on their first drink; she finally suspected that Ebba would slip into the kitchen or butler's pantry where the bar usually was located and "wolf one down" on the sly!

Henrietta from all accounts was enchanted with Frank and Bowdre who in those heady days really were "a golden couple"; she loved their company and even in her final quite ill period in the 1950s asked for nothing more than to have Frank and Bowdre to come visit as per John Walton. She was visiting the Mayses at Wrightsville Beach, North Carolina, in 1931 when a twenty-dollar check Frank had given her bounced, thereby alerting the payer to her beginning money problems! Henrietta herself would run short of the filthy lucre at times, and in the early 1930s dispatch her maid or maybe butler around to the Furniture Market at Broad and 11th Streets with a note and envelope containing her single solitaire diamond ring set in gold. She asked Bowdre to pawn the ring for the best return possible and then would reverse the procedure and send the pawn ticket later to Bowdre to redeem her ring when she again was in funds!

During these preliminary Depression days, Henrietta also was very close to her second cousin William K. (Billy) Barrett who could charm one and all and who always was ready for a party or bridge game. Henrietta probably also advanced him funds from time to time in these early days as her situation permitted.

Even if ready cash were scarce or deficient, the Alexander home on Telfair usually would provide a cordial welcome to friends, young and old. Their food was excellent and enjoyed a well-deserved reputation downtown and on The Hill. The Barretts of 805 Milledge would loan them Robert O'Brien (and particularly

CHAPTER TEN

after the 1935 fire) who not only butlered but also was a fabulous cook. Then in this era there was also Claude Tillman, the valued butler of the Tom Barretts, who after Mayor Tom suddenly died in June 1934 was sort of "deeded" to the Augusta National Golf Club by Louise Barrett. Claude Tillman and Robert O'Brien also did "moonlighting" and worked all over Augusta but mainly on The Hill. Tom Barrett left Claude Tillman a house just off Fleming Avenue, but his wife Pearl would not move from downtown, so he rented the dwelling. Messrs. O'Brien and Tillman were then but separately the Joe Willis Group of today in Augusta.

The Alexander household, largely managed by the eldest sister Mary, developed in the Depression days a favorite dish they called "goulash," although there is really no connection to the Hungarian variety; however, it is sort of a ragout of minced beef and veal highly flavored with chili powder, chili sauce, and mixed with vermicelli, tomatoes, mushrooms, etc. So the "Alexander goulash" lives on into the twenty-first century with the Mays and allied families where it is enjoyed often; it is a fine dish as one hot item on a buffet table. The late Emma Mason told me of times she went with Billy Barrett to the Alexander house for parties or a meal with Robert O'Brien in charge of the food and dining room. Genie Lehmann also recalls nights spent with the Alexanders as a friend of Anne Barrett who was so fond of "Aunt Nellie."

The end, as with all matters, finally arrived for number 1027 Telfair with the death of William J. Craig, trustee, on November 6, 1945. As John Craig's will dictated, the estate then was terminated, and all residents had to move out so the property could be sold. At this time I think only some of the ladies, certainly Mary and Henrietta, and perhaps Tom if he had returned from World War II, were living there. No. 1027 Telfair was sold to the Pontiac auto dealership ("Pontiac Master") who later sold the house again; it is now located at 3032 Pine Needle Road having been expanded if I view it correctly and all covered in a brick veneer. This data all comes from Ashby Taylor and Craig Cranston, Craig descendants both. The house as I write in July 2006 is now offered through the multiple listings at $895,000.

Pat Walsh wrote that the Alexander ladies first moved to a Henry Street house and later to the little house on the King estate; the latter was originally the kitchen part of the burned manor house and had been added on to by the Gregorinis for their visits from Italy. Henrietta gave a supper party for the Mays-Hull wedding party in August 1947 at the King estate house; her health even then was failing, but of course she made the effort because of her long friendship and love for Frank and Bowdre. This was the last time I saw Henrietta as I now recall that hot late Augusta evening on their terrace. This house has now disappeared but was used by the Alexanders in 1947 and in subsequent years.

Mary and Henrietta Alexander and Jessie Taylor finally built a small brick house at 2346 Kings Way circa late 1940s-early 1950s. Craig Cranston advised that Craig estate money built this house as the Alexander

CHAPTER TEN

ladies had all inherited from John Craig. Mary Craig Alexander survived her sisters and ended her days at age seventy-seven in the George Walton Apartments. Mary was the most serious sister and probably had taken much better care of herself all those years. Her nephew, Ashby Taylor, wrote from Decatur, Georgia, that "Aunt Mary" left everything to the Bishop Alexander Family in North Augusta. Unfortunately, I have been unable to interview or even locate any of Bishop's descendants to date. He has no marker on the Alexander/Craig plot at Magnolia Cemetery. Bishop Alexander as listed was the eldest Alexander child and is said to have descendants.

CHAPTER XI

**Bowdre Phinizy Mays, Jr.:
A Life Spent Largely Abroad**

As 1926 was well underway, Frank and Bowdre were expecting their second child, their first, Ruth Inman Mays, living only thirty-six hours in 1925. Both sides of the family were very pleased, as this would be Frankie Doughty's first grandchild and the first from Grandmother Phinizy's grandson, who was named for her own beloved son. On visits to 519 Greene Street, Mother Phinizy, as Bowdre always called her, was quite attentive to Frank, insisting she always use the elevator to the upper floors where the living and dining rooms were situated and when on the sofa or in a chair surrounding her with down pillows to make her comfortable. Unfortunately, my great-grandmother Phinizy died following a relatively short illness on November 26, 1926. Her final illness began during a trip to New York and Baltimore just six weeks before, so she never had the pleasure of my company, or me hers!

I was born early (5:00 to 5:30 a.m.) on February 4, 1927, at University Hospital, weighing in at nine pounds. The doctor signing the birth certificate was Lewis Wright, with the parents' address listed as 2817 Hillcrest Avenue, Father's occupation as "Frigidaire salesman," and Mother's as "Housewife." As Frank always went to the hospital in those days with her own linen and lacy pillows plus a private trained nurse, I am certain we were both well cocooned. The hospital stay in those days, I am told, was a week or more, and the trained nurse, who I believe was Katherine Armstrong, also moved with Frank and the newly born to 2817 Hillcrest Avenue for some time before all baby tasks were transferred to my baby nurse, Mamie Byrd.

At some point, there was a second nurse called "Nursie Coleman," who may have come on board either somewhat before or when Frank, my sister, arrived May 17, 1928 (Mary "D." Phinizy and Frank both deciding to get pregnant at the same time, their two daughters, Frank Inman Mays and Betty Palmer Phinizy, became lifelong friends as well as born cousins).

I was christened at St. Paul's Church, wearing the robe still in the family and used now by our grandchildren. This was made in Atlanta by my great-grandmother

CHAPTER ELEVEN

Mrs. Walker P. Inman and was worn also by my mother at a similar event at St. Paul's. My godparents were Uncle Marion Ridgely, Sr., Uncle Walker Inman, and Aunt Mary Lou Phinizy. All of this was duly reported in the local press in the days when such an occasion was big news! However, we began Sunday School at Good Shepherd, and I was confirmed there May 12, 1940. The parents probably couldn't be bothered to cart us downtown on Sundays, as I recall Mother at times driving us all to Good Shepherd in her nightgown and robe! One teacher I did enjoy at Sunday School was Eleanor Wright Teague, and another, for a short period, was Rodney Cohen, Jr. This was the time of the Reverend Hobart Barber, followed by the Reverends Lawrence Fenwick and Allen Clarkson. For an unknown stupid reason, I declined to be an acolyte, although the Ridgelys, who were very devout members, urged me to join the acolyte training class as Hank McGowan and Jack Sherman did. Why I refused is still unknown to me now.

I still have a few memories of 2817 Hillcrest: Willis "Sonny" Irvin riding me around the block on his horse (Mother paying him twenty-five cents); the Christmas when Santa Claus called from the North Pole (I found out years later it was really Joe Mathewson); and having a "picnic," as they called it, in the den about 1931-1932 when the electricity had been cut off due to nonpayment and we were about to move. They heated Mr. Campbell's tomato soup in a pot held into the fireplace!

I also recall Grandmother Doughty accompanied by Auntie T (Ted Ridgely) and driven by Willie Washington coming by many afternoons to take me to ride. I would snuggle between the ladies in the back seat of the Buick or Pierce-Arrow, and in chilly weather there was a fur car rug to fold over our legs and knees, as cars in those days contained no heat or air conditioning. My favorite itinerary was to drive around the residential section overlooking Lake Olmstead to a vacant lot where an old wrecked motorcar lay. "To the old car," I would direct in my childish voice! Grandmother Doughty had a lot of time for me, and I grew to both admire and love her deeply. She would tell me family stories and, to a large extent, focus on all positive aspects. She was generally a very happy person. She was my first teacher relative to family lore and how a young boy should comport himself.

Willie Washington had been with the Doughty-Inman ménage since Frank was a young girl, taking care first of horses, her pony, and, later, cars. He taught me to ride a two-wheeler bicycle when I was five or six and, following Grandmother's death in 1939, worked full time at our house in the yard, kitchen, and at table. After her death, we also had Grandmother's cook, Florrie Favors, for many years. Willie always went with us to Edisto Beach each summer and eventually married or lived with our then nurse called "Lottie," who looked after Inman, Ted, and Sam. Mamie Byrd left us to go to work for the Berry Fleming family, who took her to New York City. This must have been around the time we moved from Hillcrest Avenue. Mamie's son, Harold, later worked for Skippy Hull Boyd as cook-butler, and

CHAPTER ELEVEN

he once told me Mamie kept up to date with us through him, for she never returned to live in Augusta.

In my very early years, Mamie Byrd would take me in a stroller to Slusky's Corner on Walton Way on fine afternoons; many nurses and their young charges tended to congregate in the vicinity and perhaps rest on the low wall. Uncle Bowdre Phinizy, now married to "Miss Meta" McGowan (in 1928), came by and asked the name of several babies. Mamie told him my full name, and he asked her to tell his mother he would give her $10,000 to change my name! Frank sent him word that I was not named for him but rather my father, who of course was named for his uncle! Uncle Bowdre loved to make such jokes and "pull legs," so they say. Considering the value of $10,000 in those days, it might in retrospect have been an intelligent idea to take the money and perhaps rename me Benjamin Yancey or even Charles Phinizy after Cousin Charlie! That would have pleased another in the family!

I do not think playgroups were available in those days, as nurses were plentiful and cheap. My first schooling, therefore, was Mrs. Clark's Kindergarten on Williams Street just across from William Robinson where I went to first grade. The pretty and young Miss Sheron was my first-grade teacher and often wore a flower or ribbon in her hair. We buried "ain't" and "got" in the schoolyard one day, but that made little impression, for we often heard well-educated family and others take great and probably perverse pleasure in using such terms! Being born in February, I was a tad younger than others who began with me, and it was decided to hold me back for one year. I must have repeated first grade, finding my ultimate classmates to be the following girls and boys: Betty Boardman, Mary Barrett, Suzanne Hardy, Sally Bussey, Betty Nance, Anna Maxwell, and boys Alfred Martin, Donald Boardman, Mike Calhoun, Bill Lester, Rusty Bailie, Henri McGowan, Hoyt Kirby, Al Kitchens, Arthur Merry, John Smith, John Phinizy, Grover Maxwell, Jr., etc.

Miss Kathleen Lowe was school principal, a rather grande-dame sort with jutting bosom who always carried a large nest of keys in her diamond-ringed hand. The worst punishment was to be sent to her office; why, I never discovered, for nothing took place once one arrived.

In those days, we had seven grades, with Mrs. Arthur Fielder teaching the seventh. We graduated in 1940, and at the commencement exercises in the school auditorium, I was asked by Mrs. Fielder to make a short speech of thanks, presumably to all and sundry, but mainly the staff, and to hand out gifts to Miss Lowe and perhaps others. Donald Boardman was scheduled to perform the same chore in case one of us was away, and in any event I think he was out sick. My parents and Aunt Mary Lou attended the ceremony and seemed pleased at my public speaking debut following weeks of practice sessions where Mrs. Fielder insisted on expression and tried to teach us to avoid a monotone and use our hands to gesture.

Then on to Richmond Academy for four years, graduating in May of 1944 at age seventeen. World

CHAPTER ELEVEN

War II was in full force, so to avoid being drafted when I turned eighteen in February of 1945, my father conceived the bright idea of my joining then what was known as ASTP (Army Specialized Training Program). Under this program, I would be sent to college/university all paid for by "Uncle Sugar," continue the military training I had already begun at Richmond Academy (which had ROTC), and wear army uniforms, being a part of the Army Reserve, in essence. Then when I was eighteen, I would proceed to basic training and then return to the college to get the four-year degree, after which one would be sent to Officer Training School. A great scheme to avoid being simply used for cannon fodder! I went to North Carolina State College in Raleigh in September of 1944 by train from Columbia, South Carolina, driven to the latter by mother.

After my eighteenth birthday (February 1945), I reported to active duty but was honorably discharged after the new physical due to severe myopia. By 1945, the war in Europe was winding down, so the need for many new recruits was drastically reduced. I then obtained a government job at the Augusta Arsenal as a messenger delivering mail between the various departments by bicycle and trolley. I presume my job experience at the Augusta Post Office during several Christmas seasons eminently qualified me for this position! After three months, I entered the University of Georgia in June of 1945 for the summer session, planning to graduate in three years, which could be accomplished by adding in the summers. I achieved my goal, obtaining my BA degree in June of 1948, driving up to Athens alone early one morning and returning that afternoon. Most of the family was at the Edisto Beach house.

One seminal event occurred in spring of 1948 (although at the time I had no way of knowing the impact on my life), when Mary Barrett (now Robertson) asked me to join a group of friends for a dinner party in her honor at the Terrace Room of the Bon Air Hotel. This was a party hosted by Mr. and Mrs. Harold V. Smith, who were visiting from New York City. Mother told me how Alice Davison Smith was an Augustan whose mother, Emma, had been a close friend of Frankie Doughty. As a matter of fact, Emma's picture had been in Grandmother's scrapbook, and I later saw a portrait in the Smith's New York apartment on Gracie Square, probably painted from that same picture. Emma was lovely looking. We gathered for drinks in the Smiths' suite prior to dinner, and Mr. H. V. asked what I was planning to do with my life following graduation in June. I told him of my strong interest in Foreign Service, and he imparted some particulars of his business and its foreign operations. He was then CEO of The Home Insurance Company of New York, which operated in Central America, Cuba, Puerto Rico, and the British and French West Indies under that name and through a property and casualty consortium in other parts of the world. The consortium was founded in 1918 and known as AFIA (American Foreign Insurance Association), of which Mr. H. V. was then non-executive chairman, with The Home owning

CHAPTER ELEVEN

perhaps 25 to 30 percent. Our conversation ended in an invitation to let him know when I had definitely decided how to proceed.

Looking back a bit in deep retrospect, I guess the tales of trips to Europe by family and their friends and Grandmother Doughty's visit to Hawaii, Japan, Korea, and China in 1935 had important impact. I had sent away for a book on the US Foreign Service to learn how to go about sitting for that exam and then much regretted I had turned down Aunt Mary Lou's earlier offer of French lessons by the lady who was then instructing Craig Cranston! Daddy and John Walton took me to call on a Foreign Service officer (a Mr. Jennings) then living in Augusta following his retirement. I believe he had been an ambassador at some minor post, and when we were back in our car Daddy said he was disappointed he did not say he would call a former colleague or someone to help me! I did excel in languages at the University of Georgia, studying both Latin and Spanish to rather high levels. Aunt Mary Lou had treated me to a study trip to Mexico the summer of 1946 when I traveled with a group from a college called Trinity in San Antonio. This improved my command of the language, which I think is the easiest of the Romance variety to learn.

The summer of 1938, Aunt Mary Lou had invited me to visit at her house on Satulah Mountain in Highlands, North Carolina (about a three to four-hour drive from Augusta). There I also had great foreign exposure with Aunt Mary Lou Phinizy and Miss Tracy regaling me with their stories of travel in Europe and times in Paris, etc. We were friends with the German family the Kratinas, who had a rented house, and there were other foreign embassy persons visiting friends in the vicinity. Frederic Kratina and I were about the same age, so we saw each other often; the Kratinas came from Dresden, where they had lived for some years. Marguerite Pressly Kratina's father, Charles, had been in the United States Diplomatic Service (United States vice consul general at Paris) many years, and the distinguished old gentleman now lived with them in Augusta. The Presslys were related to Pleasant Stovall (US minister to Switzerland), and Pleasant had introduced Charles Pressly to the State Department. I also recall a German Embassy person visiting them from Washington, and we all climbed Whiteside Mountain together.

Craig Cranston was a few years older and staying with his family, who also had a house lower down on Satulah. He took little notice of me (even though his parents probably told him to show me around!) and once tried to put a match to "Sugarlump's" gonads! "Sugarlump" was a wire-haired fox terrier who had been given to Aunt Mary Lou by Frank and Bowdre years before. He was ancient by 1938 and quite crotchety, although he did love to have me take him to walk on a leash.

The time spent in Highlands also opened new vistas in that across the street were the David Blacks. Cousin Marion Black was a Phinizy, being Leonard's daughter, so my grandmother Hattie Phinizy Mays had been her first cousin. Her husband was known as "Pinky," and

CHAPTER ELEVEN

they lived in Atlanta. They had a charming daughter Anne a few years older than I who had a convertible Pontiac and, I assume, a driver's license. We went for many drives and played a lot of badminton at their court on a flat piece carved from the mountainside. She introduced me to the Cunninghams from Scarsdale, New York, who were related to the Misses Elliott, friends and neighbors of us all. Charles Cunningham and I played together and climbed Satulah, too. I suppose I had kind of a "crush" on Anne, if that is possible for an eleven to twelve-year-old idiot! Anne and her husband, David R. Berry, were killed in the Air France plane crash at Orly Airport in Paris in June of 1962. They were on the Arts Museum trip and left two sons. I had the pleasure of meeting Christopher Berry and his family in March 2001 when they came to the Phinizy family reunion with the Phinizy Swamp as the principal venue. His mother and grandparents Black were lovely people, always giving me much attention. Their chauffeur (whose name I cannot now recall) while in Highlands also gave me time, and I would spend hours talking to him about cars, as his boss, Pinky Black, was an enthusiast and, I think, also something of an inventor of automotive products.

This first summer, or maybe the next, 1939, we went for lunch one Sunday to a Highlands Country Club Cottage, which our cousins, the Hulls, Garretts, and, I believe, Neelys had rented. There for the first time, I met Jim Hull, Jr., then attending V.M.I., who came to the car to greet us. Mr. Henry Garrett, Sr. told me how, as a child, I would talk to him through the bushes dividing his lot on Walton Way from 2817 Hillcrest, where I then lived. It was a jolly crowd, and I felt right at home getting to know all these cousins on a "grown-up" basis.

Miss Bernadina Taliaferro (known as "Miss Dina") also was a guest at Aunt Mary Lou's house one summer. At one time, Miss Dina and her mother, Mrs. E. S. Taliaferro, took "paying guests" in their Hickman Road home. Dina and Aunt Mary Lou were lifelong friends, with Aunt Mary Lou helping her in case of need. Dina never married, and at one stage worked for a dentist as receptionist. Miss Dina was a sweet, diminutive lady who, at times, seemed to profess some shock or surprise at Aunt Mary Lou's blunt and to-the-point statements regarding people and events of the day. Mary Lou evidently thought her a bit naïve. Dina was always kind and told me stories about past events in Augusta. She even forgave me once for eating a major portion of her Swiss chocolate bar with almonds or hazelnuts without her permission! Back in Augusta, she often took Sunday dinner at 814 Milledge Road with Aunt Mary Lou and the Bussey and Mays families.

My great-great uncle Jake (Jacob Phinizy II) was very fond of Bernandina and her mother, to the extent that in his will, probated in 1924, he deeded his interest in the Hickman Road house (now owned by Bryan Haltermann) to them. Uncle Jake was mayor of Augusta 1901 through 1903 and also president of Georgia Railroad Bank from 1897 until his death in 1924.

CHAPTER ELEVEN

Another interesting Satulah Mountain summer resident was the Cheshire Nash family from Savannah. Their house was new, just a short walk from Mary Lou Phinizy's house, and I often was employed as an equerry to deliver notes back and forth, usually invitations to drinks or supper. Violet Nash was fun, as was her daughter Ann. Violet always came armed with a silver flask carrying her scotch, which I think was seldom around in that era. She was a great friend of Sophie Meldrim Shonnard, who also was Mary Lou Phinizy's close and dear friend. Sophie at that time lived in New York City. Violet spent many months in Highlands every year to get away from the heat; also the cooler climate appeared to dampen her allergy problem. Violet had an older daughter known as "Little Vee," while she sometimes was referred to as "Big Vee." Little Vee married Olin McIntosh, whose family owned much of the present Hilton Head Island. Lynn and I visited them at their house at Bram's Point around 1970 or 1971 when on vacation from Singapore at Hilton Head. Cheshire Nash was president of Columbia Naval Stores Company, and this crowd, including Aunt Mary Lou, Miss Tracy, and Sophie Meldrim Shonnard, all loved to discuss the US Civil War and how President Lincoln, in his 1863 Emancipation Proclamation, set free only the slaves in the rebellious states and not in the entire Union. I formerly discussed this subject in more detail in Chapter IV.

My daughter, Katherine, in 1999, began urging me to write these recollections, as it then was my seventy-second birthday. She even sent a series of questions and comments to jog the memory, and one strangely enough was, "Were you ever an escort at a debutante or cotillion ball? If so, describe it." Well, in 1947, there was a debutante group (I think for the first time since World War II); included therein were Frenchie Battey, Nancy Marshall, Betty Phinizy, Anne Claussen, Mary Jo Howerdd, and Martha Wienges, always called "String." The latter asked me to be her date for the large presentation dance party given at the original country club building by all the debs and their parents. White tie and the works, including white gloves for all plus the necessity to send a minimum of one large white orchid to one's date. Frank complained, I recall, about the twenty dollars she paid for one white, while the lavender variety cost around five to ten, depending on size! Frenchie Battey Bush recently confirmed the late 1947 date and showed me pictures of the event. There were also many other parties given to honor this or that deb, particularly during the Christmas season. My only other memory of that ball is Mary "D." Goodrich showing me the charming small bouquet or nosegay sent by Frank and Bowdre to Betty Phinizy. There was a table on which many flowers sent to honor the debs were displayed, for they could not hold or wear them all! For some reason, Frank and Bowdre did not attend, although I can recall speaking to Mary Lou and Tracy, who were holding court and surveying the scene from one side of the ballroom. Mary Lou always referred to String as "Miss Wienges"!

    Following graduation from the university in June of 1948, I wrote Mr. Harold V. Smith in New York asking

CHAPTER ELEVEN

for a business interview, as I had great interest in their international network. He responded promptly, inviting me to come see him in New York City and to advise the date of arrival. So in early September, I departed Augusta, hitching a ride as far as Philadelphia with Red Boardman, who then was attending the University of Pennsylvania. We traveled in his Studebaker coupe; these cars were among the first to roll out new models after World War II, and I think one of the Boardman family sold them at that time. We made one stop for the night en route at Roanoke, Virginia, to visit Hollins College, as I was anxious to see Ann Sydenstricker. After a fairly late night, which included surveying the view from a high hill or low mountain where we parked, we were off again. The only other details I recall were picking fresh cotton from fields along the way to fill the space below the rear window and stopping at Howard Johnson's, which then advertised thirty or more flavors of ice cream and always wanting one not on the menu!

Reaching Philadelphia around 7:00 p.m., Red offered to put me up for the night at his place, but as I wanted to move on and get settled in New York, I decided to take the train that evening. We said goodbye at the 30th Street Station, but on arriving and finding that the several hotels known to me had no free rooms at that hour, my hasty departure from Philadelphia was regretted. I had made no reservation. How stupid and naïve! Spending most of the night at Penn Station, I finally located a room early the next morning at a "fleabag" called

"Stafford Hotel" around the 34th Street vicinity. Mr. H. V. had never heard of it.

Visiting then CEO Harold V. Smith of The Home Insurance Company at their downtown (Wall Street area) headquarters at 59 Maiden Lane was a real revelation. His office was palatial, and he was treated and venerated as a king! He sent me over to his international unit, then known as American Foreign Insurance Association, to meet Ugo Guerrini, general manager. Mr. Guerrini was most cordial, and when in later years I knew him better, I found he had that rather indefinable attribute we call native charm. He was married to a Southerner, Floride Groover, who I think came from Jacksonville and who had met Ugo in Florence (his home) when on a trip to Europe. He eventually followed her to this country and had been with AFIA based in Europe before assuming his present position around 1945 to 1946. Ugo soon turned me over to his chief assistant, Lilbourne Irvine, known around New York as "Bert," who invited me to lunch at the Banker's Club on a high floor of one of the downtown office towers. Ugo also first introduced me to Ned Hitt, with whom I was to become good friends and colleagues in the years ahead. Ned came from Atlanta and was then organizing AFIA's casualty operations. He left for Japan soon after our meeting. I learned much later that his mother was a Slaton and therefore closely connected to the Butt and Doughty clans of Augusta.

The lunch was pleasant, and I found that Mr. Irvine was a close relative of kin of mine on the Phinizy side and had spent many school years in Augusta while his

CHAPTER ELEVEN

parents were in business in Brazil. He was born in Brazil and spoke Portuguese perfectly. His father had gone to Brazil in 1895 as a representative of the American Banknote Company and married a Danish lady he met there. Bert had married Dorothy Lombard from Augusta and had lived with the John Phinizy family, Dr. Irvine Phinizy being his first cousin, during some of his school years. He remembered Frank and Bowdre from his Augusta years. When we parted on the street corner following lunch, I asked if I had the job, i.e., to enter their training program for overseas service. He replied that it was up to Mr. Guerrini, and my heart and hopes took a tumble!

Immediately, I reported back to Mr. H. V., who then at once picked up the phone and asked to be put through to Mr. Guerrini, who he jokingly called a "Wop" to his telephone operator! I was told then to report for work the next day! Mr. H. V. told me I was the third Augustan he had helped with a position, and the first two had failed, whether from homesickness or inattention to work, I do not know. He hoped I would succeed and make the most of this splendid opportunity. I asked him to endorse a cheque my father had given me the morning of my departure from Augusta in an envelope marked "Last Will and Testament." He inquired, "Where did Bowdre get a hundred dollars?" and I recall being irritated when responding, "He made it!"

Mr. H. V. introduced me next to Joe Carruth, the then vice president of The Home Insurance Company's Southern Department. Joe was from Charlotte, North

Carolina, and he and his wife were childless. In these early days, they were most cordial, inviting me to dinner at their lower 5th Avenue apartment and taking me along on other outings in Greenwich Village, etc. Joe arranged for me to move to the Sloan House YMCA on 34th Street (I think that same night) and then later, a week or more, to the 63rd Street YMCA just off Central Park West. The 63rd Street "Y" was more like a residential hotel in those days, with good weekly rates, an in-house cafeteria, a library, and a health club with pool catering to residents and non-residents. This was my home until I left for Japan in June of 1949. I was very lucky to get in, as such was not easy in that era. My accommodation was a small room with a sink and mirror and also an in-room telephone, with bathroom facilities located down the hall. There was one window looking out over some rooftops.

Either Joe Carruth or Mr. H. V. also had me meet Robert (Bob) Bodet, vice president of The Home Insurance Company and a former employee of AFIA in Egypt and perhaps other countries. Bob Bodet then managed The Home's direct operations in the Caribbean and Central America and attended AFIA's board or committee meetings when Mr. H. V. so directed. Bob came from New Orleans and continued to be a friend and resource until his retirement, probably in the early 1980s. He also had been an OSS operative during the World War II days.

The AFIA "training program" at that time was rather informal, consisting of rotation to the various underwriting and claims departments where routine tasks

CHAPTER ELEVEN

were assigned; such was supplemented by study classes at the Insurance Society of New York about three nights a week after the offices closed at 5:00 p.m. Classes began around 5:30 or 6:00 p.m., lasting one and a half to two hours. I enrolled in General Insurance Practices and Marine Insurance, the latter because I had been assigned first to the Marine Underwriting Department, then headed by Anthony Muldoon, who had been in Manila when World War II began and spent the war years in Santo Tomas prisoner of war camp during the entire Japanese occupation.

My direct boss was Robert Henshaw, who had a dry sense of humor and liked two-martini lunches! I traveled to and from the office, then located at 80 Maiden Lane (the Continental Insurance Company building), by subway from Columbus Circle, only several blocks from the West 63rd Street "Y." Although I cannot exactly remember my starting salary, it was miniscule by New York, and probably all, standards in 1948! After paying the rent and transportation costs, with an allowance for food daily, there was nothing left over for emergencies or even entertainment! Some months I gave out entirely, having to borrow a few dollars until next payday (every two weeks) or arrange to take meals at the "Y's" cafeteria on "tick" until I was able to pay it all off. Once or twice, I even had to appeal to my father for funds to be sent via Western Union. I had no bank account then, and there were no credit cards!

During the work week, some of us often went to an underground luncheon spot, jokingly known as "Eat'em and Beat'em." Here one lined up to pass by the lady cashier simply calling out what one owed after choosing the food (sort of an automat environment) and eating with everyone standing at tall and round tables. Sandwiches were fifteen to twenty cents, and I enjoyed my first fried oyster sandwich, but which cost a bit more. I never ordered the hot dishes, although on cold days I longed for the hearty beef stew or other more costly dishes that many ate with relish. After leaving the subway at Columbus Circle, following work and class, if any that day, I usually stopped in at the Horn and Hardart Automat just off the Circle for supper, or dinner as they grandly called it. My standard choice was chicken a la king on rice with fresh spinach on the side taken with one hard roll and butter. If I could afford it, I might add iceberg lettuce and dressing, and on payday I always splurged, asking for lamb (freshly carved at the counter) or roast beef. I think the lamb cost about sixty-five cents, while the chicken a la king and rice, say, about thirty-five cents. On the meat days, the complete meal might cost ninety or ninety-five cents, no tip required!

I used the library at the "Y" and recall reading most of Maugham during that first winter. On weekends, I swam in the heated pool, ran on the indoor track, and occasionally took a full sun bath under the ultraviolet lights, then not considered dangerous. I also rather systematically explored New York City: Statue of Liberty, Ferry to Staten Island at five cents each way, famous museums, including the Cloisters of the Metropolitan, Frick, Whitney, Museum of Natural History, and several

CHAPTER ELEVEN

lesser known sites. I walked everywhere in fine weather, west to east across Central Park South, then twenty to thirty blocks up and down, plus the longer blocks across on the East Side, i.e., 5th to Madison, the latter to Park, to Lexington, etc. I was a great window shopper. On Sundays, the Harold Smiths had me to lunch often at their spacious and elegant 10 Gracie Square duplex apartment. Their Swedish cook, Agnes, always prepared the same menu: a large roast beef (which Mr. H. V. carved), Yorkshire pudding, roast potatoes, a green vegetable, and coleslaw made with a piquant sauce containing much mustard. For some reason, I do not recall the desserts, but they were likely ice cream, probably vanilla, for I seem to remember vaguely a hot chocolate sauce.

On occasion, there were other Sunday guests (e.g. Sophie Meldrim Shonnard and her son, Ted Coy, or once Katherine Barrett Murphy), but often I was the sole invitee. Mr. H. V. delighted in offering a cocktail he made in his bar, beautifully paneled in a lightish colored wood, and it was here where we all sat before lunch was announced or for a drink in the evening. The Smiths' large duplex apartment overlooked the square and the East River, with a beautiful view from the living room, where hung the portrait of Emma Davison mentioned before. Miss Alice and Mr. H. V. talked about Frankie Doughty and her close friendship with Emma, and how my grandmother and the Judge Barretts helped arrange their wedding long before. Harold Smith first met Alice Davison when he came to Augusta to investigate a theft of some jewelry. His career was rather meteoric, first in Philadelphia beginning as special agent of the Franklin Fire Insurance Company, which in due course merged into the Home Insurance Company, at one time the single largest writer of fire and property insurance in the United States. The Smiths had one surviving daughter, Emma Johnson, who then lived with her husband, Bucky (an executive with Marsh and McLennan Insurance Brokers), in New Canaan, Connecticut. There were several granddaughters. The Smiths often visited them on, say, a Saturday, driving from New York City.

Mr. H. V. had a Lincoln, or maybe a Cadillac Town Car (the kind where the chauffeur sat up front in the open; perhaps there was a roof which could be shut), and I often saw the vehicle waiting outside Maiden Lane to collect him as I was en route to the insurance class or subway. One evening, the Smiths invited me for dinner at "21 Club" and then on to the theatre. I think the Joe Carruths also were along, as the town car contained jump seats in the rear so five passengers were comfortable. I can't remember how I was picked up; it is likely we all gathered at 10 Gracie Square for a drink prior to dinner, but I do recall the warm reception at "21," where the Smiths were well known.

On another occasion, Aunt Mary Lou came to town to visit Sophie Meldrim Shonnard, and the Smiths sent the car and chauffeur to us for the day so we could tour the city. We lunched at "SeaFare" under the El on 3rd Avenue, and Miss Sophie had asked me to take supper with them at her apartment, then on Madison Avenue.

CHAPTER ELEVEN

Her French maid, Thérése, spoke English with a heavy accent and was exactly like what one would expect a French lady's maid of some years to be. Thérése had been with the family for many years and was quite fond of Sophie's two sons, and Aunt Mary Lou as well as me eventually by extension, calling me always "Miss Phinizy's nephew." She knew something also about the South, having lived with the family when they owned Harrietta Plantation near Charleston.

Aunt Mary Lou took me another day, early Saturday I believe, to Roger Kent (Sophie having told her the prices beat Brooks) to buy an overcoat. Roger Kent was really a "Brooks knock-off," as they say now. For sixty-five dollars, we bought a brown tweed wool overcoat, not having any heavy coat suitable for the winter rapidly approaching. I really wanted a gabardine topcoat, but Aunt Mary Lou insisted on wool, and such was a splendid decision! She made clear this was also a Christmas present for 1948. On the street following the purchase, we ran into Yancey relatives from Rome, Georgia, and they invited us to lunch with them at the St. Regis Hotel. This was Cousin Claire and her husband, Austin Clark. Claire was the daughter of Uncle Hamilton Yancey, brother of Mary Lou Yancey Phinizy. Thus, she was Aunt Mary Lou's first cousin, but they had enjoyed no real recent contact. The Clarks were an elegant looking couple, tall and well turned out so that Aunt Mary Lou insisted on returning to the Shonnard flat for her fur jacket prior to our early lunch date as she had matinée tickets.

I wrote more about the Yanceys in my Chapter II, as they were an interesting family with several memorable members. At this encounter by chance in New York, I then recalled that we had met a soldier stationed at Fort Gordon around the end of World War II, probably a son or nephew of Claire's, and he came to our house with Aunt Mary Lou, who financed my taking him out with a date for dinner.

John Walton also came to New York the autumn of 1948, staying at the Taft Hotel in the theater district. He called and asked me to take dinner with him and Adele Petit at a little bourgeois French restaurant called "La Tour Eiffel" situated on the West Side near the theaters, as he had tickets that evening. John liked to come to New York about once a year to eat well and see the latest shows. Adele, who was an Augustan, had known him always and had been studying piano in Paris when John lived in France in the 1920s. Adele had studied to be a concert pianist (with Egon Petri) and made her living now giving piano lessons to many persons in the New York City area, including Westchester County. She knew Frank's family well, and it transpired she and her sister, Almeda, had arranged the music program for Frank and Bowdre's wedding in 1924. Adele was one of the earlier liberated ladies, in that she wanted to see the world, finding little Augusta much too limited in scope. Adele opened many doors for me and made my initial stay in New York City much more bearable. She also had been fond of Grandmother Doughty, whom she called "Miss Frankie."

CHAPTER ELEVEN

Adele occasionally cooked dinner in her small East 56th Street apartment and invited me in and also introduced me to the best automat in the city (I think it was on 57th Street near Carnegie Hall) and to other eating places in her vicinity on the East Side. We both paid our own bills! She introduced Mercer French, who was related to Maisie Chafee of Augusta. I believe Mercer was her niece and often visited her in Augusta, usually during the winter. But Mercer irritated me straight off by asking if Frank was "fat" when trying to place her! The Frenches were a well-to-do and well-connected New York family who owned the French Building on Fifth Avenue. Also, she introduced the Bob Jennings who lived in the winter atop the Sherry Netherland Hotel and whom I entertained years later in Hong Kong when they came through on a round-the-world cruise, I think on the *Caronia*, of Cunard line.

I really came to admire Adele, who had succeeded on her own and who had created an interesting life for herself. She loved to travel and had seen most of Europe, spending several months in the early 1930s in Majorca during what she called her "vagabond year," liked to swim and be near the water, and had visited Japan (and, I think, China) in 1938 or 1939 on the invitation of several of her former Japanese music students. These were prominent Japanese consular and business families who had been stationed in New York. One was the Sawada family; Miki Sawada was close to Adele, and Renzo Sawada had been Japanese consul-general in New York. I met their daughter, Mary, while in Japan in 1950. Renzo came back after World War II to the United Nations as part of the Japanese delegation when that country was admitted to membership. The Chigera family was another connection, and when I arrived in Japan, Mr. Chigera was CEO of Chiyoda Bank, known as Mitsubishi Bank before the war. He invited me to lunch at the Peer's Club and then to the theater to see a Noh play with his daughter, Eiko, while I was in Tokyo. Eiko later married an executive of the bank and, at one stage, lived in New York (where we met again in the early 1960s) and in Iran.

One weekend, I walked across town to call on Adele; I had no money, and payday was the following week. She loaned me five dollars. This was the type of assistance one can never forget, nor will I! As I recall, I had depleted all funds by trying to be a big shot and taking a girl I had met through the Carruths to a New York night spot called "LaRue" that was popular then, following the Carruths' invitation to dinner at a hotel.

Looking back, I still do not know why my parents (Frank, in particular) did not take steps to put me in contact with others in New York with strong Augusta ties; for example, Anne Campbell Green, De l'aigle Munds, Boykin Wright (then a senior partner with Sherman, Sterling and Wright) or Elbert Jackson, to whom we are related on both the Doughty and Phinizy sides. Elbert had married Constance Wright (sister of Boykin) and was close to Uncle Walker Inman and even called Frankie Doughty "Aunt Frank." Of course, I was not really interested in family ties at that stage and probably lacked

CHAPTER ELEVEN

the confidence to push for such introductions. But had I known those people, my initial period in New York undoubtedly would have been much more fruitful and, in turn, made my life and these memories more interesting. I did meet Jamie Dargan, the well-known loss adjustor of Dargan and Company, one day at AFIA. He said he was married to Lucy Doughty, who would have been a cousin as she was the daughter of Dr. William H. Doughty, Sr. The Dargans are both today buried in the large Doughty plot at Magnolia Cemetery in Augusta. I believe they then lived in Scarsdale. I never heard from them!

By Spring 1949, the AFIA manager in Japan (supported by Ned Hitt in his reports) was asking for at least two men to be assigned to Tokyo to assist in soliciting and underwriting "Military Occupation Insurance" such having first been monopolized by AIU (now largely known as AIG). Our manager, Fred Provost, had been told when he first when to Tokyo in 1946-1947 to concentrate on rebuilding our pre-war Japanese agencies. But with the country basically destroyed, the only real paying business there was military which, due to one peculiarity, enjoyed a plus, yes <u>plus</u> loss ratio! This no one could understand at first; such came to pass as insurance companies were the only parties permitted to sell vehicles to the Japanese market, imports being forbidden, and the local auto industry barely functioning. We would declare a total loss, say, on a 1948-1949 Ford insured for $2,000; the wreck would bring the Japanese yen equivalent of about $10,000 on the local market, so with this salvage our net profit in this case would be $8,000 but paid to us in Japanese yen. But we needed yen to pay local expenses, and this situation as explained allowed us to avoid selling dollars for yen. At long last, AFIA Head Office finally agreed to send two young Americans to Japan: I was one and Tom McDonnell was hired as the other. Tom had a brief amount of US domestic insurance experience and was a graduate of Wesleyan University in Connecticut. There was a rush to get us off, and we departed New York City in June 1949 by a night flight on American Airlines for Los Angeles, with another short break of one or two nights at Honolulu, where we stayed on Waikiki Beach at the Halekulani Hotel.

I almost missed the flight for Los Angeles by taking too late a bus from the 42nd Street airline terminal following dinner at a Lexington Avenue fish place with Adele Petit, who had agreed at the last minute to mail some books and clothes I could not fit into my suitcases. Then in Los Angeles, we spent one day driving down to Laguna Beach, changing in the car (left on the road above the beach) and returning to find we had been robbed! Fortunately, my principal valuables (passport, etc.) were left at the hotel. After losing a day and a refueling stop at Wake Island in the very early morning, our DC-6 (or was it a souped-up DC-4?) reached Haneda Airport, Tokyo. Ned Hitt and Fred Provost were waiting and immediately whisked us to the Shiba Park Hotel near a park and downtown Tokyo. This hostelry had originally been a school with dormitory and,

CHAPTER ELEVEN

on occupation orders, was converted into a lodging for US businessmen, as the still undamaged pre-war hotels all were used by the military or civilians (then known as DACs for Department Army Civilians) employed by the military.

So in this strange environment where General McArthur was the supreme commander, there were three classes of foreigners: military (largely US but also other nationalities, such as Russian, British, Canadian, and Australian), DACs, and "foreign traders," as we then were known. If there were any diplomats around, they must have been accredited to McArthur, for as yet no peace treaty had been signed. There were in use three different currencies: MPC (military payment certificates, in theory forbidden to non-military), Japanese yen, and trader's certificates (another name for regular US currency which was used to purchase them). Except for using yen to go to a bar for beer or for a visit to a Japanese hotel away from Tokyo, our needs basically required the use of US currency. This was true of the Shiba Park Hotel and also after we had moved to our "mess" (as the Brits term them) near Omori Station.

Omori is a suburban section of metropolitan Tokyo and pre-war housed a large part of the German colony said to number 1,118 in 1933 prior to the 1940 Japanese-German treaty and then doubling. A "mess" is a shared bachelor pad, and Fred Provost had purchased a small house from the US Enemy Property Custodian. Pre-war, a German had owned it. AFIA paid $5,000 to maybe $15,000 and then spent a few more thousand on renovations. I was told the house had been owned by the head of the Nazi Party in Japan, a man named Willie Fisher. I have not traced his name to date in the Richard Sorge spy saga, which has been well told in several books. As the ruined Japanese economy was barely recovering by 1949 and there was a food shortage, a sort of PX or supermarket was opened by the Meidya Company where "traders" could buy imported food and all the trimmings with US currency. In theory, I suspect the occupation authorities thought this was one way to avoid a "black market," although in any event many items from the store would find their way directly to the "black"! Items came also from the military PXs, as many in the occupation force had Japanese girlfriends! "Foreign traders" were denied legal access to the PXs.

The entire area between Haneda Airport and the immediate suburbs of Tokyo city were still mainly destroyed in June 1949, although there were pockets here and there of rebuilding. In these bombed-out areas, all one would see were chimneys left standing and the Japanese-type safes often built next to them with an iron door. Japan was just beginning to rebuild, and it was the Korean War starting in 1950 that really gave the country the jolt needed to get the economy rapidly moving forward. The railway system by then was working well, with one car on most trains reserved for "occupation" use; taxis in Tokyo were still mainly wood-burning vehicles leftover from pre-war and later converted due to the war-time petrol shortage.

CHAPTER ELEVEN

The famous Imperial Hotel and the Tokyo Kaikan were restricted to military use, as were the golf clubs and hotels away from Tokyo, such as in Atami, Nikko, and the elegant Fujiya Hotel at Miyanoshita near Lake Hakone. But from time to time, our military or DAC friends gave us access to many of these facilities, and there were a few Chinese and even pre-war restaurants like Lohmeyer's, Ketel's (called Rheingold Bar previously and run by Helmut Ketel), and Suehiro's for Kobe beefsteaks. Then the American Club reopened post-war around 1950 in a building fully occupied by the club in Shimbun Alley, downtown Tokyo. This was a very frequent destination for lunch and dinner, as was the Press Club, where most of us from AFIA were also members, and located nearby. Shimbun means "press" in Japanese.

The first office I saw was a mess. Located on the second floor of a building near Yurakucho Station (I do not recall a working elevator), the space was far too small for our staff (comprised of both pre-war employees and new hires), the building in bad repair and quite dilapidated, no proper heating or air conditioning, but all we could find as the occupation had commandeered all the best premises. At that time, we had not been able to repossess our pre-war office in the Maranouchi Building near the front of Tokyo Station and an edifice which had withstood the 1923 earthquake with little damage. But we soon had a second Tokyo office (to be used mainly for military and foreign business with the Yurakucho office managing purely yen accounts) located close to National City Bank and the Teito Hotel. We enjoyed much more space in this building owned by Bank of Tokyo (formerly Yokohama Specie Bank, as many companies had to change their names as they were "purged," i.e. forced to [in theory at least] sever their Zaibatsu ties). Naturally as soon as the occupation ended and the peace treaty signed about 1952, many of the Zaibatsu promptly regrouped again! We first managed our military writings directed by Ned Hitt; then Tom McDonnell went to Yokohama, where we had first opened an office with Herb Schoene, son of pre-war agent in charge but who was now assigned to open new offices in Kobe and Osaka to be concerned principally with Japanese yen business and some foreign property and marine accounts.

In our new Tokyo office, I also assumed the responsibility of supervising our casualty claims department, which as explained, enjoyed a "plus-loss ratio" due to the peculiar manner of automobile salvage recoveries. As one can easily imagine, the possibilities for kickbacks and fraud were legion in this area, and I was often approached and entertained by those wanting me to award one of the legitimate car total losses to them. We also were allowed to dispose of the wrecks to Japanese garages or dealers, who then could not import new units. Fred Provost instructed me to play along and just accept the geisha parties if I chose and make the awards in the proper way following the submission of sealed bids, which tended to increase our ultimate take! This I did with great gusto!

CHAPTER ELEVEN

In late 1950 or early 1951, Tom McDonnell was transferred to Okinawa to open an office to service the American Express agency. AMEXCO then had the sole military license for a bank, which all the American military used, and insurance sales to the occupation personnel was a very natural adjunct. I then replaced Tom in Yokohama, commuting each day by train or company car, if there was a free one, but I soon purchased my own 1950 model MG for $1,200 after securing a loan from National City Bank. Provost counter-signed the note, which I then paid off monthly. The MG was black with green leather upholstery, and the only four-seater model ever introduced. I had a small garage built at the Omori House by utilizing a large part of the front left garden and really thought I was a swell driving about with the top down in fair weather. This MG had been imported into Japan from Europe by a DAC in the Yokohama Judge Advocate section and, of course, was my first car. My friend, Walter Wolff, who worked for American Trading Company, a leading import-export firm and also our pre- and post-war insured, always said convertibles were good for "picking up" girls! Naomi Hasegawa (born in Los Angeles and caught in Japan when the war broke out in December 1941) was my secretary (my first, by the way!) in the Yokohama Branch, and she has reminded me in her "memoir" that several times the US Military Police stopped me, not for an infraction of the law, but because the GIs wanted to see the MG!

In 1950, Walter Wolff, from Harrison, New York, talked me into renting a joint summer/weekend house at the coast near Hayama and down the road from Emperor Hirohito's summer palace. I don't know how I could afford this on my low salary, but it was a decision I never regretted! After passing the emperor's premises, the road turned left down past the promontory jutting into the sea and called Jogagasaki, one drove a bit and our house was situated on the right, down a narrow lane (cars left on the road then) to a Japanese-styled house, all tatami mats but with two stories and a view and yard looking out to the sea and beach below. The house came with a caretaker who would open the sliding outside blinds and Japanese Shoji doors inside. There was someone also to clean up and prepare Japanese food if we so ordered. The resident fisherman often would sell us the local lobsters (no claws) and fish. The nearest small town was Zushi, where Walter moored his sailboat (about twenty feet or more with a heavy centerboard) in the local boat basin. There was a mainsail and jib. In good weather, we went sailing every day all around the Hayama area and also circling sometimes the island of Enoshima near Kamakura. The famous large Buddha (called "Daibutsu" in Japanese) is located at Kamakura.

Our weekend house parties included usually other friends then living in Japan and the occasional business guest from abroad, with our Japanese girlfriends always in the party. Through Ed Seaver, an American working also with American Trading Company who had an attractive Japanese girlfriend called Kay (for Keiko, I believe), I met Florence Ohnishi. Kay and Florence had been school friends and spoke English well. Florence

CHAPTER ELEVEN

worked in Tokyo for an American or English legal office or later a public accounting firm but lived with her widowed mother near Zushi. I believe her deceased father was the well-known Japanese Vice-Admiral Takejiro Ohnishi (air naval officer) who had advocated a new sort of air force, the kamikaze, a suicide air force once the Japanese carriers and their best pilots had been eliminated in the war. Florence had a wonderful sense of humor and taught me a lot about the country and the Japanese character. She made friends with Walter Wolff's girlfriend, Hideko, and we all remained close companions for my entire Japanese stay and during future visits.

In the Yokohama office, we did mainly military business but at the same time were soliciting foreign commercial accounts such as Siber Hegner (Swiss), Helm & Company (British-Japanese), etc. Coca-Cola was also a large account. Our main agents were Sam Lord, son of a pre-war Sunlife Insurance of Canada agent and a Japanese mother, and a Chinese/Korean/Japanese we called Colonel Chen, as he had a Chinese Nationalist passport (probably one among several). There was also a white Russian (Serge Beilious) who had lived in Japan many years after his family left Red Russia. Kaneko-San, a very successful pre-war agent, also was on board, and Provost had allowed Kamei-Son (our last pre-1941 Japanese manager before we were closed down) to assign a Mr. Kuroda, a retired senior insurance executive from Dowa Insurance Company, to reopen our Yokohama marine underwriting and claims settling departments and to canvass for new Japanese market agents.

National City Bank, as our principal banker, helped in making new contacts; one of interest was Vera Dell'Oro, who had just returned to Japan to recover the pre-war properties belonging to her husband and Dell'Oro and Company, silk exporters. Dell'Oro and Company had very valuable land in central Yokohama in the Bund area and housing lots on the Bluff, where most foreigners had resided before the last war. Dell'Oro had originally been an Italian national and, apparently, for some of the war years he was left alone, probably by using his Italian passport at first. Vera was born Australian, was still a very handsome lady, and did not hesitate to "throw her weight around" to accomplish her objectives. She now had a US passport and had spent the war mainly in New York City. They had known the Joseph Grews (US ambassador for ten years before 1941). Mr. Dell'Oro did not come to Japan initially, so Vera built warehouses on some of the town property that she promptly rented at high rates to importers badly in need of space. At first, she built an office and living quarters near the Godowns and then later a fine home on the Bluff which I visited circa 1961-1962. She later sold out and moved to Hong Kong, where Lynn and I lunched at her final house on the Kowloon side in late 1965. By then, she was almost blind from glaucoma but still retained some looks and her vibrant personality. She died suddenly soon after.

In 1951, I took a local vacation involving visits to Kobe, Osaka, and Kyoto in the Kansai area of Honshu, and from Kobe a steamer trip on the Inland Sea with

CHAPTER ELEVEN

a stop at Takamatsu on Shikoku Island and then on to Beppu in northeast Kyushu. Beppu is a well-known resort, then noted for hot mud baths and located on Beppu Bay, an arm of the Inland Sea. I returned to Tokyo/Yokohama by train with the track then running by the sea so that the famous shrine at Miyajima Island was clearly viewed. Other business or pleasure trips took me to Nikko, Lake Chuzenji in central Honshu, where there is the well-known shrine containing the three monkeys who "see, hear, and speak no evil," to Sendai with its spectacular pine groves near the beach in northern Honshu, to Atami, then the Nice/Cannes equivalent on the coast below Yokohama, and often to the Lake Hakone region.

Then in 1951, I climbed to the top of Mt. Fuji from the Gotemba side with a small group. We drove up a few "stations" by Jeep then parked and walked up way past the timber line where we stopped to sleep a few hours in one of the stone huts. Then in the early morning dark to the summit, arriving for the impressive sunrise view and to circle the crater of the volcano, which has been quiet since 1707. There are ten stages to the climb of the 12,395-foot Mr. Fuji, and at each stage the climber has his walking stick branded with a hot iron. July and August are the only months of the year when Fuji almost completely loses its snow. My main memory from the summit is the wonderful view of the three Fuji lakes, Seiko, Shoji, and Motosu, which are said to be connected subterraneously at the bottom on one side. Lakes Yamanaka and Kawaguchi also surrounded Mt. Fuji. As the Japanese say, "It is as foolish not to climb Mt. Fuji as to climb it twice in life"!

In January of 1952, I was transferred to our office at Manila, Philippine Islands, as the New York head office thought one ought to spend time during a first tour at a non-occupation office dealing with general business. Jim Mewshaw had preceded me from Japan, and Tom Hauff was to go to Okinawa to replace Tom McDonnell. We all shared the Omori House "mess" at one time or another. I traveled to Manila on a Messargerie Maritime vessel. There were three MM French flag units named *Viet-Nam*, *Laos*, and *Cambodge*, after the then Indochinese states. I think I took passage on the *Cambodge*, which called at Hong Kong before Manila. The weather wasn't too good until we reached the South China Sea, but at less than twenty-five on my first sea voyage on a French ship, such was of little concern! Among the other passengers were the Stu Bell family from Manila (part of the Caltex Oil local establishment) and Prince Shihanouk with his then attractive girlfriend or wife (Princess Monique), who was on vacation from Phnom-Penh. Cambodia gained independence from France in 1955.

During our stop in Hong Kong, I met again Johnny Lyons, our manager, who took me to the British-owned Whiteway Laidelaw Department Store to buy some "tropical kit," i.e., white pants in Irish linen or what they called "Saigon linen." I should not have bothered, as Jim Mewshaw introduced me, once in Manila, to a fine local tailor and cobbler who would come to the office and take measurements! I was fascinated with what I

CHAPTER ELEVEN

saw in Hong Kong and could not then imagine I would be returning in about twenty-two months as AFIA manager.

Victor Bello (my new boss) came on board at arrival in Manila and took me to the Army and Navy Club where I would live. Located on a park called the "Luneta" and across from the world-famous Manila Hotel, the ANC was the perfect base for a new bachelor arrival, as most of the American community congregated there and often used the dining, pool, and tennis facilities. While the residential rooms had screens, we still slept under mosquito nets, for those pests would sometimes find their way in. My room overlooked Manila Bay with its spectacular sunsets, the most beautiful in the world and on tap almost every day!

I was put in charge of the marine underwriting and claims departments. As the majority of our business was derived from general agents, some dating back to the early 1920s, I began a round of visits to all our producers to make friends and solicit new business. There also was liaison with the leading local and foreign insurers who favored us with reinsurance proposals. I even found it possible to use my Spanish at the local Spanish Club and when visiting some of the Filipino businesses, as that tongue still was employed by many of the older families in the home and as the "social language." Some still said the Filipino personality had inculcated all the bad elements of their "colonial connections," i.e., the Chinese, Spanish, and Americans! I found most to be very pro-gringo, with the ladies very decidedly so!

Although I was asked to join an English "mess," in a nice home with a pool, I decided to continue at the Army-Navy Club which allowed me more freedom to mix with various groups. Also taking advantage of the warm outdoor-type of climate, I began tennis lessons at the ANC from Bautista, a noted local pro. Golf, which I had tried to pursue in Japan under the tutelage of Tom Hauff when we were allowed on occasion to play at Hodagaya Golf Club then under occupation control, was across the street at the Muni Golf Course built on what once had been the moat outside Intramuros. The latter is the old Spanish walled city heavily damaged by the 1945 recapture from Japanese control. During the two-hour lunch break (siesta time for many who still went home from offices), I usually returned to the ANC to swim, take lunch at the pool, and then, once or twice weekly, have a tennis lesson. The pool and courts were located in front of the club fronting Manila Bay.

The most senior AFIA General Agency was E. E. Elser, Inc., dating back to the very early days after 1918; then there was A. Soriano y Cia (Spanish/Filipino), F. E. Zuellig, Inc. (Swiss), Wise & Co. (English), Gordon Mackay, De Guzman, United Insurance, and a number of others. The Ed A. Keller Agency (Swiss) had been an important agency pre-war producer representing Franklin Fire Insurance Company but cancelled when Franklin Fire merged with The Home. This because they disliked taking on a new company, particularly since they also now had Insurance Company of North America. But eventually we prevailed and brought Keller back into the

CHAPTER ELEVEN

fold. Colonel Andres Soriano, controlling A. Soriano y Cia, general agent for the Home Insurance Company, had been close to the Philippine Commonwealth Government prior to independence in 1946 and had served under General Douglas McArthur during World War II.

Many important Philippine industries belonged to the Soriano empire, and also a number while managed by Soriano y Cia were local public companies with shares traded locally. The Soriano Agency was growing rapidly; the managers were Marciano Cordero and "Mike" Moreno, both of whom liked the "good life" and who, after a special lunch at, say, "New Europe" (probably then Manila's best and most expensive restaurant), liked to move on to a "Day Club" of which there were several on Dewey Boulevard (now Roxas Boulevard). There were ladies dying to entertain and dance, etc. Just like in the evening, except that it would be, say, ninety degrees in bright sunshine and three o'clock p.m.! But in those far-off days, there were few telephone calls from abroad, no fax machines, no emails, etc., to worry about—just cables, and not too frequently either! I also found that some of the ladies at the Dewey Boulevard clubs even spoke some Japanese, indicating that life still goes on as we all go around and around!

Victor Bello taught me a lot about the insurance business. At that time, he also supervised our operations in Guam, Hong Kong, and Taiwan so that my knowledge was expanded to include these additional territories. Bello encouraged on-the-job training, and I gave lectures on marine underwriting to our local staff and joined the Chartered Insurance Institute to prepare for their study program by mail and obtain the Chartered Insurance Institute (CII) designation. This is the approximate British equivalent of the USA's CPCU certificate with the CII title, better in non-USA markets for the most part.

On the social side, there were many opportunities to meet and party with young foreigners assigned like I was to Manila and with their wives, if any, and to be sure also with the local Filipino crowd, many of whom had some part of their education in the United States or United Kingdom. One girl I saw was Helen Lichauco, a tall willowy brunette whose father was a well-known local attorney. The girls were all great dancers and happy to know and date American bachelors. My office colleague, Jim Mewshaw, was dating Trophy O'Campo, and they later married. President Magsaysay of the Philippines gave her away, as her father was deceased, and also acted as one of their sponsors. There were home parties and evening dances at the Winter Garden (fully air conditioned) of the Manila Hotel. Many nights when not engaged, I would walk over to the Manila American Legion Club adjacent to the Army-Navy Club to take dinner, as one was allowed to sign chits and charge the ANC membership. The food was better and simple: Lapu-Lapu, the good local fish, ham steaks with rice and Salote, a local squash-like vegetable. Or I could walk across Dewey Boulevard to the Swiss Inn for Swiss-type food: rosti, sausages, weiner schnitzel, or their excellent chicken or

CHAPTER ELEVEN

shrimp curry always on their menu. Or perhaps wander a few steps further down Ermita Street to the Taza de Oro, a small café owned and run by an American lady who had several other Taza de Oros, one at Clark Field (a US airbase then) and elsewhere. The Taza in Manila offered what one would call unpretentious "home-style cooking," i.e. Lapu-Lapu, roast or fried chicken with rice, cole slaw, and good desserts.

As my first tour of duty (three and a half years) was up in December 1952, I planned to return to the United States, making stops in Europe en route, for this was my first opportunity to take in some European highlights. The winter weather was a nil consideration as I made the travel arrangement with American Express Manila. The itinerary was Hong Kong to pick up Pan Am's round-the-world daily flight to Rome, my initial destination. Then there were stops in Bangkok, then either Rangoon or Calcutta, Karachi, Basra, Iraq, and then an overnight at Pan Am's expense in Beirut. Florence by train followed Rome, by car to Nice (side day trips to Cannes, Monte Carlo, etc.), and plane to Switzerland where I rode the mountain railway to Zermatt at the foot of the Matterhorn. Then plane to Paris and London, from where I boarded Pan Am's Stratocruiser (two decks) to New York. Due to poor Atlantic weather, we were detoured to the Azores for more fuel, and during one idle chat, I found that one cordial family traveling on the plane were friends of Bert Irvine, by then the company general manager. Reporting to Head Office, which by then had smart new premises at 161 William Street, I saw Mr. Irvine, who said he wanted me to take part in a new program whereby juniors returning from their first tour would undergo additional on-the-job training at Head Office and in other friendly insurance offices—this following my leave, which was three months in total with about two and a half still to go.

Arriving home in Augusta was quite pleasant, even though I soon discovered most people really did not spend too much time hearing my stories, notwithstanding their purported interest and initial questions! They mostly were still taken with all that was happening in Augusta! During my vacation, I took my brother, Inman, and a rented car to Florida (Miami), where we flew to Puerto Rico and Charlotte Amalie, St. Thomas, Virgin Islands, for about a week in early 1953. For some reason, the Caribbean at that time interested me, although now, having seen most of it over the years, I can't imagine why!

Back to New York in March, I ran into Charles W. Barnard (Chick), just in from three and a half years in Calcutta, which was then an important AFIA branch. Chick was an Amherst graduate, and this Yankee Ivy Leaguer and Southerner hit it off well from the start. He had my kind of ironic sense of humor and a rather cynical outlook. I was back at the 63rd Street YMCA with Barnard temporarily at the Amherst Club. As we were both "retreads" (as the new trainees called us) and planning to spend some months at headquarters, four of us pooled together and sublet a rather large 1920-1930s-built apartment in a building on the corner

CHAPTER ELEVEN

of either 21st or 22nd Street and 2nd Avenue. There were two bedrooms, two baths, a kitchen, and spacious living and dining rooms. Our other roommates were Don Miller (later killed in an auto accident in South Africa) and Ed McElgunn, who came from Summit, New Jersey, and had been with Chase Bank in Hong Kong. Two or three afternoons a week, a Mr. Blankenship lectured us on the principles of basic accounting, as Mr. Irvine felt all field executives could benefit from such training. He was correct: At last I learned that one had to "debit" cash when funds were received and at the same time "credit" the account involved!

Chick was farmed out to the Talbot Bird marine underwriting office, and I was seconded to Ken Fraser's office, which was the managing agency for the New Zealand Insurance Company. We met often for lunch in the Wall Street area—retreads and trainees who also included McAllister Borie, godson of H. V. Smith. Mr. H. V. had us to lunch at The Home Insurance executive dining room, and "Mac" Borie joined our crowd often as he also shared a flat in the 23rd Street area. We noticed that Chick seemed to be seeing "a lot of movies," as he put it, many evenings; in due course this "movie" turned out to be Margaret Blue (called "Brownie"), recently graduated from Mount Holyoke (sister school of Amherst). They were married in August of 1953 in Princeton, New Jersey, with a reception following the church ceremony at the Nassau Inn. A group of us rented a car and attended; when the bridal party departed for Cape Cod later in the afternoon in Chick's Ford convertible with the top down, we gave chase like idiots and almost received a ticket for speeding. We all chipped in, and Ann Thomas bought them a silver Paul Revere bowl.

Ann was a new AFIA secretary/assistant in Foreign Branch Administration. She came from Philadelphia, being the daughter of Frank Thomas, chief executive of Fire Association of Philadelphia, one of the AFIA owners. She and her roommate, Clare Sotherland from Wilmington, Delaware, were Vassar graduates and occupied a second- or third-floor walk-up apartment in an old brownstone house on East 72nd Street. I cannot now recall whether the location was between Madison and Park or between Park and Lexington; either is still a great address! Tom McDonnell, back from Okinawa, was dating Ann heavily, and I started to take out Clare. She worked for some little-known advertising agency, but at her office one afternoon, I did meet Coles Phinizy, Jr., who must have been then beginning his career with Time, Inc.

Ann and Tom soon became engaged. Tom was assigned to Cairo, and Ann left New York at some later point to prepare their wedding and to move to Egypt. I continued to see a lot of Clare, who for some reason was not a big favorite with Barnard and others in our "mess"; I think she was rather outspoken and a bit "snooty"! She invited me for dinner often and was a good cook, at least to me in that era when I knew little about food. One of her favorites was zucchini squash; I had only eaten before the yellow variety common then in

CHAPTER ELEVEN

the South! On several occasions, we had several drinks and I would then fall asleep on the sofa while Clare was fixing the food! But keep in mind I had come directly from the office, it had been a very long day as we rose early, and I had eaten little all day! One evening just before Chick Barnard's wedding, Ann and Clare had us to dinner, and we played "spin the bottle" on the floor after dining. Clare was a good kisser and liked to neck, and the bridegroom wasn't averse to a few kisses from the ladies, either! As we left their building, we turned over several garbage cans on 72nd Street in front, and my final recollection is seeing the girls in their front windows yelling, "You naughty boys!"

We had several wild parties at the "mess," inviting mainly AFIA persons, and there were non-AFIA visitors—Sara Evans from Augusta and Amaryllis Phinizy from Greenville came and prepared dinner during one of their clothes-buying trips. Frank O'Connor, sent by Dupont for training to New York, spent a week when we had a free bed, etc. But all this came to an end when I was assigned to Hong Kong as manager, leaving New York for Los Angeles in November 1953 to meet Victor Bello, then on home leave, for an up-to-date briefing on the Hong Kong office. Bello's main theme was we badly needed more business to support that office, so this became my number one objective. I flew via Tokyo and Manila and recall seeing the Barnards (then on their first posting to Japan). My predecessor, John Lyons, and his family left Hong Kong for New York about a week following my arrival after introducing me to all business contacts and the American community at a reception at the American Club, at that time located in the Hong Kong Shanghai Bank Building, where the club had an entire floor.

I then moved from the Gloucester Hotel in downtown Hong Kong on the island up to the back side of the Peak to the Coombe Road flat rented by AFIA: two bedrooms, two bathrooms, living/dining one large area, long hallway from the front door entrance, kitchen and servant's quarters off the latter. The furniture belonged to my employer, and some of it apparently had been shipped down from Shanghai when that office closed circa 1950, for some "old China hands" told me once they remembered some pieces from Buster Brown's home establishment in China! Brown had been our last manager prior to the Communist takeover.

The company car was a new Ford Zephyr made in England. Ah Chen and his wife continued at the flat to cook, clean, wash clothes, and manage all shopping, etc. There was an Indian driver at the office named Ali and about ten others including a first-rate accountant, A. E. Noronha, whose brother was a senior officer of the local Citibank branch. The Noronhas were descendants of an old Portuguese family; there was then quite a large Portuguese/Macao-related group in Hong Kong with many employed as accountants or in banking. Our office was located on Duddell Street behind Citibank and the Club Lusitano and just off Queen's Road Central. I was very excited and rapidly studied our office and agency situation to determine my initial focus and objectives

CHAPTER ELEVEN

considering Victor Bello's first admonition: generate more premium income.

Around the time of my early days in Hong Kong, I finally discovered that genius, at least in my world of insurance, really was a question of setting specific business objectives and then accomplishing them by implementing certain strategies. This simple truth always served me well, and following it secured advancement, i.e., promotions and more money. I become known for my focus on production/expansion, or "marketing" in the current lingo, and administration, i.e., attention to detail, which is another quick definition of genius. For example, when I departed Hong Kong after about four years in 1957, our business had increased about seven times, well on the way to one million US dollars in annual premium income! The US currency then was far stronger at that time in purchasing power! Irvine's successor as AFIA president, Jimmy Nichols, told me on my return to New York in 1957 that he thought the territory might produce pounds sterling 25,000, then equivalent to about US $100,000! But I opened two new branches on the Kowloon side and in the New Territories, expanded our general agency and solicitor/broker base, sold personal accident insurance at busy KaiTak airport, and introduced many new types of casualty, property, and marine (including some hull) coverage.

Also I was lucky, in that Head Office (Bert Irvine) rehired Winston Chen, who had, as assistant manager in 1949-1950, closed our China operations after the

Communists seized control. He repatriated from Chile, where he and his wife, Helena, had emigrated from Hong Kong around 1951-1952. They reached Hong Kong in 1954 with a new baby girl, Lin. Winston Chen knew many of the Shanghai business community, now organizing new factories in the colony, and with his wife became very popular members of both the American and Chinese business communities.

We did a lot of cold canvassing together to the small Chinese insurance companies and solicited all the local banks, many of which became our agents, as these banks usually controlled nice and profitable blocs of property and marine insurance because they normally financed imports, exports, and re-exports for Hong Kong was the classic entrepot port. The local insurers would cede reinsurance and pass over lines of insurance they did not underwrite. Many of these Chinese entrepreneurs spoke little English, so Winston translated (he spoke Mandarin, Cantonese, and Shanghainese among Chinese dialects) my sales pitch. One important lifelong tenet I had learned by then was "to ask" for business openly and directly: this usually works quite well, and when employed in the mid-1950s in Hong Kong by a young sincere American, who was also taught by Winston how to present my business card (printed in English and Chinese characters) in the ultra-polite Chinese manner with both hands extended, achieved much success.

Social life was most pleasant, with clubs catering to every taste. The American Club was very active (I lunched

CHAPTER ELEVEN

there almost every workday), and there was the Ladies Recreation Club midway up the peak (known as LRC) for tennis and swimming—men allowed in the LRC only as associate members with no vote! There were two golf clubs and three courses, one of nine holes only, the Royal Hong Kong Yacht Club, and the staid Hong Kong Club, where only the "taipans" (or seniors—mainly English) were members. Through Bob Harper and his charming wife, Heather, I met her sister, Shauna Anderson, whom I dated for a long time. The Andersons were Scots, and their father the Lloyd's Registry manager locally. The Harpers were Americans who originally had been Ford Motor distributors in China but now had the sole dealership for Hong Kong. My predecessor, John Lyons, had just appointed Wallace Harper and Company as our agents when I arrived. There were many boating trips on the weekends to uninhabited islands and beaches in the New Territories where I learned to water ski (always on two boards!) and tried to use an underwater breathing (SCUBA) apparatus, which I never liked! One weekend, I went with several American Consulate General friends to the larger island, Lantau. There we climbed the peak of 3,100 feet, camping out for the night and returning to the city the next day in a British Naval vessel that gave us an unexpected lift from Silver Mine Bay.

Winston and Helena Chen knew from Shanghai days the Negro/Filipino band now playing nightly at a restaurant/night club in Wanchai or maybe North Point—I think this was called the Majestic, or was it Sunning? The band would play all our favorite tunes.

At that stage, the dance rage locally was cha-cha-cha, mambo, and rock and roll. A Chinese instructor gave lessons to the Chens and Shauna Anderson and me, and a crowd of us would take over the dance floor as the orchestra played the latest cha-cha-cha hits. Late at night we then would visit the open-air sidewalk eateries on the Wanchai waterfront to eat with chopsticks Chinese noodles prepared in front of us; many coolies as well as well-heeled types local and foreign were our eating companions at these stalls. The coolies were always in their undershirts and shorts, including jinrikisha operators.

In 1954 or 1955, my brother Inman paid me a visit from his US Air Force station in Japan. He stayed with me in the company flat on the Peak, and I enjoyed introducing him to the local environment and the pleasures of the colony at that time. One day, I presented Inman to the military attaché at the US Consulate General, who arranged for him to return to Japan as a "free-loader" on a RAF military plane. Included among the illustrations is a photograph of Inman taken in Japan by Gould Barrett, who also was in the Air Force and then stationed in Korea but visiting Inman in Japan. Inman recently wrote that while in Hong Kong he played golf one day at the Royal Hong Kong Golf Club with Tsufa Lee, an insurance agent of AFIA Hong Kong but originally from Shanghai. They enjoyed tiffin and drinks on the club verandah with various British Colonial types after the match, and Inman wrote it was really a scene from a Somerset Maugham story! I arranged also for Inman to

CHAPTER ELEVEN

meet Walter Wolff in Tokyo as well as Lance La Bianca, then assistant manager for AFIA Japan.

After about four years, I left Hong Kong circa August 1957 for long leave and reassignment. I did take several "local vacations" in 1954 and 1955 or 1956, one to visit British North Borneo, Sarawak, Singapore, Saigon, and Hanoi and another on the Lloyd Triestino vessel *Victoria* from Hong Kong to Colombo with stops at Manila and Singapore. Good friends, the Rob Kennedys and Johnny Soongs, were also passengers on this sailing en route to Europe while I left the ship at Colombo, visiting Kandy in central Ceylon to see Buddha's tooth, staying a couple of days at the Galle Face Hotel in the capital, and making another side trip to see the beach and hotel at Mount Lavinia on the coast south of Colombo. Then by BOAC flying back to Hong Kong after a day and night pause in Singapore with John and Sally McTeer. John was Getz Brothers manager; we became good pals from my arrival in Hong Kong in November 1953 when we both were new in town and living at the Gloucester Hotel. I was best man at John's wedding to Sally King, an attractive English girl, in 1954, I think, and sometime thereafter they were transferred to Singapore.

Jack Lilley and I left Hong Kong in 1957 together by Pan Am, Jack leaving the plane in Beirut where his girlfriend, Ellie, met him. Ellie was Norwegian and a Pan Am stewardess based in Beirut. They later married and lived a long spell in Bogotá, Colombia, where Jack continued to work for Mobil Oil, called Standard Vacuum in some locations, being a joint venture with Standard

Oil (now Exxon). I flew to Rome en route to Sicily, where I rested a few days staying in Taormina at the very fine San Domenico Palace Hotel. Mt. Aetna volcano was spewing plumes of fire almost every night, all clearly seen from the hotel terrace. I also stopped in Naples to make my first visit to Pompeii and Sorrento and to spend a few days on Capri, where I stayed in Ana Capri at a hotel (Cesar Augustus) near Monte Solaro and the Axel Munthe Villa called "San Michele." A great panorama of the island from Ana Capri, as I recall. Rather disappointed in the Blue Grotto, but I did climb to the headland to see the remains of Tiberius's palace at the Villa Iovis. Next by train to Venice and on to Interlaken in Switzerland hoping to have a clear day to visit or see the Jungfrau. But, alas, a veil of cloud spoiled the day so that the rail trip was cancelled, and I went on to Berne. Walter Wolff, then living in Hamburg, happened to be in Zurich on business, so we met up, as I had planned also to visit Zurich to see Bob Harper, who was in a Swiss Sanatorium recovering from a touch of tuberculosis, which was endemic in Hong Kong. Then Paris and boat-train to Le Havre, where I took the French liner *Flandre* for New York—my first transatlantic crossing, on a medium-sized vessel, in first class, too, although most evenings I ended up in tourist where the group was more lively!

After reporting to my bosses in New York on Hong Kong, I was offered the post of General Manager Colombia. This was an important country operation with the main office in Bogota and sub-branches

CHAPTER ELEVEN

in Cali, Pereira, Manizales (coffee country), and Barranquilla on the Caribbean coast. Important general agents functioned in the key cities of Cartagena, Medellin, Bucaramanga, and also in Bogotá itself. Home Insurance and Hartford Fire Insurance were operating as our two American companies; we also owned and ran La Continental de Seguros, our Colombian Company, which was useful when a local insurer might be preferred. There were several hundred employees, including two other Americans, a manager in Cali and an assistant in Bogota.

I was replacing Lloyd Benedict, who later joined Johnson and Higgins and launched the J & H International department. Lloyd had transferred from our large office in Brazil about three years earlier and had done a superb job in reorganizing the entire country operation, then badly in need of what they now call "reengineering." My main job was leading the staff and encouraging new business production throughout the country as we were then seeing increased competition from the large purely local insurers [La Colombiana, Suramericana, Bolivar, Tequendama (managed by our former Colombian manager Robert Chapman), etc.] who were making loans to desirable large accounts in exchange for their insurances.

I arrived in Bogota in late November 1957, flying from New York City on the daily Avianca evening flight. I think this Constellation plane trip was a nonstop or perhaps one-stop only at Miami. This was after a visit to Augusta and also following another trip to the Caribbean, where I sampled Antigua, St. Kitts, St. Martin, and a short stop in Anguilla. This basically cured my focus on the Leeward Islands! The early evening of my departure day, our president, Jimmy Nichols, and his wife, Itala, took me to dinner on 14th Street at Luchow's. Afterwards they insisted I call the H. V. Smiths to bid them goodbye and then put me in a taxi, or was it the airport bus to the airport? Lloyd Benedict and Bill Manson were at the Bogota airport (a wild scene before the new El Dorado terminal opened a few years later), whisking me promptly to the new Hotel Tequendama Intercontinental.

The Tequendama was my home for about a month or more until I located an apartment. This was in a small building, sited around Carrera 3rd with Calle 71, containing just three apartments plus one small ground-floor studio apartment next to the entrance and garages. The building was owned by an Englishman with a Colombian wife who lived nearby in a separate house. After a spell in one of the upper floor flats facing the street, I managed to acquire the rear ground unit which boasted its own private garden all enclosed by a tall brick wall. A good-sized living room, one bedroom used as the dining room (although when alone I had supper served in front of the fire in the living room, for Bogota's residences are normally not heated or cooled centrally), nice entrance hall, master bedroom and bath plus a small room which could be a single bedroom or office, kitchen, and servant's room/bath. Maria lived in the latter, cooked, did all the shopping, housework including laundry, and left

CHAPTER ELEVEN

after lunch Saturday (we then worked a half day) for her day off, returning in time for supper Sunday.

I remember trying out my Spanish immediately at the hotel when ordering a sandwich for lunch from my room. That first night, the Benedicts and Mansons took me to "Balalaika" for dinner; this was a restaurant operated by White Russians who had escaped Russia following World War I into China, eventually immigrating to Colombia. There were a number of White Russians accepted by Colombia at the end of World War II; one was Katherine Senichenko, a capable secretary in our Bogota office, and her family. There was also an insurance broker named Golovine who placed businesses with us.

Lloyd escorted me around town for many introductions, mainly on foot, for our offices, on two floors of the Citibank Building, were located in the then business center. I was glad to note that the high altitude of 8,500 feet did not disturb me as it does some. One call was on John Moors Cabot, US ambassador and specialist in Latin America, who told me he did not really care for the Far East where he once was posted, I believe, in China. Mr. Cabot was a real Yankee Brahmin! Another to W. R. Grace and Company, an important client, and to McAllister y Cia, long-time general agency for the Hartford Fire Insurance Company. The McAllisters were an interesting family, presumably of English-Scottish ancestry, who were direct descendants of persons who had settled in Colombia after helping Simon Bolivar defeat the Spanish in 1824. There were a number of old Colombian families of the same ilk, i.e., one named Crane, who all had Anglo-Saxon or Scot surnames. There were two important insurance brokers—Gordon Lawry (an American ex-AIG) dealt mainly with Johnson and Higgins from his office in Bogota, and Ernie de Lima in Cali was correspondent of Marsh & McLennan,—and we did much business with both, principally on American accounts.

Our office staff was first-rate, with sound underwriting managers and excellent claim staff (claims headed by lawyer Dr. Alberto Copete), great secretarial support in English and Spanish, and our own internal audit department, which was much expanded during my time. Managers in the branches could focus on new business development with support from the country-wide marketing department in Bogota directed by Bill Manson. I visited all branches as soon as possible; my command of Spanish was a great hit, as most of the local managers preferred to speak their language, which of course was a necessity with several, and most of the office staff and many clients.

In Manizales on my first visit, our manager confessed late one night after we had dined with our most important producer in town, Elias Hoyos, who controlled many coffee accounts, he wished Latin America had been settled by the Anglo-Saxons instead of the Spanish. If so, he felt his country and many others in South America would have made much more progress; naturally I tried to at once disabuse him of this scenario, but this heart-to-heart conversation does reveal

CHAPTER ELEVEN

some little chink in the Latin personality. I wish I had then read "What Makes Sammy Run," a business article dealing with the foreign and even Latin temperament, for it points out that the boss, in this case me, always must interface often between the local executives and colleagues at headquarters if there is to be success. Many first-rate local people just will not easily accept pressure and orders from abroad if such clashes with their innate idea for a better way to do things or impinges (so they think) on their honor or veracity relative to some business problem or recommendation. To intervene was a good technique I began to learn and practice when confronted then and later with local emotions and quite prickly personalities.

There was the Anglo-American Club near the center, and one could walk there for lunch, as I often did. The Club Campestre (country club) was situated in the then outer suburbs on the fringe of one of the best residential districts. Many foreigners and leading Colombian citizens were members, and our company owned a share providing me and my successors with a membership. We also owned one share at Los Largartos, a smaller newer club used by the Bogota Branch manager, Armando Gutierrez, who in addition was a member of The Gun Club, useful for lunch and near our offices. There were several acceptable restaurants downtown, and "El Pollo Dorado" soon opened: specialité roast chicken from the spit with excellent crispy French fries and salad. In those days chicken in Colombia was more expensive than beef!

The Hotel Tequendama Intercontinental then was new and was sort of a "new town social center," not quite downtown and across the street from the Corrida Arena, where ladies would lunch or take tea and coffee, and a group of young Colombians would "hang out," as the present vernacular puts it! The American Chamber of Commerce had their monthly meetings and lunches there, and there was in addition to the coffee shop-restaurant a bar and a separate formal restaurant with orchestra and dancing virtually every night. I soon met many of the "Tequendama crowd," probably initially introduced by one American bachelor around my age who worked for the hotel as an assistant manager. I cannot now recall his name, although I can still see him in my mind's eye! One Colombiana, Amparo Cubillios, had some schooling in the United States, and we dated some with one introduction leading to another—Amparo later turned up in Singapore about 1968 then married to an American named Brown who worked for one of the oil service companies. The Browns dined at home with us at least once, and we saw them at some parties. One of Amparo's friends was Edith Martinez who I later saw and dated in New York during the bachelor period. She came originally from Barranquilla.

A friend from Hong Kong, Mike Collins, arrived with Ford Motor, and through this contact my circle then expanded; Mike married the daughter of an American government official around 1959 in a large church wedding with reception following at the Hotel Tequendama. I was an usher-groomsman, and soon

CHAPTER ELEVEN

thereafter Mike was assigned to Manila where we next met in the early 1960s. Around this time Dixie and Rick Coleman (he was with Celanese Corp.) invited me for dinner, Thanksgiving, I think, and introduced Jean Patterson from Texas, now in Bogotá working for one of the larger American oil exploration companies. Jean was an attractive blonde who was popular with all even though her facility with Spanish was close to nil. We had some good times; one long weekend a group of us flew to Cali for some local fiesta and the special Corrida then presented. Most of the town was "en fete," or better said, "en fiesta," and we sort of fancied we were Hemingway-like in another Pamploma but without the running of the bulls through the streets!

I stayed on to visit our Cali branch after the party. Meanwhile, I was studying and making plans to open branches in Bucaramanga town and in Santa Marta on the Caribbean coast and next in Cartagena on the coast and Medellin, a large industrial city in the interior, as our general agents were aging and required help in both locations. Collections from agents and brokers also required almost daily attention. I was also getting to know all local and foreign competitors; in some cases we were co-insurers or reinsurers with companies such as La Andina (Royal of UK) and Nacional de Sequros (a French-owned enterprise) managed by Bernardo Saiz de Castro (former subagent of J. Planas who had at one time before World War II and even after had been our important agent). Now Planas was working full-time for Pan-American Life of New Orleans. Bernardo later turned up in Brussels as ambassador, but I missed seeing him there. We also worked with Albingia (partly German controlled), Fenix de Colombia (Phoenix UK), and many others. Reaseguradora de Colombia was the first local resident reinsurer with all local companies owning shares. The general manager was Rodrigo Vasques, and after our office closed, I would, on occasion, go to the Reaseguradora premises up the street and join Rodrigo and a few colleagues in their daily bridge game. In early 1959, I was invited to joint the Junta (Board of Directors) of Asecolda, the insurance industry rate-making and tariff body.

Around this time, Richard Nixon made his celebrated swing to South American as vice president of the United States. There were riots in Venezuela and Peru as I recall, but complete calm prevailed when he reached Bogota. A local junta then was in power. There was a reception given in his honor at the Palacio Nacional by the president of Colombia, and I shook his hand as I went through the receiving line also telling him why I was living in Bogota. I met Nixon again in 1968 at the US ambassador's house in Singapore just before he announced again; Haltermann accompanied him on this trip to Southeast Asia and was seen at this meeting.

Quite suddenly, circa 1959-1960, W. F. (Chick) Cushman died of cancer, and Nichols, our president, decided to reorganize New York Headquarters into a regional management for sections of the world, as formerly all overseas branches and areas had reported

CHAPTER ELEVEN

to Vice President Cushman. I was invited to return, promoted to secretary (insurance terminology for, say, assistant vice president but a board-elected officer of the company) and put in charge of the Far East area including Japan, Korea, Okinawa, Taiwan, Hong Kong, Guam, and the Philippines. This area later was extended to include Singapore, Malaysia, Indonesia, Thailand, Viet-Nam, Brunei, Burma, India, Nepal, Ceylon, and Pakistan. The general idea was to travel in the area once or twice a year, focus on expansion and marketing where profitable, and encourage the overseas branches and agency officials.

By 1965, another important change was when I moved to Singapore to open a regional office in the field to which all local branches in that area would report. My first visit abroad under the new New York regime lasted about three months, from September through December of 1960, and I landed in New York from Hawaii the same day of the horrendous United airplane crash in Brooklyn! I worked in Manhattan, living in apartments first on E. 71st Street and 3rd Avenue, then E. 74th Street and 3rd, for about five years. There were trips at least once a year to the region and another special assignment of several months in 1964 to the Caribbean, at our branch in Trinidad/Tobago and visits to a number of agents in Jamaica, Bahamas, etc. Every year I managed to vacation in Europe, and those travels, including Portugal, Spain, Greece, Beirut, Italy, Switzerland, Pakistan, Egypt, Austria, France, Belgium, and Holland, provided a useful foundation in later years for actual work during my domicile in Europe and the Middle East.

Initially I regretted accepting the call to leave the field where I was "top dog," but my theory then was to never decline any promotion at that embryonic stage of my career; also my father and Aunt Mary Lou had urged acceptance. H. V. Smith told me he had felt the same way and had sat at his desk in New York with tears in his eyes on his day of arrival! But there were some compensations in that I soaked up useful data relative to our worldwide business, met most of our managers around the globe, and interacted with many insurance brokers who placed overseas business from their New York offices. However, the one best thing that happened in my entire life did occur during my New York City sojourn.

Such was my encounter with Lynn Alexander from Dallas in 1964 at a party held in the St. Regis Hotel roof ballroom. This was a dance given on subscription by a committee composed of, say, "late twenty- and thirty-somethings" as they term them now, with one or two "older ladies" steering the committee which Lynn and I later did join, too. Of course, all committee members were to introduce new blood and attract participants. There were several black-tie dances every season, fall, winter, and spring, and perhaps other functions, too. Jane Burns-Dugdale first introduced me to the group and, in turn, I had met Jane through Hudson and Skippy Hull Boyd. Jane's half-brother Earle also was a member, and there must have been Russian antecedents, for I now recall a thé dansant, also at the St. Regis roof,

CHAPTER ELEVEN

where Jane introduced me to Serge Obolensky, who that late Sunday afternoon was dating Virginia Chow, then at the United Nations but whom I had seen earlier that year in Hong Kong. Old Elsa Maxwell also was at that party and pointed out to me. The white Russian community in the 1960s still was active in the city and held various fundraisers. The Owen Cheathams then lived in New York City at River House and had me to dinner during the wedding festivities for Marion Boyd. Later Celeste was kind in sending several other invitations to events she sponsored, such as her Diamond Ball, etc., where I think I escorted Lynn.

Lynn reports she considered me pompous and stiff on our first date; there was some difficulty in locating her after our first meeting at the St. Regis roof, for following our dance when I asked for her telephone number, she replied, "Butterfield 8," alluding to the then popular Elizabeth Taylor film where she plays a call girl! The next date was to the theater with supper afterwards at the Café Pierre, where there was a nightly combo for dancing and good food. She had a bad cold and said later she would have cancelled except she knew I had tickets to some show. Then at least one or two of the "Committee" dances, then held at the Hotel Ambassador East on Park, and finishing 1964 with New Year's Eve at a party in a large Park Avenue flat followed by renting a limo/driver by chance on the street and going to some very late-night place Lynn knew on the West Side. There I became very amorous, and we smooched all the way back to the East Side in a taxi. Shepherd's Disco was then the rage, and we went often—and on occasion to El Morocco (known by regulars as "Elmo's"), and Lynn now says she thought I was quite a swinger at the time (even calling my tuxedo the "uniform"!) and always ready for a party, etc. She now says I deliberately misled her! I say I saved her from the perils of the fast and furious life of New York City!

I asked her to marry me in late January 1965 around the time of the Johnson inauguration; her parents were then in Washington, DC for the ball, and I called their hotel to ask for her hand. Her father replied by telling me to talk to her mother, to whom he handed the phone! Mary Alexander visited New York soon after, and I took Lynn and her mother to L'Veau d'Or for dinner. The wedding was scheduled for June 5, 1965, at "The Little Church Around the Corner" on East 29th Street with reception following at the Regency Hotel, then new, at Park and 61st Street. I took Lynn to Augusta in March to meet the family; Aunt Mary Lou entertained young and old at a large supper party at 814 Milledge Road. Miss Tracy and Mr. Rod had us for drinks, including a prenuptial cake, and Frank Mays Hull invited the family to an old-fashioned Sunday dinner (middle of the day), after which we returned to New York. Tracy, Mary Lou, and Betty Boardman Witham all said they were coming to our wedding.

A few weeks later, I flew to Dallas to bond further with the Alexander clan with whom I stayed. One night, the Herb Marcuses had an elegant supper party for the older friends of the parents and Lynn's best buddies

CHAPTER ELEVEN

from school and the University at Austin. Included was Bill Crowley (and his wife), manager from the AFIA branch in Dallas.

I was told the groom had to entertain the night prior to the wedding and decided to consult Adele Petit, Alice Smith, and Sophie Meldrim Shonnard. Adele found I could have a Westbury Hotel party in a private room including food and drinks for the wedding party and all out-of-town guests for about $300 to $400. Alice said she might arrange it at the Colony Club provided no one of a certain religious persuasion came, and Miss Sophie then leaped to the occasion and to my rescue in deciding to give the party at her spacious and charming apartment on East 57th Street, near Sutton Place. Then Aunt Mary Lou objected, saying Sophie was not well and telephoning me (at first, as I recall) to decline the offer and then when Sophie stood firm, she finally acquiesced on condition that she would send a case of champagne while I was instructed to provide all the spirits, i.e. bourbon, scotch, gin, and maybe vodka or Canadian, as I do not think we drank much vodka (except in a Bloody Mary) in that era!

The party was perfect in its setting with plenty to eat and drink, a long seated table in the dining room and smaller tables in the hall and, I think, library. There were toasts, but as Betty B. Witham later said, mostly to do with the speaker and not devoted much to Lynn and Bowdre! For instance, Earle Cabell, then in the US House of Representatives from Dallas, sounded like he was still on the floor of the House, and Tracy Cohen talked of her own honeymoon in December 1909 with Rod, and the private railcar they left Macon aboard—such had two bedrooms, and she said both were used their wedding night!

As Miss Sophie's friend, Nona Park, was the daughter of William McAdoo and had been and still was actively involved with the Washington scene, there was some community of interest. Both Sophie and Nona seemed quite taken with Linda and David Underwood from Houston and had known about the Underwood family plantation in Louisiana called Rosedown. Sophie, of course, knew my mother and sister Frank, and it transpired she had dated Jim Hull's father ages ago. Sophie also took a strong interest in Mrs. Charles H. Phinizy, Jr., widow from Greenville, South Carolina, with the same married name as her old hostess and Aunt Mary Lou's dearly beloved mother. Sophie and Amaryllis Phinizy also were both in the high-end "rag trade," even if at somewhat different price levels!

After the dinner, Aunt Mary Lou and Nona Park started a bridge game with Jim Hull in the den, presumably to indicate we all should depart; no one seemed intent on leaving, so Mary Lou told me Sophie "is a sick woman" and to leave now! We did, with the Underwoods, and took a taxi to the King Cole Bar at the St. Regis Hotel, then a stroll on a gorgeous early June night up Fifth Avenue. Mother came to my apartment around 9:00 a.m. June 5, and we went for a hot breakfast at a place around the corner on Third Avenue. Afterwards, I slowly packed and made some telephone calls: the first

CHAPTER ELEVEN

to Miss Sophie to thank her for the spectacular party and to urge her and Nona to come to our wedding. Rob Kennedy came by to collect some furniture pieces I had sold, and I made final arrangements with the concierge for the arranged sub-let of my lease. My best man Inman Mays arrived around 2:00 p.m. following my lunch on a can of jellied beef consommé. I had no appetite! We then taxied to the Westbury Hotel on Madison Avenue to leave my bags as we were to leave the next morning for Bermuda to begin our honeymoon of about a month. To the church on East 29th Street where we waited in a small room off the church altar section but having a view of the street so we could watch arrivals. Ted and Sam Mays, our usher-groomsmen, came, and I have a vague memory of showing Mother around the church and, in particular, the very small adjourning chapel which she admired a lot but which was too tiny for all our guests.

When I was standing near the altar awaiting the bride's arrival, Mother, in the first right pew, told me how beautiful Lynn looked. I recall she was with the Jim Hulls and "Legs" (Henry) Gardner. Mother refused to look directly at the camera at the reception but was charming and gracious to one and all. However, I was a little uptight, objecting to the man who I guess was a hotel "wedding planner"-type as he directed us to feed each other cake and wanted me to perform the "garter" lifting procedure; this I just refused! The Underwoods urged me to have a drink and stop making waves, so I relaxed after a bit, we danced, cut the cake, and talked to our guests at what was really a beautiful reception in a large handsome room well appointed with flowers, furniture, and Lester Lanin's band playing all our favorite show-type tunes. "Mountain Greenery" was one favorite we requested several times. Our chauffeur, Roosevelt Zanders from Harlem, who was driving us joined the party at some point (some opine Jim Hull invited him) and went over to sit with Aunt Mary Lou, Tracy Cohen, and Alice Smith. This caused some consternation, for those three Southern ladies then decided to depart rather hurriedly; Jim Hull and I stopped them by the door, and a picture, now in our wedding album, was taken of this encounter. In retrospect, I think these granddames also were irritated that not enough attention was paid to them at the reception; if so, I do regret it. Lynn's mother, Mary Alexander, made an elegant picture and was a gracious hostess to all.

We finally changed in bedrooms upstairs and left in sort of a teary farewell for the Hotel Westbury, again driven by Roosevelt. To the airport early the next morning, a Sunday where the Herb Levines came in their Rolls to say goodbye. The American Express travel representative also was on hand to present Lynn with an orchid corsage which she didn't want to wear, thinking all would know we were flying Pan American to Bermuda on our honeymoon! Pan Am upgraded us, I think, so that we sat in the front lounge section of the 707 jet drinking Bloody Marys most of the way. We went directly to the Coral Beach Club, where we had a small cottage directly facing the beach; when an English employee came to bring us

CHAPTER ELEVEN

something soon following our arrival, I introduced him to "Miss Alexander"!

After a peaceful week in Bermuda, where we went to one party given by the AFIA agents and by chance ran into a Bermuda friend from Hong Kong days at the Coral Beach Club, we departed by British Air at night to London in direct transit to Geneva. Walter and Maike Wolff then were living at Nyon, a suburb of Geneva, and Walter met our flight and conveyed us to our guest-house/bed and breakfast fronting the lake and near their own small house. After a few days in Switzerland, we flew to Nice Airport, picked up a car, and drove to Cap-Ferrat where we stayed some six or seven days at the Grand Hotel situated just on the tip of the "Cap." We made many day trips up and down the coast (St. Tropez, Cannes, Eze, Monte-Carlo, Menton, Grasse, Juan les Pin, Cap d' Antibes, St. Paul de Vence, etc.) and just relaxed at the great hotel pool, called in English "Sun Beach." We lunched there often, walked all about Cap-Ferrat and, on Sunday, went to the morning service at the little English church at Beaulieu. Dawson and Betsy Teague from Augusta had the parish that summer and dedicated the service to us, Betsy playing the organ in the loft joyfully! One night we had a festive dinner with them at a famous old restaurant in Villefranche, where we had a table on the terrace outside and facing the harbor. I think that was the evening when John Profumo and his party sat behind us at another table. His scandal was then the talk of the day in London and elsewhere usually labeled "L'Affaire Christine Keller"!

IS LIVING WELL STILL THE BEST REVENGE?

The Teagues were at the Nice airport to see us off to Rome via Pan Am. We stopped a few days at the Hotel Massimo de la Azeglio, a favorite of Vera Dell'Oro and where we had a good rate. Their kitchen was rather well known too, but we did not like much the location near the main train station and the old Grand Hotel. We accomplished some sightseeing, and Peter Fornacca, a friend from our Rome office, was hospitable in every way. We left by night-sleeper for Brindisi, arriving rather early the next morning; but as our Olympic air flight to Corfu did not depart until, say, 3:00 p.m., we took a day room at a Jolly Hotel. Arriving later that day in Corfu, we taxied directly to our hotel on a beach outside of town. The resort was run by the Swiss, and I had booked a week; the price seemed reasonable, and I knew Swiss food and management to be first rate. As soon as Lynn saw our room and bath, her first remark was that such reminded her of a child's camp! Concrete floor, no air-conditioner, and the lawns were filled with what seemed to be holiday trippers from the UK on package tours! The food, which was American Plan, wasn't bad though, and the beach was nice with sports such as water-skiing provided behind a motorboat.

We went into town after a day to see if we could move into the Corfu Palace Hotel, which was air-conditioned, for this was still June in Greece! Everything was fully booked, as Queen Anne-Marie of Greece was about to give birth at Mon Repos, the royal family estate on Corfu! We then negotiated with the Swiss, who had no difficulty in filling our room, and decided to move on

CHAPTER ELEVEN

to Athens earlier than planned. We had booked at the Grand-Bretagne Hotel on the main square, Syntagma, but wanting a pool we switched after arrival to the new Athens Hilton, opened about 1963 and one of their really luxurious hotels in the chain. The rooms were large and all bathrooms in marble, which I later discovered could be much cheaper than wood in Greece.

Lynn being now happy in air-conditioned splendor, we set about seeing all in about three or four days. I had been once in Athens but Lynn never, so we went to the various museums, climbed up to the Acropolis, Mt. Lycabettus, visited the Herodes Atticus Theater (still in use), the Royal Palace to see the Evzones stand on duty, the oldest section of the city known as the "Plaka," the Arch of Hadrian, and several old churches, including the nineteenth-century cathedral. We took a one-day trip to the islands near Athens/Piraeus, including Hydra, Poros, and Egina. I acted badly on this trip, principally because the bus took us last back to the hotel from Piraeus, but the unpleasantness began on the boat when I complained about the quality of the food and threw my stale bread roll against the wall, thereby mortifying Lynn, who stopped speaking to me. Fortunately, we made it up after I apologized very contritely! We had a nice dinner that night in the Taverna of the Hilton.

On to Istanbul and its Hilton located above the Bosporus separating Europe from Asia Minor. When checking in, we were offered one room overlooking the front and the Bosporus Strait at one price and another on the back garden side for a lower sum; naturally

I chose the latter, not being told there was a circus in full force nearby every night! As this hotel also was not fully air-conditioned, the result was some noisy nights! I learned later that "once in a lifetime" is a pretty good guideline, and, in addition, that you only regret (usually) what you don't do!

AFIA owned 50 percent of a Turkish insurance company, so I visited with the local management, who also took us to dinner at a restaurant owned and managed by a white Russian whose wife acted as sort of the friendly receptionist! This was the first of many visits over the years to that restaurant whose name I have forgotten. Good Russian food always—borsch, chicken Kiev, caviar, sturgeon, and shashlik. We also learned that Greek food, coffee, etc., all really derive from Turkey, considering that the Turkish Ottomans occupied what is now modern Greece for over 400 years. This data on food of course includes feta cheese.

This was the first trip for both of us to Istanbul, so we eagerly went on tour to see all, if possible, during our stay. We made good progress in what had been the "old Constantinople" and soon had visited Topkapi Palace, Saint Sophia (now a mosque), Blue Mosque, Dolmabahee Palace, the Hippodrome, Grand Bazaar, Suleyman Mosque, Galata Bridge spanning the Golden Horn, then to Kariye to view the wonderful mosaics. There also was a drive up the Beyoglu district past the handsome former European embassy buildings from the time of the Ottoman Empire when Constantinople was the capital.

CHAPTER ELEVEN

One afternoon we took a small launch and went up the Bosporus to the Black Sea (it is very dark); we must have gone into the water on this trip as there are pictures of me in bathing trunks. On the same excursion, we went to see several smaller palaces built directly on the water, and we stopped once on the Asia Minor side. This was before the completion of the huge steel bridge now connecting both sides of Istanbul. And so on to the end of our wonderful and special honeymoon, as one morning we boarded Pan Am's daily round-the-world flight for Beirut, from where we were due to depart the same night on British Air to Singapore, soon to be our new temporary home.

Antoine Argaropoulou came to the Beirut Airport to collect us, as Tom Hauff, a friend and long-time colleague, was then away on vacation. I had first known Antoine in Cairo when I stopped by when he was busy closing up the AFIA office due to the Nasser nationalization of all insurance. This was in 1961 or 1962. Antoine was an "Alexandria Greek," as many called them, and soon repatriated himself and family, with many other "Alexandria Greeks," back to the land of their forebears. He later opened the very successful Marsh and McClennan brokerage office in Athens. We drove along the Corniche by the sea to the City Center, ending up for an early dinner on the terrace of the St. Georges Hotel.

Beirut then was in its prime; some termed it "the Paris of the Near East," and it was the undoubted vacation playground for the entire Arab world. Money flowed widely, and Beirut was the banking center of the Eastern Mediterranean extending down to the oil-producing countries. Pipelines of oil flowed through Lebanon to the Mediterranean.

Our flight was on time, bags checked to Singapore, and we managed three seats to ourselves, making privacy and a bit of "smooching" an easy task! There were stops, I think, then in Karachi and Calcutta prior to touching down around the mid-afternoon of the next day, say, a nine- or ten-hour trip in the air. We were in the dark until Calcutta, when we were allowed to disembark. Lynn went to the terminal restroom and when she came out excitedly reported that there was a cleaning woman inside with a large gold ring in her nose—and she wanted a tip! I told her she was going to see not only nose rings but many finger rings, many earrings on one ear, toe rings, and a multitude of other strange sights in the days to come!

Bill and Barbara Krall (he was manager for Singapore/Malaysia) and my old friends from Hong Kong, Winston and Helena Chen (he now worked for Insurance Company of North America in Singapore), met us. Bill said he had taken a leave flat for us at Meyer Court on Meyer Road; this was the building where he lived which fronted the water in the Katong area. The Kralls had all of us to dinner at their flat that night and cooked steaks on their terrace. The flat we occupied was fully furnished on a lower floor and rented by an English couple then away on vacation. The flat came with a Chinese couple, Ah Khoon and his wife; she was

CHAPTER ELEVEN

the Amah (maid and cleaner) while the husband cooked, ran the household, and acted as butler.

Then early the next morning I was off to the office, ready to attack with our new decentralization plan under which the Southeast Asia area would now report to the new regional office I would establish in Singapore. The region included Guam, Taiwan, Hong Kong, the Philippine Islands, Indonesia, Indo-China, Thailand, Brunei, Singapore, and Malaysia with India and Pakistan added later.

I was back in my element, but Lynn complained she was stuck out in postal district #21, while all our friends and the people she was meeting daily all lived in districts 9, 10 or 11, with few exceptions. So I told her to look only for a house or flat in one of those codes. She found a super house in Queen Astrid Park (Code 10) for the equivalent of $500 monthly; I turned it down stupidly and the search continued until we found a small bungalow for about $250 (Code 11), and the owner agreed to upgrade the interior as Lynn wanted. The bungalow had two bedrooms and two bathrooms, plus a large wrap-around veranda where we normally took all meals and sat. The bedrooms only were air-conditioned. There was a large garden on two levels with wonderful tropical plantings, and a Malay gardener came every day to trim, replant, cut, and sweep.

We were lucky to inherit the two old-school Amahs (called black and whites, as they always dressed in black pants and starched white tops) from some friends with Mobil Oil who were leaving on transfer. They were Ah

IS LIVING WELL STILL THE BEST REVENGE?

So and Ah Ho and soon became close members of the family with the arrival of Tracy in 1966 and Katherine in 1969; for years these Amahs had worked for Standard Vacuum (previously joint venture of Standard Oil, N.J, S.O., California, and Mobil), Ah So as the baby Amah and Ah Ho as a ladies' maid. Ah So also had developed cooking skills quite acceptable for simple western dishes, so in our home we were very well looked after by these experienced hands who ran the home, i.e., ordered groceries, waited table, cooked, cleaned, and did all washing, Ah Ho being a genius with a man's shirt! The moment one dropped a garment, it was whisked away! However, these Amah sisters were extreme snobs and always insisted on working for the number one executive in a business! They knew the "number ones" from all others in the community!

We lived in our first home in Brizay Park for about two years. Then in search of larger quarters, Lynn found a newly constructed home on Narooma Road; this was a "sort of the best house on the street" situation, but at $600 monthly, then termed a bargain—with the large influx of new people coming in now that Indonesia had reopened following the fall of Sukarno and with new oil tracts discovered off Malaysia, the Narooma Road house could soon command a monthly rental of $2,000 or more! We had a five- or six-year lease!

We lived in Singapore seven and a half years, had Tracy and Katherine at Mount Alvernia Hospital, both of whom were christened by Anglican ministers, and Lynn developed a fine home establishment for us all.

CHAPTER ELEVEN

The girls also developed English accents from their preschool days. She was a devoted mother and soon had a large cadre of friends in the American community in addition to friends from the Chinese, English, and other expatriate resident communities. Her mahjongg skills were perfected along with bridge with ladies and also with couples at night. She played some tennis and, for the first time, started golf at the Royal Singapore Golf Club. I concentrated on expanding our business and, by evolution, assuming the responsibilities heretofore exercised by the headquarters in the United States.

When I arrived in mid-1965, we had eight branches in Guam, the Philippines, Hong Kong, and Singapore/Malaysia. By January 1973 at my departure, we had new offices in Bangkok (replacing one agency), two in Indonesia having reopened 1966, several more in the Philippines, new offices in Brunei, Kuching, Sarawak, two in Borneo (East Malaysia), a sub-branch at Jurong, Singapore, and new branches in Malaysia at Penang, Ipoh, and Malacca, for a new total of twenty-one, with India and Pakistan, of course, in addition! There also was a representative office in Saigon, Vietnam. The government of India nationalized property and casualty insurance circa 1972, and I went to New Delhi with a group of US and UK insurers to negotiate the best deal possible. As the Indians did not just seize our portfolios, as had happened elsewhere, we received compensation and also salvaged several key trained executives from our Indian staff for work in the Southeast Asia area.

IS LIVING WELL STILL THE BEST REVENGE?

I was the first foreign insurance executive to return to Indonesia following Sukarno's downfall and recall boarding the KLM flight Singapore to Jakarta one early evening in December 1965 on an almost empty plane which hit the usual "bump" as we crossed the equator en route! Mr. Soenarto (our number one local executive before nationalization) met me at the dilapidated terminal which had flooded due to heavy rains, as I remember the water all over the cement floor. There were few or no street lamps lit due to the endemic electricity shortage, and the Hotel Inter-Continental was almost empty! Thus the initial stage for securing our license back and whatever assets remained, i.e., one house built in a residential area with all funds and bonds virtually worthless due to hyperinflation. Lynn accompanied me on some of my business trips so that over our seven and a half years in Singapore she had visited most of Southeast Asia plus at least one or two trips to India which we both savored immensely.

Once we took a short vacation from Calcutta and flew to Bagdogra and then by tiny narrow-gauge rail and taxi to Darjeeling, which lies at about 6,000 feet. Darjeeling is the stop en route to Sikkim and from the higher "Tiger Hill" one, if lucky, can glimpse Mount Everest as the sun rises. We put up at the old-fashioned but charming Windermere Hotel, owned and run by the Tinkerbelle Tendufla family (part English and part local, probably). The old mother or a relative was the dining room receptionist, and each bedroom was in sort of a connecting series of cottages, all with fireplaces that burned brightly

CHAPTER ELEVEN

each morning and evening. We were lucky, as after being called early one morning around 4:30 a.m., we drove in a jeep up Tiger Hill wrapped in warm wool blankets to see if Mother Nature would permit us to view the famous Mount Everest, and all of a sudden the sun began to peep over the horizon, the clouds and mist seemed to part, and there was Everest flying its renowned snow plume! But the sighting lasted only a few minutes, for the clouds rolled back in and Chomolungma (as the Tibetans call Everest) was obscured again. We did have a grand view of Kanchenjunga (28,146 ft. high) from Tiger Hill, which I believe is about 1,500 feet higher than Darjeeling. Once jetting from New Delhi towards Bangkok, there was a perfect clear day, and at our high altitude I had a fantastic view of the entire Himalayan range, including Everest at 29,028 feet.

We were rather active in the American Community, as my business dictated such, and one year I was president of the American Club while Lynn was active in the American Women's Association. I chaired the Insurance Committee of the International Chamber of Commerce, for in that era American businesses decided not to form a separate American Chamber. I was asked to head the American Association, a kind of business committee fostered by the US Embassy, but declined this knowing I would leave Singapore in January 1973.

We entertained at home mainly with buffet dinners for, say, eighteen to twenty-four, and this was relatively easy, for besides the dining room seating ten to twelve, we had a large covered terrace with several round and square tables seating up to twelve. Besides our own staff of two, we engaged one or two bartender/servers depending on the crowd. The living room and another terrace off that could easily accommodate the cocktail hour. Afterwards we often danced on the terrace or played charades if the group was not too large.

Ford Motor had operated an assembly plant in Singapore since well before World War II; it was in this plant that the British General Percival signed the surrender to the Japanese on February 15, 1942. Ford was insured by our company, and we were friends with the local management. The local Ford managing director invited us to a black-tie dinner party around 1970-1971 in honor of the visit of CEO Henry Ford, II, then touring New Zealand, Australia, etc. This was a so-called "high-level affair" in a private room at the old Raffles Hotel, and we found to our mild surprise a fun group, having expected government officials plus others of that ilk. The guests mostly consisted of the Ford travel party from their private plane and other business personages we knew in Singapore. Christina Ford (then I believe Henry's second and beauteous wife) was tall and fascinating and wore a handsome pearl bracelet containing a large emerald in the clasp; there was an attractive English lady introduced as Evelyn de Rothschild (said to be Henry's great and good friend) and several other jet-setters whose names I do not now recall. At dinner, I sat next to the wife of Ford's vice president for the area, including Australia, New Zealand, and Asia in general, and she candidly regaled me with amusing anecdotes

CHAPTER ELEVEN

relative to their trip, i.e. who did what, where, how all the entourage were getting along, etc. There were really some choice stories! All the Ford ladies were mad about Lynn's sparkly Indian caftan (handmade in Bombay), which out-shown their Valentinos or whatever!

In October 1972, I was offered a transfer to Brussels as resident vice president for Continental Europe, the Middle East, and Africa (excluding South Africa). Lynn was delighted to anticipate cooler weather and a real change of seasons away from tropical Singapore. So, in January 1973, we packed and, with many a tear, said our goodbyes. The Amahs were the real problem, as they had been with the girls from birth and loved both dearly. We even toyed with taking them with us, but after having had Ah So in the United States one month while on vacation, we knew this would not really work over time. I flew on directly to Europe alone, Lynn, Tracy, and Katherine going to Hong Kong a few days later to obtain winter clothes before transiting to Dallas to stay with Lynn's parents prior to joining me.

While in Hong Kong, Lynn ran into Danny Kaye at the Dynasty shop in the Peninsula Hotel; Danny kept Tracy and Katherine amused and laughing with his mimic action and funny faces while Lynn looked at clothes. Finally in late January, they came on the daily Sabena jet from New York, Lynn very elegant in a new mink coat from Neiman-Marcus secured at a favorable sale price and with her father's discount!

We first lived in a small duplex apartment on Rue du Buisson which runs on one side of the small Jardin du Roi just off Avenue Louise. This had been rented by my company predecessor and really was a rather elegant European flat on two levels, with several other flats in the same building. There was ample garage space in the basement with an automatic door to the street; however, the flat was small by Far Eastern standards, particularly those in Hong Kong and even Japan. As soon as Lynn saw the narrow building, she said the space must be small. But at least the flat option removed us quickly from the hotel, so we moved in as soon as our shipment of furniture and other goods arrived. The latter was badly water damaged by the climatic change on the winter ocean voyage from Singapore to Northern Europe; some clothing was wholly ruined, and certain furniture pieces required refinishing.

Lynn had Tracy and Katherine entered in schools after surveying all possibilities and began to search for a stand-alone house and garden, which she finally located around October 1973 at 18 Chemin du Putdael, a narrow one-way street laid with cobblestones and said to be the sole remains of an old Roman road. This was located in the Brussels quarter or commune of Auderghem, which was multi-lingual—French, Flemish, and German speaking, the three official tongues in Belgium. Our rented house in Brussels was brick painted white with a Federal look or a bit Regency. There was a small square garden in the rear planted with two apple trees and bordered all around with tall cedars so that we had privacy. Opening out from French doors in the dining and breakfast rooms was a flagstone terrace with

CHAPTER ELEVEN

the garden beyond. The front entrance hall, a small den, bathroom, and garage were located on the ground floor with a staircase leading up to the main hall. On the main level were the living, dining, breakfast room, powder room, and kitchen, with another stairway up to the bedrooms and baths on the third floor. Lynn even had a small dressing room containing a basin. Here we lived for nine years in a wonderful central location; one could walk to shops and the bakery (the one that makes bread for Rob's, the best food emporium). Our club, Chateau St. Anne, was a five-minute walk and provided a good table, tennis, and swimming as well as allowing us to meet many Belgians and other foreign nationals who also were members. The school bus stopped at the head of our street to take the girls to and from school, and my office at 40 Avenue du Arts was about fifteen to twenty minutes or less, depending on traffic. The girls were now at St. John's International School in Waterloo, although Katherine first had attended a kindergarten called "Brussels Sprouts"! St. John's was a private school with classes in English but French instruction compulsory each day. Both girls excelled here, Tracy on the tennis team and Katherine with her academics. They both learned fluent French with a good accent.

The Zaventam Airport was only a ten to fifteen-minute drive, and in these early days this proved very useful since I was on the move visiting brokers, agents, and our branch offices in Belgium, Holland, Germany, France, Spain, Portugal, Italy, Greece, Scandinavia, the Middle East, and Africa. We had about 1,000 staff members in total with premium volume turnover of US $200 million per annum plus investment income. I now occupied one of the several most-senior posts in the company, and when promoted to full corporate vice president at the head office level in late 1973, I considered myself well en route to eventually becoming a strong candidate for president/CEO of the entire company! I was extremely well motivated and eagerly devoted myself full time to expanding our business on a profitable basis and, where necessary, reducing our exposures in losing markets. Lynn wondered how I could devote so much time to an enterprise I did not own!

Lynn felt I was away too much in these early days, thereby missing some activities with the children, but as time moved on, the trips were shorter (usually during the week), and we also began to take the girls on European jaunts to France and other destinations. There were visits with Tracy and Katherine over the years to Italy (Rome) and then Florence plus Pisa and on to Venice for Easter one year; to the Riviera, Cannes, and Mougins to visit the Walter Wolffs, to Paris, Loire Valley, and Provence and then Toulouse, to Pau and Carcassonne in the border regions of France; Eugenie le Bain to Biarritz and Bordeaux, plus many visits to Holland, Germany, another Easter time in Salzburg, Viénna, Austria, and all around Belgium often. Several trips were made to London and throughout England and Scotland—some with the girls too; once we had brother Inman with us as he first flew from New York to Brussels and then joined us in London where we stopped at the Chester Square

CHAPTER ELEVEN

home of Sherry and Tom Hauff, then on vacation in the United States.

During the school's winter vacation period, the girls went with their St. John's class to what was known as Les classes de Niege, a week spent skiing and studying in Switzerland in a French-speaking Canton resort. Their command of French improved to a high level under daily instruction, and Lynn soon spoke and understood most French rather fluently, even if there were a few grammatical errors. She has a great proclivity in copying accents, which proved useful, and also rapidly acquired acquaintances, some of whom became our good friends. We are still in touch today with Belgian and American friends we knew from our residence in Brussels and last visited with several during our summer 2001 occupancy of the Arthur Maixners' spacious flat in the Belgian capital.

At the risk of a little "name-dropping," it may be of some interest to the reader to learn that while living in the European Union capital, we had the opportunity to meet many visitors, both business personages of note and government officials, at large receptions or luncheons sponsored by the American Club, American Chamber of Commerce in Belgium, or the Belgo-American Association. These personalities included David Rockerfeller (whose personal secretary had come to our wedding in New York), Winston Churchill II (grandson of the wartime British leader), General Alexander Haig (NATO top gun), Sheik Armani (Saudi Arabian Oil Minister), CEO Walter Wriston of Citibank, Prince Albert (now King Albert II of Belgium), Leonard Firestone, Anne Cox Chambers, and Charles Price, the final three all US ambassadors to the Belgium Court, and many other business and political leaders (i.e., Senator Kit Bond from Missouri) from the United States and other countries. In Belgium, the United States has three ambassadors: to the king, to NATO, and to the European Union. We met most of them over the years and knew Chambers and Price quite well. Both came to our house.

Lynn was an active member of the American Women's Club, which maintained their own clubhouse, and both the Association Belgo-Americaine Senior and Junior Ladies Groups. One was asked to join these Belgo-Americaine bodies, and here we met many prominent Belgian couples in the business and social worlds who had interest in US ties. I was asked in time to become a director of both the American Club and the American Chamber of Commerce, and lunched frequently at the Circle Gaulois, a Belgian club near my office housed in an old building to the rear of the park fronting the town royal palace. Some say one of the balls before the Battle of Waterloo was held here. The Circle Gaulois was pure old-fashioned Brussels at its best with good food and rather "shabby style." I rather think the continental equivalent of a leading London Club—but with a superior cuisine! Once a year the club held a diplomatic dinner honoring those principals located in Belgium and where the club members were mainly in "habit" (white tie/tails with decorations and, as the British say

CHAPTER ELEVEN

"gongs") and all ladies in long dresses and jewels. Food and drink were elegant at these affairs. Once the King and Queen of Sweden came to lunch, and His Majesty (related to the former and beloved late Queen Astrid of Belgium, whose son was then King Baudouin) made his remarks to the assembled company in perfect English which apparently he spoke better than French. The king was accompanied by Queen Silvia, a beautiful and gracious German/Brazilian lady, then heavily enceinte with their first child.

In late 1982, I was recalled to our headquarters in New York City, as the new president, Paul Butler, who was hired away from AIG, decided to eliminate the regional offices in favor of a more centralized management/underwriting structure in the United States, our world headquarters. At the same time, I assumed new responsibilities, to include Government Affairs/International Relations, as Butler felt this to be an essential unit lacking in our organization. This job also included finding ways to have company spokespeople, and particularly our president, at the forefront when insurance/financial services were being worked in Washington and abroad. At this time, the United States and other countries were at last recognizing that the service industries, e.g., banks, insurers, travel/tourism entities, communications, and electronic/fiberoptic industries, were rapidly replacing many old "rust-belt" companies in contributing to a more favorable balance of payments for our trading economy. We wanted to be leaders in negotiating more favorable terms in certain foreign markets for

United States insurers, as many countries had imposed restrictions over the decades on non-national insurance company operations. My counterpart at AIG was Ron Shelp, from Montezuma, Georgia, and the author of *Beyond Industrialization*, which Butler told me was "ghost written"! Shelp had worked the service industry issue to great effect so that the AIG CEO, Maurice Greenburg (known to friends as "Hank"), had received much good publicity.

I set about at once to seize upon some very worthwhile business proposition to emanate from our president, who could espouse it and therefore become another key spokesman. But in two years, I never quite found the ideal subject to embrace, even though we did become involved in many issues with our own government and abroad. There were many visits to Washington, to Europe, and to the Far East in pursuing our objective of more freedom for service companies. The Department of Commerce and United States trade representative were strong allies, as were our State Department career diplomats and the United States Chamber of Commerce in Washington, DC. It was a real novelty to learn at first hand how the Washington, DC establishment really functions and to see the lobbyists and politicos at their so-called work!

We bought a house in Chatham, New Jersey, about a one-hour commute to my office on William Street in lower Manhattan; William runs perpendicular to Wall Street more or less straight, as most of these early lower New York Streets at one time had been probably mere cow paths! The girls entered Chatham Township high

CHAPTER ELEVEN

school, Tracy a sophomore and Katherine in eighth grade. We had American friends and their children from Belgium residing nearby, and they aided them in soon adapting to the local mores. As a matter of fact, both finally married their initial Chatham sweethearts, first known at this school! We came South in late 1982, December as I recall, to Jim and Karen Hull's wedding, and again to Greenville to attend Carol De l'aigle Hull's marriage to Fred Palmer in 1983. The girls also came with us on this latter occasion. We all visited Cape Cod, Martha's Vineyard, and Nantucket in 1983 and 1984 on vacation, staying in Edgartown with Betty and Tom Bonner Bowring, who had come to see us in Brussels (along with Martha Fleming) in 1980, and also seeing the Chick Barnards at their Orleans, Cape Cod, house.

In early December 1983, Lynn joined me for the Interhemispheric Insurance Conference held that year in San Francisco at the Fairmont Hotel, where we also lodged. This gave me an opportunity to see some Latin American friends I had not seen since the mid-1960s while working in Colombia. Our last night in San Francisco, we invited Pat Walsh and Susie Pearsall to drinks and dinner at Jack's (old San Francisco). We finished off at the bar atop the Mark Hopkins Hotel, as Pat continued to fill us in on Augusta even though he had by then lived in San Francisco for years; he knew it all, never forgot any detail and remained fully au courant by almost daily telephone calls! We had not been in touch since our wedding in 1965 when he was living in Paris, and I think we talked on the phone from Cap Ferrat. He liked Lynn a lot.

While Lynn and a small group took a one-day tour to the Napa Valley, I visited the Fireman's Fund Insurance Head Office, where I heard a rumor to the effect that the AFIA owners were selling, probably to Cigna, itself a merger in 1982 between Insurance Company of North America (The United States' oldest insurer, founded in 1792) and Connecticut General Life Insurance Company, which, incidentally, already owned about 15 percent of AFIA through their property and casualty subsidiary, Aetna Insurance Company (sometimes called the "Little Aetna"). But back in New York, no one took my input seriously, and at our annual meeting the following week, our disingenuous Board of Directors said nothing. We learned later, however, that the deal had been basically agreed upon just prior to our annual meeting followed by dinner at the Downtown Association, a club where I also had membership. This is an example of how the unexpected can happen suddenly in the modern United States business climate!

Cigna had its own international property, casualty, marine, reinsurance, and life operation—while considerably smaller than AFIA's (one-third or a bit more in size in gross premium volume), the purchase did seem to make much economic sense, as it overnight catapulted Cigna up to first or second place, depending on the expert analysis, in international business for a United States company. Interestingly, Insurance Company of North America (INA) was a founder of AFIA in 1918

CHAPTER ELEVEN

but withdrew in the late 1920s to work abroad on its own. When the takeover for about US $450 million plus reinsurance and other assumption guarantees was announced in late 1983, I feared the "mushroom syndrome" might affect me directly; such is defined as "first you are kept in the dark, then one is cultivated, and then later canned"! On the other hand, Cigna needed executives who had performed well and experienced hands who knew the international markets and how to grow the business. AFIA operated in many countries where Cigna had no license, so in-house capability was immediately required. On the opposite side, however, there were to be staff reductions in many areas due to the dual existing organizations. I was lucky in making the transition to Cigna, so by the summer of 1984, I accepted an assignment to the INA-Cigna area office in Athens, Greece, as senior vice president for the Eastern Mediterranean, Middle East, and Africa (excluding South Africa). Thus back to the former decentralized AFIA structure with local area units managing and underwriting our business in a given territory and reporting final consolidated numbers to headquarters. I was very happy and looked forward to no more commuting to New York City from New Jersey!

Tracy started her freshman year at the College of Charleston in late August 1984, with Lynn and her sister driving her down, as Lynn had broken a bone in her foot in a fall on Nantucket! Katherine, just in her sophomore year at Chatham Township and with her new beau Brett in the picture, was furious at the thought of moving to

IS LIVING WELL STILL THE BEST REVENGE?

Greece! I left on the Pan Am nightly flight to London en route to Athens in the early days of September. Several of our Africa and Middle Eastern broker connections had London offices, and I was asked to visit them prior to reaching Athens. This I did, stopping at the Park Lane Hotel after spending the first night, following an approximately 8:00 p.m. arrival at Heathrow, at the Strand Hotel, sort of a "fleabag," in a single with no private bath or air conditioner. The Strand, just off lower Oxford Street, was finally suggested by the taxi driver after the Hilton and others contacted were fully booked by the late hour. Our London office had not given a credit card number to secure the reservation for late arrival, even though there was difficulty in booking anywhere due to the many visitors then in the city. After calling on agency, brokerage, and company connections who all supported our Africa/Middle East business, I took the daily morning British Air flight nonstop to Athens. George Khoury and George Liakakos met the plane and drove me to the Athens Hilton. It was September 4 or 5, 1984, and I was delighted to be back in the field again and eager to attack the new job challenge.

I spent these early days reviewing our business and contacts, talking with the staff underwriting our various portfolios, and preparing our tentative budget and 1985 business plan to present to the our president in late September in New York City. This return to New York included my final stay in our Chatham house, which Lynn was readying to sell. She called me one night at the Athens Hilton in October to discuss an early offer

CHAPTER ELEVEN

(giving us a very nice profit after about two years) just before she flew to Athens to spend a week or ten days house hunting and to inspect a few places already offered to me. Lynn discovered an unfinished dwelling at 4 Panos Street in the Athens suburb of Ekali, a rather perfect location situated about nine miles above central Athens, but only, say, five or six from our office site.

Ekali is above the smog, with a nice view of Mt. Parnassus and the Tatoi area, land owned by the exiled Greek royal family. Tatoi was the site of their country home, which we visited on weekend walks, and the location of the royal graves commencing with George I, the Danish Prince who accepted the crown in 1863 as an eighteen-year-old and ruled until his death in 1913. Our house was built sort of like a German block house, two stories with a flat roof and basement and owned by a Greek engineer and his wife then working in Frankfurt. While Germanic in spirit and looks in a very modern way, the house was centrally air conditioned and heated which then was most unusual in Greece! The utilities were the finest-known modern German and European products—so fine, in fact, that when a subsequent problem arose, local experts claimed such units were not suitable for a country like Greece! They did not understand how they worked! There was some nice woodwork employed inside and even marble steps leading down to the basement. We then again learned that in Greece marble is cheaper than wood!

The house finally would be complete in March 1985 except for the garden fence and a few other details, so

Lynn, Katherine, and our Dandy Dinmont dog named "Dandy" for Frank Inman Mays, planned to arrive in Athens in late January so that Katherine could enter the second term of her sophomore year at the Athens American School. Within seven to ten days back in school, Katherine was happy and had discovered several persons in Athens who knew her former classmates in Brussels or who had themselves been at school in Belgium.

While she still missed her Chatham friends, at least she was not discontent and morose, as on her arrival when I first saw them at the Athens terminal. "Dandy" was still drunk from the eleven-hour flight and preflight medication she had imbibed! We then stopped at the Athens Hilton for some thirty days until our effects arrived and the house was ready. Dogs were welcomed, provided they registered and gave one paw print on the hotel registration card! After the first day when Lynn took Katherine to school, she took the school bus that came to the bus stop across the street from the Hilton. She did not get off at that stop the first afternoon, and Lynn almost became panic-stricken rushing back to her hotel room to find her in tears. It was her first day at a strange school, and she had left the bus at an earlier stop. That evening, Steve Liakakos and his father, George (a Cigna employee), came by; Steve also was a student in the high school, and he promised to take Katherine around and make introductions when she arrived the next morning. That was the real beginning, for Katherine soon began to excel in both her studies

CHAPTER ELEVEN

and school leadership activities. Her first girlfriend was Emily Stearns, daughter of the United States ambassador, and she rapidly made many others of various nationalities. Katherine graduated in June 1987 with a plethora of honors, both academic and social, made many friends of various nationalities, and was elected "Prom Queen" at the final celebration.

My new post was really unique in that we managed both the Arab world—including the entire Persian Gulf region, United Arab Emirates and Oman, Saudi Arabia, Pakistan, and Turkey—together with Israel, Cyprus, Greece, Bahrain, Malta, and Africa where we had operations in Egypt, Ivory Coast, former French Colonies of Cameroon, Mali and Senegal, Liberia, Nigeria, Kenya, and Zimbabwe. Insurance brokers and agencies supporting this business were located both in the countries themselves and in Paris, London, Athens, and Istanbul. The only places where there existed Cigna operations were Saudi Arabia, United Arab Emirates, Abidjan, Ivory Coast, and Monrovia, Liberia. Hence, only in these territories was a decision required on how to merge or proceed with parallel operations. In Ivory Coast, we easily merged the two offices using Colina Insurance Company, Inc. (a Cigna vehicle) as our underwriting company; in Monrovia, we just continued with the two agencies, one for INA and changing the St. Paul carrier for a Cigna insurance entity so that the combined operation probably accounted at that time for 50 percent or more of the entire local admitted property/casualty market!

Saudi Arabia was Cigna's large area producer, and their Saudi operation was certainly better spread, diversified, and, after my first visit, I decided better managed with a focus on growth than was the Riyadh Insurance Company, the AFIA unit in Dammam on the East Coast. We also controlled 100 percent of the Cigna business whereas AFIA had Saudi Arabian and Japanese shareholders owning about 49 percent of the company. We also had a few problems with our Saudi sponsors/shareholders, so I decided, after much analysis and discussion with headquarters, to sell our share of Riyadh to the Saudis and concentrate on the Cigna operation. The business AFIA controlled would be transferred to the Cigna entity; and the Salem Rizk and Khouja agencies would continue as separate Cigna operations in Jedda on the West Coast. As for Dubai and Abu Dhabi, United Arab Emirates, I finally obtained the agreement of the INA general agency to permit the small AFIA branch and agency to continue following the registration of a Cigna-owned company for the new Cigna branch.

I was on the road a good deal commencing fall 1984 and well into 1985 addressing the integration and other business problems, e.g., what to do about the stagnant situation of our Turkish company lacking an active manager and Cigna having no real control with our 49 percent ownership, the need to reduce property/marine commissions in Israel, how to do something really effective in Pakistan where INA had to be registered to replace Home Insurance, collections from the INA agency in Dubai were a constant problem, how to get more from our Bahrain

CHAPTER ELEVEN

reinsurance connection, and whether we replace Reliance Insurance in Oman by INA since the Omani insurance law prohibited the entry of any additional or replacement companies. The foregoing just to provide a small dose of items we initially had to work. I had some very fine support from our Athens area office staff, and from Head Office, so we went ahead and solved our key objectives one by one, including the replacement of several AFIA registered insurance companies in Greece, Cyprus, Israel, etc., all of which was done in good time after many complaints from agencies representing them for years.

Lynn went with me on several business trips to Istanbul, Israel, Rome, Paris, London, and Brussels, but she missed Nairobi on several occasions and now regrets this. During our six years in Greece, we also took Tracy and Katherine to Istanbul to sample the Turkish atmosphere. In the Grand Bazaar, one rug salesman asked Lynn how many camels she wanted for the beautiful nubile Tracy, who then turned beet red! Our family also spent a number of weekends touring Greek Islands by sailing yacht as guests of George Koumbas, an important agent/broker in Athens. On various occasions, we sailed in waters around both the Ionian and Aegean Islands, visiting over time, to name a few, Corfu and surrounding islands, Kefalonia/Ithaca, Spetses, Skiathos and Skopelos in the Sporades Group, Mytilini (Lesbos) from where the Turkish coast is visible, etc. On another occasion, Lynn and I took a short cruise on a Greek ship that called at Mykonos, Rhodes, Ephesus in Turkey, and Patmos. The girls also saw much of Greece island life during their vacations and even invited friends from the United States to Athens.

While residing in Greece, we had friends visit from Belgium and elsewhere. These included the Van Dierendoncks, Jeff Wrights, De la Failles, Coppins, Arthur Maixners, Dudley Smiths, Bob Morrows from Mexico City, etc. In addition, cousins and friends from home, including Laura Phinizy (then teaching at the best Greek private school), her parents the Stewart Phinizys, Tommy Johnsons, Pat Dolan with Betty Bowring and Bruz and Kitty Boardman all dropped by. Sam and Sandra Mays's daughters, Ruth and Margaret, visited as did Sandra herself and her "group" when in Athens as a part of their 1989 tour. The Barnards came from Cape Cod at the end of the Danube and Turkey journey they much enjoyed.

Tracy graduated from the College of Charleston in May of 1987 in a beautiful ceremony on the campus grounds attended by her parents and Aunt Jan O'Reilly; then Tracy went on to a paralegal school in Atlanta and shortly thereafter became engaged. After much discussion, her wedding was scheduled for May 20, 1988, at Church of the Good Shepherd in Augusta. Lynn and Tracy organized a charming late spring afternoon affair with the support of good friends and family.

By 1989, our office was well on its way to US $100 million in turnover, our settled goal. But suddenly another change at headquarters when a new president came on board and began his new regimen, which can be fairly named "The Re-Engineering Epoch," as it

CHAPTER ELEVEN

turned out the new management favored a strong focus only on the eight to ten foreign countries providing the bulk of our business, even though it was next to impossible to do other than break even at best in some of these markets. In the international insurance world, a wide spread of risk over many countries throughout the globe is a good tactic and even a necessity! Many of the smaller country operations were consistently profitable, and many streams do make a large river, as the Chinese say! Cigna still had difficulty in understanding how to manage business from foreign-incorporated subsidiaries, there was little future vision relative to Africa, the Middle East, or territories like Pakistan and Cyprus or those of the former Eastern European block, and Headquarters never appreciated the money to be made in "troubled waters," e.g., the Middle East and in parts of Africa. While I was not privy to all of the foregoing until I had departed Athens in mid 1990, it now seems obvious such a new policy was adopted with the parallel objective of reducing costs, i.e., staff, office expenses, and commissions in order to prepare the property, casualty, and overseas divisions for ultimate sale, as did happen later. In the long run, we would be closing down in many countries.

As I had planned to retire after my sixty-fifth birthday in February of 1992, Cigna, wanting to have all management succession settled well in advance, offered a new contract whereby I would spend the final one and a half years of my career at the Philadelphia Head Office assisting Executive Vice President Nick Steffey with

Eastern Europe (site of potential new operations) and other overseas issues. Steffey was then responsible for all foreign branches and regions. Lynn, while enjoying her life in Greece, was content, as Katherine could join us following her graduation in January 1991 from American University in Washington, DC with a degree in Art History. Philadelphia would be a new and interesting experience for us all, and not least we would be closer to Tracy, now married and living in Connecticut. There was also the huge question of retirement, and to where?

We owned property at Hilton Head Sea Pines and a lot in Augusta. But why not take a year or two off and maybe live in Brussels, London, or Paris for a bit in a rented flat until we took a final decision? All of this influenced my agreement to transfer to Philadelphia in August 1990. We stopped at the Schloss Hotel in Kronberg after leaving Athens for Frankfurt via Lufthansa and also visited Berlin, Potsdam, Dresden, and London en route. In Philadelphia, Lynn found an attractive townhouse on Delancy Street between 2nd and 3rd in the "old city." We planned to move into the house in late September following the arrival of our shipment from Greece with another part put in temporary storage in Atlanta. Lynn then returned to Athens to pack up and say goodbye.

Several weeks after our arrival, I went on a mission to Bulgaria with a group from the United States Chamber of Commerce in Washington, DC. The group was advising on the opening of the country to foreign investment, including the previously nationalized insurance

CHAPTER ELEVEN

industry. This was part of Cigna's study for the newly "freed" countries previously comprising Eastern Europe. We met all senior local government officials, including the president, prime minister (who spoke perfect English), and for me the state insurance managers, one of whom was assigned as my "guide" for the entire stay. The first Gulf War, or initial standoff, took place in August 1990, and I was interviewed several times and spoke at the Insurance Institute Annual Dinner in New York City in September concerning my recent experience in the Middle East. On that occasion, I predicted Saddam Hussein would probably withdraw from Kuwait once he knew the first Bush president and our allies would fight; how wrong I was! We were in New York at the Waldorf Astoria the night (January 16, 1991) the first Gulf War began to attend a dinner at the Council for Foreign Relations. Tom Brokaw was to be the dinner speaker, but we heard on the taxi radio en route to the council that the Baghdad bombing had commenced; Tom never showed up, but we listened to his news reports on a huge TV moved into the dining room. So much then for "foreign resident experts" considering my earlier prediction!

After Lynn and Nellie, our King Charles spaniel, arrived in Philadelphia, we lived for about a month in a suite at the Warwick Hotel. This was about a short block from Rittenhouse Square, so very convenient for walks with Nellie, who for the first twenty-four hours or so did not want to void at all. Then to our townhouse on Delancey Street between 2nd and 3rd in the Society Hill old town and a short walk from the famous Independence Hall and Liberty Bell. We had no car initially and rented our parking space in the rear of the house to a neighbor; but this allowed us to really explore Philadelphia on foot. We walked everywhere in good weather; I even walked to my office or took a bus on inclement days. We found the city to be surprisingly friendly for a large one and made some new friends and even reacquainted ourselves with the Stan Brownes, who lived around the corner in a wonderful old three-story townhouse on 2nd Street. Stan and Libby had been in Brussels for some years with his law firm, and we continued to see them at church, first at the Anglican in Belgium and then at old St. Peter's (near our house) in Philadelphia.

Katherine graduated with her BA in Art History from the American University in Washington, DC in January of 1991. We attended the ceremony, where she received her degree Magna Cum Laude. Katherine then joined us in Philadelphia, where she secured a job on her own credentials at the Philadelphia Museum of Art in the old print department. She also could use her French in this position and loved every minute of her work. Katherine occupied the finished basement of our townhouse, and this permitted her to save most of her low salary; but the experience and adding PMA to her museum resumé was what really counted! Katherine and dog Nellie slept together!

We continued to discuss the final retirement location: Augusta, where we still owned a lot, Hilton Head Sea Pines with our Briarwood condo redone and

CHAPTER ELEVEN

extended as permitted by the regime, or just take our time and spend a year or two headquartered in Brussels, London, or Paris. We already knew the United States would be the ultimate spot, but where? We drove to Augusta in November and met with Brad Bennett, who introduced us to John Sandeford, a well-known local architect. We hit it off immediately, and John later sent us in Philadelphia a picture of an Atlanta Regency house built years ago for Mills B. Lane. Plans in detail followed as by then Lynn decided on Augusta as our permanent homesite. I concurred, as we preferred not to live full-time in a vacation environment. Our new home was supposed to be completed by December 1991. In the meantime, we finally acquired a car and took several more short trips to Augusta, to Vermont to see the Hauffs in Manchester, to Cape Cod to visit the Barnards in the middle of "the Perfect Storm," and then on to Boston where we had not been before. I was in Manhattan on many occasions for business meetings and also in Washington, DC working on Eastern European prospects. Katherine was back in touch with her Chatham, New Jersey, friends, and her high school beau now was also back in the picture visiting us in Philadelphia. We were all together in Philadelphia for Christmas 1990, including Tracy from Connecticut.

We left Philadelphia in early December 1991 after spending our last night at the new Ritz-Carlton Hotel, Nellie being relegated to the kennel for the final days while we were packing up. Although I did not really realize the impact then, I was about to embark on one of the last great adventures in life, i.e., retirement, even though the official date was March 1, 1992, as per my work contract. This amounted to about forty-three and a half years of service with two different companies! Thirty-six and a half of those career years were spent living and working abroad. Lynn was somewhat skeptical about having me around all day, and I was also suffering "buyer's remorse" a bit, wondering if Augusta was really the correct decision for both of us. My final thoughts and retirement conclusions will be conveyed in Chapter XII "Coming Back to Augusta and L'envoi."

CHAPTER ELEVEN

Harold V. Smith, CEO Home Insurance and Chairman AFIA – HVS was my mentor who gave me my "start" in the insurance world.

IS LIVING WELL STILL THE BEST REVENGE?

Inman Mays when in Japan mid-1950's

CHAPTER ELEVEN

In Singapore, Lynn, Tracy, and Katherine 1971

IS LIVING WELL STILL THE BEST REVENGE?

Bowdre and Mrs Bowring during the Bowring and Martha Fleming visit to Brussels in 1981. "Bloodies before breakfast"

CHAPTER ELEVEN

*Our "Great Gatsby" scene in our Athens, Greece,
garden circa 1986-1987.*

IS LIVING WELL STILL THE BEST REVENGE?

Reception honoring Judge Frank Mays Hull in 1997 following her elevation to the 11th Circuit Court of Appeals at our Conifer Place house.

Brother Ted Mays in a happy mood at the 1997 reception for our family "Judge" in a corner of the living room at our Conifer Place house.

CHAPTER XII

B.P.M., Jr.: Coming Back to Augusta with Epilogue and L'envoi

As I indicated in the final sentences of Chapter XI, we arrived in Augusta in early December 1991 with some small feeling of trepidation. This was largely caused by wondering if we had made the best decision relative to our retirement locale. While we rather rapidly learned Hilton Head was not the ultimate community we sought due to its growth and the constant resort atmosphere, still there had been the opportunity to live perhaps in Brussels, London, or Paris for a year or more prior to taking the next step. Of course our new house, slated and promised to be ready December 1, still was in the final interior-finishing stage! Hence, we moved into the Hampton Inn with our dog Nellie and set about the numerous tasks everyone faces in a move. Furniture and all personal household effects came from Philadelphia and from storage in Atlanta once our new abode was fairly habitable just before Christmas. Katherine, second daughter, came to join us for the first Christmas in Augusta, and Lynn even found and decorated a half-dead Christmas tree on December 24!

Our new Regency-façade home at 76 Bristlecone Lane was a hit with all (even with the architect John Sandeford who rather rudely told Stewart Hull, "It's turned out better than I expected!"). This was due to its curb appeal (similar to an older white painted brick Mills B. Lane Atlanta home on Muscogee) and the interior flow. The four and one-half baths, great closet space, an entrance hall unencumbered by a second-floor staircase, with roomy living, dining, and separate library areas all contributed to our happiness and the general approbation of the many who visited. Lastly, the high ceilings, ten, eleven, and twelve feet in all the first-floor rooms, conferred a spacious and older ambience over all. Our friend Rex Pruitt helped Lynn with furniture placement and picture hangings. By my sixty-fifth birthday, February 4, 1992, we were partially ready to celebrate and invited about twenty-five to a chili and polenta supper party. The dining room still contained a sizeable black trunk packed with most of our silver with pictures in some areas unhung and leaning against the walls.

CHAPTER TWELVE

I learned that almost every day in Augusta was different and found old hands like me, once on the local turf again, fit in easily and just reassumed relationships without much further ado! One just "picked up" after a long hiatus of many a moon and soon was up to date. Many people, although professing interest in my life away, soon were back on the "Augusta situation" in no time at all! I did discover a new interest in mainly the older generations (still with us) whom I had known and remembered as a kid or young adult as I could now interact with them more or less on equal terms. Again and again I wished I had listened more as a child to the conversation of the adults who in many cases now were deceased. There were still many questions to be asked pertaining to the Augusta life in past years. My mother at age eighty-eight did supply some input as did Emma Mason, Genie Lehmann, Margaret Twiggs, and Mary Lou Bussey, particularly relative to my own family and other "movers and shakers" of the past! The late Teto Barrett was a real joy in recounting many past stories and times. Teto and my mother, were contemporaries and about the same age.

At first I felt a bit out of my bailiwick with no office to attend after a career of forty-four long years and no help in dealing with the mundane daily problems of life. I conjectured long about retirement at only sixty-five: was I really correct in planning to leave at this age? I found myself spending a lot of time just "looking for things" as another retiree once so aptly put it! But soon I found retirement to be a great gift in that, properly organized, one had time to read, travel for pleasure rather than for business as in the past, and focus mainly on the remainder of one's short time as a resident of planet Earth.

Betty B. Bowring, my old friend from grammar school days at William Rob, soon was saying, "Lynn and Bowdre took Augusta by storm!" Doubtless a fine compliment but certainly principally due to Lynn's wonderful disposition, calm efficient demeanor, rather quick sense of humor, and with at all times an enthusiastic wholehearted approach and commitment. Lynn had made many moves around the world but at all times managed to replant herself and our family in these both foreign and US locations with ease. We actually thrived as she mainly made our lives prosper in each new environment. She met the right people and always was a popular member of American/international groups consisting primarily of ladies.

In Augusta, after some months, Lynn knew many more people than I did! She volunteered for the newly formed Morris Museum of Southern Art in 1992 and The Sacred Heart Cultural Center serving both as a director for several years. She was asked to join several garden clubs and became a member of three. She was called (probably a trifle maliciously) "The Garden Club Queen" but retorted that many ladies in Augusta also had two garden club memberships plus sewing, card, and book clubs whereas she concentrated only on the gardens!

CHAPTER TWELVE

Pat Walsh in his typical way wrote Lynn from San Francisco when he heard she had been asked to join The Sand Hills Garden Club: "As you have been made aware, I'm sure, that for a lady in Augusta is the ne plus ultra." Aunt Mary Lou Phinizy and Tracy Duncan Cohen would have been delighted that Lynn indeed had taken her place in Augusta so soon after arrival and made so many new friends and supporters.

Since 1992, we have taken a number of trips abroad: the first in 1993 to Ireland, a first for us, to visit Bunny Davis and "Mr. D"; 1994 back to Greece and a week in Spain; Lynn alone took two trips to Italy and France with ladies from Augusta and Texas, I believe in 1995-1996; we went to Brussels, Switzerland, Austria, Prague, and again to Ireland to see Bunny in 1997 and ending in London; in 1998 a return to Brussels and Germany for the Achenbach wedding by the Rhine River including side trips to Berlin and Dresden, etc; to Bermuda in 1999 for the Boardman-Copenhaver nuptials; Seabourne Cruise (starting from Rome) in the Mediterranean mid-2000 ending in Paris following stops at Marseilles and Aix-en-Provence to see the Jeff Wrights. Finally a month spent in Brussels summer 2001 including side trips to Amsterdam and Paris returning home just prior to "9/11."

Lynn returned to the Pacific in 2008, joining a group from Garden Club of America, and went to China for two weeks. She visited all the important tourist sites including Beijing and Shanghai. When we lived in Singapore (1965-1973), US citizens usually were not able to travel to China in that era.

We in addition have seen new parts (at least to us) of Georgia (Thomasville, Macon, Columbus, LaGrange, Milledgeville, Brunswick, etc.) plus making many road and flying trips to the Northeast and to Chicago to see Tracy, Katherine, and their families. Tracy has three charming girls (Mary Inman, Elizabeth Law, and Katherine Drake Olmsted), and Katherine our only grandson, Alexander Mays, and his sisters Kerrigan Russell and Charlotte Foley Bunker.

We had a happy visit to New Orleans with Red and Ann (in their plane) and the Newton Quantzes in 1995 and again to New Orleans in 2004 for a Garden Club of America Board of Associates outing. Several Georgia Trust Rambles opened new Georgia vistas as did road trips to Memphis, Nashville, Natchez, Jackson, and Montgomery to view special museum exhibits. There have been as well several visits to Texas for a wedding and to visit family in Dallas.

For a number of years we have gone to Hilton Head in late summer when Tracy, Katherine, spouses, and grandchildren join us for a week at the beach. They usually also visit Augusta before/after the seashore portion.

Lynn went with Mary Ann Douglas to Santa Barbara in 2007 for another G.C.A. Board of Associates gathering. We had air tickets booked to Brussels for October 25, 2006, but have been forced to postpone this planned trip to Northern Italy, Paris, and Brussels due to a projected move to Brandon Wilde in late 2006. This came

CHAPTER TWELVE

about suddenly; we had been on the list only about two years as a "form of insurance," but an offer of a unit we liked in "The Big House" seemed too interesting to reject. So we go from 3,990 square feet in our "dream house" to a bit over 1,700 square feet. Our new abode is just like a spacious New York City apartment. Lynn will be the "teenager" at Brandon Wilde, but we made a joint decision on the transfer. Contemplating the future, we do believe our plan is the intelligent one although we had originally said the next time we moved from our house would be in a box! We have now lived here more than fourteen years, the longest time anywhere in our married life and built the house with a ramp on one rear door and with wide doorways throughout, never anticipating a "live" departure!

Commencing in 1993, we rented our house to Mr. and Mrs. Arnold Palmer for Master's Week in April for the next ten years or so; when Arnold played his final fiftieth Masters round in 2004, we rented to his children including his last caddy, Grandson Sam Saunders. Arnold and his late wife Winnie always were perfect guests and true patterns for a lady and gentleman! One winter we stayed with Sherry and Tom Hauff as the Palmer guests in a condo at Bay Hill Club near Orlando. Then we drove on to Boca Grande to visit Barry and Donnie Stout on the West Coast and decided Boca Grande has our vote for "numero uno" in that part of Florida!

We made another trip to both the West and East Floridian Coasts in 2002, taking in Sanibel, Sarasota, Naples, Boca Raton, Palm Beach, Ormond Beach, and Ponte Vedra. Our favorite stop on the East Coast is Jupiter Island, where we stayed with the Charles Falcones in December 2003 at their elegant house facing the ocean.

Lynn for the first time since Singapore has taken up golf again; she has taken lessons with friends and attended one golf clinic at Sea Island. Betty Bowring, our past local club ladies champion who also won the Club Championship at Edgartown Club, Martha's Vineyard, said Lynn shows much promise if she will devote more time and practice to the links. Lynn is well coordinated, unlike me, so I foresee great improvement for her. Playing at the country club is simple during the week (no tee times needed) most of the year, excepting of course some hot summer months. My own exercise activity is a brisk three-mile walk at least five days a week outside in clement weather or inside on the Health Central or Family Y track in bad or the too-hot conditions in summer. We also have a treadmill to use at home.

We had what was called a "celebration" for my seventieth birthday at 519 Greene Street, the Old Phinizy House, where my father was born. An evening black-tie affair with music and supper of chicken hash and cheese grits served following a long cocktail session. Around 200 guests including some from out of town whose presence was much appreciated. For my seventy-fifth a dinner party at home when the following doggerel was read:

Happy Birthday Bubba
I'm glad that your my hubba!

CHAPTER TWELVE

Before we start the cheers
Let's go back a few years–

When I was twenty-four
He took me off to Singapore
Bowdre's heart began to beat faster
'Cause he knew that there he would be called
Master!

What a happy time he had
Working, playing and becoming a Dad
Life in the tropics was fun and hot
But soon it was time to head for another spot.

Off to Brussels we went
No challenge too great for this gent!
There he was a real survivor
Made easier
'Cause he still had a driver!
Ten great years we spent in Brussels
Enjoying endive, chocolates and mussels.

One day to New York he was called—
"Oh My", he cried with disdain
"I'll have to go to work on the train!"
After two years in the US of A
'Twas time to once again go far away.

This time Bowdre was full of smiles
For we were off to the Grecian Isles!

What could be better
Than going to the land of Feta?

Six great years we spent
Enjoying everywhere we went
Until-Bring out the packing crates
It was back to the United States!
This time to Philly
Where the winter was pretty chilly
Bowdre worked in his office high above
The City of Brotherly love
Then as retirement neared
It was back to where he was reared
Now in Augusta to stay
And we are happy today.

So let's all drink a birthday toast
To the man I love the most!

    Love from Lynn-February 4, 2002

A Birthday Tribute for Dear Old Dad

There once was a man named Bowdre
Who greeted everyone with "Howdy",
    Now he's turning 75,
    And should be glad to be alive,
Before he ends up in the plot with Grandma Doughty.

CHAPTER TWELVE

At an early age he caught wanderlust
And in the kitchen always likes to create a fuss,
    He loves good books,
    And his special reading nook,
Even though all those WSJs and Gusty Chronicles are collecting dust!

So on this special day, it's time to reflect
And even though we're not there to genuflect,
    We wanted to say Hip Hip Hooray,
    And here's a little toast from miles away,
"Best wishes to YOU (Bubba our dad) with love and respect."

    Happy Birthday!!!
    Love,
    Tracy and Katherine

These Southern Aristocrats

Who wear many hats,
Father, son, husband, brother,
Know many facts,
Social historian, insurance, traveler,
Whose ancestral mansions
Have become Elks clubs and chicken runs,
Or Hatcher centers at least,
Where we enjoyed your 70th anniversary feast,
Let us now pause

IS LIVING WELL STILL THE BEST REVENGE?

To join our applause
For a man who's eaten mussels in Brussels
And dined on tuna albacore in Singapore,
Who wears the Brooks Brothers golden fleece
And knows the kings of Greece
Backward and forward, a country clubber
Who answers to the nickname of "Bubber,"
A moniker which hardly suits him in any way,
Too red neck, too familiar for our wonderful
Bowdre Phinizy Mays.

-- Starkey Flythe

CHAPTER TWELVE

Walking "Rowley" on Brandon Wilde Campus (Circa 2008-09)
"Rowley" is widely known as "Top Dog"

IS LIVING WELL STILL THE BEST REVENGE?

Lynn and Bowdre at Thanksgiving Dinner Augusta Country Club (Circa 2008)

CHAPTER TWELVE

Lynn and Bowdre in Country Club Living Room for Assembly Spring Party, May 2010

EPILOGUE AND L'ENVOI

So here "I be" having turned eighty-five, very content and happy, even though there is a certain air of finality associated with any bio sketch. The world's really a mess, but life, I find, is great: still a mixed bag of blessings and endless paradoxes! I started out at an early age with a thirst for knowledge as well as an urge to see and learn all about the world. Mr. H. V. Smith gave me the initial chance, but it was my own work and taking full advantage of all opportunities that carried me to the current stage. While it may be a strong start to have connections open doors, don't forget that these same people usually are also rather adept at closing them should one fail or play on the job! I used to say in a rather cynical way that a large income was the best recipe for happiness ever heard of, but now I know that good health is also an important factor in the formula!

When first abroad in Tokyo in 1949-1950 at the ignorant age of but twenty-two, I met many of the "Old China Hands" (as they were always known), meaning men who had worked in and known pre-world War II China or Japan as businessmen. Their nationalities ranged from American to Brits plus many other countries also including "White Russians." The latter had left home during the aftermath of the Russian 1917 Revolution and settled principally in North China and Manchuria. These "Old China or Japan Hands" always talked about their grand past years and the interesting lives they remembered. This excluded, naturally, the years some had spent in Japanese prisoner-of-war camps as enemy aliens. Many were stranded in Japan or China and were not lucky enough to be exchanged in 1942 on the famous *Gripsholm* voyage from the Orient to Lourenco Marques, Mozambique. Since then I have always tried to determine if indeed one's past was really any more appealing than the present: probably depends some on luck, ones age, and in what activity at the time one was engaged. In any event, even in those immediate post-World War II days, we happily could deal and work without daily cheap telephone calls, email, and fax messages flooding the desks with an ever-increasing volume! Life in those days still seemed exciting to me!

Then there appears to be the rather unhealthy maintenance of blogs (aka web logs) by many with a specific agenda that kids and gullible persons accept as gospel or the truth. These blogs in fact are a computer-generated alternate reality world where users spend time playing and interacting. People spend hours a day roaming around seeking friends, giving opinions, and picking up trends. There is a "social-mentoring" site where users can create their very own "home page" with pictures and look for friends or hunt for lovers. I read that many of the kids who frequent "MySpace" are interested in sex and attractive partners, but no surprise here so don't stop the presses yet! These kids say they spend a lot of spare time "chillin"; they don't read much with the usual answer: "I don't have time to read!" This presumably accounts in part for the rather abysmal English language skills we hear often on TV and on occasion read even from college graduates! Some opine blogs are healthy and permit one to both divulge and find remedies to various stresses in living. If so, what did we do before the onset of blogs?

Of course I know we can't turn back the clock; hence, the new and ever-growing technology is bound to continue its invasion! Nevertheless, we must wonder about these internet start-ups which grow without any real business model or plan to make money. The monetization strategy is still uncooked but presumably is the job of the venture capitalist for the future.

On the contrary, cloud computing is one business model that helps companies reduce costs by purchasing computing power when needed. This also allows a business to respond quickly to changing situations as such arise.

IS LIVING WELL STILL THE BEST REVENGE?

One serious problem, seemingly almost endemic, in the current United States is the "political correctness" situation. This theory or belief by some has been elevated to extreme and ridiculous levels in one's daily life. "Political Correctness" is the recent cause of many asinine decisions by government and the judiciary involving race, religion, the workplace, and other aspects of human existence. If we could abolish "Political Correctness" tomorrow, this would eliminate one evil from our lives.

Recently I have noticed that the United States is rapidly becoming a large country of a mainly leisure-time mentality. For example, there now are more sports medicine college graduates than engineers in this early twenty-first century. The trend to a more and more service (as opposed to industrial) economy has been the reality for many years and may not be too harmful as it allows the USA to outsource jobs abroad where the labor is cheaper. At the same time, we then can concentrate on higher-level technology and scientific gains from the laboratory or factory. Nevertheless, the lack of new engineers for one is a disturbing sign for the future and may mean the increasing importation of engineering experts from abroad and eventually a complete loss to other countries of the previous USA pre-eminence in many technical fields. To bring closure (a favorite word in these days of repeated rampant terrorism) to this chapter and epilogue, let me briefly state some core business beliefs and lifespan conclusions:

EPILOGUE AND L'ENVOI

- Never substitue the actions of e-mailing, texting, and teleconferencing for time to think and be creative in your work and problem-solving or time meeting people in person and establishing personal business relationships.
- Be very cognizant of well-known true and tried business principles such as "Parkinson's Law, Peter and Rhino Prinicples".
- Avoid inflation in management staff levels, titles, and meetings (some held just to decide whether to have one!) or unncessary travel.
- Shrouds have no pockets, and you usually regret what you don't do.
- Life is no dress rehearsal so don't delay or put off what can be done today.
- Hope the good Lord treats and endows one well, for physical appearance and attitude/personality have much to do with success. Good looks help build confidence; many assume that the inner spirit and mind go hand in hand with handsome folk. I have observed many who in normal life do better than maybe their efforts merit alone!
- The better schmoozer and enthusiast customarily wins out! Glibness also can triumph!
- Genius is really devoting the time and effort to diligently attend to the details so that one's ultimate objectives are reached.
- Concentrate on the opportunities, not the problems, always remembering it is possible to find problems to every solution!

- Focus on sales, production, or whatever it is called in one's business, as this is the most important key to advancement, money, and progress on up the ladder. This refers to all businesses, whether the professions, merchants, or industrial manufacturing. There always are sales receipts to be garnered no matter the market, while, at the same time, pros and cons to every business decision you will make!
- Always ask for business from all contacts, repeatedly if necessary.
- Avoid paralysis by analysis!
- Ask many questions and challenge all business proposals and recommendations, for due diligence is always essential in every organization. "Why" is a useful word to constantly employ!

As I read somewhere long ago: "Heureaux qui comme Ulysse a fait un beau voyage." The Romans called him Ulysses, the Greeks Odysseus. He was a King of Ithaca and fought in the Trojan War. Homer wrote of the ten-year voyage of Odysseus in returning home to Ithaca. Most can agree that the most optimum satisfaction in one's life is indeed to make a happy voyage!

The C. P. Cavafy 1911 poem "Ithaka" always has appealed to my sense of travel and a long and happy life. Thus I end with this verse written most appropriately by one of the "Alexandria Greeks," i.e., one born to Greek parents in Alexandria, Egypt, the site of a large Greek population pre-Nasser.

EPILOGUE AND L'ENVOI

ITHAKA

As you set out on the journey to Ithaka,
wish that the way be long,
full of adventures, full of knowledge.
Don't be afraid of Laistrygonians, the Cyclops,
angry Poseidon, you'll never find them on your way
if your thought stays exalted, if a rare
emotion touches your spirit and body.
You won't meet the Laistrygonians
and the Cyclops and wild Poseidon,
if you don't bear them along in your soul,
if your soul doesn't raise them before you.

Wish that the way be long.
May there be many summer mornings
when with such pleasure, such joy
you enter ports seen for the first time;
may you stop in Phoenician emporia
to buy fine merchandise,
mother-of-pearl and coral, amber and ebony,
and every kind of sensual perfume,
buy abundant sensual perfumes, as many as you can.
Travel to many Egyptian cities
to learn and learn from their scholars.

Always keep Ithaka in your mind.
Arriving there is your destination.

But don't hurry the journey at all.
Better if it lasts many years,
and you moor on the island when you are old,
rich with all you have gained along the way,
not expecting Ithaka to make you rich.

Ithaka gave you the beautiful journey.
Without her you would not have set out on your way.
She has no more to give you.

And if you find her poor, Ithaka did not betray you.
With all your wisdom, all your experience,
you understand by now what Ithakas mean.

Note: In 1990, we (Lynn, Bowdre, and Katherine) visited Ithaka during a private cruise of the Ionian Sea Greek Islands. We were guests on the yacht of Dora and George Koumbas, our charming Greek friends. What a lovely and dramatic way to end our own Greek sojourn of six happy years!

In the final analysis, what remains is the story of one's life: in the end, it's the sole thing any of us will really own!

EPILOGUE AND L'ENVOI

A man and his dog --1928

A man and his dog --2001

"Self explanatory" (*2001 in our Augusta Garden*)
with Nellie

THE END

BIBLIOGRAPHY

General:

Augusta Chronicle and *Augusta Herald*, various articles.

Augusta Country Club 1899-1999, Centennial Book, 1998 by Eileen Stulb

Bell and Crabbe. *The Augusta Chronicle (1785-1960)*. Athens: University of Georgia Press, 1960.

Cashin, Edward J. *The Story of Augusta*. Spartanburg, SC: Reprint Company, 1991.

Dutcher, Salem and Charles C. Jones. *Memorial History of Augusta*. Syracuse, New York: Georgia D. Mason & Company, 1890. (Also used for Chapter VIII relative to the King Family)

Garden Club of Georgia, Inc. *Garden History of Georgia 1733-1933.* Savannah, Georgia: Kennickell Printing Company, reprinted 1976.

Spalding, Phinizy. *The History of The Medical College of Georgia.* Athens: University of Georgia Press, 1987.

The Story of The Augusta National Golf Club by Clifford Roberts, 1976, Doubleday & Co., Inc.

White Columns in Georgia. Parkerson, New York: Bonanza, 1952. (Gift of Clay and Catherine Boardman)

Chapter IV: **Private World of M.L.P. at 814 Milledge Road.**

Hines, John E. and Kenneth Kesselur. *Granite on Fire.* Austin, Texas: The Episcopal Theological Seminary of the Southwest, 1995.

Jackson, Chevalier. *The Life of Chevalier Jackson, an Autobiography.* McMillan, 1938.

Chapter V: **Potpourri of Milledge Road Minutiae: Who Was Who on Milledge?**

Augusta Georgia: The Garden City of The South. Augusta, Georgia: Ridgely-Tidwell Co., , reprinted by Tidwell Graphics, 1984.

Cumming, J.B.. *Sketch of the Descendants of David Cumming.* Privately printed and edited by Mr. Bryan Cumming, 1925.

Cumming, Mary G. Smith. *Two Centuries of Augusta.* Augusta, Georgia: Walton Printing Company, 1926.

Haltermann, Bryan M.. *From City to Countryside.* Lamar Press, 1997.

BIBLIOGRAPHY

Lowrey, Jacob H. *Augusta — Yesterday and Today: The Hill's Old Homes*. Junior League, 1950.

Montgomery, Dr. C. J. *Old Homes of The Sand Hills*. Circa 1914 or before.

Moore, Dr. Victor A. III. *A History of The Good Shepherd*. Spartanburg, South Carolina: The Reprint Company, 1995.

Chapter VIII: **The King Family in Augusta and Europe**

Angelesey, 7th Marquess of, *One-Leg*. New York: Morrow, 1961.

Barzini, Luigi. *The Italians*. London: Harmish Hamilton, 1964.

Brandon, Ruth. *The Dollar Princesses*. London: Weidenfeld, 1980.

Ciano, Edda. *Mussolini, My Truth*. London: Weidenfeld, 1977.

Ciano, Galeazzo, *Diary 1937-1943*. New York: Enigma Books, 2002.

Crawford, Francis Marion. *Ave Roma Immortalis*. London: Macmillan, 1900.

De Castellane, Marquis Boni. *How I Discovered America*. New York: Knopf, 1924.

MacColl and Wallace. *To Marry an English Lord*. New York: Workman Publishing, 1989.

Maugham, Robin. *Somerset and all the Maughams*. New York: New American Library, 1966.

Memorial booklet on John Pendleton King.

Montgomery. *Gilded Prostitution (1870-1914)*. Routledge, 1989.

Moseley Ray. *Mussolini's Shadow, the Double Life of Count Galeazzo Ciano*. Yale University Press, 1999.

New York Times Magazine of January 14, 1917, containing Pendleton King article on Youssoupoff, Murder of Rasputin.

Obolensky, Serge. *One Man in His Time*. New York, McDowell, 1958.

Smith, Jane S. *Elsie de Wolfe*. New York: Atheneum, 1982.

ABOUT THE AUTHOR

Bowdre P. Mays, Jr., a native of Augusta, Georgia, is a retired international insurance executive who spent most of his forty four year career abroad in the Orient, Middle East, Europe, and South America. He and his wife, Lynn, reside in Augusta, Georgia, and have two daughters, both born in Singapore, and six grandchildren.

Made in the USA
Columbia, SC
20 March 2020